SOUTH ASIAN SOVEREIGNTY

This book brings ethnographies of everyday power and ritual into dialogue with intellectual studies of theology and political theory. It underscores the importance of academic collaboration between scholars of religion, anthropology, and history in uncovering the structures of thinking and action that make politics work. The volume weaves important discussions around sovereignty in modern South Asian history with debates elsewhere on the world map.

South Asia's colonial history – especially India's twentieth-century emergence as the world's largest democracy – has made the subcontinent a critical arena for thinking about how transformations and continuities in conceptions of sovereignty provide a vital frame for tracking shifts in political order. The chapters deal with themes such as sovereignty, kingship, democracy, governance, reason, people, nation, colonialism, rule of law, courts, autonomy, and authority, especially within the context of India, Bangladesh, and Pakistan.

The book will be of great interest to scholars and researchers in politics, ideology, religion, sociology, history, and political culture, as well as the informed reader interested in South Asian studies.

David Gilmartin is Distinguished Professor of History at North Carolina State University, USA. His current research focuses on the legal history of India's electoral institutions as they have evolved from a colonial past and changed in relation to evolving visions of the people's sovereignty. His earlier books include *Blood and Water: The Indus River Basin in Modern History* (2015), *Civilization and Modernity: Narrating the Creation of Pakistan* (2014), and *Empire and Islam: Punjab and the Making of Pakistan* (1988).

Pamela Price is Professor Emerita of South Asian History at the University of Oslo, Norway. She began her research on political culture working on colonial South India and has published, among others, *Kingship and Political Practice in Colonial India* (1996). Moving onto post-colonial topics, she edited *Power and Influence in India: Bosses, Lords and Captains* (2010, with Arild Engelsen Ruud). A collection of her articles appears in *State, Politics, and Cultures in Modern South India: Honour, Authority, and Morality* (2013).

Arild Engelsen Ruud is Professor of South Asia Studies at the University of Oslo, Norway. He writes on issues of democracy and politics in South Asia, specifically West Bengal and Bangladesh. He is the author of *Poetics of Village Politics: The Making of West Bengal's Rural Communism* (2003), co-editor of *Power and Influence in India* (2010, with Pamela Price), and co-author of *Mafia Raj* (2018, with Lucia Michelutti et al.).

Exploring the Political in South Asia

Series Editor: Mukulika Banerjee, Director, South Asia Centre and Associate Professor, Department of Anthropology, London School of Economics and Political Science

Exploring the Political in South Asia is devoted to the publication of research on the political cultures of the region. The books in this Series present qualitative and quantitative analyses grounded in field research, and explore the cultures of democracies in their everyday local settings, specifically the workings of modern political institutions, practices of political mobilisation, manoeuvres of high politics, structures of popular beliefs, content of political ideologies and styles of political leadership, amongst others. Through fine-grained descriptions of particular settings in South Asia, the studies presented in this Series inform, and have implications for, general discussions of democracy and politics elsewhere in the world.

Books in this Series

The Politics of Caste in West Bengal
Edited by Uday Chandra, Geir Heierstad, Kenneth Bo Nielsen

Politics, Landlords and Islam in Pakistan
Nicolas Martin

Emotions, Mobilisations and South Asian Politics
Edited by Amélie Blom and Stéphanie Tawa Lama-Rewal

South Asian Sovereignty
The Conundrum of Worldly Power
Edited by David Gilmartin, Pamela Price, and Arild Engelsen Ruud

For more information about this series, please visit: www.routledge.com/Exploring-the-Political-in-South-Asia/book-series/EPSA

SOUTH ASIAN SOVEREIGNTY

The Conundrum of Worldly Power

Edited by David Gilmartin, Pamela Price, and Arild Engelsen Ruud

Routledge
Taylor & Francis Group
LONDON AND NEW YORK

First published 2020
by Routledge
2 Park Square, Milton Park, Abingdon, Oxon OX14 4RN

and by Routledge
52 Vanderbilt Avenue, New York, NY 10017

Routledge is an imprint of the Taylor & Francis Group, an informa business

British Library Cataloguing-in-Publication Data
A catalogue record for this book is available from the British Library

Library of Congress Cataloging-in-Publication Data
A catalog record for this book has been requested

ISBN: 978-1-138-32359-9 (hbk)
ISBN: 978-0-367-31270-1 (pbk)
ISBN: 978-0-429-29920-9 (ebk)

Typeset in Bembo
by Apex CoVantage, LLC

CONTENTS

Notes on contributors *ix*
Acknowledgements *x*

Introduction: South Asian sovereignty: the conundrum of worldly power 1
David Gilmartin

PART I
Law, religion, and sovereignty in India **35**

1 Sovereign struggles: governance and *mathas* under British imperial rule in South India 37
Pamela Price

2 The guru as legislator: religious leadership and informal legal space in rural South India 58
Aya Ikegame

3 Time and the sovereignty of the people 78
David Gilmartin

PART II
Kingship reconfigured 107

4 Deities, alliances, and the power over life and death: exploring royal sovereignty and its tenacity in a former princely state in Odisha 109
Uwe Skoda

5 Dynastic continuity and election in contemporary Karnataka politics 136
Caleb Simmons

6 Circuits of protection and extortion: sovereignty in a provincial North Indian town 150
Lucia Michelutti

PART III
The nation and the sovereign imagination 173

7 Messianism and the Constitution of Pakistan 175
A. Azfar Moin

8 Sovereign sensibilities: *Gunday* and the nation as the self 196
Arild Engelsen Ruud

Afterword: we have other ideas 216
Jonathan Spencer

Index 227

CONTRIBUTORS

David Gilmartin is Distinguished Professor of History at North Carolina State University, USA.

Aya Ikegame is a social anthropologist and works as Associate Professor at the Institute for Advanced Studies on Asia, University of Tokyo, Japan.

Lucia Michelutti is Professor of Anthropology at University College London, UK. She is the author of *The Vernacularisation of Democracy* (2008) among other works.

A. Azfar Moin is Associate Professor of Religious Studies and History at the University of Texas at Austin, USA.

Pamela Price is Professor Emerita of South Asian History at the University of Oslo, Norway. She writes on modern political culture in South India.

Arild Engelsen Ruud is Professor of South Asia Studies at the University of Oslo, Norway. He writes on modern political culture in India and Bangladesh.

Caleb Simmons is Assistant Professor of Religious Studies at the University of Arizona, USA. He specialises in religions of South Asia, particularly Hindu kingship.

Uwe Skoda is Associate Professor for India and South Asia Studies at Aarhus University, Denmark. He focuses on political anthropology and on visual culture.

Jonathan Spencer is Regius Professor of South Asian Language, Culture, and Society at the University of Edinburgh, UK. He has worked in Sri Lanka since the early 1980s.

ACKNOWLEDGEMENTS

The idea for the volume began with a retirement conference for Pamela Price held at Oslo University in December 2013, entitled 'Why history? On the Relevance of Cultural History for the Study of Contemporary South Asia'. We want to thank the funders for that conference, the Departments of Archaeology, Conservation and History and of Culture Studies and Oriental Languages at Oslo University. We also wish to thank all of the participants: Paul Brass, Gunnel Cederlöf, Manuela Ciotti, Lars Tore Flåten, Ute Hüsken, Aya Ikegame, Norbert Peabody, Erling Sandmo, Hilde Sandvik, Uwe Skoda, Jonathan Spencer, and Claus Peter Zoller. Their ideas on the importance of cultural history for the evolution of South Asian studies provides the intellectual backdrop to this volume. It was in the wake of that conference that the editors decided to focus on the history of sovereignty in modern South Asia, the increasing interest in which, we believe, represents one critical, recent turn in intellectual approaches to cultural history.

David Gilmartin would like to thank the National Humanities Center, Research Triangle Park, North Carolina for fellowship support during the time of the writing of the introduction to this volume in 2017–2018.

Thanks go to Uwe Skoda for providing the photograph that we have used on the cover. The picture, taken in October 2016, shows the worship of swords during Dasara in the former princely state of Bonai in Odisha. On one level, the picture references a central occasion when swords, representing the goddess, were worshipped inside the palace. But it also captures, we believe, something of the critical ineffability of concepts of sovereignty, particularly in the face of the structural and historical tensions between sovereignty and worldly rule that chapters in this volume have attempted to explore.

INTRODUCTION

South Asian sovereignty: the conundrum of worldly power

David Gilmartin

The term sovereignty is ambiguous and contested. But its value as a focus for argument and research is that it captures a set of universal tensions relating to the operation of power and its legitimacy. Central to the notion of sovereignty is that worldly power alone cannot legitimise itself. While sovereignty's meanings have changed over time and place, it is a term whose discussion requires us to engage both with *processes of* power, including the wielding of violence and coercion as critical elements in social order, and with *ideas about* power and its ultimate sources of legitimacy (both in elite and popular understandings). Moreover, its analysis points to the *irresolvable* tensions that the operation of legitimate power – and the wielding of ruling force – inevitably crystallise. To remain vital, the exercise of sovereign authority entails appeals to an ultimate source of authority conceptualised as standing apart from the everyday worlds of power and social interest – whether cosmic power, sacred authority, disinterested reason, or popular will. Yet sovereignty, while appealing to *extrapolitical* sources to legitimise authority, also entails a deep engagement with the *political* power (including violence) necessary to establish order in society itself. Without *both* of these, sovereignty falters.

The word 'sovereignty' (in its most common modern usages – and as a key element in the modern international order) is one with a distinctive history in European political and intellectual history and its development in modern India is impossible to understand without that context. But the tensions in the imagining of (and legitimising of) political authority that it captures have far older roots, including deep roots in South Asia. In critical ways, the conundrum of modern sovereignty is strikingly illustrated by the 'conundrum of the king's authority' captured in the writings of the Sanskritist, J. C. Heesterman. In Heesterman's argument, the effective projection of kingship in ancient India depended on the ability of the king to do two contradictory things at once: to stand apart, as an outsider, from the webs of hierarchy and dependence that defined the worldly politics of his kingdom *and* – at the very same time – to bind himself to those very same networks, thus mobilising the resources, political connections, and violence necessary to maintain effective worldly order (Heesterman 1985a: 108–127). As Heesterman argued, the irreconcilable contradictions between these roles defined an 'inner conflict of tradition', evident not only in ideas relating to kingly sovereignty, but also in the contradictions marking fundamental conceptions of power more basically. This was manifest, for example, in what Heesterman delineated as the opposing cultural styles of Kshatriyas and Brahmans, linked in the first case to the deep dependencies inherent in social hierarchies, and in the second case to the imagining of forms of power rooted precisely in the independence from such social bonds – thus enabling connections to the extrapolitical powers shaping the universe (Heesterman 1985b: 10–24).

Heesterman himself drew on a long academic tradition of Indological writing on kingship and sovereignty. But our aim in this volume is not so much to engage with this tradition directly as it is to suggest that the concept of sovereignty itself, as a vehicle for understandings of modern political order, provides a framework in which differences between modernity and the worlds of Indian 'tradition' can be dissolved in the interest of understanding not the 'inner conflict of tradition', but the inner contradictions of political (and state) power in all its forms of operation and legitimation. To hone in on South Asian sovereignty specifically, as we do in this volume, is not to search for forms of sovereignty that are distinct from those elsewhere, for forms of sovereignty in modern South Asia are inexplicable without grounding in the sovereign political and intellectual frameworks associated with modern colonialism as a worldwide phenomenon. But a focus on South Asia at the same time reveals – and in particularly striking ways – how modern, universalising visions of sovereign power have intersected with subcontinental history to define a distinctive set of historical tensions. The very premises necessary for the establishment of sovereignty – as distinct from the specifics of governance and rule – have repeatedly opened forms of subcontinental rule to potential moral challenge. The reliance of effective sovereignty on both the political and the extrapolitical has guaranteed that the exercise of sovereignty has always been a balancing act. In this sense, these chapters represent both a contribution to the study of the politics of modern South Asia, and a case study that illuminates the 'conundrum of worldly power' inherent in the concept of sovereignty on a worldwide scale.

*

The existing academic literature on sovereignty is large, though it is significantly fragmented by differing disciplinary approaches. As Hent Kalmo and Quentin Skinner note at the start of their recent collection of essays on the concept, 'pointing out, or deploring, the relative ambiguity of the idea has itself become a recurring motif in the literature on sovereignty' (Kalmo and Skinner 2010: 1). Not everyone who writes on sovereignty even agrees on precisely what the concept addresses. And this fragmentation is particularly marked when reviewing the strikingly different disciplinary approaches shaping contemporary writing on sovereignty.

Perhaps the largest body of writings on sovereignty relates to its role in international relations and to the construction of the modern state system. Here, sovereignty is usually seen as a fundamental attribute of legitimate state authority, a concept mediating between power relations and international law. Its history is embedded within the modern state system that, as Robert Jackson puts it, 'originated in the controversies and wars of sixteenth and seventeenth century Europe', and then spread around the world, the so-called Westphalian system. In this Eurocentric framing, sovereignty was a distinctly European concept, standing 'in marked contrast to ideas of authority in other parts of the world before Western imperial states intervened and established themselves as a global, and no longer a merely European or Western, system of authority' (Jackson 2007: ix). Defined in significant part by the linking of state authority to bounded territory, the underlying meaning of sovereignty in this framework lay in its shaping of an emerging state system defined by individual state *autonomy* as the defining feature of a worldwide system, a system in which rulers, freed from the power of external religious authority, claimed a right to autonomously govern their own territorially demarcated spaces, pushing toward a monopoly of force in these spaces, even as they participated in the shared values of a larger state system (Howland and White 2009: 3).[1]

Yet, the ironies in a story constructed around the 'spread' of this originally western European system on a worldwide scale are manifold and conceal the deep tensions between the universalising claims underlying understandings of sovereignty and the pervasive concepts of difference and inequality underlying its application. Within the framework of international law, sovereignty developed as a concept during the nineteenth century precisely as a mechanism for excluding (and thus in fact denying practical autonomy to) non-European peoples because they were viewed as having developed neither the 'civilised values', nor the administrative means, on which such claims to individual state autonomy could be based. The principle of sovereignty was used, in other words, to confer on the most powerful European states what amounted to a 'right of recognition' (Anghie 2007). In practice, the system of sovereign states thus became a legitimising foundation for the projection of power by a handful of western European empires, whose violation of the autonomy of non-European societies became normative as they competed on a worldwide scale for resources, markets, and strategic position (Anghie 2007: 75–82).

Critically, however, if modern concepts of sovereignty thus developed in significant part to justify a world system of deep inequalities, their universalising underpinnings were also critical in undergirding the projection of European power. Central among these principles was the (enlightenment-derived) imagining of human reason as the ultimate, universalising source for world order, an imagining embodied in institutions of bureaucracy, military organisation, law, markets, science and technology, all seen as standing apart in their formal rationality from the particularities of culture that shaped inequality and consigned non-European societies to a lower place within a civilisational hierarchy. In this distinctly European view, inequality was precisely a product of the failures of these societies to have developed the underlying forms of internal state organisation, systems of production, military technology, and 'moral knowledge' – all based on 'reason' – that would have allowed them to resist such European penetration.

'Reason', of course, is a notoriously difficult term to define. But in its relationship to modern meanings of sovereignty, the term is used here (and indeed was commonly used in the nineteenth century) in the Kantian sense, that is, to signify the ultimate core of autonomy that in Kant's conception made individual humans human. As Raf Geenens puts it, it was a vision of practical reason – a concept synonymous, in effect, with individual autonomy – that came to underlie sovereignty as a vision of autonomy, the ultimate source of willed action, 'transcending mere societal or economic mechanisms' (Geenens 2017: 502–503). The key to reason's power lay in the fact that it operated *in* the world (through human volition) but was not wholly *of* the world. In this, the autonomy of reason was much like earlier conceptions of the sovereignty of the divine, at once an emanation of will and an embedding of that will in the ineffable mysteries of the cosmos, in this case, the mysteries of human consciousness. And yet, if emanating, like divinity, from a place far removed from the operation of society, it was nevertheless a power that had the capacity to order and transform society. The autonomous power of human reason was made visible through the new forms of collective access it offered – preeminently through 'science' – to the seemingly hidden, 'occult forces' of nature and the universe (as Alexander von Humboldt put it), which were tapped to transform and reorder human material life. It thus opened a window for tapping into cosmic forces emanating from a place beyond the more immediate operation of worldly politics, and it was in this that the sovereignty of reason gained its most powerful purchase on the modern imagining of power.

Yet critical also to this story was that this vision of individual human autonomy was only actualised in the world through what might be called human 'development'. On one level, this was reflected in complex nineteenth-century European debates on how an 'enchanted', autonomous self, capable of reasoned detachment from the world, could exist in relationship to the social and natural pressures that also, inevitably, shaped individual lives. The human 'self' was a contested nineteenth-century construct, subject to innumerable theories about how the influences of nature and culture were related to the cultivation of ultimate human autonomy.[2] Few doubted in the nineteenth century that social and aesthetic influences were critical in some ways to reason's full development.[3] But most agreed that the clearest marker of reason's realisation lay in individual self-direction and independence, a product of maturation and education, and the master template in the nineteenth century for understanding the world's actual inequalities, which were framed not only in terms of differences *among* individuals, but also in terms of differences *between* classes of individuals and societies, all imagined within a hierarchy of maturation linked to cultural access to the cultivation of reason. This was a vision powerfully reflected in the German concept of *Bildung* and one perhaps most clearly projected in Mill's vision of the transformative power of education. In practice, these underlying assumptions about inequality were easily collapsed into the far more visible heuristics of gender and race as cultural (and biological) justifications for the pervasive inequalities on which this vision of sovereignty was based. Fluid visions of social difference as modelled by individual 'development' thus easily took on a harder edge. But underlying the plausibility of a developmental vision of difference lay the *visible* differences in education, wealth, technology, and military power that were the hallmark of the era of high European imperialism.[4] These defined, in effect, a tautology of common sense, simultaneously the cause and the effect of a vision of Europeans as occupying the highest rung of development – and thus of favoured access to reason's sovereign power.

Sovereignty and rule

But if critical for the story of modern sovereignty, this highly abstracted vision of reason's power did not mean that it was translated into a single template of *rule*. Far from it. European colonial empires frequently made use of indigenous, non-European structures of power as foundation for the establishment of stable order, justifying varying forms of rule by their pragmatic engagement with realities of order and power in *the real world* as they saw it. This, in fact, came to define colonial sovereignty's central tension.[5] If sovereignty depended on human consciousness (manifested in 'reason') as the ultimate source of autonomy and will in the universe, this could only find worldly fulfillment in conditions of order, which required measures of force, violence – and pragmatic adaptation – in a world in which the full 'development' of reason remained, in European eyes, a still largely European (and, indeed, white male) phenomenon.

In some areas, particularly in Asia, there had, in fact, been significant expansions of rationalising bureaucratic structures in the early modern period well before the establishment of European forms of colonial rule – a reminder that enlightenment visions of reason can in no way be conflated with the discovery of rationalising forms of rule. Indeed, elites associated with earlier structures of rule proved critical in these areas to the practical establishment of colonial rule (Lieberman 2009). In South Asia, as Rosalind O'Hanlon has written, the centuries before the establishment of British rule 'witnessed a "paper revolution", as state bureaucracies expanded in the drive to raise revenues, develop judicial procedures, and accurately document proprietary rights and obligations' (O'Hanlon 2014: 281, 2013). These centuries were also an era of growing sophistication in commercial arrangements and modes of accounting, without the existence of which the effective extension of European trading into Asia would not have been possible (Bayly 1993). But even as reliance on literate, rationalising scribal and commercial elites proved central to the effective establishment of colonial order, the principles underlying the indigenous social positions of these elites were generally consigned by the British to a social world divorced from sovereign reason, that is, to a realm of caste, patronage, and religion ('custom' and 'tradition') that occluded these elites in British eyes – however important they were to British rule – from sharing in the *ultimate* sovereign authority of the Europeans. The sharp distinction between worlds of status and contract, articulated by Sir Henry Maine as fundamental to reason's progress, in fact provided a master narrative for the shift from inherited position, and from a social order linked to lineage and custom, to a sovereign order defined by autonomous, reasoned, individual choice, which the British saw as the defining foundation for (and legitimiser of) their own distinctive – and ultimately worldwide – order of sovereignty. This provided, as Karuna Mantena argues, the most powerful 'alibi of empire' (Mantena 2010).

And yet the tension between ultimate sovereign principle and the reality of accommodation to the needs of local order defined also the pervasive tensions in this sovereign projection. In practice, British colonial rule was marked by a welter of complex state forms, all imagined at the intersection between colonial legalism/reason on the one hand, and pragmatic forms of domination (including significant violence) justified by adaptation to sometimes intractable on-the-ground realities, on the other. As many scholars have argued, this created a complex mix – marked by the projection of what some have called overlapping, layered, residual, informal, shared, or quasi- 'sovereignties' – all growing out of the mechanisms by which imperial European states encountered and worked through indigenous forms of authority as they built their own structures of rule.[6] Sometimes these were embedded in formal structures, as in the legal construction of 'protectorates', or 'princely states' as in British India; sometimes they were embedded in the construction of the British administration itself. Tracking these complex forms – and the older, indigenous visions of sovereignty that sometimes lay behind local projections of authority within the British system – is critically important for understanding how expanding European imperialism actually operated, and for understanding how the stability of colonial rule depended critically on the ways these forms played to multiple audiences.[7] European visions were hardly always hegemonic, and appeals to older framings of sovereignty changed over time, sometimes supporting forms of significant resistance to the authority of Europeans themselves, sometimes assimilated to support colonial sovereign claims.

Yet, in assessing such myriad manifestations of imperial 'sovereignty', it is critical to note that such multiple forms of adaptation in no way signalled a challenge for the British to their overarching vision of reason as providing sovereignty's *ultimate* cosmic roots. Rather, they signalled the 'conundrum of worldly power' underlying sovereignty's manifestations, the ongoing contradictions between power's ultimate roots and its worldly forms. Cosmic justifications for sovereignty were frequently at considerable odds with the realities of stable domination; indeed, the tension between these was often so marked in the eighteenth and nineteenth centuries that it was easy to label the rhetoric of 'reason'-based sovereignty as nothing more than a form (as Stephen Krasner puts it) of 'organized hypocrisy', in which claims to sovereign authority differed so fundamentally from the practice of rule as to create significant moral dissonance. In its actual operation, sovereignty inevitably entailed, as Krasner argues, the appeal to legitimising principles that were systematically violated in application, whether in forms of internal state control or in inter-state relations (Krasner 1999).[8] Indeed, it was precisely the pervasiveness of universalising sovereign rhetoric amidst the actual violence and coercion of colonialism that opened the doors to bitter critique from some of those colonial elites most exposed to the rhetorical construction of reason as the key to sovereign power. Not uncommon views on the British discourse of sovereignty were reflected in Hasrat Mohani's comments in the Indian Constituent Assembly in 1947 on the British offer of Dominion Status: 'They [the colonial powers] are past masters in the art of jugglery of words and double dealing', he said. 'They say one thing and mean quite another.'[9]

Yet, to understand indigenous reactions to the structure of colonial sovereignty more broadly, it is also critical to note that such seemingly hypocritical contradictions between cosmic principles and worldly practice were hardly peculiar to the new European forms of sovereignty associated with colonialism – or even to modern sovereignty more generally – but were intrinsic to the very character and structure of sovereignty itself as a concept – and were well understood as such. They were found in most older projections of sovereignty as well – in Europe and in India alike. If the content of the modern sovereign claims of reason were new, in other words, the 'conundrum of worldly authority' that marked the structural deployment of sovereignty as a concept certainly was not.

To analyse what *was* new, it is thus useful to begin with a brief discussion of the *continuities* between colonial and earlier, indigenous sovereign conceptions and practice. And we can find one useful entry point into this discussion if we take seriously European efforts to project their sovereign claims into the language of 'civilisation', thus suggesting the most fundamental ground for claims to continuity with earlier practice. Appeals to 'civilisation' were pervasive in nineteenth-century European sovereign rhetoric, and for many recent scholars of imperialism no word more clearly calls attention to the hypocrisy of imperial sovereign pretensions than this one. But the use of the term also suggests the deeper structural continuities in sovereignty's history. Within the context of 'civilisation', 'exemplary centres' were those sites where the core, cosmic, universalising principles of sovereignty were most visible. But such principles gained powerful resonance only in juxtaposition to the 'peripheries' associated with the patricularised identities, politics, and conflicts most associated with the cultures and lives of the far-flung peoples Europeans conquered.

Critical to the civilisational meanings of 'centre' and 'periphery', however, this juxtaposition was not simply a geographic one, but one shaped also by the tension between avenues of access to the universal principles of power organising the cosmos and the everyday worlds of social and political relations shaping everyday life. If the 'centre' in the context of 'modern' civilisation thus lay in a geographical sense in the capitals of the great European empires, with their magnetic attractions for colonial pilgrims, glimpses of modernity's many emanations were evident at a range of key sites in more peripheral regions: in the coming of railways, for example (or in the great railway stations of India's port cities), or in the provincial high courts (with their projections of the sovereign power of reason and law), or in the mysteries of science and technology, circulated through publications and taught in schools, which opened vistas on the hidden powers of the universe tapped through the structures of 'modernity' that lay at the core of sovereign power. In this sense, 'centres' of civilisational power (and thus of sovereignty) could be glimpsed at 'hot spots' scattered across the landscape. But perhaps most important, they could also be imagined as operating (in a non-geographical sense) on individuals' interior selves, defining those aspects of the self that opened to the structure of power in the universe even as social lives were embedded in the 'peripheries' of the localities. In a 'civilisational' framework the contrast between centre and periphery can thus be seen as a metaphor defining also the internal cultural tensions that shaped the lives of the mediatory elites who were so important to imperial structures.

As a civilisational form, 'modernity', with its underlying roots in individual human autonomy, thus showed deep structural continuities with earlier civilisational forms, however different the cosmic visions and varied political structures that may have underlain them. The same complex character of 'centre' and 'periphery' can be seen, for example, in Sheldon Pollock's discussion of the 'Sanskrit cosmopolis', stretching for nearly a thousand years across multiple political entities (and thus with no single *political* 'centre'), from the region west of the Indus to Southeast Asia. Here, amidst a variety of local forms of rule and cultural practice, it was the Sanskrit language itself, the 'language of the gods', that modelled with its elaborate forms and cultivated rules a vision of ultimate order, a 'central' reality somehow deeper than that reflected in the worldly competition for power, which it both legitimised and existed in tension with (Pollock 1998, 2006). In a universe where interactions between gods and humanity defined the cosmos, it was perhaps the epics that provided the most powerful templates for projecting this deeper 'reality' onto multiple and varied worldly settings. Some scholars see a 'Persian cosmopolis' that operated in similar ways in the era immediately preceding the arrival of the British in South Asia. The role of Persian as a civilisational language certainly operated against a very different, post-Mongol cosmic backdrop, in which humanity's links to the cosmos were defined, as Azfar Moin has shown, by millennial expectations and enchanted genealogy, whether in the form of the diverse sufi holy men who dotted the social landscape, or in the sovereign authority of rulers claiming divinely illumined descent, as in the case of the Mughals (Moin 2014). But Persian, too, operated, as Muzaffar Alam has written, as an 'overarching' imperial idiom, linked to a vision of cosmic balance, even as the Mughals used it to 'negotiate the diversities of Indian society' (Alam 2004: 144). All such visions of 'civilisation' were built on deep conceptual tensions between the powerful cosmic pull of an extrapolitical 'centre' (that is, a 'deeper' source of power and order in the universe) and the worldly pull of politics as it operated on multiple 'peripheries'.[10] A structure for sovereignty marked by deep moral and political tensions was thus as familiar to most Indians as it was to the British.[11]

But there were undoubtedly critical shifts that also sharply *differentiated* modernity's civilisational forms from earlier civilisational structures, which are critical for understanding modern sovereignty as it evolved in South Asia. One critical difference, of course, lay in the very intensity of economic and resource exploitation and commodification associated with the era of European colonialism, which brought new, *economic* conceptions of centre and periphery into the mix.[12] But central also were the different *systems of knowledge* through which the universe's powers were brought to earth – and translated into power and rule. Underlying the new vision of disinterested reason as the key to ultimate power was a vision of knowledge predicated not fundamentally on genealogy, or on a world of interacting gods and men modelled through great epics, but on the intrinsic autonomy of individual humans themselves, and their ability through reason to stand apart from the social and natural worlds (in which they were otherwise embedded) in order to understand and control them. This generated a powerful imaginary not only of order, but also of 'progress', an aspirational model for many indigenous, educated colonial elites, suggesting an avenue through which they too could share in the underlying foundations of sovereign authority by participating in this structuring of knowledge.

Perhaps most importantly, it also imparted a distinctive pattern to the structure of British colonial control. The key to this lay, as many analysts of modernity have noted, in the power of such objectifying knowledge to stand above and conceptually frame *the world as it actually was*, that is, to encompass, even as they stood apart from, the social/cultural/material realities they encountered in the colonised world. As Timothy Mitchell has argued of British rule in Egypt, this power to *frame* the social world was projected into multiple structures of colonial control.[13] The most powerful policies of British control in the second half of the nineteenth century were thus directed toward *encapsulating* (and thus protecting and authenticating) the many worlds of Indian culture and social relations that the British saw as necessary to the stability of their Indian polity, even as the sovereignty of reason – modernity's civilisational 'centre' – provided an overarching and universalising frame for containing these 'peripheral' forms of culture and social organisation.[14] Such a vision was embodied in British administration and law, from massive revenue and ethnographic surveys, to censuses (with their numerical imaginaries), to the ways that the structuring of Anglo-Hindu and Anglo-Muhammadan law encompassed 'indigenous' legal systems (with their links to earlier civilisational dispensations) within rationalising legal procedure. The centrality of this British vision of sovereignty was embodied in Queen

Victoria's proclamation of 1858, a sort of covenant underlying British promises to recognise ancient Indian 'customs and usages' – and rights to property – even as they were brought within the ordering frame of sovereign British protection and 'the equal and impartial protection of the law' (as if the law stood apart from the worldly interests of power). The contrast between the extrapolitical authority of the state, as a rational orderer, and the opposing realm of the embedded social and cultural structure of indigenous society, was thus brought to the very centre of the strategies through which the sovereignty of reason was translated into rule – even as it remained apart (as a frame) from the world it made sense of.

The sovereignty of the 'people'

Such visions of modern sovereignty took distinctive colonial form in India. But as a product of universalising principles they hardly developed independently of the larger trajectories of sovereign thinking in Europe, which underwent critical transformations in the nineteenth and twentieth centuries, particularly with respect to the ongoing evolution of the concept of the sovereignty of the 'people'. The sovereignty of the 'people' has been much written about – and its history is complex. Rooted initially in visions of the autonomous, reasoning, individual self, it was an evolving idea projecting an imagined collectivity based on such individual autonomy, an emerging challenge in the seventeenth and eighteenth centuries to divine right kingship. The concept of the people's sovereignty thus acted as a revolutionary force in the English revolution of the mid-seventeenth century and in the French revolution over a century later. But the concept was one with multiple meanings, linked to a variety of interests, and with little consensus on what it might imply in terms of forms of rule.

Indeed, the sovereignty of the 'people' gained its greatest vitality not as a blueprint for a particular form of rule at all, but as a sovereign imaginary casting the 'people' as an entity abstracted from actual social life – an *extrapolitical* collectivity existing somehow anterior to the operation of actual worldly power. In a wholly worldly sense, the people were, of course, inescapably divided by interest, class, sect, gender, status and faction; they were in this sense everything and nothing when it came to the specifics of a system of rule. The key to the projection of the people as a sovereign unity thus lay in the modelling of the 'people' precisely as a supra-political imaginary, a source of ultimate power *authorising* rule, the 'constituent sovereign that establishes government rather than the governing sovereign' (Yack 2001: 522).[15] Though this vision of 'constituent power' evolved in multiple forms in western Europe, it came to provide the ultimate foundation for most modern forms of 'constitutional' government, and the most prominent (though hardly the only) way in which the sovereignty of the people – rooted in the enchanted autonomy of the individual self – ultimately took worldly form.[16]

But as a concept evolving in tandem with the new concepts of individual state autonomy shaping international conceptions of modern sovereignty, even this conception was marked by (at least) two deep-seated contradictions. The first contradiction related to the 'people's' relationship to the vision of individual maturation and development as a key feature of the sovereignty of reason. Though this idea by no means disappeared as the concept of the people's sovereignty evolved (and was reflected, for example, in ongoing nineteenth- and twentieth-century conceptions of voting defined and limited by age, gender, race, and lack of property-holding status, all seen as markers of incomplete 'development' toward the ideal of the sovereign self), the concept of the 'people' nevertheless also gained increasing purchase in popular thinking as a vision of community mobilised through the immediacy of symbolic public action – action suggesting an equality of individual affect, devotion, and sacrifice as expressions of claims to individual autonomy – that could not be easily contained within 'developmental' visions.[17] Such tensions were reflected also in ongoing debates among intellectuals on the nature of the autonomous self (and of the human will) and on the very meaning of 'reason' (sometimes, though by no means always, contrasted with 'emotion') as a frame for individual sovereign autonomy.

This was related to a second, and perhaps even more dramatic contradiction, relating to how the 'people' were to be mobilised as a foundation for autonomous *state* sovereignty. The ultimate power of the concept of popular sovereignty lay in its universalism, in its links to universalising conceptions of individual freedom, will and practical reason as the ultimate keys to a human consciousness imagined as having the power to stand apart both from nature and from the social in order to exert influence over the world. As a sovereign concept, the 'people' gained its greatest sovereign power through this universalism. But to be effectively mobilised as a source of sovereignty for individual states, the concept had also to be grounded in the territorially and culturally *particular*, associating each sovereign 'people' with a specific territory and state. One nineteenth-century answer to this seeming contradiction lay in the development, as Charles Taylor has described it, of the concept of individual *authenticity*, of the idea that all human beings, whatever the universality of their individual autonomy, each had also his or her own distinctive *way* of being human. Individuals, in other words, carried in their very humanity their own essential and unique personalities, and with a moral imperative to be true to themselves. Such a vision, as Taylor notes, shaped the nineteenth-century evolution of the idea of distinctive 'peoples' (Taylor 1994: 28–33). Sovereign 'peoples', like individuals, were at once carriers of the universal and the particular, on the one hand projected as unities standing apart from everyday culture and politics, yet on the other hand carrying their own intrinsic cultural essences and particular 'personalities', often (though not always) linked to the specificities of language.[18]

But a paradox nevertheless remained, for the requirements of sovereignty as an ultimate, extrapolitical source of power required that such a vision of the 'people' also be cast in opposition to the *lived* forms of culture that shaped 'society', the term used increasingly in the nineteenth century to describe the collection of sociologically interacting individuals and groups who occupied a state's territory.[19] If the 'people' were thus imagined as a single collective self, a self with its own intrinsic, essentialised culture, this vision of the people also stood in contradistinction to the imaginary of 'society', the realm of the people as worldly, socially embedded human beings (in the plural), defined by their interactions, divisions, social conflicts, and economic interests/competition. These were, in a sense, the 'people's two bodies', a concept modelled on Ernst Kantorowicz's notion of the 'king's two bodies' in premodern Europe, the one mortal (and social), the other immortal (and abstracted from society), as a foundation for kingly sovereignty (Kantorowicz 1957).[20] It was, in essence, the immortal body of the sovereign 'people', rooted in the mysteries of 'enchanted' individual autonomy and 'authenticity', that was conjoined with the 'located' or sociological body of 'society', defined by its worldly networks of economic connections, competing interests, social and class dependencies, and lived socio-cultural interactions. These two bodies were essential to the people's sovereignty, and yet in ongoing and inescapable tension.

In practice, it is hardly surprising that the conceptual separation between these 'two bodies' of the people was frequently a hazy one, which led to forms of popular politics in Europe that sometimes mixed uneasily a vision of the 'people' as a product of abstract individual autonomy (and reason), with a politics of socially embedded cultural competition, driven by appeals to affect and devotion to symbols of identity that were necessary to imagine the 'people' as sovereign within the modern state system. The tension between these visions was often mediated by the state, which acted to order and regulate 'society' even as its power was itself increasingly conceptualised as authorised by the 'people'. It was in this context, in fact, that the concept of the 'nation' gained its greatest traction, both as a culturally grounded name for a spatially-located 'people', but also as a field for cultural and status competition in society. Indeed, this was the framework in which the idea of the 'nation-state' took on increasing significance in international relations, particularly in the years following World War I.[21] It was a concept whose spread was authorised in the wake of the worldwide political crises of the first half of the twentieth century as much by the state's need to limit the destabilising political implications of the people's sovereignty as to tap into it as a source of ultimate sovereign legitimacy.

*

Not surprisingly, changing ideas about the nature of sovereignty in Europe (and in the world at large) had significant influence on the course of sovereign conceptions in India. But they intersected with the distinctive forms in which sovereignty had developed in India during the British colonial era – and with older, evolving Indian ideas on the nature of legitimate political authority – in complex ways. This collection of chapters makes no attempt to cover all the varying aspects of the operation of sovereignty in modern South Asia, a huge subject. It is rather an attempt by some historians, anthropologists, and scholars of religion, to suggest some key themes for thinking about the evolution of sovereignty in South Asia as it played out in the colonial era and subsequently in relationship to the worldwide transformations associated with modern forms of sovereignty.

The chapters in the volume are divided into three sections, which explore three of the most contested and critical aspects of the ways that sovereignty functioned in colonial and post-colonial South Asia. The first section looks at the role of law as a key to British constructions of imperial sovereignty in India, and examines the ways in which the British concept of the 'rule of law' in India, as a manifestation of the sovereignty of reason, both displaced older notions of sovereignty, and yet, at the same time, built on older notions, and drew older ideas of sovereignty into the structure of the British system. As all the chapters in this section show, an examination the 'rule of law' also takes us beyond narrow questions of political theory in India and into questions also relating to the relationship between sovereignty and religion. The second section looks at the complicated story of kingship in South Asia, both during the colonial era and within the democratic order that succeeded it. Here the tension between law as an expression of rule-bound sovereignty is brought into direct juxtaposition with visions of embodied sovereignty represented in the person of the king. Though kingly sovereignty was in some ways challenged in modern thinking by reason, by law, and by the people as the *ultimate* founts of sovereign authority, there is no doubt that images of embodied sovereign power have continued to carry significant weight in South Asia (and elsewhere) – and have developed in a sometimes close, if paradoxical, relationship to the 'sovereignty of the people'. The final section turns our attention to the nation and to the tensions between 'nations' and 'peoples' as a problem that continues to shape debates on the meaning of sovereignty, not only in independent India, but also in Pakistan and Bangladesh.

I. Law, religion, and sovereignty in India

The concept of the 'rule of law', in its relationship to sovereignty, remains one of the most important arenas for discussing the history of sovereignty in modern South Asia. Law lay at the very heart of British representations of their regime as a manifestation of the sovereignty of reason – whatever its accommodation to the realities of worldly power – and remains one of the most powerful legacies of the colonial regime. Yet, the significance and meaning of the 'rule of law' – as a manifestation of sovereignty – remains a sharply contested subject among historians of South Asia.

Debates over the relationship between law and sovereignty in South Asia have their roots in the debates of modern European political theory. The importance of monarchical authority to social order was widely recognised in early modern Europe, but the dangers of vesting unconstrained authority in a monarch without the constraints of law were also the focus of considerable attention. It was this tension that lay behind Hobbes' vision of a contract among the people, ceding all power to the king (as an embodiment of the abstract people taken as a whole) in the common (and reasoned) interest of maintaining worldly order. More significant in the evolution of British conceptions of law's relationship to sovereignty was Locke's vision of a contract among the people to constitute a realm of law to stand between the ruler and the people and to constrain both. Law in this sense was separated from rule; conceptually, it existed prior to the operation of power (however much implicated in it) since it emanated in imagination from a past social contract between the people and the ruler. And yet, while thus imagined as antecedent to the state (and thus a constraint on its power), law still served in this framing as a powerful instrument for the projection of state authority.

In India there has been a considerable amount of writing on the 'rule of law' as a concept central to the sovereign claims of British imperial authority. The British themselves frequently projected law as the central element in their own association with reason and progress – a position perhaps most powerfully expressed in the writings of the Law Member of the Viceroy's Council in the early 1870s, Sir James Fitzjames Stephen. As Mithi Mukherjee has noted, Stephen saw British sovereignty as a 'bridge' carrying India's multitudes from a world of violence and superstition to one of 'orderly, peaceful and industrious' life. This bridge rested in Stephen's view on two equally important 'piers'. One pier was military power, without which order in India was impossible. But the other pier was what Stephen called 'justice'. 'Justice' (linked powerfully in Stephen's thinking to the rule of law) was the 'ultimate end', in Mukherjee's terms, that justified colonial sovereignty (Mukherjee 2010: 72–73). And the key to this vision of 'justice', as Mukherjee argues, was procedural fairness and disinterest, rooted in the autonomy of reason, a principle Mukherjee calls 'justice as equity'. As a key to sovereignty, the power of the 'rule of law' thus lay precisely in its imagined detachment from the culture and politics of Indian society, a principle self-consciously projected as distinct from (and even the antithesis of), the very military power that was equally necessary – given the current state of Indian society – to the effective establishment of rule.

This was an oft-repeated British projection of 'justice' in India. Yet critics (both contemporary and subsequent) have questioned whether the 'rule of law' in British India – as an actual system – could in any way be characterised as structurally independent of the colonial state's overt executive and military power, particularly given the law's often highly racialised execution (De 2012: 72–73). This has been underscored by scholars such as Nasser Hussain and Elizabeth Kolsky, who have detailed the critical role of race in shaping the law's actual operation (Hussain 2003; Kolsky 2010). Indeed, for many, British claims to uphold a colonial 'rule of law' that operated independently of executive power was just another example of sovereignty's 'organised hypocrisy'. As David Washbrook has written of property law in the Company period, for example, the fiction that the law 'treated and protected private property as if it existed at a remove from the state', was 'pure farce' (Washbrook 1981: 665).

But if the law courts, particularly in their everyday operation, were deeply in thrall to the needs of the colonial state, it is nevertheless also true that the imagining of the law as an autonomous force standing apart from the direct exercise of power, whatever the general operation of the courts, was one that gained a significant hold in India, not only on the imaginations of the British themselves, but also on the imaginations of a cohort of Indian elites – particularly those trained in the law but including a significant segment of the Indian middle class as well. In part the imaginative appeal of law in such circumstances was captured by E. P. Thompson in his classic statement in *Whigs and Hunters*; as a potential check on the authority of the state, the law had only to call the state to account occasionally to project the fiction that the law's sovereign authority transcended elite class capture and constrained state violence (Thompson 1976: Conclusion). As De notes, it was certainly significant that 'the legal public, that is the professional sphere of lawyers and judges, had deep faith in it' (De 2012: 86).[22] And although few British officials bought into the idea of a social contract between the 'people' and the colonial state authorising the law as an autonomous realm, there were nevertheless multiple ways in which the law carried powerful intimations of sovereignty that bridged any hard racial lines between the British and key groups of Indians, both with respect to the law as ideology and with respect to its institutional operation.

There were two areas in particular in which the distinctive structure of the 'rule of law' in colonial India – in spite of its undoubted association with state violence – still resonated with pre-existing Indian assumptions about sovereignty, and in ways that were to have significant implications for the construction of sovereignty after 1947. Perhaps the most important was the law's strong professional appeal, through its emphasis on disinterested proceduralism, with forms of power long associated in the subcontinent with renunciation, self-denial, and even asceticism. This was a conception of sovereign independence associated particularly with Brahmans, as Heesterman discussed in his contrast of the cultural styles of Brahmans and Kshatriyas noted earlier. Indeed, the law offered an entrée for many high-caste Indians to the principles of sovereignty defining the colonial state's claims to power, even as it offered independence from the direct control of the colonial bureaucracy – and the hierarchies of landed authority with which it was connected. The rhetoric of the 'rule of law' powerfully resonated in this connection with earlier conceptions of sovereign authority that allowed it to gain significant purchase in certain strands of Indian thinking.[23]

Of perhaps only slightly less importance, however, was the manner in which the law provided a framework for the recognition in India for certain types of popular customary and religious 'rights' in India as ostensibly 'authentic' expressions of an autonomous realm of Indian culture – even if this realm of culture remained in tension with the detached (and reasoned) principles marking the 'rule of law' as, at least in British eyes, a 'higher' sovereign realm. The roots of this vision of the 'rule of law' can be found in the Company period, and in the projection of a legal framework within which rights were 'discovered' and protected by the state, as if their claims to authenticity conceptually preceded the direct power of the colonial state.[24] But it gained formal recognition in the

Queen's proclamation of 1858, in which the government bound itself to respect 'ancient rights and usages' as a central element in its projection of the 'rule of law' as a framework for sovereignty that could be conceptualised as transcending the state's military authority. Though hardly defining the law as independent of political influence, the recognition of such 'rights' was widely projected as a kind of covenant, defining the law's authority as binding even on the colonial state itself (a reading that found expression in numerous popular petitions and court actions). This was the case also for landed property rights, which at times took the form in colonial India of a contract with the state (a powerful conceit, though one the state retained the power to sometimes abrogate), but which were more commonly rooted in the more binding language of 'ancestral' inheritance, as in Queen Victoria's proclamation itself. On one level, this was a structure critical to the mechanisms by which British rule sought to subsume indigenous forms of culture and leadership within a framework of legal proceduralism that reflected their own, superior sovereign authority as the bearers of reason. But it was at the same time a structure that recognised the authenticity of indigenous 'rights' based on religion, caste, and lineage, and offered to them the sovereign sanction of the 'rule of law' – thus potentially constraining even the power of the state. This too resonated with many indigenous ideas about sovereign authority, and it was a structure that was to leave important legacies for the operation of the 'rule of law' as a frame for sovereignty, even after India's independence.[25]

The actual ways that these principles played out in the law's workings in colonial India were complex. Pamela Price's chapter on the history of litigation relating to Hindu *mathas* (monasteries, or *maths* as it is more commonly transliterated in north India) in Madras Presidency in the nineteenth and early twentieth centuries illustrates the critical relationship between the 'rule of law' as an expression of sovereign authority and the operation of local authority linked to religious institutions. By tracking a long series of court cases relating to authority in such mathas, Price shows us the consequences of the colonial state's use of the law to adjudicate – and in the process try to encapsulate – longstanding forms of institutionalised religious authority. A history of these cases shows clearly how the courts sought in many ways to 'protect the status of matha heads', (p. 52) underscoring the importance of religious lineage and of a renunciatory style in shaping and stabilising religious authority of these institutions under the colonial regime. Here we can see clearly how the law provided a sovereign frame in which the legitimate authority of these leaders was recognised within the British system in the language of legal claims. Yet, at the same time, as Price also shows, the very process of encapsulating this structure of religious authority, a process in which matha heads were deeply complicit as they competed for state recognition and control over matha property, had important implications for perceptions of the relationship of religion to sovereignty. Appeals to lineage and a renunciatory style of authority were adjudicated by the courts not with respect to the *ultimate* religious validity such claims carried, but in accord with their relationship to past practice (or custom), evidence of which was evaluated through the higher authority of legal procedure and independent reasoning and argumentation. Price's chapter thus points toward transformations in the very meaning of 'religion' that the linking of sovereignty to the 'rule of law' may have encouraged. British court adjudication came to be largely predicated on the separation of personal religiosity (however valued) from the management of 'worldly' institutional religious affairs, which, in accord with the state's sovereign principles (and, increasingly, the views of an educated middle-class 'public' as well), were subject to procedural rationality and reason.

As Price's article implies, such conflicts point to the critical impact of changing conceptions of sovereignty in transforming the very meanings attached to 'religion'. Indeed, assessing the operation of the 'rule of law' through the lens of sovereignty gives us new perspectives on the often-conflicted meanings of 'secularism' in colonial India and beyond. At the core of colonial secularism was the projection by the state of a source of cosmic power (disinterested human reason) that transcended the particularities of all worldly religions. From this perspective, the role of the courts 'secularized' the authority of the leaders of the mathas, whose institutional leadership was now defined as deriving not from cosmic principles, but from the socially embedded positions and customs which marked the mathas as part of 'society'. They were thus, like other social institutions, subject to reasoned regulation. Yet this development was hardly without contradiction. For if the law embodied a claim to sovereign power transcending religion, its structure also gave to the language and institutions of religion, and to custom, a central – perhaps even privileged – place in the ordering of the society on which it acted.

The particular resonances between the 'rule of law' and renunciatory styles of religious authority in India are explored directly by Aya Ikegame in her chapter on the influence of a matha-based guru in Karnataka in post-independence India, with the backdrop provided not just by the 'rule of law', but by the larger framework of the 'sovereignty of the people', with all its intrinsic paradoxes. For Ikegame, the fundamental paradox in the law's relationship to the people's sovereignty was laid out by Rousseau. As Rousseau saw it, it was only the 'people' whose sovereign 'general will' could authorise the social contract establishing the law. But, at the same time – paradoxically – it was only the contract itself (that is, the law) that could actually bestow such authority on the 'people' to enter into such a contract. As Ikegame notes, a partial answer to this paradox – at least for Rousseau – lay in the conceptualisation of a worldly legislator or lawgiver who could embody the 'people' (presumably as an expression of individual reason), while at the same time standing apart from the human passions that the law was intended to control. The law was associated, in other words, with a lawgiver who, as Ikegame puts it in quoting Rousseau, 'could see all the passions of men without experiencing any of them'. (p. 61) Here we can see an image of sovereign power of law rooted in the human capacity for reasoned detachment from worldly political interest, and embodied in the image of what Ikegame thus calls 'the sovereign renouncer', a figure at once associated with the law, with the people, and with the cosmic forces shaping the universe that had long been associated with religion. Yet, in exploring the figure of the guru as judge at his *Nyaya Peetha* ('seat of justice'), Ikegame also shows the entanglements of his adjudication with the myriad conflicts of local 'society', including local communities, mining companies, and the power of the state in multiple guises. In describing the tensions inherent in these interactions, her account thus provides a window for thinking about how the 'rule of law' and the 'sovereignty of the people' have conceptually intersected in India – even as both imaginings have drawn on powerful, older assumptions about religion and culture.

In the final chapter in this section, David Gilmartin tracks the relationship of law and sovereignty on a larger political canvas, that is, through India's twentieth-century transition from colonial rule to the formal enshrining of the 'sovereignty of the people' in India's Constitution. The projection of competing *temporalities* was a key, from the beginning, to the way that the British attempted to reconcile the universalism of their own claims to sovereign power, as the bearers of modern reason and law, with their practical exclusion of Indians – and Indian 'society', locked into a 'traditional' past – from sovereignty's 'enchantments'. This temporal displacement had long been central to the structure of British sovereignty. To rule in India, as Maine put it, the British had 'to make their watches keep true time in two longitudes at once' (Maine 1875: 37).[26]

Not surprisingly, it was against the backdrop of this temporal duality that the most serious challenges to the British association with the 'rule of law' arose. There had, of course, long been Indian leaders who had asserted their own association with the law's sovereignty as a claim to share in British imperial power – and who had at times used the law to try to call British power to account. But it was Gandhi who launched the most sweeping challenge to the competing temporalities underlying the disjunction between the law's sovereignty and the practical structure of British rule. Hardly reflecting the maturation of reason, the 'rule of law' in British India was, as Gandhi saw it, nothing but an artefact of colonial power and politics pure and simple. Indeed, a far truer commitment to disinterested reason (and truth) – and to the *concept* of the 'rule of law' – was to be found in the socially detached self-control of the *satyagrahis* whom Gandhi mobilised to challenge the British. He thus used his technique of *satyagraha* to project an alternate vision of law that fundamentally challenged the temporal duality underlying the claims of the British. Gandhi's vision of *swaraj* (or sovereign autonomy) was tied to a vision of law and sovereignty that was *at once* rooted in Indian tradition and *at the very same time* temporally modern in its appeal to the sovereignty of reason (and widely recognised as such internationally).

Yet, Gandhi's vision of the people's sovereignty was still marked by its own contradictions, for – in an echo of European ideas of reason's maturity as a mode of becoming – it rested on its own deeply developmental vision of law's relationship to India's still less-than-self-controlled 'masses'. During India's nationalist movement, his visions thus competed with other projections of the sovereign 'people', including projections of sovereignty with far less reference to the self-discipline of law. Perhaps most powerful among these was the international socialist vision projecting the 'people' as the class-based carriers of a modern, worldwide revolutionary tradition embedded in capitalism's inherent contradictions and in its own vision of progressive time. This rested on a powerful image of the 'people' as an immanent, revolutionary force, even if their inchoate spirit required representation by socialist-inspired party leaders, operating both within, and outside, the Congress.

Such competing framings of the 'people' played themselves out after 1947 within a constitutional order that continued to define the relationship between the state and the sovereign 'people' by juxtaposing multiple temporalities, associated on the one hand with the law and the 'people' in a process of 'becoming', and on the other with the people as the bearers of a revolutionary mission, whose spirit would be channelled by the state. The tension between these was evident even in debates over the temporal meanings attached to the constituent power of the 'people' in the promulgation of the Indian Constitution itself. For some, the 'people', as the *ultimate* source of the Constitution (whoever the document's actual historical authors), stood apart from worldly time, their sovereign power embodied in a vision of the Constitution as Law, which was anterior to the time-bound affairs of state governance and parliamentary politics.[27] In such a vision, the sovereign power of the 'people' was brought into everyday time only during the cyclical holding of elections, which were sharply constrained by legal procedures. But for others the people's voice remained immanent in politics, invoked in popular protest and public performance, and embodied in the state's own embrace of the progressive socialist vision embodied in the Constitution's Directive Principles for the state.[28]

Such conflicted understandings of the people's sovereignty exploded during the years leading up to Indira Gandhi's Emergency. But they were hardly resolved even with the end of the Emergency and the restoration of electoral democracy that brought it to an end. Such conflicts continued to shape contestations over the law as a manifestation of the sovereignty of reason, and the relationship of the law to the public performance of sovereignty not only through elections, but also through popular protest. If the end of the Emergency led to a significant weakening in the state's claim to the revolutionary mantle of a socialist 'people' (a weakening reflected in the turn toward capitalist 'liberalisation'), subsequent contestations surrounding sovereignty related not just to the 'rule of law' but also to visions of *embodied* sovereignty, associated both with the 'people', and with old imaginaries focused on the enchanted bodies of Indian kings.

II. Kingship reconfigured

Whatever sovereignty's association with ineffable cosmic forces, many of its most powerful manifestations have been associated in modern South Asia not with seemingly impersonal forces, like law, but with 'enchanted' human bodies – and it is for this reason that debate relating to the continuing modern vitality of tropes of kingly sovereignty in India represents one of the most important and sharply contested areas in the academic scholarship on modern sovereignty's interpretation. Academic debates relating to the fate of kingly sovereignty in South Asia have taken two very distinct forms. One line of debate relates to the distinctively South Asian story arising from the subcontinent's history of colonial rule. Within this story, forms of kingly sovereignty maintained their significance under colonial rule as icons of 'tradition', deliberately preserved in the status – and wide importance – given to 'little kings' as intermediaries within the structure of colonial sovereignty. The result was the perseverance (even, perhaps, flourishing) of kingly *styles* of leadership in popular politics and culture under the Raj, even as these styles came under critique from 'middle-class' elites who saw kingly styles as precisely a calculated colonial mechanism for distancing Indians from the *ultimate* sources of the modern sovereignty of reason under the British.[29]

These tensions took on new significance with the constitutional recognition of the sovereignty of the 'people' after 1947, when images of embodied kingly sovereignty gained new meaning in the context of elections, serving in some cases as a vehicle for the expression of the 'people's' own, autonomous sovereign voice, even as the processes of elections were encased in legal proceduralism. The success of the descendants of ruling families who deployed kingly styles of political performance were easily interpreted as signs of divine favour now carried through the people themselves (as Caleb Simmons suggests in his chapter), an association of the people's sovereignty with forms of divine power that transcended the impersonal forms of legal and bureaucratic authority that in fact framed the holding of elections. As Pamela Price has shown elsewhere, dramatic examples of the continuing vitality of kingly sovereignty in India can thus be found in the images cultivated by a range of popular politicians in late twentieth-century India. These include many who used associations with film, and the images of older kingly styles, to find new media for kingly sovereign performance, as, for example, in the styles of leadership cultivated by leaders like MGR in Tamil Nadu or N. T. Rama Rao in Andhra Pradesh (Price 1989, 1996). This can be seen also in the ongoing vitality of dynastic politics in patterns of Indian political representation, however much such forms have continued to come in for 'middle-class' critique (Chandra 2016).

But debates on kingly sovereignty in South Asia have taken another prominent academic form as well, and one extending well beyond the specificities of South Asia. At the heart of these debates lies the scholarly concept of 'political theology', the idea that modern sovereignty, whatever its associations with reason, has continued to draw heavily on templates of divinity. Visions of a unitary, anthropomorphic God, with power over life and death, have thus provided, as some have contended, powerful frames for conceptualising the ultimate roots of modern sovereignty. The most influential strands in the development of this approach to sovereignty derive from the work of Carl Schmitt in the 1920s, and from its more recent elaboration in the work of Giorgio Agamben

(Schmitt 1985; Agamben 2005). Both of these thinkers emphasised what they called the 'exception' as the key to understanding the ultimate source of sovereignty, a vision of ultimate power transcending law, just as the ultimate authority of God transcended the order of nature in the form of the miracle. An emphasis on the 'exception' in political theology thus represented precisely an appeal to embodied power (on the model of divinity) as a form of power transcending not only human law and reason but also human ethics – indeed, that transcended *all* of society's cultural bonds (thus reducing humanity to Agamben's 'bare life'). Like the sovereignty of reason, this was a powerful vision of sovereignty as an extrapolitical force. But for Schmitt in particular, a political theology rooted in the sovereign model of an anthropomorphic God with ultimate power over human life and death, was precisely a response to what he saw as the inability of the 'rule of law' alone, even in a secular age, to provide the vital sovereign centre – that is, an expression of *will* – necessary to compel order in the time of significant political uncertainty in Europe following World War I.[30]

Some analysts of sovereignty in South Asia, notably Thomas Blom Hansen and Finn Stepputat, have taken up this model to contrast what they call 'de jure sovereignty', as reflected in 'the legitimate right to govern', and what they call 'de facto sovereignty', or the 'right over life', reflected in the personalised wielding of sovereign violence (Hansen and Stepputat 2006: 301–302; see also Hansen and Stepputat 2005). Here the sovereignty of the law and of kingship are clearly juxtaposed as co-existing, yet opposing, frameworks for sovereign authority, drawing on different principles. Yet such a framing is necessarily in tension with a vision of sovereignty deriving from access to an *ultimate* source of cosmic power. And this problem points in turn to the question as to how applicable the *particular* theological model of Schmitt and Agamben might be for South Asia – or for the history of kingship in South Asia. As we have seen, the purchase of the 'rule of law' as a concept among key groups in South Asia could also be linked to 'political theologies', that is, to models of cosmic power conceived of as accessible through forms of internalised self-control, self-restraint, and ascetic self-denial – avenues for access to power as compelling for some as the image of the king as the wielder of divine violence.[31] Some scholars have thus been skeptical of the application of Schmittian models of 'political theology' to South Asia, particularly in the face of complex South Asian ideas about the more permeable flows of divine power across the 'thresholds' between the invisible and visible worlds at the boundaries between life and death, such as have been analysed in the recent work of Bhrigupati Singh (2012: 383–407).

Whatever the controversies surrounding these ideas, however, there is little doubt that they point us toward the importance of analysing kingly models in shaping a significant range of popular ideas about sovereignty (including the 'people's sovereignty'), in South Asia as much as in other parts of the world.[32] Such questions provide a backdrop for the three chapters in this section. In the first two articles, Uwe Skoda and Caleb Simmons focus on the transformations in the perceptions of authority surrounding two very different 'little kings' in modern times, one in the Bonai region of Odisha, the other in Mysore in the South. Skoda takes us, via an analysis of royal chronicles, to the roots of the common tensions that many historians and anthropologists have found in premodern South Asian kingship more generally – most notably the tension between the king as 'outsider', and, as such, a wielder of a 'power over life frequently tied to a similar power of the deities' (p. 111), and the king as the bringer of local order through 'insider' alliances with local leaders and the engagement with and protection of specific local communities, dramatised through the patronage of temples and ritual.[33] Skoda emphasises how these contradictions were negotiated through relations with local goddesses, and manifested in ritual, most notably at the pan-Indian festival of Dasara, which produced what he calls a 'sacrificial polity' (associated with the king's ultimate control over life), even as this power was limited in the actual relations of these kings with a shifting array of local power holders. But Skoda also provides evidence of the increasing attenuation of this ritual world under overarching British authority and colonial law – and even more so after the establishment of the new democratic order of the Republic of India. His story could thus be read as one showing the sapping of kingly images of sovereignty in the face of the new sovereign claims of law and of the 'people'. Nevertheless, as he argues at the end, his story is far less one of popular disaffection from kingship as a worldly 'divine manifestation', than it is one of a decline in the Bonai royal family's ability to mobilise the resources necessary to make the public performance of kingly sovereignty compelling. If the current heirs to Bonai's kingly traditions have thus fallen on hard times, Skoda's story points to the ways that ideas of kingly sovereignty, linked to changing forms of religious ritual and patronage coming from new sources, can still be mobilised in local politics in conflicts over local resources, such as those increasingly being exploited by mining companies and new forms of politics.

The complex relationship between worldly violence and the projection of kingly sovereignty as a manifestation of the favour of the gods lies also at the heart of Caleb Simmons' chapter. Focusing on the modern history of the Wodeyar princely house in Mysore, Simmons argues that in the days before the British colonial takeover of Mysore, it was preeminently the successful wielding of violence, through military conquest, that provided the foundation for kings to assert that their rule was also blessed by divinity. The successful assertion of worldly force and power provided the most powerful evidence of divine favour (and provided as well – critically – the ritual resources to dramatise it). The worldly and other-worldly foundations of sovereignty were, in this sense, inseparable. But this fundamental link between the successful wielding of violence and divine selection was broken, as Simmons argues, during the colonial era. With the British responsible for installing the Wodeyars in power, the connection between the Wodeyars' own wielding of worldly violence and their projection of divine selection was far less compelling. Nevertheless, a link between worldly power and divine favour powerfully re-emerged with the establishment after 1947 of a system of democratic elections, a new form of worldly combat, linked not to violence but to votes. Indeed, with the repeated election of Srikantadatta Wodeyar to parliament, the sovereign people themselves could now be imagined as the carriers of a new form of divine mandate that took worldly shape through success in electoral politics. On a small scale, the people's sovereignty could thus here be imagined to be actualised, and to be associated with divine favour, through the kingly persona of the man the people themselves had elected.

Such a link between electoral success, and conceptions of both kingly and popular sovereignty, can in fact be seen in the structures of patronage shaping contemporary electoral politics in India far more broadly (Piliavsky 2014). But the relationship between the local wielding of violence and the claim to a sovereign mandate appears as far more central – and yet far more problematic – in Lucia Michelutti's contribution, which focuses on western Uttar Pradesh, a region known, as she puts it, for the 'endemic violence' deeply ingrained in the cultures of its 'dominant castes, such as the Jats, Yadavs, Gujars and Thakurs' (p. 153). Here too we see an image of kingly sovereignty projected as a culturally sanctioned (and perhaps divinely sanctioned) form of authority rooted in the requirements of social order, a frame within which the wielding of kingly *danda* (force), as laid out in ancient texts such as the *Arthashastra* and the *Mahabharata*, has long remained central to conceptions of sovereign authority. But in sharp contrast to the world of Srikantadatta Wodeyar in Simmons' story, the role of the king as both a protector of and a source of power over the local community seems largely lacking here in any of the forms of restraint (or renunciation) associated with the 'rule of law'. In spite of the backdrop provided by elections, 'kingly violence' seems to shade very quickly into racketeering and extortion, that is, into a world of 'mafia raj' where power – and violence – does indeed seem to justify itself. The system is epitomised by 'Raja Bhai', a successful politician and government minister – and a 'hero' to local Rajput and Yadav informants – whom Michelutti evocatively characterises as simply a 'kingly (*raja*) gangster who kills with impunity' (p. 163).

So, what then, exactly, is the relationship between kingship and the 'people's sovereignty' that we can see in this local context? If the 'people' are to be seen as manifested in such embodied forms of worldly power, then we have here a vision of the 'people' of a very distinctive sort. On one level, of course, it is not difficult to see in this story precisely a manifestation of 'popular' values, as Michelutti suggests in her linking of the 'macho' values underlying this system to the pervasive forms of violence against women that characterise Rajput and Yadav families. Gender is central to this story. The 'popular values' driving this system, are, in fact, values closely linked to the striving for masculine honour and status among the men of the martial and backward castes in this region more generally. But what is noteworthy is the seemingly complete disappearance here of a vision of the 'people' as an abstract entity, a sovereign collectivity imagined to transcend the social worlds in which the competition for honour, wealth, and protection that she describes occurs. If there is an imaginary of an abstractly equal 'people', standing apart from the social hierarchies and conflicts of this world, it is seemingly a 'people' coterminous only with the bounds of these *particular* castes, and thus one with none of the universalising, human resonances relevant to the authorisation of formal, legal power. Nor do we see significant evidence of law as a counterpoint to *danda*. Law is simply another form of worldly power that is subsumed within a structure of kingly calculation.

And yet, there is no doubt that the vision of sovereign 'kingly' authority wielded by the men described by Michelutti is also one imagined as authorised by the sovereignty of the 'people' in a certain sense, that is, by the idea that kingly power (and the use of violence) binds these 'little kings' (or kingly protectors) to their followers within a structure of electoral competition.[34] That this form of sovereign claim has been shaped not only by old traditions of kingship, but also by the structure of India's colonial past, and, perhaps most importantly, by the contemporary structure of electoral democracy and by the prominent role of caste within it (as a critical, competitive essence of identity framed through the law's structuring of reservations), remains critically important. One way to characterise this world of local power is to follow Hansen and Stepputat in labelling this as a form of de facto sovereignty, that is, a vision of sovereignty largely decoupled, in its relatively unconstrained linkages to local violence and intimidation, from the realms of legitimate de jure sovereignty undergirding the official claims of the state. But it is also important to ask whether these forms can ever be separated (except for narrow heuristic purposes). For, as we have suggested here, it is arguably the relationship between these forms, however conflicted (and even, seemingly, oppositional), that points us toward sovereignty's deepest meaning – and deepest contradictions.

III. The nation and the sovereign imagination

The final section of the volume focuses on how concepts of sovereignty can help us understand that form of 'imagined community' that we call the *nation*, a concern that takes us back to the relationship between the distinctive cultural framings of the 'people's sovereignty' that have emerged in South Asia and the universalising, idealised visions of state autonomy that have shaped the modern, international order. The idea of the *nation* has long borne a close relationship to the modern concept of the people's sovereignty as the bedrock of the international state system. But to confront the *distinctions* between 'nations' and 'peoples' is also to confront sovereignty's deepest tensions. As we have already seen, the historical projection of the 'people' as a *sovereign* entity has generally required that they be abstracted from the conflicted social relations and cultures of the particular 'societies' that they have also constituted; that is, that they be imagined as transcending social particularity in order to serve as a universalising source of unity authorising rule. But when imagined as a 'nation' within the modern state system, a people had, of necessity, to be also saturated with cultural particularity, for only then could they be mobilised as a source of sovereign authority for a *particular* 'nation-state', a state autonomous and distinct from every other (and thus claiming a legitimate place in the international order of nations). In the tension between 'people' and 'nation', between the universal and the particular, lies the heart of the conundrum of worldly rule.

We have already discussed briefly how this contradiction has been navigated, in part through the common association of nations with distinctive definitions of 'cultural authenticity', or cultural *essences* imagined as somehow anterior to actual social life – and thus distinct from the lived cultural differences marking every 'society' – and yet each different from every other. In creating such essences, 'national' history itself has frequently come to the rescue, converting complex stories of social conflict into narratives of the worldly unfolding of prepolitical cultural essences.[35] In this way the 'nation' too could be imagined as *unitary*, and standing apart from everyday politics and social division, even as it also defined a 'people's' cultural particularity. Yet, the practical projection of such essentialised cultural identities has always remained in significant tension with the actual politics of internal cultural, class and gender divisions within *societies*, not least in the production of 'minorities'. This has been an important element within the politics of all of South Asia's varied post-independence political systems.

It is this context that both Azfar Moin and Arild Ruud explore in their chapters in the final section, not only the importance of contrasts between a 'national' essence and cultural 'others' (both external and internal) in defining the foundations of sovereignty, but also the complex ways that these struggles have come to be embedded in internal social and political conflicts and divisions, and, indeed, in the internal struggles that have marked efforts to create the image of an individual 'national' self.

Moin's story focuses on the dramatic case of the Ahmadis in Pakistan, a messianic and missionary sect that originated in the late nineteenth century, whose members were subsequently, if gradually, anathematised in Pakistan after independence. To understand this phenomenon, Moin casts it not only against the backdrop of conflicts over the nature of sovereignty in Pakistan after its creation in 1947, but also against the backdrop of political theology. Before the colonial era, the dominant vision of sovereignty among Muslims in India was tied to what he calls 'messianism', a sovereign vision he associates with the Safavids and Mughals (and with a world dominated by Sufis), who invested sovereignty in the divinely illuminated bodies of messianic individuals and lineages, whose power stood above all of society's own 'religious and cultural distinctions' (11). But this vision was deeply undercut by the slow-moving collapse of the Mughal empire and by the new structures of knowledge and power brought by the British in the nineteenth century, including the 'rule of law' and, ultimately, the concept of the sovereignty of the people. Significant for Moin's story, however, is that this gradual relegation of messianism to the status of a 'subordinated knowledge'[36] was associated not only with the new visions of sovereign power accompanying the British, but also with the reassertion of older, competing (and universalising) political theologies among Muslims themselves, most notably a doctrinal theology of absolute divine transcendence that stood in opposition *both* to the messianic sovereign vision of the Mughals *and* to the new sovereign dispensation of the British.[37] This played out in increasing contestation among the ulama in British India focusing on how new visions of Muslim 'community' were negotiated in relationship to existing worldly hierarchies of status and mediation on the one hand, and to direct personal commitment to the authority of divinely inspired texts on the other.[38]

Multiple – and conflicting – conceptions of sovereignty in fact shaped the emergence of Pakistan in 1947 as a Muslim state, including models drawing on the colonial 'rule of law'. But of increasing importance for some Pakistanis were models that had grown out of the deep internal conflicts shaping Muslim thinking under the British, particularly relating to the ultimate 'sovereignty of God', and its relationship to the new state. This was an idea that was mobilised directly in the Objectives Resolution passed by the Constituent Assembly of Pakistan in 1949 – and later incorporated into the preamble to Pakistan's Constitution. The idea of the sovereignty of God was a quintessentially universalising vision, for to assert it was to demand, in effect, each individual's *ultimate* loyalty to God as an act of volition transcending the social bonds of worldly hierarchies, a commitment that Moin (following Jan Assmann) labels as 'total religion'. It is not hard to see this resonating also in some sense with the concept of the sovereignty of the 'people', for the sovereignty of God was brought to earth, in effect, through autonomous individual commitment, theoretically transcending all social positionings, and vesting sovereignty in an imagined unity of a Muslim community bound by this vision of religion. But the relationship of this political theology to worldly power was clearly a subject of ambiguity, as perhaps most clearly reflected in the fact that the Objectives Resolution itself 'delegated' the sovereignty of God not *to* the 'people' but *through* the 'people' to the Pakistani state.[39]

Questions of sovereignty were thus caught up in all sorts of contestations and divisions within Pakistani politics in the decades following partition. Given this, it was perhaps not surprising, as Moin argues, that in the moment of most severe crisis in the foundations of Pakistani sovereignty, following the splitting apart of the country's two wings in 1971, the anathematising of the Ahmadis provided a new foundation for the reassertion of messianic sovereignty. The Ahmadis, who were projected in their messianic origins as an affront *both* to God's transcendent sovereignty *and* to the unity of the Pakistani people, became the scapegoat for the assertion of a new messianism attached to the sovereign claims of the (now more narrowly territorialised) Pakistani people themselves. A 'doctrinal messianism' (linked to the sovereignty of God) was now embodied also in a 'sociological messianism', as Moin puts it, associated with the leadership of Zulfiqar Ali Bhutto, the populist 'saviour' figure who presided in the early 1970s over the Pakistani state's official classification of Ahmadis as non-Muslims. Though this hardly resolved fully the tensions between the universalism of sovereignty's claims – linked ambiguously both to the sovereignty of God and to the 'rule of law' – the production of an internal 'other' reveals in Moin's story the ongoing tension between an imagined sovereign 'people' attuned to the transcendent, and the reality of a 'national' politics linked to the territorial authority of the Pakistani state and cast against the backdrop of Pakistan's internal divisions.

Similar issues can be tracked, though in very different ways, in Arild Ruud's analysis of the meanings of the 'people' and the 'nation' in Bangladesh – an analysis he opens up through the remarkable window provided by recent online reactions to a Bollywood movie. The concept of the 'sovereignty of the people' is one that, as Ruud notes, is deeply entrenched in Bangladesh's Constitution and among Bangladeshis themselves (and associated with the Bangla language). But if the notion of the sovereign Bangladeshi 'people' as an imagined unity, standing above and apart from society's divisions, is an important one in this context, it can hardly be fully separated, as Ruud's analysis shows, from the culturally grounded frames – and forms of political power – through which such a vision of sovereign autonomy has been commonly projected, and debated. In this case the backdrop to the story lies in the deep Bangladeshi unease about the cultural influence of their powerful neighbour, India, whose ability to compromise the essence of Bangladeshi nationhood – and unity – through the hegemony of their cultural production and circulation, lies at the heart of the story.

The significance of online critiques of the 2014 film, *Gunday* ('goondas', or hoodlums), lay in part in the medium, in the manner in which individuals could, in a sense, stand apart in such an online context from their specific, 'located' social positions, asserting their own autonomous identification with the Bangladeshi 'people' (in answer to the film's portrayal of India, rather than Bangladeshis themselves, as responsible for Bangladesh's independence from Pakistan in 1971). But, as Ruud shows, the construction of a sovereign self through such symbolic associations was never fully separable – even in an online setting – from the divisions of class, gender, and political affiliation that defined social position – and shaped debates about the meaning of the 'nation'. Indeed, gender in particular framed the cultural meaning of sovereign independence and autonomy for many individuals in the largely male audience who participated in this commentary. Issues of challenged manhood lurked only slightly underneath many of the expressions of hurt, anger, and humiliation at the movie's failure to recognise what was a linked sense of personal and national autonomy. If the projection of a unitary 'nation' thus transcended – in imagination – all social differentiation, the realities of its connections to the imaginings of individual autonomy only highlighted the anxieties associated with the social realities of dependence and cleavage within the complex social structures and political divisions of Bangladeshi society. As both Moin's and Ruud's chapters show, politics have remained critical to imaginings of the 'nation', even as the image of the 'nation' has been widely projected as apolitical, bound up with visions of the cosmos and the self, transcending social life.

*

The contradictions inherent in the juxtaposition of the political and the imagined apolitical are thus intrinsic to discussions of sovereignty. To write about sovereignty is difficult because we are always concerned, simultaneously, with the operation of politics, often in its most violent and controlling forms, and with imaginings of *ultimate* power that both shape and transcend – and thus, theoretically, can also be mobilised to control – politics, as if from a moral, cosmic position standing apart from the world. Papers in this volume track key aspects of this relationship with respect to law, to kingship, to the people, and to the nation. In doing so, they provide us a glimpse of the underlying 'conundrum of worldly power' that the problem of sovereignty crystallises in South Asia, both in its distinctive South Asian forms and in relation to the international currents that have defined conceptions of modern state sovereignty. In structuring the volume, we have also attempted to underscore the critical intersections – and oppositions – between the self-denying power of the 'rule of law' and the embodied forms of kingly and personal sovereignty that have been central to modern sovereignty's evolution. Though much work needs to be done if we are to understand how sovereignty operates as a concept in South Asia's politics, the articles in this volume open a window on what the study of South Asia has to contribute to the study of sovereignty as a worldwide undertaking.

Notes

* Thanks to the History Department at North Carolina State University for a lively discussion of, and suggestions on, the first half of this Introduction. I also want to thank my colleague, Tony LaVopa, for comments and discussion over many lunches relating to sovereignty and ideas in the European Enlightenment.

1 The relationship between individual state autonomy and shared 'systemic values' (which include openness to market forces and participation in formal and informal international organisations) continues to be debated. See Sheehan (2006).

2 For a history of the idea of the 'self' in western European thinking, see Seigel (2005).

3 Here again, Humboldt provides an important model. His work underscored powerfully the separation between a scientific and an aesthetic vision of nature. But he underscored the critical importance of both of these on the development of human consciousness, however unresolved the tensions between them remained. 'His pages embody less a harmonious fusion than a frustrating gap between the scientific and the aesthetic, between detailed observation and phenomenological perceptions of the natural world.' Yet his influence was 'far-reaching' (Pettinaroli and Mutis 2013: 8).

4 The critical element of *material* success (through technology) as the key underpinning also for the *moral* claims of ultimate sovereignty is suggested by the ways this was used to frame civilisational hierarchies. See Adas (1989).

5 Here, colonial sovereignty was also linked to older traditions of rule defined by the protection of the realm, or, what came to be referred to as 'reasons of state'. The sovereign imperative to maintain *worldly* order (in the face of the ever-present threats of disorder in the *world as it was*) was thus frequently in tension with the higher claims of sovereign authority in Europe and in the colonies alike. For a detailed intellectual history of this concept in the evolution of the concept of the modern 'nation-state', see Hont (1994).

6 There is a large literature dealing with this; see for example Benton (2007: 54–67) and Benton (1999). For India, see Sen (2012: 227–242).

7 In this volume, an example of the complex background to the negotiations of rulership under the British is provided by Caleb Simmons in his discussion of Mysore.

8 It should be noted, however, that Krasner's approach to 'hypocrisy' is somewhat different from that adopted here. For him, it is a manifestation, in effect, of rational choice.

'At times rulers adhere to conventional norms or rules because it provides them with resources and support (both material and ideational). At other times, rulers have violated the norms, and for the same reasons. If rulers want to stay in power and to promote the security, material, and ideational interests of their constituents, following the conventional practices of Westphalian and international legal sovereignty might or might not be an optimal policy' (p. 28). The argument here is that this 'hypocrisy' is less a product of rational choice than of the 'conundrum of power' itself, requiring rulers to appeal to universalising principles detached from the particularities of worldly power, even as they manipulate these particularities to establish order.

9 Constituent Assembly of India Debates (Proceedings), August 20, 1947. Volume V. (http.// 164.100.47.194/loksabha/writereaddata/cadebatefiles/C20081947.html)

10 Critical to this model of 'centre' and 'periphery', however, was that however deep the tension between them, they were also mutually constitutive. Pollock notes this clearly in his discussion of the 'cosmopolitan' and the 'vernacular'. As 'the cosmopolitan is constituted through cultural flows from the vernacular', he notes, 'so the vernacular constructs itself by appropriation from the cosmopolitan' (Pollock 1998: 25). In this framing, civilisation always takes different forms in different localities, even as the patterned contrast between the cosmopolitan (or universal) and a multiplicity of particularities also constitutes its unity. One can, of course, see the structure of 'modernity' in much the same way, that is, as a civilisational phenomenon that is in its very nature both a unity and at the very same time plural, thus suggesting the problematic character of emphasising the concept of 'modernities', as some do, as an alternative to the concept of a singular 'modernity'. It was intrinsic to the concept of modernity that multiple particularities, different *ways* of being modern *in the world*, was intrinsic to the singular concept of 'modernity' itself.

11 In actual practice the British tended more frequently to link their own civilisational ancestry to the Roman Empire than they did to earlier Sanskrit or Persian civilisations. But that hardly changes the similarities in form linking the British to these earlier 'civilisations'. For some discussion, see Gilmartin (2017).

12 Antony Anghie thus notes how a vision of higher civilisation opened up the world to exploitation in the ostensible name of the 'good' of the world as a whole, a vision of the 'good' linked to European positivism and to the naturalisation of the peoples being exploited (Anghie 2007).

13 As Mitchell puts it: 'The reorganisation of towns and the laying out of new colonial quarters, every regulation of economic or social practice, the construction of the country's new system of irrigation canals, the control of the Nile's flow, the building of barracks, police stations and classrooms, the completion of a system of railways – this pervasive process of "order" must be understood as more than mere improvement or "reform". Such projects were all undertaken as an enframing, and hence had the effect of representing a realm of the conceptual, conjuring up for the first time the prior abstractions of progress, reason, law, history, colonial authority and order' (Mitchell 1988: 179).

14 To say that the British 'protected and authenticated' custom and cultural practice is not, of course, to suggest that this structure of 'encapsulation' did not, in actual fact, induce significant change, as several of the chapters in the volume show.

15 This concept of 'constituent power' as an operational frame for popular sovereignty has received wide treatment. For one discussion, see Kalyvas (2005).

16 For a recent collection of historical essays on the variety of conflicts and meanings surrounding the history of the people's sovereignty, see Bourke and Skinner (2017).

17 The wide variety of popular perceptions of sovereignty in the early and mid-twentieth century, many relating to caste and religious messianism, is captured in Milinda Banerjee's discussion (Banerjee 2018: chapters 4 and 5).

18 The relationship between language and the definition of a 'people' has often been noted, but it is important to note the difference between Benedict Anderson's argument relating to the links between language, print capitalism, and 'nation', and the

argument here. The role of print markets and circulation in the imagining of linguistic 'identity' was no doubt extremely important historically, as Anderson argues. But the foundation of language as the key to the inner essence of a sovereign 'people' hinged on the specific *form* of language's imagining, that is, as a 'quality' of the self existing somehow outside history (and thus capable, ironically, of public expression in multiple languages – as, for example, in the significant reliance in many vernacular language movements in India, on publication in English). For Anderson's argument, see Anderson (1998).

19 For a discussion of the shifting usages of the term 'society' and its movement in the nineteenth century from an older meaning associated with sociality and fellowship toward its modern definition as 'our most general term for the body of institutions and relationships within which a relatively large group of people live' is discussed by Raymond Williams. This shift is what opened 'society' to objectivizing 'sociological' analysis, and what converted it (as an imagined 'entity' of interacting groups and individuals) into a potential target for state action (Williams 1985: 206–209).

20 For a discussion of the 'people's two bodies' in the context of popular sovereignty in Anglo-American tradition, see Morgan (1988: chapter 4). The form in which this vision of the king's two bodies found its perhaps clearest expression in British thinking in colonial India was in a form mediated by the thinking of Thomas Hobbes, who merged the body of the 'people' with that of the king, thus justifying highly authoritarian rule. For a discussion of such a formulation by Sir Alfred Lyall, and its critique by early Indian nationalists, see Banerjee (2018: 7–19). As Banerjee notes, this Hobbesian vision associating the 'people' as the contractors for the sovereignty of a unitary democratic state even influenced the language of sovereignty as debated in the Constituent Assembly (pp. 245–251).

21 As John Kelly and Martha Kaplan note, 'the term "nation-state" is less than a century old. It appears in the English language only in reporting on Wilson at Versailles. It appears in no major dictionary of the English language before 1950, though it is in all of them by 1970. The nation-state as the uniquely legitimate solution to the formulation of sovereignty in international law is a very new idea.' John Kelly and Martha Kaplan, 'Legal Fictions after Empire,' in Howland and White (2009: 170).

22 For an argument that some high courts did assert independence from the Government, see, Chandrachud (2015).

23 This of course oversimplifies the complex processes that drew Brahmans to the law in colonial India; for an overview, see Washbrook (2010: 597–615).

24 This process has been elaborated by Washbrook (1981: 652–654). The state, as Washbrook puts it, recognised (or 'discovered') 'entrenched ascriptive (caste, religious and familial) status as the basis of individual right', as if such rights were thus anterior to the state's power. The complex relationship of such 'rights' to the state's use of force was played out dramatically, to use just one example, in the Benares House Tax hartal of 1811. This was a critical early challenge to British rule, in which the British were clearly ready to use force to collect their revenue demands, even in the face of protest. But ultimately, the structural outcome of the crisis was one in which the British recognised the binding authority of past (customary) *forms* of taxation, even as the people accepted the government's right to tax.

25 Detailing the legacies of this construction of the law's sovereign authority is beyond this introduction, but it undoubtedly provides a critical backdrop for understanding the powerful claim in independent India for religious and caste-based 'rights' that are projected as anterior to the state's authority and thus deserving of the law's sovereign protection. It is also important for understanding the politics of reservations in India in the post-Mandal era.

26 India was a place where, as Maine wrote, 'a large part of ancient Europe survives' (Maine 1875: 24).

27 This was the view that found ultimate expression in the Supreme Court's 'Basic Structure' doctrine, according to which the Constitution's fundamental structure, deriving

from the constituent authority of the 'people', stood outside political time, and could not be changed even by the formally legal process of constitutional amendment.

28 For a discussion of sovereignty as performance, in many contexts, see Benite, Geroulanos and Jerr (2017).

29 Forms of kingship were, in fact, given an ordered place within British imperial structure, defined by titles, honours and darbars in an empire-wide hierarchy with the British monarch at its apex. See Cannadine (2002).

30 Schmitt was also skeptical of the people's sovereignty as a concept, which he saw as rooted in a mechanistic, scientific view of the universe, imagined to operate without a decision-making centre.

31 For some speculation on the implications of these theological forms, see Azfar Moin's chapter in this volume.

32 Indeed, the importance of 'imagined' sovereigns has thus, as Milinda Banerjee persuasively argues, often played as important a role in shaping politics as the appeal to real kingly figures. 'Imagined and imaginary rulers', he writes, 'were almost drawn out of the mist, by a conjuror's sleight of hand, by anti-colonial nationalists or peasant actors, to articulate their political demands' (Banerjee, 2018: 398).

33 Interestingly, Skoda also notes the lack of any indigenous term quite equivalent to the English 'sovereignty.'

34 Michelutti in fact elaborates on this much further in her book on Mathura (Michelutti 2008).

35 'National' histories have thus often projected the cultural characteristics of a people as existing originally in embryo, as it were, before finding actual lived expression in the context of society. In one powerful explication of this form of history, Daniel Lord Smail explores the common biological metaphor in the late nineteenth and twentieth centuries of history unfolding from an original 'seed' (Smail 2008: 74–78). The search for a national history transcending the history of lived politics also suggests why mythology and history sometimes merged in nationalist historical constructions, a common occurrence in India. The significance of this in the development of monarchical images in early Indian nationalism is discussed in Banerjee (2018: chapter 3).

36 Moin takes the phrase from Bayly (1996: 330).

37 The role of new forms of colonial authority in stimulating internal debates among Muslim themselves on the relationship of sovereignty to existing traditions of embodied, hierarchical cultural authority on the one hand, and to scriptures on the other, was powerfully delineated many years ago in Geertz (1968).

38 Such competition was played out, for example, in debates among the ulama, for example in the polemics in the first half of the nineteenth century between Fazl-i Haq Khairabadi and Shah Ismail Shahid on the meaning and ethics of mediation, which provided a backdrop for the later conflicts between Deobandis and Barelvis over questions of saintly and Prophetic intercession. See Tareen (2015).

39 The text read: 'Sovereignty over the entire universe belongs to Allah Almighty alone and the authority which He has delegated to the state of Pakistan, through its people for being exercised within the limits prescribed by Him is a sacred trust.'

References

Adas, Michael. 1989. *Machines as the Measure of Men: Science, Technology, and Ideologies of Western Dominance*. Ithaca: Cornell University Press.

Agamben, Giorgio. 2005. *State of Exception*, trans. by Kevin Attell. Chicago: University of Chicago Press.

Alam, Muzaffar. 2004. *The Languages of Political Islam: India, 1200–1800*. Chicago: University of Chicago Press.

Anderson, Benedict. 1998. *Imagined Communities: Reflections on the Origin and Spread of Nationalism*. London: Verso.

Anghie, Antony. 2007. *Imperialism, Sovereignty, and the Making of International Law.* Cambridge: Cambridge University Press.
Banerjee, Milinda. 2018. *The Mortal God: Imagining the Sovereign in Colonial India.* Cambridge: Cambridge University Press.
Bayly, Christopher A. 1993. 'Pre-Colonial Indian Merchants and Rationality', in Mushirul Hasan and Narayani Gupta (eds.), *India's Colonial Encounter: Essays in Memory of Eric Stokes*, pp. 3–24. New Delhi: Monohar.
Bayly, Christopher A. 1996. *Empire and Information: Intelligence Gathering and Social Communication in India, 1780–1870.* Cambridge: Cambridge University Press.
Benite, Zvi Ben-Dor, Stefanos Geroulanos, and Nicole Jerr (eds.). 2017. *The Scaffolding of Sovereignty: Global and Aesthetic Perspectives on the History of a Concept.* New York: Columbia University Press.
Benton, Lauren. 1999. 'Colonial Law and Cultural Difference: Jurisdictional Politics and the Formation of the Colonial State,' *Comparative Studies in Society and History*, 41 (3): 563–588.
Benton, Lauren. 2007. 'Empires of Exception: History, Law, and the Problem of Imperial Sovereignty,' *Quaderni di Relazioni Internazionali*, 8: 54–67.
Bourke, Richard, and Quentin Skinner (eds.). 2017. *Popular Sovereignty in Historical Perspective.* Cambridge: Cambridge University Press.
Cannadine, David. 2002. *Ornamentalism: How the British Saw Their Empire.* Oxford: Oxford University Press.
Chandra, Kanchan (ed.). 2016. *Democratic Dynasties: State, Party, and Family in Contemporary Indian Politics.* Cambridge: Cambridge University Press.
Chandrachud, Abhinav. 2015. *An Independent, Colonial Judiciary: A History of the Bombay High Court During the British Raj, 1862–1947.* New Delhi: Oxford University Press.
De, Rohit. 2012. 'Emasculating the Executive: The Federal Court and Civil Liberties in Late Colonial India, 1942–44', in Terence C. Halliday, Lucien Karpik, and Malcolm M. Feeley (eds.), *Fates of Political Liberalism in the British Post-Colony: The Politics of the Legal Complex*, pp. 59–90. Cambridge: Cambridge University Press.
Geenens, Raf. 2017. 'Sovereignty as Autonomy', *Law and Philosophy*, 36 (5): 495–524.
Geertz, Clifford. 1968. *Islam Observed: Religious Development in Morocco and Indonesia.* Chicago: University of Chicago Press.
Gilmartin, David. 2017. 'Imperial Sovereignty in Mughal and British Forms', *History and Theory*, 56 (1): 80–88.
Hansen, Thomas Blom, and Finn Stepputat (eds.). 2005. *Sovereign Bodies: Citizens, Migrants and States in the Post-Colonial World.* Princeton: Princeton University Press.
Hansen, Thomas Blom, and Finn Stepputat. 2006. 'Sovereignty Revisited', *Annual Review of Anthropology*, 35: 295–315.
Heesterman, Jan C. 1985a. 'The Conundrum of the King's Authority', in *The Inner Conflict of Tradition: Essays in Indian Ritual, Kingship and Society*, pp. 108–127. Chicago: University of Chicago Press.
Heesterman, Jan C. 1985b. 'India and the Inner Conflict of Tradition', in *The Inner Conflict of Tradition*, pp. 10–24. Chicago: University of Chicago Press.
Hont, Istvan. 1994. 'The Permanent Crisis of a Divided Mankind: Contemporary Crisis of the Nation State in Historical Perspective', *Political Studies*, 42: 166–231.
Howland, Douglas, and Luise White (eds.). 2009. *The State of Sovereignty: Territories, Laws, Populations.* Bloomington: Indiana University Press.
Hussain, Nasser. 2003. *The Jurisprudence of Emergency: Colonialism and the Rule of Law.* Ann Arbor: University of Michigan Press.
Jackson, Robert. 2007. *Sovereignty.* Cambridge: Polity Press.

Kalmo, Hent, and Quentin Skinner (eds.). 2010. *Sovereignty in Fragments: The Past, Present and Future of a Contested Concept*. Cambridge: Cambridge University Press.

Kalyvas, Andreas. 2005. 'Popular Sovereignty, Democracy and the Constituent Power', *Constellations*, 12 (2): 223–244.

Kantorowicz, Ernst. 1957. *The King's Two Bodies: A Study in Medieval Political Theology*. Princeton: Princeton University Press.

Kolsky, Elizabeth. 2010. *Colonial Justice in British India: White Violence and the Rule of Law*. Cambridge: Cambridge University Press.

Krasner, Stephen D. 1999. *Sovereignty: Organized Hypocrisy*. Princeton: Princeton University Press.

Lieberman, Victor. 2009. *Strange Parallels: Southeast Asia in Global Context, c.800–1830*. New York: Cambridge University Press, vol. 2 (Mainland Mirrors: Europe, Japan, China, South Asia, and the Islands).

Maine, Henry Sumner. 1875. *The Effects of Modern Observation of India on European Thought*. London: John Murray.

Mantena, Karuna. 2010. *Alibis of Empire: Henry Maine and the Ends of Liberal Imperialism*. Princeton: Princeton University Press.

Michelutti, Lucia. 2008. *The Vernacularisation of Democracy*. New Delhi: Routledge.

Mitchell, Timothy. 1988. *Colonising Egypt*. Berkeley: University of California Press.

Moin, Azfar. 2014. *The Millennial Sovereign: Sacred Kingship and Sainthood in Islam*. New York: Columbia University Press.

Morgan, Edmund S. 1988. *Inventing the People: The Rise of Popular Sovereignty in England and America*. New York: Norton.

Mukherjee, Mithi. 2010. *India in the Shadow of Empire: A Legal and Political History, 1774–1950*. Delhi: Oxford University Press.

O'Hanlon, Rosalind. 2013. 'Contested Conjunctures: Brahman Communities and "Early Modernity" in India', *American Historical Review*, 118 (3): 765–787.

O'Hanlon, Rosalind. 2014. 'Gods in the Courtroom: History, Sacred Space and Proprietary Rights in India', in *At the Edges of Empire: Essays in Social and Intellectual History of India*, pp. 235–301. Ranikhet: Permanent Black.

Pettinaroli, Elizabeth M., and Ana Maria Mutis. 2013. '"Introduction" to "Troubled Waters: Rivers in Latin American Imagination"', *Hispanic Issues On Line*, 12.

Piliavsky, Anastasia (ed.). 2014. *Patronage as Politics in South Asia*. Cambridge: Cambridge University Press.

Pollock, Sheldon. 1998. 'The Cosmopolitan Vernacular', *The Journal of Asian Studies*, 57 (1): 6–37.

Pollock, Sheldon. 2006. *The Language of the Gods in the World of Men: Sanskrit, Culture, and Power in Premodern India*. Berkeley: University of California Press.

Price, Pamela. 1989. 'Kingly Models in Indian Political Behavior: Culture as a Medium of History', *Asian Survey*, 29 (6): 559–572.

Price, Pamela. 1996. *Kingship and Political Practice in Colonial India*. Cambridge: Cambridge University Press.

Schmitt, Carl. 1985. *Political Theology: Four Chapters on the Concept of Sovereignty*, trans. by George Schwab. Chicago: University of Chicago Press.

Seigel, Jerrold. 2005. *The Idea of the Self: Thought and Experience in Western Europe Since the Seventeenth Century*. Cambridge: Cambridge University Press.

Sen, Sudipta. 2012. 'Unfinished Conquest: Residual Sovereignty and the Legal Foundations of the British Empire in India', *Law, Culture and the Humanities*, 9 (2012): 227–242.

Sheehan, James J. 2006. 'The Problem of Sovereignty in European History', *American Historical Review*, 111 (1): 1–15.

Singh, Bhrigupati. 2012. 'The Headless Horseman of Central India: Sovereignty at Varying Thresholds of Life', *Cultural Anthropology*, 27 (2): 383–407.
Smail, Daniel Lord. 2008. *On Deep History and the Brain*. Berkeley: University of California Press.
Tareen, SherAli. 2015. 'Competing Political Theologies: Intra-Muslim Polemics on the Limits of Prophetic Intercession', *Political Theology*, 12 (3): 418–443.
Taylor, Charles. 1994. 'The Politics of Recognition', in Charles Taylor, et al. (eds.), *Multiculturalism: Examining the Politics of Recognition*, pp. 25–73. Princeton: Princeton University Press.
Thompson, Edward P. 1976. *Whigs and Hunters: The Origin of the Black Act*. New York: Pantheon Books.
Washbrook, David. 1981. 'Law, State, and Agrarian Society in Colonial India', *Modern Asian Studies*, 15 (3): 649–721.
Washbrook, David. 2010. 'The Maratha Brahman Model in South India: An Afterward', *Economic and Social History Review*, 47 (4): 597–615.
Williams, Raymond. 1985. *Keywords: A Vocabulary of Culture and Society*. New York: Oxford University Press.
Yack, Bernard. 2001. 'Popular Sovereignty and Nationalism', *Political Theory*, 29 (4): 517–536.

PART I

Law, religion, and sovereignty in India

1

SOVEREIGN STRUGGLES

Governance and *mathas* under British imperial rule in South India

Pamela Price

British imperial sovereignty in directly ruled South India was not statically grounded, but was continually under construction in the course of the nineteenth century. Important were processes of engagement and discussion in colonial courts of law. Judicial officers could not take refuge in simple pronouncements from codes and regulations, but were compelled to use discursive reason and moral argumentation in meeting with a wide range of figures from subject communities. Because of the highly segmented nature of these socio-political communities, judicial officers were engaged in the encompassment of local sovereign statuses within the imperial state. The political needs of the state were served because, in the public, adversarial proceedings of litigation, subject institutions suffered the undermining of their appeal among important classes in the population. I have earlier discussed this process with reference to former little kingdoms which engaged in litigation as *zamindaries*,[1] revenue estates (Price 1996). In this chapter I examine this process with another type of political segment, large domains of Hindu *mathas* ('monasteries').

At the end of the eighteenth century, administrators of the presidency of Madras had to contend with religious chiefs, along with little kings and rural bosses, in competition for political allegiance.[2] There existed across the presidency network domains of mathas, some controlling thousands of villages, manned by members of spiritual lineages under the leadership of lineage heads, gurus. Widely honoured and respected, matha gurus sat on thrones and the wealthy among them went on elaborate processions with royal insignia. Colonial armies secured the Pax Britannica, but it was in the exercise of colonial moral order that the reframing of renouncer rule would take place. New meanings of renouncer leadership evolved, not in some frozen 'legal sovereignty' (Hansen and Stepputat 2006: 296–297), but in sovereign displays of reason in processes involving public sphere elites.

In the course of the nineteenth century, British imperial notions of appropriate management and protection of property coincided neatly with the political undermining of matha domains. Imperial sovereignty was constituted around notions of 'the rule of law' (Ocko and Gilmartin 2009), and imperial rule of law found illegitimate certain actions which supported the sovereignty of matha guru heads.[3] The maintenance of matha guru status required the personal distribution of matha resources, while the protection of endowment property constituted an important element in the delivery of imperial justice. Thus, guru notions of spiritual sovereignty clashed with imperial beliefs in the proper separation of the religious sphere from worldly property, and matha heads came to be stigmatised as corrupt. This chapter investigates processes through which the constitution of imperial sovereignty involved the discrediting of matha domain rule. I use conflict involving matha heads at the famous pilgrimage site of Tirumala Tirupati Devastanams (TTD) to illustrate my points.[4] Litigation involving this site attracted wide attention and at the end of the nineteenth century one course of TTD appeal cases, 'The Hathiramji Mutt case', as it was called, became the most famous litigation of the day (Ramaswamy Aiyar n.d.: 273).

Imperial rule of law was epitomised in judicial rulings in the Anglo-Indian legal system. In British understanding, imperial judges stood apart from conflicting forces and desires in society and made decisions according to disinterested discourses of reason. The ideal was a vision of 'justice as equity' (Mukherjee 2010), fairness administered by an imperial state which could be fair *because* of its absolutist separation from the governed. In this vision the state operated free from the religious principles of Indian society. The extent to which the judiciary was an arm of the executive in colonial India has, of course, been debated since the nationalist movement. A recent contribution is a study of the Bombay High Court which argues for considerable independence on the part of the judiciary and mutual respect between Indian and British justices (Chandrachud 2015). In Madras Presidency district and appellate court judges appeared to take care in deciding which law and/or usage to apply and in examining evidence offered in court.[5] Judicial efforts were persuasive, and by the end of the nineteenth century, elites in the public sphere commonly accepted 'rule of law' as the proper constitution of state sovereignty. The very existence of law courts in which suits could be and were instigated against officers of the state made a powerful impact on imperial subjects and played a major role in the constitution of imperial sovereignty (Mukherjee 2010: 46–48). Imperial claims to be purveyors of justice held credence when the state provided public forums where displays of discursive reason could result in the humiliation of its own officers.

In this study I focus on an area of colonial litigation in which judges argued in such a way as to support the imperial state against the sovereign influence of heads of Indian mathas. The adjudicators based their arguments on a British understanding of the proper separation of the 'religious' from the political which belied the significance of mathas in pre-colonial governance.[6] Their argumentation appeared disinterested, at the same time as it served the political goals of the imperial state. Because of widespread preoccupation with religious reform among Indian actors in the public sphere in the nineteenth century, judicial decisions critical of matha leadership were commonly perceived as serving social needs.

In this study of processes in the construction and maintenance of imperial sovereignty, then, we find a curious confluence of images of authentic Indian spiritual practice. Ordinary people, it appears, continued to honour and revere guru heads of mathas, while reform-enthused elites accepted the sovereign right of imperial justices to remould guru domain leadership. Cultural and social change conspired to produce collaborators among elite imperial subjects as the Anglo-Indian legal system shaved the prerogatives of spiritual potentates. However, imperial 'rule of law' required some give and take between the rulers and their various constituencies, and judicial practitioners moved cautiously.

Mathas were centres of spiritual lineages concerned with sacred learning and worship. They had been associated with the sovereignty of pre-colonial regimes and by early modern South India, some matha heads were the spiritual sovereigns of vast domains. The renouncer heads of mathas were sources of knowledge of *dharma* (cosmic, moral order) and right practice and had played roles in managing conflicts in early modern South India (see, for example, Prasad [2007: 206]; Vail [1985: 139]). In the nineteenth century, heads of mathas could be 'religious potentates' who managed large holdings of agricultural land and were administrators at major temples with extensive landed endowments (Washbrook 1976: 187).

In imperial courts judges found heads of mathas to be incompetent at best and, more commonly, avaricious and intriguing breakers of the law. Judges held that a matha head, as a renouncer, should be withdrawn from 'worldly' concerns. This view was contrary to much matha practice before the consolidation of British rule, as matha heads and their lineage members administered the affairs of matha domains and served in dispute management. More than that, renouncer gurus were 'expected to give gifts to devoted persons who approached them' (Vail 1985: 139). In such redistribution, matha heads purveyed spiritual qualities; they were 'gracing others with power [*shakti*]' (Vail 1985: 140). When matha administrators engaged in the redistribution of resources in the tending of their domains, imperial officials labelled such activities as 'misappropriation' or 'malversation'.

In the imperial understanding of rule of law, besides the protection of persons, the protection of property lay at the basis of justice, and the protection of property was a secular issue. Issues involving property were to be decided, not in terms of religious principles, but according to the defining formula for legal judgement, 'equity, justice, and good conscience'. Under these circumstances matha heads appeared as embezzlers of matha and temple funds. As imperial sovereignty was constituted and performed, over time the scope of matha heads was contained. Checking the expenditures of matha gurus, officials were enacting the assumed moral superiority of British governance, dealing with Indian institutions of transcendent values presumably gone astray. In 1909, arguing a point of law, the British Chief Justice of the High Court at Madras appears to have made a common observation when he said, 'The fact [is] that the heads of Mutts have more or less frequently abused their position' (PC 1920: 69).

In the course of the nineteenth century, actors in the public sphere of the new middle class, including major figures of the Indian legal profession, came to share the imperial view of contemporary matha leadership. Matha heads acquired a poor reputation elsewhere in the subcontinent, as well (see, for example, Sarkar [1997], Kasturi [2009], and Kasturi [2016]). There was less acceptance of the many paths in renunciation which had emerged. Throughout British India, litigation involving mathas contributed to notions which juxtaposed the approach to religion of a reasoned 'public' against those who simply followed 'custom', including supposedly corrupt forms of practice (Gilmartin 2015: 377).

Heads of mathas in South India were commonly respected by ordinary people (e.g. Mudaliar 1974: 36, 49), but, in the evaluation of public sphere elites, the moral authority of the heads came to be undermined (see, for example, Venkatachalapathy 2012: 31). In courts of law, members of spiritual lineages demeaned each other with accusations of wrongdoing. From the mid-nineteenth century, Indians who were interested in reform of practices and beliefs in worship and sacred study pressured the imperial government to expand its oversight and control of the administrations of mathas and the temples they were associated with.[7]

Theological change and activities of publication in South India were among the results of the meeting with Protestant Christianity. We find this in the careers of major reformers Arumukam Navalar (1822–1879), Ramalinga Swamigal (1823–1874),[8] and Mayuram Vetanayakam Pillai (1826–1889) (Ebeling 2010). Publications and public discussion of religious change in general emerged from the 1840s with the career of Arumukam Navalar in Sri Lanka and India. Blackburn observes that Navalar 'proposed that Saivism be purified by reviving its ancient texts and eliminating later-day corruptions' (2003: 144). Apart from issues of texts and ritual, reform attention turned to concerns which imperial officials voiced about the administration of temple and matha property. From the 1860s and 1870s petitions, memoranda and addresses appeared in the public sphere arguing that the imperial government should take greater action to protect the endowments of temples and mathas (Mudaliar 1974: 31).

It is one of the paradoxes of imperial rule that Indians became active participants in the formal depoliticisation of institutions of worship and sacred learning, the undermining of spiritual-political authority and scope for action. Members of spiritual lineages instantiated British notions of imperial sovereignty as they took part in processes of competition which were managed in bouts of litigation in the Anglo-Indian legal system. Early in the nineteenth century rivals for authority, status and/or wealth in temples and mathas began to discover imperial preoccupation with the 'misappropriation' of religious endowments and sought to undermine their rivals with such accusations.[9] Such charges were not only the cause of disgrace, but – when 'proven' – also could be the basis for removal from a position of authority in a temple or matha. In litigation, interactions among lineage members lay open to public view in novel ways. Court proceedings were public and commented on in newspapers. Judgements were published in organs like the *Indian Law Reports* and discussed in the *Madras Law Journal*. Imperial procedures and institutions sought to mould matha heads into an official vision of the meaning of their vocation, one that simultaneously protected the sovereignty of the state. The politics of imperial legal procedures, as matha heads and their rivals adapted to the new dispensation, involved negative representations of the parties in litigation.

Regimes, temples, and mathas

From at least the tenth century in South India, warrior leaders seeking ruling legitimacy endowed worship in temples and acted to manage conflicts in the institutions (Appadurai 1981; Heitzman 1997). Protection of worship in these and other ways was an important constituent of royal sovereignty. In a later political development, ruling houses in early modern South India sought the services of the heads of spiritual lineages and they endowed mathas, places where members of a spiritual lineage lived and where the teaching of the lineage founder might be transmitted. Spiritual lineages produced figures who played important roles in the consolidation of ruling regimes. Under the expanding Vijayanagar empire, for example, heads of spiritual lineages facilitated imperial protection of major temples in conquered areas by organising and managing endowments funding worship (Appadurai 1981: Chapter 2; Stoker 2016). Establishing mathas proved to be a flexible means for the expansion of imperial economic and political control (Stoker 2015). In early modern South India, then, there emerged across South India network domains consisting of large and small mathas, attached to temples, propagating sacred learning, and serving the needs of ruling lords, local and far away. Heads of powerful mathas were beholden only to the heads of major ruling houses[10] and used, themselves, monarchical symbols as part of the representation of their authority, both within mathas and when they went on procession. They headed spiritual domains in polities with strong elements of segmentation.

Mathas appear not to have gone into decline while ruling houses were battling with each other and European forces in the eighteenth century (see, for example, Price [forthcoming] and Simmons [forthcoming]). J. H. Nelson, imperial officer and historian, wrote about early nineteenth-century Madurai district, for example, that 'the principle Pagodas [temples] with their enormous establishments, their officiating priests, &c., were managed by a Dharmakarta, or trustee and manager for life who . . . was usually a monk and guru'.[11]

We need to look more closely at the qualities of a matha head. To begin with, he had been found appropriate to be initiated into a spiritual lineage and had engaged in the disciplines of renunciation and learning taught in that lineage. Renunciation included leaving his birth family for the brotherhood of the lineage and forsaking marriage. His leadership as the head of a major matha would be anchored in this lineage membership. As a general function of renunciatory disciplines, his shakti or spiritual power had become awakened, but as an initiated matha guru, his shakti was pure and concentrated (Vail 1985: 124, 126–127). An eminent guru was believed to have become 'fully realized' with divine power, and in his soul-body dwelt the formless God (Vail 1985: 127–128). His matha provided a centre of 'sacredness'.[12] Burghart observed that a renouncer saw 'himself as a great king. His senses do not rule him, rather he rules his senses and he gives visible expression of his rulership by appropriating the regalia of the terrestrial king' (1996: 47).

As we have seen, a matha head's power lay also in his engaging in exchange, including giving and receiving gifts (Vail 1985: 139).[13] Redistribution through gifting was highly political, associated with honour and authority. It appears that a powerful matha head was one who practiced skillful and appropriate redistribution, of both material and spiritual values, the two conjoined. Vail notes, 'The blessed gifts which the [renouncer] gives are thus especially important for the [devotees] in affecting their spiritual progress because the [renouncer's] qualities and so he himself are contained within the material gifts' (1985: 135–136). Data from an extensive High Court judgement dealing with the history of the network domain of Dharmapuram Adhinam shows heads in the *adhinam* (head matha) and network mathas continuously making gifts, large and small (ILR Madras 1887). Several heads distinguished themselves by the extravagance of their largesse (Price forthcoming). As I have argued elsewhere (Price 1996: 78–79, 84–85), there was power in gifting, dharmic power and, similarly, the power of sovereign protection. To guru gifting was added spiritual power.

Matha gurus' membership in and headship of a spiritual lineage gave them the right to organise particular celebrations and to carry out particular rituals. Thus was their lineage-linked personal disinterestedness regularly represented, elements of their sovereign authority in their domains. This perceived disinterestedness had contributed to their mathas' being lavishly endowed and their predecessors selected to manage temples. Ruling houses and substantial figures continued to endow mathas after the establishment of the presidency, though royal endowments greatly declined in the first half of the nineteenth century (ILR 1887).

Challenges to British imperial sovereignty lay in the reverence and awe with which heads of great mathas, secure in their lineage membership, were received by ordinary and elite groups in early nineteenth-century South India. Add to this that they served to manage disputes in their domain and we can see that they represented a model of disinterested authority which competed with that of enactors of imperial sovereignty, judges of the Anglo-Indian legal system. Rule-bound in their discipline with a commitment to equity, imperial judges themselves had a renunciatory aspect in their work. Over the course of the nineteenth century, austere in approach, they pronounced a narrow vision of matha renunciation which separated the religious from the political and mirrored their own distance from societal interests. Unfortunately for the reputation of matha gurus, the disinterestedness of imperial judges appealed to the self-denying personal ethos of Brahmans and high-caste non-Brahmans who dominated the legal profession and the public sphere. When members of the new public were looking back in time to 'purer' religious traditions of ascetic withdrawal, judicial critique of allegedly profligate matha gurus found a willing audience. On those occasions when judges found actions of gurus and priests to constitute simply 'religious' practice (rather than being corrupt), these practices were labelled as 'custom' in court usage and were thus drained of sovereign meaning.[14]

Administration at Tirumala Tirupati Devastanams

As the East India Company (EIC) expanded its territorial control in the seventeenth and eighteenth centuries, it approached institutions of worship and learning with care, taking on responsibilities as occasions arose. Agents of the state had played roles in pre-colonial dispute processing in temples, so this was a role for the EIC that found acceptance in localities. Because of the vast revenue-producing properties of these institutions, they came under the oversight of the Board of Revenue, established in 1789. By the early nineteenth century the imperial regime had assumed uneven supervision, varying from district to district, of the management of religious endowments. With the aim of regularising imperial involvement and in recognition of the importance of this activity the presidency government passed Regulation VII of 1817, confirming the right of officers of the Board of Revenue to undertake such supervision. The preamble to the Regulation justified this assumption of authority with reference to the 'misappropriation' of endowments (PC 1874: Judgement of the Judicial Committee). There had developed an official proclivity to view both temple and matha administrators as appropriating institutional resources for purposes officially categorised as not pertaining strictly to worship and sacred learning. According to this reasoning, the original purposes of endowments were not being honoured.

The superintendence of accounts according to British notions of appropriate expenditure was only one aspect of Regulation VII. The regulation operated further such that missionaries came to believe that Christian institutions were being neglected. By the 1830s they and their allies in India and Britain succeeded in convincing officials in the East India Company that the reigning policy constituted 'official patronage' of idolatry (Mudaliar 1974: 17). Formal withdrawal from government administration began in the 1840s (Mudaliar 1974; Appadurai 1981), though Presler finds that the Government of Madras resisted giving up control: 'the details and intensity of control were modified . . . [or] control was simply shifted to other agencies or buried in hidden institutional arrangements' (Presler 1987: 16). Still, withdrawal from 'interference' was the official line.

One of the effects of imperial preoccupation with temple and matha endowments was the attempt of rivals in temple and matha affairs to discredit each other by alleging misappropriation. This tactic became the major tool for faction leaders to employ in a struggle for dominance in the management of the celebrated pilgrimage site, Tirumala Tirupati Devastanams (TTD). That vast complex of more than 30 temples, located in the southern part of today's Andhra Pradesh, was considered by the government to be of interest to 'the whole Hindu community' (Mudaliar 1974: 20). The site maintained a pan-Indian reputation and annually attracted thousands of worshippers, bearing gifts – some of great value – with which to honour and propitiate the gods. The Government of Madras became involved in the administration of the TTD in 1808 (PC 1907: 295).

In 1843 the government appointed one matha head over another (from a different matha) as trustee, that is, as chief administrator, of the affairs of 19 temples at the site, including the two most important and wealthiest, Sri Venkateswara Swami and Sri Govindaraja Swami. With this appointment the government was to withdraw formally from involvement in the affairs of TTD, in keeping with the new imperial policy. The favoured matha head came from a north Indian spiritual lineage that maintained a matha at the site, the Hathiramji matha, possessing 'considerable endowments'.[15] The matha head is referred to as *mahant* in the court documents and he and his lineage subordinates were *bairagis*, Vaishnavite monks. The matha head who was *not* favoured as TTD trustee was called the *pedda jiyangar* ('big' jiyangar),[16] from a matha called the Pedda Jiyangar's Mutt (matha). The position of pedda jiyangar was supported by a *mirasi*[17] and he had major responsibilities of management at five of the temples at the TTD, including the two most important temples mentioned previously.[18] His main subordinate in his matha was the *chinna jiyangar* ('little' jiyangar,) who would succeed to headship of the matha when his superior died. The chinna jiyangar had responsibilities of management at less important temples of the TTD. Both renouncers were Sri Vaishnavites of the Tenkalai sect.[19] At the TTD there were also families with inherited income and privileges (mirasis) in the worship and management of temples. These *mirasidars* were also Sri Vaishnavites, at least some of whom were of the Vadagalai sect. At the TTD, as at other temple sites in South India, competition and conflict existed between Tenkalais and Vadagalais.[20]

The first Hathiramji mahant trustee at the TTD was Seva Doss (served 1843–1864). Seva Doss received from the imperial government a grant (*sanad*) that outlined in general terms his powers and responsibilities at the TTD. The government included in the sanad that the trustee was to be neutral in dealing with the two sects, so it appears that the Hathiramji lineage's lack of membership in either sect counted in the mahant's favour.

Leadership at the site, with its 30-odd temples of varying significance, was relatively decentralised. Management was carried out through the services of the mirasidars, who had inherited their rights to responsibilities. Some of these persons were entitled *dharmakarta* (administrator, 'protector of a temple'). The pedda jiyangar's title was dharmakarta, as well. The common practice in South India was that there was only one person entitled dharmakarta at a site of worship and he was the highest authority in matters of administration. The practice at the TTD, however, was for the title to be used severally. Over the course of the century pedda jiyangars played on possible imperial misunderstanding of the practice at TTD as they argued that they, as 'the' dharmakarta, should be the official trustee/chief administrator at the site.

The mahant of Hathiramji matha was not one of the dharmakartas at the TTD and in the course of the litigation here, a mahant did not claim such. The government gave the mahant the title of *vicharanakarta*.[21] It appears that previously the mahant's main official connection with the TTD had been in the capacity of an inherited right (*inam*)[22] at one of the temples to carry out 'certain services'.[23]

In keeping with the preoccupations of the imperial state, the sanad of 1843 focused on the vicharanakarta's rights and responsibilities regarding TTD property. Seva Doss was 'put . . . in possession of the 19 Devastanams . . . the [treasure] boxes and locks, keys &c.' (PC 1907, 239). He was to 'safely secure all the property belonging to the Devastanams' and he was instructed that '[t]he accounts of receipts and expenditure relating to the Devastanams shall be regularly kept and shall be open for inspection when required' (PC 1907: 239–240). Broadly, the vicharanakarta had responsibility for 'each and every matter relating to the Devastanams such as the making of Pooja [worship] . . . according to mamool [custom]' (PC 1907: 239). If the temple staff, including the pedda jiyangar and chinna jiyangar, neglected their duties, the mahant was to 'deal with them in the same manner as Sircar [government] had been dealing with them' (PC 1907: 240).

The general nature of the sanad directions gave rise to increased occasions for conflict in the TTD leadership. For example, did the mahant or the pedda jiyangar punish those temple servants who were negligent, but who were also subordinates of the pedda jiyangar? But that was a relatively minor issue in the long run. Of greater importance as far as pedda jiyangars were concerned was that the outline of the mahant's rights and duties in the sanad corresponded with pedda jiyangars' understanding of their *own* position of leadership at the temple complex.

There several issues to consider here. First, Hathiramji mahants did not belong to a Sri Vaishnavite lineage. The mahants were appointed as the superior authority over the Pedda Jiyangar Matha without being a guru for lineage members of that matha. The pedda jiyangars had not taken vows of obedience to the mahants.

Second, the pedda jiyangars believed that the superior status of their lineage, and thus their special role vis-à-vis the TTD site, had not been recognised when Seva Doss had been appointed in 1843. After the death of Seva Doss in 1864, a pedda jiyangar seemed to think that he could convince the government that it had acted in error with the earlier appointment. Initiating a law suit, the pedda jiyangar was in the seemingly hopeless position of asserting his sovereign status in a process which confirmed imperial sovereignty. But, from the point of view of the pedda jiyangar, the TTD had existed for centuries and could well outlast the British regime.[24]

Pedda jiyangars conceived of their position as being in a direct line from the renowned twelfth-century theologian and founder of Sri Vaishnavism, Ramanuja. They conceived of Ramanuja as their lineage guru and pedda jiyangars bore that guru identity in themselves as a status inherited in the lineage. In the suit from 1868 the pedda jiyangar described Ramanuja as the person who had 'enlarged' the development of the TTD site and had 'regulated the liturgy and framed and systematized' the management of 'all religious and other affairs' of the temples at the site (PC 1907: 215). The historical Ramanuja travelled and taught throughout South India, was involved in the organisation of temple worship at various sites (Appadurai 1981: 75), and may have founded the Pedda Jiyangar Matha.[25] However, the major development at Tirupati from a small collection of shrines to the complex of temples occurred between 1350 and 1650, a process beginning 200 years after the death of Ramanuja (Appadurai 1981: 93). The pedda jiyangar may well have believed that the honour of TTD site expansion belonged to the founder of his matha. He was also, though, appealing to the imperial preoccupation with property. His lawyers were most likely aware that the rulers of Ramnad Zamindari in Madras Presidency could have strengthened their argument to be the dharmakarta of the great pilgrimage temple at Rameswaram if they had been able to prove that their ancestors had been the prime endowers of that site.[26]

The pedda jiyangar's mirasi rights suit ended with a compromise agreement between the pedda jiyangar and the mahant. However, the cessation of conflict was only temporary. The innovation in organisation among renouncers which the imperial government orchestrated was deeply resented at the TTD, with the resentment being directed in public against those who had been appointed to the new status. The effect of this misfit was political involution, as pedda jiyangars burrowed deeper and deeper, exploring the possibilities for undermining the Hathiramji mahant as imperial policy evolved over the course of the century. The rhythm of the conflict was informed by government attempts to respond, as we shall see, to repeated calls in the public sphere for closer state supervision of temple and matha endowments.

Competition among TTD renouncers

Beginning with mahant Seva Doss, but increasing in intensity after his death in 1864, pedda jiyangars sought to discredit the mahant vicharanakartas. The main tactic was to convince the government to dismiss specific vicharanakartas on the basis of accusations of waste and embezzlement. Generations of pedda jiyangars and their faction mates lodged accusation after accusation of mahant wrongdoing. Thus was mathu guru distributional practice stigmatised in processes of litigation competition. Seva Doss' successor at Hathiramji matha, Dharma Doss (1864–1880), faced open hostility from the beginning of his tenure. The pedda jiyangar tried to convince the government to appoint a committee over him shortly after his succession. That effort failed, Dharma Doss explained, and he added that the pedda jiyangar, 'who is always jealous of the power of the Mahant . . . has harassed him with several complaints ever since he came to the management without successful results' (PC 1907: 147).

Suits could be contemplated because, partly in reaction to the Rebellion of 1857, the Imperial Legislature passed the Religious Endowments Act XX of 1863. This act legalised the disconnection of the government from the direct administration of institutions of worship and sacred learning which we have seen was formal imperial policy from the 1840s. Act XX of 1863 divided institutions into two classes, one in which persons connected in some fashion to an institution could institute law suits against trustees, managers, superintendents or members of the committees on charges of fraud or neglect of duty. The court could award damages and remove trustees and managers (Mudaliar 1974: 27).

In a suit instituted in 1867 the TTD plaintiffs (pedda jiyangar faction fellows) alleged that Dharma Doss had 'usurped and misappropriated' approximately Rs610,905 (PC 1907: 143), a strikingly large amount.[27] E. F. Eliott, the acting judge in the Civil Court of Chittoor, examined the charges and found that some of the expenses of Dharma Doss (described as embezzlement in the plaint) were justifiable and that some of the charges made against him were 'puerile and factious' (e.g. PC 1907: 167, 168). After 24 pages of careful examination, he decided that Dharma Doss was liable for approximately Rs225,458, a considerably lesser sum.

The plaintiffs included in the charges against Dharma Doss a loan for Rs500,000 that he had given the Zamindar of Karvetnagar, head of a prominent ruling house in the locality. They argued that the security for the loan, a taluk with an annual income of Rs180,000, presented too many uncertainties. Judge Eliott in the Civil Court found that a safer investment of temple funds would have been in government securities, but that Dharma Doss 'appears to have acted throughout *bona fide* and with the intentions for the good of the Devastanam [TTD]' (PC 1907: 172).

The judge found that the mahant's poor management in general had not helped his cause. Dharma Doss' failure to keep the money from the matha separate from the TTD funds had given the faction opposed to him openings to say that the 'mixing up of money' was done 'purposely' (PC 1907: 179). The mahant had been negligent, but Eliott found there was not 'satisfactory proof that he has actually embezzled' (ibid.): 'the fault all lies in a laxity of administration and an *ineffete* [sic, emphasis in the original] and imbecile management much to be deplored, more than as the result of fraud or culpable negligence. . . . It must be clear that these ascetics are not men of business practically and cannot make efficient managers' (PC 1907: 181). Eliott here voiced the view of the proper renunciatory concerns of a matha head which was common in the legal profession. He most likely thought that he was determining the law, rather than creating it, since judges were not properly engaged in making law in social and religious matters.[28] Judge Eliott decided that there was no point in dismissing Dharma Doss, because another ascetic would fail similarly (PC 1907, 182); at least Dharma Doss had now acquired some experience in administration of the temple complex. Both parties appealed the decision to the High Court, which decided that Dharma Doss owed the TTD the sum settled on by judge Eliott and that, following somewhat Eliott's reasoning, he would not be dismissed. Before examining the High Court decision, we shall examine how Dharma Doss aggravated the tension that existed between him and the pedda jiyangar.

Dharma Doss' skills as a manager were criticised by the judge, but factional animus at the TTD was probably also directed against his having expanded his role in local affairs with temple funds. He appears to have been one of the 'religious potentates' mentioned by Washbrook in his discussion of local structures of political power in late nineteenth- and early twentieth-century Madras presidency (1976: 187). The plaintiffs (opposed to the mahant) specified 'Devastanam funds which . . . are . . . being advanced by him on loan &c., to others for his own advantage and profits' (PC 1907: 143). Spectacular was the large loan to the Karvetnagar zamindar. The estate at the end of the nineteenth century was 943 square miles in area, containing 667 villages.[29] With such a generous gesture to a ruling house, Dharma Doss greatly enhanced his status as a matha head. The pedda jiyangar and his faction fellows would try in various ways to diminish him.

When the 1867 embezzlement case was heard in the High Court, in their judgement of 1870 justices Holloway and Collett took an approach very different from Civil Court judge Eliott in considering the culpability of Dharma Doss. Their opening comments signalled their attitude to matha heads and temple administration in general: 'To talk of the preservation of the funds of any institution of this character would be idle. They have always been funds for embezzlement and what embezzlement has left will speedily be swallowed up in litigation' (PC 1907: 185). The justices did not agree with the lower court's assessment that the mahant's actions were the result of a lack of administrative skills: 'Now, no doubt exists of this man's fraudulent conduct. That he deserves removal is clear, but whether his removal is expedient is a wholly different question' (PC 1907: 186). They stated 'that his *predecessors* [emphasis added] defrauded before him and that his successors, if we should nominate them would, commit fraud also there is as little doubt. It is not the question of replacing a dishonest man by an honest one but of replacing a dishonest man of substantial means by one certainly as dishonest and more hungry' (ibid.). (Dharma Doss had only one predecessor as vicharanakarta at TTD, so it seems that the judges were speaking generically.) Litigation assaults following this case continued to take their toll on the reputation of the mahants. End-of-century TTD litigation would result in radical attempts to rearrange the relationship of the mahants to the TTD.

Judges, public sphere activity, and schemes of matha administration

Increasingly from the 1870s public sphere actors wrote petitions, memoranda, and addresses to the government asking that the official policy of neutrality be given up and that imperial institutions be devised to manage temples and mathas (Mudaliar 1974: 31). There was conviction among elite Indians that Act XX of 1863, which set up temple management committees and facilitated the instituting of court cases, was ineffective in preventing 'misappropriation' of temple and matha endowments. Leading Indian lawyers and administrators started an association, the Dharmarakshana Sabha, in which members endeavoured to keep track of religious endowments and to file suits for the removal of trustees or the settling of schemes of management (Mudaliar 1974: 31, 37; Washbrook 1976: 190). Lawyers in particular were convinced of the value of reform through law and the role of law in assisting or impeding progress in India (Price 1989: 171).

The first attempt to compose a bill to strengthen imperial engagement in the management of temples and mathas was that of an Indian member of the Madras Legislative Council in 1871. Both Indians and Britons continued in the decades following to search for legislative solutions that the central imperial government would approve. The Government of India was cautious, however, expressing fear of civil unrest if governmental machinery was set in place which gave across-the-board interference in the administration of religious institutions. In 1900 the Government of India observed, in defence of executive inaction, '"Even the mass of the Hindu worshippers did not appear to feel any appreciable grievance in the present system of the management or recognize the existence of any evil that called for remedy"' (Mudaliar 1974: 36). There had been in the 1880s, however, a turn in policy showing an imperial interest and perceived responsibility in this area by expanding the jurisdiction of the judiciary (Presler 1987: 25, 26). Section 539 of the Civil Procedure Code, added in 1887, gave the courts the power to modify the trusteeship of endowments either by adding new trustees or appointing a committee 'or in any other way that the Court deems fit' (PC 1907: 371). Through the application of this measure, the mahants of Hathiramji matha experienced the severe reigning in of their scope of action by a district court.

In 1898 two TTD mirasidars instituted a suit against mahant Ramakisore Doss (1895–1900), alleging that he had embezzled the outstanding sum of Rs627,000 and asking for his dismissal. Following in the possibilities provided by section 539, the plaintiffs included a request that the court settle a scheme of management that would prevent further 'abuses'.[30] The mahant made a statement denying the charges, but he was murdered before all of the argumentation on his behalf was heard (PC 1907: 361). His successor two months later was included in the case as Ramakisore's legal representative and the argumentation continued. In his judgement in 1901 the District judge found it unnecessary to examine the charges for embezzlement, since Ramakisore was dead, but he noted that in a similar case against the mahant decided earlier, he had found wrongdoing amounting to Rs50,674–14–2, about 8 per cent of what was originally alleged (PC 1907: 366).

The issue of a new scheme of management of TTD finances, under section 539, received close attention in the course of the litigation. When Ramakisore made his statement of defence at the beginning of the proceedings, he argued that section 539 could not be interpreted to allow modification of the original constitution of the trusteeship in 1843 (PC 1907: 360). The case for the mahant was weakened, however, because his advocate, V. Bashyam Aiyangar, one of the most distinguished at the Madras bar, agreed that 'the management of the Devastanam was being mixed up with that of the Mutt, that this was objectionable and that a scheme for the removal of these evils might be formulated' (PC 1907: 361). With one mahant murdered and his successor a young man of barely 18, it seems that the lineage at Hathiramji matha was not in a strong position even with regard to their own lawyer.

The justices at each level of adjudication devised a different draft of a scheme of management of TTD finances, with the District and High Court solutions being appealed against. Final adjudication in the case came in the Judicial Committee of the Privy Council in London in 1907, nine years after its institution in the District Court.

When the case for the mahant was heard in the Judicial Committee, a principle objection to the scheme proposed at the High Court was that it would 'lower the position of the Mahant and weaken his authority.'[31] The Privy Council justices decided on a scheme which would leave the mahant as the sole trustee, but without rights and responsibilities which were previously his regarding the disposition of the property (cash, jewels, land, etc.) of the TTD. The District Court was to appoint a treasurer at a salary who would have 'custody' of temple property which he was to manage according to rules framed by the District Court.[32] Scope for action of the vicharanakarta lay in that he would annually made a budget, and he would decide the use of the surplus income from the temples. The treasurer would distribute the funds under consideration and the District Court would have to be applied to if the mahant's expenditure were to exceed Rs5,000 beyond the budget. The scheme was enacted and provided the main framework for the administration of the TTD until the 1930s (Kumari 1998: 130).

Two of the most prominent lawyers in South India, V. Bhashyam Aiyangar (1844–1908) and S. Subramania Aiyar (1842–1924), were involved in the litigation which led to the mahant's loss of financial control at the TTD. Such was the widespread respect for Bhashyam Aiyangar that he could take the lead, even as counsel for the mahant, in arguing for a new structure of management for the TTD. At one point the wealthiest lawyer in South India (Price 1989: 163), Bhashyam Aiyangar '"was almost invariably consulted by important men on all occasions of domestic disputes, settlements of property and commercial and other legal transactions"'.[33] Subramania Aiyar, one of the two High Court justices when the decision for that case came down in 1905, was the fulcrum of a major clique of Brahman lawyers in Madras City (Price 1989: 169). Subramania Aiyar's commitment to the oversight of temple and matha administration extended beyond his 1905 reform judgement, as he served as president of the association to monitor religious endowments, the Dharmarakshana Sabha (Washbrook 1976: 257). Powerful Indian lawyers, both Brahmans, facilitated the financial confinement of the mahant.

The central Government of India was pleased that the conflict had been resolved through litigation.[34] In general, though, Madras public sphere reformers wanted increased, comprehensive executive action. It would be Indians, in power under diarchy (dual rule) established with the Montagu-Chelmsford reforms of 1919, that would shape the role of the executive with regard to temples and mathas. The non-Brahman Justice Party, established in 1916, won the most seats to the Madras Legislative Council and so provided an Indian minister who took responsibility for religious endowments as a 'transferred' subject.

The bill which eventually created the Hindu Religious Endowments Board (Madras Act II of 1927)[35] gave rise to considerable controversy. The formal legislative debate of the bill lasted over three years, with the bill's supporters arguing for historical precedents in South India for state 'protection' of temples (Presler 1987: 29). Opponents to the bill attacked it as 'flagrant intervention' and a betrayal of the imperial guarantee of noninterference in religious affairs (ibid.). One of the results of legislative deliberations was the inclusion of mathas within the scope of the new board. The judicially derived model of the reclusive matha guru prevailed as a Select Committee argued that "'*Maths* as an institution exist for the spiritual welfare of the disciples and the *matadhipati* is an ascetic and could as such have no interests other than those which are proper and subserve [sic] the interest of his disciples'" (Mudaliar 1974: 45).[36] The formulators of the Act argued that it would be possible to establish state oversight of the properties of a matha without controlling 'the person' of the matha head (Mudaliar 1974: 52). The shrinking of the political person of the matha head was thus broadly institutionalised, as the state, with an expanded legislative council with elected Indian members, centralised control.

Conclusion

Curiously, in 1907 as it gave an important role to the District Court in managing finances at the TTD, the Judicial Committee asserted that '[s]ubject to this scheme the Vicharanakarta's position [is] to remain as before'.[37] We can understand this statement as an example of imperial representation of the regime as protecting cherished native customs and institutions. As discussed earlier, officials maintained an image of matha heads that reflected ancient notions involving strict withdrawal, romanticising the 'ideal of the sages of vedic lore' (White 2009: 244). They were unaware that renouncers' activities and relationships could be important elements in their spiritual engagement (Khandelwal 2004: 34). Judges took varying views as to whether the perceived failures at mathas was due to faults in the structure of management or the moral character of the mahants, but they shared the sentiments of Subramania Aiyer and Davies in describing mahants in 1905 as 'celibates supposed to have little or no concern with worldly affairs' (PC 1907: 479). The justices of the Privy Council could, thus, very well assume that restricting the mahant's access to the property of the TTD would not alter his appropriate position with regard to the temple complex.

The imperial regime had proceeded cautiously, appearing in various ways to protect the status of matha heads, at the same time as judges pronounced on the meaning of that status. In 1874 the Judicial Committee decided in favour of the matha head at the great Rameswaram pilgrimage temple against the ruling house of Ramnad, giving the spiritual lineage top managing authority (PC 1874). There were limits to how far this protection would reach, however. In 1884 the High Court of Madras dismissed the Rameswaram matha head for the embezzlement of Rs.14,855. He was charged with criminal breach of trust and sentenced to simple imprisonment.[38] A Hathiramji mahant was found guilty in 1890 of having taken from the TTD gold coins worth Rs.175,000 and was sentenced to 18 months of rigorous imprisonment (PC 1907: 204). Such strenuous measures could safely be taken toward high-ranking matha heads when there was widespread acceptance among public sphere elites that certain types of moral regulation were constituent of imperial sovereignty.

It has been beyond the scope of this study to investigate the development of notions of appropriate renunciate behaviour in the colonial judiciary. Interesting but insufficient is the observation of Ashis Nandy, that the British ruling classes were greatly attracted to the self-denying asceticism of (the older) Hindu traditions, because of the importance of '"sexual distance, abstinence and self-control"' in their own notions of masculinity.[39] Concerning debates in Indian public spheres generally, Knut Jacobsen reports that, amidst religious revivalism, by the 1890s the attractiveness of a 'new ascetic puritanism' rendered the sanyasi the '"quintessential bearer of Indian spiritual culture"'.[40]

Such a preoccupation goes some way to explain the attention given to M. K. Gandhi's emergence as a renouncer in the Indian nationalist movement, following a simple ascetic style. The power which he acquired through his spiritual and physical disciplines was to be used in engagement against the imperial state, in the renunciation-in-the-world of himself and others. While equipped with a legal education and practical experience of the law, Gandhi rejected the imperial courts and the participation of practicing lawyers in the Congress movement. The locus of sovereignty in India was not to lie in reasoned discourse performed by detached officers of the imperial state. It was to be found in self-controlled persons, *satyagrahis*, whose own moral discipline rendered them detached from social influences even as they engaged with the world, performing acts of self-rule in peaceful resistance to the empire (Gilmartin 2015: 381–382). As Gilmartin points out, Gandhi's version of ascetic truth included the expression of international ideas of popular sovereignty, providing a background for the emergence of support in an independent India of the sovereignty of the 'people' in electoral democracy (Gilmartin 2015: 382).[41] It is noteworthy of imperial success, however, in promulgating '"British justice"' in the Anglo-Indian legal system, that, as Chandrachud points out with reference to the Bombay High Court, judges who had served in the colonial regime transitioned easily into being judges on the decolonised High Court (2015: 2).[42] Gandhi and other nationalists had been sentenced in the Bombay High Court, but overall respect for 'the rule of law' was such that imperial-era adjudicators could continue under the new dispensation.

The rule of law in Independent India protects the sovereignty of the 'people', importantly through the operations of the Electoral Commission (Gilmartin 2009). Still, the person of the ruler strikingly captures voters' imaginations. Kingly political styles are often assumed by wielders of power, as Lucia Michelutti illustrates in this volume. But as Paul Brass and W. H. Morris-Jones suggested more than 50 years ago, saintly idioms also hold appeal amidst regimes of greater and lesser self-seeking corruption and sporadic violence (Morris-Jones 1963; Brass 1965: 55). For this reason, perhaps, in 2017 the party of Hindu nationalism, the BJP, chose Yogi Adityanath, head of Gorakhpur Math, to be the Chief Minister of the north Indian state of Uttar Pradesh. Spiritual domains, otherwise, flourish. As Aya Ikegame shows, in her chapter in this volume and elsewhere, in Karnataka in South India, leaders of mathas continue to acquire sovereign aspects (Ikegame 2010: 59; Ikegame 2012: 57).

Notes

* My gratitude to David Gilmartin, Kristin Hanssen, Ute Hüsken, Arild Ruud, and members of the Oslo South Asia Symposium for reading and commenting on various drafts of this piece.

1 I italicise a foreign noun the first time I use it.

2 The term 'religious chiefs' is one used by Appadurai to characterise powerful heads of spiritual lineages (1981: 93).

3 The head of a matha was the guru, spiritual leader and chief administrator, of the lineage that was based there. In this piece I use the terms matha head and guru or matha guru interchangeably.

4 Devastanam means temple.

5 I make this observation as a result of the research involved in, *inter alia*, Price (1996), Price (2013a), Price 2013b), and Price (forthcoming).

6 The scholarship of Appadurai (1981) pointed to importance of this distinction for imperial approaches to India 'religious' institutions, at the same time as he drew attention to the significance of the patronage of temples in medieval state formation.

7 Mudaliar (1974) traces this development; however, I differ with her assessment of the meaning of the actions of temple and matha administrators.

8 See the discussion in Raman (2013: 22–27).

9 Arjun Appadurai (1981) argued that charges of misappropriation in temples could be a screen for conflicts over authority, articulated in the distribution of temple honours. A summary of arguments related to the public-private distinction and the political in relation to state formation is Haldén (2013).

10 Privy Council (hereafter, PC) 1874. Rajah Muttu Ramalinga Setupati and others v. Perianayagum Pillai, Guardian &c., The Judgement of the Judicial Committee, p. 9, quoting J. H. Nelson, *The Madura Country: A Manual*, Part III, Chapter 7, p. 162.

11 Ibid. Judgement of the Judicial Committee, p. 8.

12 Meister (1990: 236), quoting David M. Miller and Dorothy C. Wertz, *Hindu Monastic Life: The Monks and Monasteries of Bhubaneswar* (Montreal: McGill-Queen's University Press, 1976), p. 176.

13 I am grateful to Sondra Hausner for drawing my attention to this point, in a discussion of her work (July, 2016).

14 I am grateful to David Gilmartin for this insight (correspondence, 2017).

15 PC (1907) Prayaga Doss Jee Varu v. Tirumala Anandam Pillai Purisa Sriranga Charylu Varu and another. The Case for the Respondents, 2.
16 The term jiyangar is formed when the honorific *garu* is added to *jiyar,* meaning in this case the religious head of a matha. http://dsalsrv02.uchicago.edu/cgi-bin/philologic/search3advanced?dbname=tamillex&query=jiyar&matchtype=exact&display=utf8
17 Mirasis gave entitlement to lands which provided income, as well as specifying rights and privileges.
18 PC 1907, O.S. No 485 of 1894, Court of the District Munsif of Tirupati, 321.
19 Sri Vaishnavism emerged in the Tamil Country in the tenth century, combining Sanskritic Vaishnavite traditions with devotional Tamil Vaishnavite traditions from the early medieval period. The two main sects among Sri Vaishnavites were the Tenkalais and the Vadagalais.
20 A discussion of the Tengalai and Vadagalai sets and conflicts is found in Appadurai (1981).
21 Koutha Nirmala Kumari translates vicharanakarta as 'administrator' (1998: 124).
22 A tax-free grant of land.
23 PC (1907) Case for the Respondents, 3.
24 In other matha litigation as well one finds matha administrators seeking precedents that lead to future claims for status and power (Price forthcoming).
25 According to contemporary tradition, Ramanuja spent a year at Tirupati (Anon 2003).
26 PC (1874). The High Court decision referring to Ramnad endowing came in in 1865. *Zamindaris* were revenue estates, often formed from the domains of petty kings and chiefs and in this way incorporated into the administration of the presidency.
27 I will try to provide a sense of the magnitude of this sum with reference to other sums provided in the documents of PC (1907): the salary of a peon (Rs. 3 and a half/month); a TTD lawyer (Rs. 20/month); the treasurer of the TTD (Rs. 35/month); Pedda Jiyangar (Rs. 50/month). The annual income of the extremely popular Sri Venkateswara Swami temple was between 200,00–300,000 rupees.
28 Sturman has shown that this was a common practice in imperial adjudication (2012).
29 The Imperial Gazetteer of India (1908). http://indpaedia.com/ind/index.php/Karvetnagar_Zamindari.
30 PC (1907), O.S. No. 31 of 1898.
31 PC (1907) Judgement of the Lords of the Judicial Committee of the Privy Council, 2.
32 PC (1907) Judgement of the Lords of the Judicial Committee of the Privy Council, p. 3.
33 Price (1989: 164) quoting C. P. Ramaswami Aiyar, *Biographical Vistas: Sketches of Some Eminent Indians* (London, 1968), p. 131.
34 Presler (1987: 26), quoting G.O. 627 28 May 1912.
35 The successor to the Hindu Religious Endowments Board after independence was the Hindu Religious and Charitable Endowments (Administration) Department.
36 In her study Mudaliar is sympathetic to the social and political forces which called for radical reform of temple and matha administration.
37 PC (1907) Judgement of the Lords of the Judicial Committee of the Privy Council, p. 4.
38 PC (1893) Judgement of the Lords of the Judicial Committee, p. 1. With simple imprisonment no hard labour is required.
39 Referred to in Haberman (1993: 55), quoting Ashis Nandy, *The Intimate Enemy: Loss and Recovery of Self under Colonialism* (Delhi: Oxford University Press, 1983), 10.
40 Jacobsen (2018: 57), quoting Matthew James Clark, *The Daśanāmī-saṃnyāsīs: The Integration of Ascetic Lineages into an Order* (Leiden: Brill, 2006), p. 8.
41 See also Gilmartin's chapter in this volume.
42 Only the outgoing British Chief Justice did not continue (Chandrachud 2015: 2).

References

Anon. 2003. 'Sri Ramanuja Shrine at Tirumala Gets a Facelift', *The Hindu*, February 28. www.thehindu.com/thehindu/fr/2003/02/28/stories/2003022801310600.htm (Accessed June 8, 2013).

Appadurai, Arjun. 1981. *Worship and Conflict Under Colonial Rule: A South Indian Case*. Cambridge: Cambridge University Press.

Blackburn, Stuart. 2003. *Print, Folklore, and Nationalism in Colonial South India*. Delhi: Permanent Black.

Brass, Paul. 1965. *Factional Politics in an Indian State: The Congress Party in Uttar Pradesh*. Berkeley: University of California Press.

Burghart, Richard. 1996. 'Hierarchical Models of the Hindu Social System', in Richard Burghart, C. J. Fuller, and Jonathan Spencer (eds.), *The Conditions of Listening: Essays on Religion, History and Politics in South Asia*, pp. 35–58. New Delhi: Oxford University Press.

Chandrachud, Abhinav. 2015. *An Independent, Colonial Judiciary: A History of the Bombay High Court During the British Ra, 1862–1947*. New Delhi: Oxford University Press.

Ebeling, Sascha. 2010. *Colonizing the Realm of Words: The Transformation of Tamil Literature in Nineteenth-Century South India*. Albany: State University of New York Press.

Gilmartin, David. 2009. 'One Day's Sultan: T. N. Seshan and Indian Democracy', *Contributions to Indian Sociology*, 43 (2): 247–284.

Gilmartin, David. 2015. 'Rethinking the Public Through the Lens of Sovereignty', *South Asia: Journal of South Asian Studies*, 38 (3): 371–386.

Haberman, David L. 1993. 'On Trial: The Love of the Sixteen Thousand Gopies', *History of Religions*, 33 (1): 44–70.

Haldén, Peter. 2013. 'Fundamental But Not Eternal: The Public-Private Distinction, From Normative Projects to Cognitive Grid in Western Political Thought', *Small Wars and Insurgencies*, 24 (2): 211–223.

Hansen, Thomas Blom, and Finn Stepputat. 2006. 'Sovereignty Revisited', *Annual Review of Anthropology*, 35: 295–315.

Heitzman, James. 1997. *Gifts of Power: Lordship in an Early Indian State*. New Delhi: Oxford University Press.

Ikegame, Aya. 2010. 'Why Do Backward Castes Need Their Own Gurus? The Social and Political Significance of New Caste-Based Monasteries in Karnataka', *Contemporary South Asia*, 18 (1): 57–70.

Ikegame, Aya. 2012. 'The Governing Guru: Hindu *Mathas* in Liberalizing India', in Jacob Copeman and Aya Ikegame (eds.), *The Guru in South Asia: New Interdisciplinary Perspectives*, pp. 46–63. London: Routledge.

The Imperial Gazetteer of India. 1908. 'Karvetnagar Zamindari'. Oxford: Clarendon Press. http://indpaedia.com/ind/index.php/Karvetnagar_Zamindari (Accessed June 7, 2018).

ILR. Madras. 1887. 'Giyana Sambandha Pandara Sannadhi v. Kandasami Tambiran', *Indian Law Reports*, 375–508.

Jacobsen, Knut A. 2018. *Yoga in Modern Hinduism: Hariharānanda Āraṇya and Sāṃkhyayoga*. New Delhi: Routledge.

Kasturi, Malavika. 2009. '"Asceticising" Monastic Families: Ascetic Genealogies, Property Feuds and Anglo-Hindu Law', *Modern Asian Studies*, 43 (5): 1039–1083.

Kasturi, Malavika. 2016. '"This Land is Mine": Mahants, Civil Law, and Political Articulations of Hinduism in Twentieth Century North India', in Daniela Berti, Gilles Tarabout, and Raphaël Vois (eds.), *Filing Religion: State, Hinduism, and Courts of Law*, pp. 230–259. New Delhi: Oxford University Press.

Khandelwal, Meena. 2004. *Women in Ochre Robes: Gendering Hindu Renunciation*. Albany: State University of New York Press.

Kumari, Koutha Nirmala. 1998. *History of the Hindu Religious Endowments in Andhra Pradesh*. New Delhi: Northern Book Centre. https://books.google.no/books?id=Ob5REUVgpVMC&pg=PA126&lpg=PA126&dq=vicharanakarta&source=bl&ots=c1q6gfbjV8&sig=FJFBaHQtoSJjNb0FGib2qjLPUic&hl=no&sa=X&ved=0ahUKEwiBpp

mWuqXPAhXCiywKHYHzDv8Q6AEIHjAA#v=onepage&q=vicharanakarta&f=false (Accessed September 23, 2016).

Meister, Michael. 1990. 'Asceticism and Monasticism as Reflected in Indian Art', in Austin B. Creel and Vasudha Narayana (eds.), *Monastic Life in the Christian and Hindu Traditions: A Comparative Study*, pp. 219–244. Lewiston: The Edwin Mellen Press.

Morris-Jones, Wyndraeth H. 1963. 'India's Political Idioms', in C. H. Philips (ed.), *Politics and Society in India*, pp. 133–154. London: Allen and Unwin.

Mudaliar, Chandra Y. 1974. *The Secular State and Religious Institutions in India: A Study of the Administration of Hindu Public Religious Trusts in Madras*. Wiesbaden: Franz Steiner Verlag GMBH.

Mukherjee, Mithi. 2010. *India in the Shadows of Empire: A Legal and Political History, 1774–1950*. New Delhi: Oxford University Press.

Ocko, Jonathan K., and David Gilmartin. 2009. 'State, Sovereignty, and the People: A Comparison of the "Rule of Law" in China and India', *The Journal of Asian Studies*, 68 (1): 55–133.

Prasad, Leela. 2007. *Poetics of Conduct: Oral Narrative and Moral Being in a South Indian Town*. New York: Columbia University Press.

Presler, Franklin A. 1987. *Religion Under Bureaucracy: Policy and Administration for Hindu Temples in South India*. Cambridge: Cambridge University Press.

Price, Pamela. 1989. 'Ideology and Ethnicity Under British Imperial Rule: "Brahmans", Lawyers and Kin-Caste Rules in Madras Presidency', *Modern Asian Studies*, 23 (1): 151–177.

Price, Pamela. 1996. *Kingship and Political Practice in Colonial India*. Cambridge: Cambridge University Press.

Price, Pamela. 2013a. 'Acting in Public Versus Forming a Public: Conflict Processing and Political Mobilization in Nineteenth Century South India', in Pamela Price (ed.), *State, Politics, and Cultures: Honour, Authority, and Morality*, pp. 59–95. New Delhi: Orient Blackswan.

Price, Pamela. 2013b. 'Kin, Clan, and Power in Colonial South India: Queens and Slaves in the Politics of Reproduction', in Pamela Price (ed.), *State, Politics, and Cultures: Honour, Authority, and Morality*, pp. 96–125. New Delhi: Orient Blackswan.

Price, Pamela. Forthcoming. 'Network Tensions and Conflicts in a Tamil Spiritual Lineage Under British Imperial Rule'. In *Beyond the Monastery: The Entangled Institutional History of the South Asian Maṭha*.

Privy Council. 1874. *Rajah Muttu Ramalinga Setupati and Others v. Perianayagum Pillai, Guardian &c., Appeal to the Judicial Committee*, London. Decision: March 18. Consulted at the Library of Lincoln's Inn, London.

Privy Council. 1893. *Ramalingam Pillai v. Vythilingam Pillai: Appeal to the Judicial Committee*, London. Decision: July 15. Consulted at the Library of Lincoln's Inn, London.

Privy Council. 1907. *Prayaga Doss Jee Varu v. Tirumala Anandam Pillai Purisa Sriranga Charylu Varu and Another: Appeal to the Judicial Committee*, London. Decision: February 8. Consulted at the Library of Lincoln's Inn, London.

Privy Council. 1920. *Nataraja Tambiran v. Kailasam Pillai: Appeal to the Judicial Committee*, London. Decision: June 7. Consulted at the Library of Lincoln's Inn, London.

Raman, Srilata. 2013. 'The Spaces In Between: Ramalinga Swamigal (1823–1874), Hunger and Religion in Colonial India', *History of Religion*, 53 (1): 1–27.

Ramaswami Aiyar, C. P. n.d. 'Some of the Early Leaders of the Madras Bar', in V. C. Gopalratnam (compiler), *A Century Complete (A History of the Madras High Court), 1862–1962*, pp. 270–276. Madras: Madras Law Journal Office.

Sarkar, Tanika. 1997. 'Talking about Scandals: Religion, Law and Love in Late Nineteenth Century Bengal', *Studies in History*, n.s., 13 (1): 63–93.

Simmons, Caleb. Forthcoming. 'Curious Penpals: An Examination of the Role of *Maṭhas* in Ṭīpū Sultān's Letter to the *Jagadguru* of Sṛngēri', in *Beyond the Monastery: The Entangled Institutional History of the South Asian Maṭha*.

Stoker, Valerie. 2015. '*Darbār, Maṭha, Devasthānam*: The Politics of Intellectual Commitment and Religious Organization in Sixteenth-Century South India', in Rosaline O'Hanlon, Christopher Minkowski, and Anand Venkatkrishnan (eds.), *Scholar Intellectuals in Early Modern India: Discipline, Sect, Lineage and Community*, pp. 130–146. London: Routledge.

Stoker, Valerie. 2016. *Polemics and Patronage in the City of Victory: Vyasatirtha, Hindu Sectarianism, and the Sixteenth-Century Vijayanagara Court*. Oakland: University of California Press. http://doi.org/10.1525/luminous.18.

Sturman, Rachel. 2012. *The Government of Social Life in Colonial India: Liberalism, Religious Law, and Women's Rights*. Cambridge: Cambridge University Press.

Vail, Lise F. 1985. 'Founders, Swamis, and Devotees: Becoming Divine in North Karnataka', in Joanne Punzo Waghorne and Norman Cutler (in Association with Vasudha Narayanan) (eds.), *Gods of Flesh/Gods of Stone: The Embodiment of Divinity in India*, pp. 123–140. Chambersburg, PA: Anima.

Venkatachelapathy, A. R. 2012. *The Province of the Book: Scholars, Scribes, and Scribblers in Colonial Tamilnadu*. Ranikhet: Permanent Black.

Washbrook, David. 1976. *The Emergence of Provincial Politics: The Madras Presidency, 1870–1920*. Cambridge: Cambridge University Press.

White, David Gordon. 2009. *Sinister Yogis*. Chicago: University of Chicago Press.

2

THE GURU AS LEGISLATOR

Religious leadership and informal legal space in rural South India

Aya Ikegame

Anthropology of the sovereign paradox

In recent years, anthropologists have revealed practices and effects of sovereignty that are radically different from the normative definition of the sovereign state, typically characterised as a vested authority enjoying the monopoly of legitimate violence in a territory with clear boundaries (Geertz 2004: 579). What anthropologists call a sovereign goes beyond, or far below, the level of a nation-state. At the same time, the workings of the state, in a conventional sense, have also become an object of anthropological enquiry (Fuller and Bénéï 2001; Das and Poole 2004; Gupta 2012; Mbembe 1992; Sharma and Gupta 2006; Spencer 2007). From vigilantism in post-Apartheid South Africa and big men or political brokers in western India, to street gangs in Africa and 'public' transport systems provided by the local mafia in Siberia (Buur 2003, Buur 2005; Jansen 2005; Gordon 2004; Hansen 2005; Humphrey 2004), all have been considered as 'sovereign performers' (Hansen 2006) or 'localised sovereigns' (Humphrey 2004). Anthropologists have questioned and destabilised the image of the nation-state by looking at irregularity and divisions within the supposedly unified and unifying sovereign nation-state, treating the state not as static but instead as a performance, by 'reconstructing imaginations of the state, their discursive lives, and their practical effects' (Feuchtwang 2004: 587, see also Hansen and Stepputat 2001; Fuller and Bénéï 2001; Das and Poole 2004; Spencer 2007).

Grounded ethnographic investigations have revealed that these sovereign-like figures whose work provides vital social services play an essential role in maintaining some degree of social stability, bringing justice through the use of both legal and illegal means in places where legal state provisions are inaccessible or non-existent. Their contribution is significant, since policy makers and development agencies continue to consider and refer to such places simply as 'failed states'. Anthropological works on state bureaucracy have also examined how the state actually controls and surveils its population (Gupta 2012; Mbembe 1992). It has been clearly demonstrated that the state does not exercise its power in a cohesive and self-conscious way. In fact, it works in an extremely arbitrary fashion, and its very arbitrariness and illegibility produce a structural violence that is felt most by the people at the margins of society (Das and Poole 2004; Gupta 2012). While the working of the state within society reveals its inconsistency and arbitrariness, the nation-state which is treated like an individual 'person' also emerges as not so autonomous nor indivisible. Aihwa Ong (2000, 2012) has argued that in an era of rapidly globalising capital and power, the state must be 'flexible' and 'gradual' when it becomes necessary to compromise or reduce the degree of autonomy and indivisibility in order to ensure its own survival.

While the anthropology of sovereignty has uncovered the inconsistency and irregularity of the supposed autonomous and indivisible figure of the sovereign, Clifford Geertz has urged us to see 'less Hobbes, more Machiavelli: less the imposition of sovereign monopoly, more the cultivation of the higher expediency; less the exercise of abstract will, more the pursuit of visible advantage' (2004: 580). It is an interesting invitation which neatly summarises the major current trend within anthropology. 'Less Hobbes, more Machiavelli' (580) might also explain another major concern within the anthropology of sovereignty: violence. Aligning with the Schmitt-Agamben line of understanding, Hansen and Stepputat suggested the following:

> The key move we propose is to abandon sovereignty as an ontological ground of power and order, expressed in law or in enduring ideas of legitimate rule, in favor of a view of sovereignty as a tentative and always emergent form of authority grounded in violence that is performed and designed to generate loyalty, fear, and legitimacy from the neighborhood to the summit of the state.
>
> *(Hansen and Stepputat 2006: 297)*

In short, sovereignty can range in size and scope from a street to a nation, but it maintains its foundational moment in its ability to kill. Violence is undoubtedly a crucial aspect of sovereignty in many parts of the world where other forms of security are largely undermined or absent. This is also true within western democracy, when citizens are placed at the margins of the state rendering them unable to claim rights that they have: Guantanamo Bay is the ultimate example of this. Giorgio Agamben's work thus has been extremely influential in the anthropology of sovereignty.[1] His concepts, such as 'sovereign ban' and 'bare life', bring together both Schmitt's political theology and Foucault's biopower, but anthropology's relationship with Agamben does not necessarily go deeper than theoretical inspiration. Agamben's understanding of sovereignty and what the anthropology of sovereignty has empirically demonstrated do not always coincide. Actually, ethnographical examples may be suggesting something far more fundamental. For example, the person of *homo sacer* or *bare life* – the central figure in his theory, whom anyone could kill with impunity but who cannot be sacrificed (Agamben 1998) – cannot simply be extended to anyone, even when her/his life is extremely precarious and dependent upon an authoritarian regime. However, Akhil Gupta, for instance, shows that the poor in India, to whom the state failed to deliver the benefits of development, are nonetheless enthusiastic participants of democracy at different levels and they do not feel that they are far from being excluded (2012: 17). Examples, such as this, suggest that the dynamics of exclusion and inclusion should be considered differently.

There is another danger in applying Agambenian theory in the anthropology of sovereignty. Although Foucault's view on sovereignty is limited by regarding it as an archaic form of power (Hansen and Stepputat 2005: 16), it is significant that he also sees the same mechanism of sovereignty at work in any form of power relationship from a family to a kingdom. More importantly, he emphasises the fact that 'sovereignty is never shaped from above' but 'is always shaped from below' (Foucault 2003: 96). Our Agambenian inclination does not allow us to examine how people might surrender their own freedom in order to constitute a sovereign. For Foucault, people do so purely out of fear and desire for a strong will, but – as Hobbes observed in *Leviathan* – such surrender may come from a mutual contract under which each individual voluntarily gives up some rights in order to maintain certain individual rights.[2] To address those shortcomings in the anthropology of sovereignty, this chapter will engage with different and less studied sets of sovereign issues: self-rule, trust, and governance.

The growing recent academic interest in sovereignty, especially within political theory, law, and international relations, has revealed strong historical contingency within the politics of sovereign theory. The different definitions of what sovereignty is or does vary tremendously, representing diametrically opposed views. For some, sovereignty is equated with rule and the jurisdiction of law; for others, however, sovereignty is the capacity to violate the very law it creates. For some, sovereignty is a unifying force for autonomy and self-rule, while for others it is an oppressive power over citizens who demand political freedoms. Some insist upon its absolute and indivisible core nature, and others suggest that it can be sharable, partial and divisible (Brown 2008: 251–252). These oppositional views do not simply come from disciplinary or political differences, but the paradoxical aspect lies in the very core of sovereign configuration. Some theorists, such as William Connolly, see potentiality in the very gaps and fissures that occasionally emerge between the two contradictory faces of sovereignty (2005: 131–148). Connolly asks if we could perhaps envisage a more inclusive and democratic ethos in this very paradox. This places Connolly at a distance from the sovereign paradigm described by Agamben, in which sovereignty is closely tied up with biopolitics, with which it forms an inescapable conjunction.

Although his theory has not been much reflected in contemporary discussions of sovereignty, Jean-Jacques Rousseau saw this paradox as a crucial constitutional moment for popular sovereignty. His most influential work, *The Social Contract*

(2007 [1762], hereafter *SC*) begins with a riddle: 'Man is born free, and everywhere he is in chains' (*SC*, book 1, ch. 1: 28). This famous and probably most quoted line of Rousseau was often mistakenly understood as meaning that in order to be free again, we must break the social chains; but this was in fact a concise expression of the sovereign paradox. In his argument, the people, who constitute the general will, are sovereign. It is the people who authorise the social contract; however, it is the contract itself that bestows authority on the people. Therefore, 'the cause would have to become the effect' (*SC*, book II, ch. 7: 43). To solve this dilemma, Rousseau introduces the figure of the wise legislator or lawgiver, who reconfigures 'the masses into a unified, autonomous people capable of making its own laws' (Inston 2010: 397; see also Connolly 2005: 134–136). The wise legislator is an outsider who can 'see all the passions of men without experiencing any of them' and who transforms every individual 'into part of a greater whole' (*SC*, book II, ch. 7: 42). The wise legislator, though, does not entirely solve the paradox of Rousseau's theory of popular sovereignty. Connolly, for example, asks how this fictional wise man could bring an ethos of self-rule where people still live with undemocratic customs and norms. In other words, how could he found 'a democracy in a place that is not already democratic?' (2005: 135).

This chapter examines the ways in which rural citizens of southern India constitute religious leaders as sovereign-like figures and how, through this authority, they have tried to govern their own everyday life. Our particular example comes from an informal arbitration court, called *Nyāya Pītha* (seat of justice), run by the head of a *maṭha* (Hindu religious institution) in Sirigere, a village in the Chitradurga district in the state of Karnataka. We will see how his role is conflicted, as he stands as an embodiment of the people as a sovereign and a wise legislator who may bring a democratic ethos and encourage self-rule, while, at the same time, standing outside of society.

The sovereign renouncer

The French sociologist Louis Dumont (1980) has argued that the renouncer in Asian traditions attains a transcendent position beyond rigid 'caste' hierarchies. By cutting off kinship ties, a renouncer becomes 'an individual-outside-the world' (ibid.: 185). Through renunciation, 'a man can become dead to the social world, [and] escape the network of strict interdependence' (ibid.: 184). For Dumont, the renouncer is the only individual in the sense that he could 'become to himself his own end', as in the west (ibid.: 185). Yet, unlike in Dumont's structural formula, gurus in South Asia, most of whom are celibate renouncers, are not quite the ideal type of western individual-citizen. Rather, they present another dilemma of sovereign paradox. The authority of a guru comes from his transcendence from the community and social connections, but to be an effective leader he needs to understand social norms and be able to utilise networks of power and recourses. The Indologist, J. C. Heesterman succinctly demonstrated exactly the same paradox in his reading of classical Indian texts on kingship (1985: 108–127). The paradox, the 'conundrum of the king's authority' as he put it, is a fundamental and insoluble 'conundrum' in Indian political thought. In ancient Indian texts, the king – any king – is automatically an embodiment of transcendent moral order (*dharma*), but simultaneously, he needs to be subjected to the norms and customs of the community. This is a tricky manoeuvre by which, to be an effective ruler, 'the king has to belong to the community and at the same time he must stand outside so as to guarantee his authority' (ibid.: 117). As David Gilmartin (2014) has argued, this paradox is not unique to ancient Indian kingship but touches upon a more universal and contemporary problem. The idea of a 'sovereign people' that lies at the heart of modern electoral law ensures that a sovereign individual is free from any 'undue influence' and able to make her/his own 'free choice'. Paradoxically, however, in order to make a decision, the voter needs to be a part of the public where one cannot avoid interests and influence of the community (2014: 131–132). Transcending networks of influence, patronage, kinship, relationships, and affection is fundamental to the ideal of a modern citizen but is a nearly impossible task to achieve.[3] Both the Indian king and modern sovereign individual are required to 'perform a precarious balancing act' (Heesterman 1985: 115) and in many ways it is 'a gamble' (112).

The sovereign-renouncer model seems to resolve, to some extent but not entirely, the difficult juggling act of transcendence and embeddedness. The social death that the renouncer goes through gives him a transcendent position of 'an individual-outside-the world'. At the same time, unlike Dumont's understanding, the first social death creates another new kinship. In eighteenth-century northern India, many *chelas* (or *cela*), servant-disciples of the 'ascetic armies', were child slaves purchased or stolen by their guru-commanders (Pinch 2012). It was believed that the involuntary nature of their 'social death' or cutting off their original family bonds made them even more loyal and devoted to their gurus than other members who had joined voluntarily. The social death can form a variety of interesting but unexpected social bonds. Those who joined voluntarily might have conflicting affinities with the guru and their natal family, but slave-chelas do not. The lack of kin thus creates even stronger ties between the guru and disciples. A similar understanding of kinship and renunciation can be found in the modern-day southern state of Karnataka, where many lower castes and former untouchable communities have begun to form caste-based *mathas* or monasteries, and enthroned young renouncers from their community as the heads of their caste-mathas (Ikegame 2010, 2012). The dilemma that the renouncer-guru becomes the very embodiment of the caste/community from which he had transcended himself is, at least partially, resolved by the idea of new kinship. As I have argued elsewhere, by cutting off kinship ties, or by going through a 'social death', the guru forms a new bond of kinship with the community at large (Sood 2006; Ikegame 2012). The political shift that many lower castes are making, from secular caste associations to more religiously infused mathas, is crucial to creating a renewed sense of belonging and a new form of leadership. One elderly gentleman who helped to establish mathas for the Kuruba (traditionally a shepherd caste) in the early 1990s once said to me rather philosophically: 'In the case of the caste association, [everyone starts saying] it is mine, it is mine, but in the case of matha, it becomes ours' (Ikegame 2012: 56). This wonderfully expresses why the guru is an ideal form of sovereign-performer and how the guru captures many people's political imagination in contemporary South India. The renouncer does not belong to a particular person, he thus can be owned by 'us' all. Through renunciation, the guru becomes, simultaneously, the individual-outside-the Community and an embodiment of the community from which he distances himself. The logic of renunciation is therefore a paradox of sovereignty; he is not a part of the community but is the community itself. This is also an example of the extraordinary ability of the guru to 'count-as-one' (Copeman and Ikegame 2012: 18). The differences and heterogeneity of a group of people are transcended and they become one with the guru embodying them. This makes the guru a very special type of sovereign. However, the logic alone does not secure him an absolute position. The logic of sovereign-renunciation has to be constantly demonstrated and performed by gurus, and the devotees themselves continuously examine how the guru lives up to this ideal.

There is another important logic to legitimatising the guru as a sovereign. It is widely believed that because of his lack of kin, he cannot be corrupted. With an unprecedented number of corruption cases reported in the media on an almost everyday basis, suspicion towards democratically elected representatives is growing. But as one of my interviewees told me: 'How much can one *sanyāsi* [renouncer] possibly spend?' The very kin-less-ness of the renouncer assures he is an incorruptible leader. Unlike politicians, who inevitably embezzle public money in order to support their families and relatives, the renouncer remains clean and selfless. This logic of celibacy as a sign of political incorruptibility extends beyond sanyasis: members of transgender communities of *Hijras* have been successfully elected in Indian local elections. Through a violent process of castration, they become seen as truly selfless (Cohen 1995, 2004) and can thus even be representatives of a spiritual Hindu nation (Reddy 2003).[4] The media report on the marital status of Narendra Modi, just before he became the prime minister of India after the electoral success of his Hindu nationalist party Bharatiya Janata Party (BJP) in May 2014, also confirms the longevity of the political legitimation of celibacy since M. K. Gandhi.[5] Just before the election he publicly admitted for the first time that he was married. Since Modi started his political career as a *pracharak* (full-time worker) of the Hindu fundamentalist organisation Rashtriya Swayamsevak Sangh (RSS), many believed that he was celibate. According to their internal rules, pracharaks must lead a disciplined life, remain celibate, and devote their life to propagating the RSS ideology. The sudden revelation shocked many, but the fact that Modi's marriage was a child marriage (he married his wife when he was 17) and that he lived with his wife for only a couple of years was somehow enough to satisfy Modi supporters. The anti-Modi camp criticised him for abandoning his wife and leaving her in near poverty for 40 years. The logic of renunciation might have escaped the secular-minded anti-Modi critics. His very cruelty ironically enhances his sanyasi-like status. The more suffering his wife endures, the more dedicated and selfless his public image becomes.

The logic of the sovereign-renouncer model regained its intensity at the time of economic liberalisation and growing social inequality. However, not all sanyasis could automatically attain sovereign-like status. The guru is not a source of ultimate power, but, as Bruno Latour puts it, an *effect* of power. The power of the guru is merely an illusion unless people obey his orders (1986: 268). A guru is thus constituted by the people themselves. In the following, we demonstrate how the guru manipulates existing associations, links and networks and cuts his ties to them if necessary (Strathern 1996). This very practical ability, upheld by the idea of sovereign renouncer, convinces people to surrender themselves at his feet. The paradox of the sovereign encountered by Rousseau, however, surfaces again. Does he encourage a democratic ethos or remain a tyrant?

The guru's court

The Nyaya Peetha, or 'seat of justice', is an informal court run by Taralabalu Jagadguru Brihanmath, a Hindu matha in the village of Sirigere in the Chitradurga district of central Karnataka, southern India.[6] For many years, disputes have been settled in the matha in an *ad hoc* fashion. In 2002, Dr Shivamurthy Shivacharya Maha Swamiji – I shall call him Sirigere guru – radically modernised this informal settlement. Being tech savvy and an internationally renowned Sanskrit scholar,[7] Sirigere guru has created a systematised and comprehensive database of cases brought to his court. Now each dispute is given a case number, and at the end of each hearing the Sirigere guru dictates the summary of the dispute. His assistant then transcribes it and keeps a record in the database; all the petitions, counter petitions, and related documents are also carefully filed. By June 2014, the total number of disputes amounted to nearly 3,200 cases. Not all of the cases are solved. Some of them went on for several years before they saw some sort of resolution; some were simply discontinued because the accused parties did not turn up. The material for this chapter comes from recorded court hearings, interviews with the guru and people involved, summaries of past hearings kept in the database, and petition and counter petition letters that were submitted to the Nyaya Peetha. In this informal court, Sirigere guru acts as the sole judge. He listens to the claims of both sides and tries to settle the disputes. The nature of the disputes varies from failed marriages to village disputes. Most of the cases are to do with family discord about marriage and inheritance within the Sadaru Lingayats – a relatively low-status sub-caste of the dominant landed Lingayat caste – who are also devotees of the Sirigere Taralabalu matha. Although this court still functions as a kind of caste panchayat of the Sadaru Lingayats, the court itself is open for any caste or religion. Anyone can bring their problems in the form of a petition letter. Then s/he will be identified as a 'petitioner' (*arjidāra*). On the same day, the petitioner will be given a date for the first hearing – often within two to three weeks – and a case number. The court then informs the other party or 'defendant' (*prativāda*), and asks them to come and receive the blessing of the guru on that specific date. Since many cases concern family disputes amongst the Sadaru Lingayat community, most accused parties would not refuse this order from the matha. Even in cases of non-Lingayats, many of them live in nearby villages where Lingayats are still dominant, in both a numerical and political sense, so they will not ignore the guru's order.

Despite the fact that the Nyaya Peetha is located in the religious institution (matha), and the religious leader (guru) is their only judge, there is no divine or supernatural legitimation of his judgement. Unlike other religious courts, such as Dharmasthala in south-western Karnataka, where the accused has to take a sacred vow to follow the order or promises he himself has made, in the Nyaya Peetha both parties simply have to sign the agreement. I myself have never encountered the guru referring to any sacred scripture or divine presence in order to validate his decision. The large courtroom keeps old religious texts and numerous trophies the guru has received which might give some sort of awe or religious feel, but the entire process is oddly 'secular'. This seemingly 'secular' nature of the Nyaya Peetha is probably deliberate. In the early twentieth century, Lingayat (or Veera Shaiva) leaders, including gurus, very self-consciously projected Veera Shaivism as modern and rational. For example, they have selected and compiled sayings (*vachana*) of Veera Shiva saints to appeal to modern – in other words, secular, rational and egalitarian – sensibilities (Boratti 2009; for a detailed analysis of modern identity formation of Lingayats, see Ripepi 2007).

Following the tradition of modern Lingayat sensitivities, the Sirigere matha regularly invites an activist from a rationalist organisation to perform an anti-superstition demonstration in front of young students who study at the matha-run schools. At the beginning of the demonstration, he performs 'miracles' such as producing sacred ashes from his hand, piercing his cheek and hanging a lime through the pierced hole, keeping a fire on top of his head, and so on. He then invites students to come and learn how to do the tricks. All the students immediately reproduce the same miracles/tricks. Debunking miracles shows what Lingayats want to project their religion to be. A clear distinction has to be made between their enlightened modern religion and the superstition or blind beliefs into which uneducated folk are drawn. Sirigere guru performs neither a 'miracle' nor a divine sanction precisely because he is a leader of this rational religion. His judgements are, therefore, based on 'common sense'. He also sometimes refers to the existing state law and matches his decisions with it. This demonstrates that the relationship between his informal legal space and the formal state law is not oppositional but continuous, and that they are sometimes complementary to each other.

Village self-governing, the guru, and the state

When I ask people why they come to the Nyaya Peetha rather than formal courts, many immediately answer that they do so because the guru's court is cheaper, faster, and more efficient. It is worth noting that this list of the practical benefits of local informal arbitration – low cost, swiftness, and efficiency – has a long history of its own. It is widely believed that 'traditional' forms of dispute resolution were widely popularised and promoted by M. K. Gandhi during anti-British agitations. During the civil disobedience movements of 1920–1921 and 1931, Gandhi, who himself was a trained lawyer, advised the Non-cooperation Committee to include a boycott of law courts by lawyers as well as a boycott of government schools and colleges by parents or scholars. He advocated the idea that the civil courts were an agency of British rule that imposed coercive sanctions, and that truly indigenous Indian arbitration would work better because it relied on public morality (Galanter 1972: 54–55; see also Gandhi, *The Law and The Lawyers*).

Shriman Narayan, a well-known Gandhian social reformer, published the *Gandhian Constitution for Free India* in 1946 with a foreword by M. K. Gandhi. In this volume, Narayan states:

> Justice was cheap and fair. Modern courts, on the contrary, are very expensive; even very ordinary cases are disposed of only after months, if not years. The complicated judicial procedure promotes endless dishonesty and falsehood.
>
> *(Narayan 1946: 97)*

> The Gram Panchayats shall be entrusted with the dispensing of Justice, . . . the poor peasant need not go out of his village, spend hard-earned money and waste weeks.
>
> *(1946: 98)*

Like Shriman Narayan, many of Gandhi's associates were enthusiastic about the idea of promoting village *panchayats* (village councils) as bases of a local system of justice, although Gandhi himself was in some ways hesitant about the efficacy or even existence of such institutions. He was asked in 1925 what should be done if someone borrowed money from *khadi* boards and then failed to return it; his answer was to take them to court, since the idea of panchayat is 'as good as non-existent' (quoted in Bates 2005: 174). Gandhi believed that thanks to the degradation of the caste system and the 'evil influence' of British government, the 'noble institution' of panchayat had fallen into desuetude and must 'be revived at any cost, if the villages are not to be ruined' (quoted in Bates 2005: 175). As Crispin Bates has put it, Gandhi was thus 'a believer, but hardly an unequivocal champion of self-government' (175); the concept of panchayati raj has, however, become a major pillar of the ruling Congress government's rural development policy.

Indian nationalists or post-independent politicians were not the first to become enthusiastic about the local informal justice system. Ironically it was the British who first recognised the existence of village courts and the role of village headmen and panchayats as effective arbitrators of local disputes. As early as the 1820s, British officers reported the working of village panchayats in various places of India (Matthai 1993 [1915]: 162–202). Some supported village justice enthusiastically since it was believed that the accused would tell the truth in front of their fellow villagers, and the decision made by the panchayat would be taken more seriously. The major reason for the promotion of village courts by the British was, however, much more practical. They thought it would help to reduce the burden on existing magistrate courts, which had already been overwhelmed by the numbers of petty cases. Similarly the British were at the same time interested in codifying the local 'traditions' of irrigation management by village councils (Mosse 2001). The relationship between centralising state authority and the moral 'village republic' was thus never oppositional, but as David Mosse clearly demonstrated, the interest of the state in village governance can be seen as 'the corollary of the extension of centralised state power rather than its reverse' (2001: 166).

Despite the enthusiasm amongst British officers towards village legal institutions, by the early twentieth century, dissatisfaction with aspects of community arbitration was expressed. In the 1910s, there was vocal opposition against the Madras government as it continued to uphold the Madras Village Courts Act of 1889 which gave some official backing to village courts. The Madras High Court claimed that due to the progress of transport, communication, and trade, the isolation of the village community was destroyed, and the patriarchal influence of the headman consequently weakened, while at the same time the accessibility of the regular courts had become more widely known. As the number of authorised legal practitioners also increased, thanks to the spread of education, the Court argued that it would be 'to the interest of these classes to promote the regular courts instead of the primitive village tribunals' (quoted in Matthai 1993 [1915]: 189). They also pointed out that recognition of village courts did not help to reduce the numbers of cases brought to them. This substantiates Gandhi's reluctance to promote the village court system.

How can we situate the guru's court in the legal culture of modern India? On a discursive level, the guru and the people coming to his court often distinguish it from the state legal system in an interesting way. During the guru's court hearings and the interviews with the villagers, both the guru and the villagers emphasise the contrast between formal law (*kānūnu*) and morality (dharma). This does not mean that they think the state law is immoral, unlike the anti-British ideology of the pre-independence era, but they believe that the state law has its limit. Despite their vocal preference for the Nyaya Peetha, many people are happy to go to local government courts if the situation looks better there. Many come to the Nyaya Peetha either because the nature of their case can be regarded as 'illegal' according to formal law, or – although this is rarer – because one party has already gone to the regular court and the other wants to fight on different ground at the Nyaya Peetha. In the former case, they believe that they could not obtain justice within formal law. For example, the 'first wife' who wants to secure a share of her husband's property after he has committed himself to a so-called 'second marriage' – a marriage that is religiously sanctioned but not legally recognised – cannot possibly go to a formal court to achieve the arrangement she seeks.[8] The share of the property she might achieve through the guru's court would be much more valuable than the small monthly maintenance for a divorcee that is currently specified in Indian law. Moreover, neither side wants to bear the shame of a divorce. In several cases concerning former temple lands, which I have analysed in detail elsewhere (Ikegame forthcoming), villagers who wish to recover their 'common property' could not appeal to a formal court, because it was they who had deviously nominated different individuals as legal cultivators-cum-owners of the land in order to evade the land reform of the 1970s.[9]

The guru himself once told me in a private conversation that the reason why his court at his matha works is because he 'has the moral authority'. Morality (dharma) is the domain of his sovereignty. He can make the law within this domain. Moreover, the very limitations of the state law create his domain, where justice is waiting to be recovered. This is not a domain where the state has yet penetrated, but the domain where the state is, as Talal Asad has argued, 'continually both experienced and undone through the *illegibility* of its own practices' (2004: 279, emphasis in original). In other words, the state undermines its role as creator and executor of the law through its own legal complexity, ambiguity, and contradiction.

While his court creates a moral domain outside of the state law, the guru tries to operate within the state legal system and even seeks to obtain official legal backing for his decisions by using the recently revised Arbitration Act within the state. This seemingly contradictory aspect of the Nyaya Peetha can be seen from the background and functions of mediators (*madhiyasṭhagāra*) who act as a go-between for two parties. They are self-appointed voluntary mediators and there are two prominent mediators at the Nyaya Peetha. One is a retired *tahshildar*, a local government officer who deals with matters related to land, tax, and revenue, and the other is a former district level panchayat president. Both mediators are very knowledgeable about legal processes and regulations, and they not only give advice to the involved parties but also explain legal situations to the guru. The guru also makes frequent phone calls to lawyers during the hearings to ascertain the legal status of certain issues. There is thus a clear intention not to cross the legal boundaries of the existing laws. If he concludes that certain cases – typically those of severe domestic violence and violent attacks against individuals – should be dealt with as criminal cases, he immediately calls the police. Interestingly, not only does he refrain from deliberately crossing the boundaries, but he also sometimes actively seeks legal backing from the civil courts. I witnessed him advising people to go to a local civil court and even helping them to find a lawyer who would be sympathetic to their problems. The idea was that the lawyer would not contradict the decision that the guru himself made. In several ways, therefore, the guru's court acts as an extension or an agent of the state, and will have the same verdict in the formal court.

The case examined in this chapter is a dispute between local mining companies and four villages near Sirigere. The case originally started in 2003, when three local mining companies brought a complaint against the village of Muttugaduru, claiming that the villagers had been blocking the road that led to the railway station for 15 days – preventing the passage of lorries carrying ore.[10] The leaders of four villages affected by the transport of iron ore from the mining site to the local railway station were then summoned and were asked to submit a written complaint against the mining companies. From the summaries of the court hearings, we can see that the blocking of the road was sometimes carried out in an organised fashion under the order of village leaders. However sometimes a group of youths simply set up an ad hoc 'toll booth' by putting up a large picture of the previous Swamiji or local goddesses and demanding donations-cum-fees from each lorry driver who passed through. The mining companies wanted to stop all obstructions on the road and in exchange for this they were willing to accept most of the villagers' demands. The villagers then asked for compensation for crops damaged by pollution from the iron ore, as well as money for repairing the road. They also demanded strict regulations concerning the safe driving of lorries, and funding for local developmental projects.

In his judgement, the guru ordered the villagers to stop any blocking of the road. He also ordered the mining companies to deposit a certain sum of money for the purpose of constructing a new road and for further rural development. The mining companies were happy to accept the judgement of the guru's court. Since 2003, two mining companies have deposited the astonishing sum of 220 million rupees, equivalent to 2 million GBP. This particular court case is still ongoing (at the time of writing) and has become a platform for anyone who wishes to negotiate with the mining companies. Lorry owners, drivers, and even mine workers have appeared in the court, pressing their claims for higher rental fees for their lorries, wage hikes, and so on. So far, it might seem as if the guru's court is functioning as a parallel state that is able to solve local disputes successfully. During the interview with representatives of one of the local mining companies[11] who brought the case to the Nyaya Peetha, they said that the reason why they went to seek the guru's help was that it was easier to deal with one leader (=the guru) rather than several local leaders. One of them said 'there were several villages we had to negotiate with. Each village has not only one, but several leaders. And then (we need to think about) different caste groups! But if we go to the guru, all the leaders would listen to the guru. It made much more sense to go to see the guru'. The Sirigere guru, for them, is a leader above all other leaders. Leaders who belong to different localities and different caste groups would obey him. This particular local mining company was keen to demonstrate their eagerness for corporate social responsibility (as they showed me a sleek PowerPoint presentation all about their CSR prior to my interview) and they have provided a 'mobile hospital' (a van regularly visiting villages for health checks), toilet facilities, water filter systems, computers for local schools, and so on.[12] They have enough money to do many things to keep the residents happy (or quiet), but they often rely on the guru for negotiating with villagers and the state.

During my visit to the Nyaya Peetha in late August 2013, people were discussing the construction of two kilometres of reinforced concrete road from Sasalu railway station towards Sirigere. Since this road was used for the transportation of iron ore, the mining company was ready to pay for the entire cost of construction, which was 20 million rupees (around 200,000 GBP in 2013). The tender was given to a local construction company with a good reputation, and they were willing to start the construction as soon as possible. But they still needed a sanction from the state government. The request for the sanction was sent sometime in May, but by late August they had not yet heard anything. The villagers and representatives of the mining company asked the guru to intervene. During the course of the meeting, held in a village school hall, the guru made a phone call to a state minister and made him promise there and then that he would provide the necessary sanction within a week. The sanction indeed came within three days. The act of calling a politician and fixing things in front of the public was a compelling demonstration of the guru's power. In this game of power, politicians always behave like humble servants.

Electoral concerns may be a tool that a guru with a large devotional constituency can employ, but the size of his 'vote bank' does not automatically ensure his political power. The latter also relies upon his ability to forge networks and cut those ties at the right moment. Our Sirigere guru seemed to have mastered this art of political networking rather well. This is even more impressive when we consider the fact that the then state government was formed only just a few months earlier.[13] A left-leaning Kannada tabloid newspaper, *Gauri Lankesh* has reported how effectively the Sirigere guru establishes his alliance with political parties by using a political broker or intermediary.[14] The newspaper claims that a former government engineer-turned-developer called Shanmukappa joined the Hindu nationalist Bharatiya Janata Party (BJP) in 2008 in order to forge a tie between the matha and the newly elected member of the Legislative Assembly, Chendrappa, from the local constituency of Holalkere. For this, Shanmukappa was, the *Gauri Lankesh* claims, given lucrative construction projects and then named as chairman of the Bengaluru International Airport (BIA). After the Lingayat political giant B. S. Yeddyurappa fell out with the BJP and launched his own party, Karnataka Janata Paksha (KJP), in late 2012, Shanmukappa resigned as chairman of the BIA and joined the KJP along with Chendrappa. By early 2013, it was clear that Chendrappa was going to lose his constituency; the matha started supporting the Congress Party. Immediately after the election was announced, Shanmukappa joined the Congress. Allegedly, Shanmukappa gave financial support to H. Anjaneya, the Congress candidate for Holalkere constituency, and the matha also stood behind him. After Anjaneya's victory in May 2013, many state officers belonging to the Sadaru Lingayat community were transferred to Chitradurga district where the matha resides. I am not in a position to substantiate this allegation made by the newspaper, but the state minister whom the Sirigere guru then called on the day of the meeting in a school hall was this same H. Anjaneya.

The fact that the guru's sovereignty works precisely because he stands outside of the state does not mean that he can operate without the state. As was apparent in the mining dispute case, the reality is quite the reverse. Many activities of the matha require support or indeed authorisation from the state. The state is not at all monolithic or coherent, but a penetrable and to some extent manipulable entity. His act of publicly calling an influential politician to get things done is a clear demonstration of the nature of sovereigns in South India. He can stand outside of society as a renouncer and has the authority to demarcate morality from immorality, but what makes his court effective still largely depends on his ability to manipulate the state apparatus. Of course, the state and non-state sovereigns do not always work harmoniously. The illegibility of the state does occasionally declare the moral activities of the guru to be illegal. In 2009, income tax officers from the central government raided Sirigere Talarabalu matha. Allegedly, the large sum of money deposited by the mining companies was suspected to be a form of tax evasion; at least this is the story that villagers believe. The money was instead transferred directly to a local development trust that the guru ordered villagers to establish.

The sovereign domain of the guru is a space where the distinction between morality and immorality, legality and illegality, and the personal and impersonal is blurred and one penetrates the other. Only the guru and the state have the authority to draw the line as sovereigns. And yet, these lines are constantly shifting and being redrawn.

The sovereign who decides

When it comes to village disputes, the Sirigere guru seems reluctant to give any immediate decision. He often asks village representatives to go back to their village and make a list of their demands. The guru said in a private conversation that he was trying to give more power to village leaders. His encouragement of village decision-making power is, however, not always popular, especially amongst young villagers. Some expressed dissatisfaction, as they believe that the guru favours only village leaders, and some even feel that the guru is too sympathetic to the mining companies. Meanwhile, the very same person strongly believes that only the guru can make a final decision. After complaining about his favouritism towards village elders, one young villager stated:

> Because of the matha, mining is still running. If the Swamiji says: 'you should stop', the mining will stop within three days. Mining will not stop due to the infighting between us. Multinational companies have lots of money and they can buy many people. Even if Chief Minister of Karnataka says [to stop], the mining won't stop, but the Swamiji says [to stop], the

> mining will stop. But the workers will face problems, [this is the reason] why he does not do it.[15]

Because of 'infighting', villagers cannot reach any decision easily. One of the villagers told me about when one person in a village was hit by a mining lorry and badly injured:

> After the accident, eleven lorries were stopped. It was during the month of January which is the most busy month for mining. Swamiji was not in the matha, but all the representatives were there. Swamiji was in Chikkamangalor and Shimoga. Everyone waited until Swamiji came. He came later the night. Everyone went home. By 11.30, everyone has left, there were only 10, 15 people stayed to have his judgement. Swamiji said that 'if you go home now, there will be a wife and child waiting for you. If I go home, there is nobody for me. Since the morning until 11.30, you are still testing my patience. You want more pain than this?'[16]

He narrated this episode in order to show how dedicated and self-sacrificing their Swamiji is and that he is therefore highly respected. This story also conveys how desperately villagers need the decision made by their guru. It seems that they are unwilling to negotiate with mining companies or lorry owners by themselves. The role of the guru here is not only to interpret morality as a disinterested outsider or to 'get things done' as an efficient fixer, but also to decide what the final settlement is. And yet, this is contradictory to what the guru tries to do in order to recover village self-rule that may or may not have existed. Rousseau's dilemma comes back here. Does the guru imbue people with an ethos of self-rule, or simply prevent it?

The position of the Nyaya Peetha is crucial here. The guru's court works above the level of village politics and yet still strongly influences it. This opens up a new political space for some, especially those who are less powerful. Other village disputes often involve elected village panchayat leaders or traditional village heads as the accused (Ikegame forthcoming). For some, the Nyaya Peetha could be a place for counter-politics. The mining company case, as we have seen in this chapter, has become an open platform for everyone who has a grievance against mining companies. In August 2013, a group of low-wage unskilled workers came to the Nyaya Peetha and demanded a wage hike. There were also lorry drivers who demanded the same. While the mining company representatives were explaining the wage structure, one young mining worker shouted: 'How many years do we need to work in order to become skilled workers?' The definition of an unskilled, semi-skilled, and skilled worker was based purely on the educational qualification of the worker. Many local engineering colleges now offer a variety of diplomas and degrees in mining. Those who do not have any education cannot advance their career in mining at all. Village elders do not seem to care about such issues, and the guru has so far done nothing to change it.

The Nyaya Peetha is not a radically transformative body, but is rather conservative. Some might see it as a guardian of the existing social structure. The judgement of the guru does, however, create another space beyond village politics. Villagers who patiently waited for the guru could not decide themselves, but this may not be because they were incapable of deciding, but because there were too many embedded interests competing with each other. Village politics may not allow them to speak up in public. However, the Nyaya Peetha is the space where everyone, potentially, has an equal voice. The voice of the young miner may be ignored, but at least he could speak.

Conclusion

The state does not always actively intervene in the sovereign space of the guru – nonetheless it does so occasionally. The existence of the state is often felt by rural citizens as a massive entity of remoteness, incomprehensibility, inefficiency, and indeed illegibility, yet simultaneously they do rely on the state in order to obtain permissions, documentations, and many sorts of developmental benefits. The Sirigere guru aptly called the state 'a slow-moving elephant' and mocked local state officials for providing a mere postal service, passing papers from one government department to another. The power of the guru 'to get things done' attracts people to his court, precisely because he has an ability to make the state, at least partially, work for their benefit. He achieves this by apparently being a selfless individual, or ideal renouncer (Ikegame 2012), who can be a repository of trust for all parties within a dispute, through the logic of sovereign renouncer. The role of the guru as a familiar, local level developmental and judicial broker, who also acts as a gatekeeper in dealings with the local state, is thus pivotal. And yet, a guru provides something more.

The rural citizens of Karnataka constitute their guru as a sovereign by submitting themselves. Rousseau's social contract did not happen in a remote past or prehistory of human society, but as Latour argued, 'the origins of society are still with us today' (1986: 270). But they do so not from blind faith or ignorance. They are capable of organising themselves, as shown in this chapter in the collective blocking of a road, but they could gain more by following the orders of the guru. By doing so, they secured from local mining companies at least a portion of something to which they thought they were entitled. Aspiring to be a wise legislator, the guru does not impose his decision upon people but tries instead to restore the power of village elders. Villagers, on the other hand, see different political possibilities in his ability to make the final decision. Here, we see the contradiction that Rousseau placed at the centre of his theory of popular sovereignty. Do people chain themselves in order to be free or do they abandon freedom in order to escape social restrictions? Either way, the guru and his informal court offer a glimpse into a different politics where the guru refuses to be a strong sovereign while the people force him to be one. This ambiguity and shifting foundation of the guru's position is not a reflection of the inability of people to be political, but the very opposite. In contemporary rural Karnataka, there is no single coherent locus – whether it is a village, caste, or kin network – within which politics can be clearly expressed. The guru's court connects village politics to larger political spheres and his sovereignty opens up a space in which villagers can participate in re-evaluating the vital moral and political issues that concern them. The sovereignty of the guru is fragile one. It can be easily undermined by the state, and his exceptional nature of being 'outside of society' needs to be constantly demonstrated and examined. Yet, this unstable terrain is precisely where people can find an alternative ethos for the exercise of more inclusive democratic practices.

Notes

1 For a critique of the use of Agamben in anthropological writings, see Jennings (2001).
2 For less draconian Hobbes, see Prokhovnik (2008: 55–77).
3 A similar theoretical formation of modern democracy and citizenship is found in historical sociology of Weber (1978 [1956]). He argued that a person becomes citizen only when s/he cuts and moves away from ties of religion, kin, clan, caste and tribe (1260).
4 Some sadhus go through castration as an extreme form of asceticism (van der Veer 1988: 121). Recent news articles suggest that in the controversial guru-led organisation Dera Sacha Sauda, some men were forced to be castrated.
5 BBC News. 2014. 'India Election: BJP "Bachelor" Modi admits marriage'. www.bbc.co.uk/news/world-asia-india-26970397.
6 For the modern development of mathas in Karnataka, see Nair 2019.
7 Dr Shivamurty Swamiji has developed computer software on Sanskrit grammar based on famous Panini's treatise in the fifth century BC and made it available online. www.taralabalu.org/panini/
8 A majority of cases brought to the Nyaya Peetha are related to the division of land and other assets. A large proportion of such cases are derived from 'second marriages'. Second marriages are justified when the first wife failed to reproduce or she had personal problems with in-laws. Most of the second marriages are arranged between two families and second wives often come with dowry.
9 The successive land reforms in Karnataka in the 1970s were believed to be relatively successful in terms of enforcement although they did not bring the more fundamental social transformation that some other states managed to achieve (Thimmaiah and Aziz 1983; Deshpande and Torgal 2003).
10 The Nyaya Peetha Case no. 398/03.
11 Interview June 3, 2014 near Sirigere, Karnataka.
12 The most popular project initiated by the mining company was the construction of a temple. Villagers also liked the fact that small contributions they make whenever they used the health check van went towards the running of the temple. Small toilets the company built in front of each house did not seem to be popular and indeed not many actually used them.
13 The former ruling party, BJP, suffered a spectacular electoral defeat and the Congress gained a majority within the state assembly in May 2013 in Karnataka.
14 *The Gauri Lankesh* on August 28, 2013 by T. N. Shanukha.
15 From the interview with villagers in Muttugaduru, August 2013.
16 Ibid.

References

Agamben, Giorgio. 1998. *Homo Sacer: Sovereign Power and Bare Life*. Stanford: Stanford University Press.

Asad, Talad. 2004. 'Where Are the Margins of the State?', in V. Das and D. Poole (eds.), *Anthropology in the Margins of the State*, pp. 279–288. Santa Fe: School of American Research Press.

Bates, Crispin. 2005. 'The Development of Panchayati Raj in India', in C. Bates and S. Basu (eds.), *Rethinking Indian Political Institutions*, pp. 169–238. London: Anthem Press.

Boratti, Vijayakumar M. 2009. 'The "Discovery" of Vachanas', *South Asia: Journal of South Asian Studies*, 33 (2): 177–209.

Brown, Wendy. 2008. 'Sovereignty and the Return of the Repressed', in D. Campbell and M. Schoolman (eds.), *The New Pluralism*, pp. 250–272. Durham: Duke University Press.

Buur, Lars. 2003. 'Crime and Punishment on the Margins of the Post-Apartheid State', *Anthropology and Humanities*, 28 (1): 23–42.

Buur, Lars. 2005. 'The Sovereign Outsourced: Local Justice and Violence in Port Elizabeth', in Thomas Blom Hansen and Finn Stepputat (eds.), *Sovereign Bodies*, pp. 192–217. Princeton: Princeton University Press.

Cohen, Lawrence. 1995. 'The Pleasures of Castration', in P. Anderson and S. Pinkerton (eds.), *Sexual Nature, Sexual Culture*, pp. 276–304. Chicago: University of Chicago Press.

Cohen, Lawrence. 2004. 'Operability, Bioavailability, and Exception', in A. Ong and S. J. Collier (eds.), *Global Assemblages*, pp. 79–90. Malden: Wiley-Blackwell.

Connolly, Willam E. 2005. *Pluralism*. Durham: Duke University Press.

Copeman, Jacob, and Aya Ikegame. 2012. 'The Multifarious Guru: An Introduction', in J. Copeman and A. Ikegame (eds.), *The Guru in South Asia*, pp. 1–45. London: Routledge.

Das, Veena, and Deborah Poole (eds.). 2004. *Anthropology in the Margins of the State*. Santa Fe: School of American Research Press.

Deshpande, Satish V., and Vijaykumar N. Torgal. 2003. 'Land Reforms in Karnataka: Impact on Beneficiaries', *Economic and Political Weekly*, 38 (44): 4647–4649.

Dumont, Louis. 1980 [1966]. *Homo Hierarchicus: The Caste System and Its Implications*. Chicago: University of Chicago Press.

Feuchtwang, Stephan. 2004. 'Comments to Geertz', *Current Anthropology*, 45 (5): 587.

Foucault, Michel. 2003 [1997]. *Society Must Be Defended*. London: Penguin.

Fuller, Christopher J., and Véronique Bénéï (eds.). 2001. *Everyday State and Society in Modern India*. London: Hurst.

Galanter, Mark. 1972. 'The Aborted Restoration of "Indigenous" Law in India', *Comparative Studies in Society and History*, 14 (1): 53–70.

Gandhi, Mohandas K. 1962. *The Law and the Lawyers*. Ahmedabad: Navjivan Publishing House.

Geertz, Clifford. 2004. 'What Is a State If It Is Not a Sovereign? Reflections on Politics in Complicated Places', *Current Anthropology*, 45 (5): 577–593.

Gilmartin, David. 2014. 'The Paradox of Patronage and the People's Sovereignty', in A. Piliavsky (ed.), *Patronage as Politics in South Asia*, pp. 125–153. Cambridge: Cambridge University Press.

Gordon, Robert. 2004. 'Popular Justice', in D. Nugent and J. Vincent (eds.), *A Companion to the Anthropology of Politics*, pp. 349–366. Malden: Blackwell.

Gupta, Akhil. 2012. *Red Tape: Bureaucracy, Structural Violence, and Poverty in India*. Durham and London: Duke University Press.

Hansen, Thomas Blom. 2005. 'Sovereigns Beyond the State: On Legality and Authority in Urban India', in Thomas Blom Hansen and Finn Stepputat (eds.), *Sovereign Bodies*, pp. 169–191. Princeton: Princeton University Press.

Hansen, Thomas Blom. 2006. 'Performers of Sovereignty', *Critique of Anthropology*, 26 (3): 279–295.

Hansen, Thomas Blom, and Finn Stepputat. 2001. 'Introduction', in Thomas Blom Hansen and Finn Stepputat (eds.), *States of Imagination*, pp. 1–38. Durham: Duke University Press.

Hansen, Thomas Blom, and Finn Stepputat (eds.). 2005. *Sovereign Bodies*. Princeton: Princeton University Press.

Hansen, Thomas Blom, and Stepputat, Finn. 2006. 'Sovereignty Revisited', *Annual Review of Anthropology*, 35 (1): 295–315.

Heesterman, Jan C. 1985. *The Inner Conflict of Tradition: Essays in Indian Ritual, Kinship, and Society*. Chicago: Chicago University Press.

Humphrey, Caroline. 2004. 'Sovereignty', in D. Nugent and J. Vincent (eds.), *A Companion to the Anthropology of Politics*, pp. 418–436. Malden: Blackwell.

Ikegame, Aya. 2010. 'Why Do Backward Castes Need Their Own Gurus?', *Contemporary South Asia*, 18 (1): 57–70.

Ikegame, Aya. 2012. 'The Governing Guru: Hindu Mathas in Liberalising India', in J. Copeman and A. Ikegame (eds.), *The Guru in South Asia*, pp. 46–61. London: Routledge.

Ikegame, Aya. Forthcoming. 'Trust and Trusts: The Guru and Devotee-citizens in Rural South India'.

Inston, Kevin. 2010. 'Representing the Unrepresentable: Rousseau's Legislator and the Impossible Object of the People', *Contemporary Political Theory*, 9 (4): 393–413.

Jansen, Steffen. 2005. 'Above the Law: Practices of Sovereignty in Surrey Estate, Cape Town', in Thomas Hansen and Finn Stepputat (eds.), *Sovereign Bodies*, pp. 192–217. Princeton: Princeton University Press.

Jennings, Ronald C. 2011. 'Sovereignty and Political Modernity: A Genealogy of Agamben's Critique of Sovereignty', *Anthropological Theory*, 11 (1): 23–61.

Latour, Bruno. 1986. 'The Powers of Association', in J. Law (ed.), *Power, Action and Belief*, pp. 261–277. London: Routledge and Kegan Paul.

Matthai, John. 1993[1915]. *Village Government in British India*. New Delhi: Low Price Publications.

Mbembe, Achille. 1992. 'The Banality of Power and the Aesthetics of Vulgarity in the Postcolony', *Public Culture*, 4 (3): 1–30.

Mosse, David. 2001. 'Irrigation and Statecraft in Zamindari South India', in C. Fuller and V. Benei (eds.), *Everyday State and Society in Modern India*, pp. 163–193. London: Hurst.

Nair, Janaki 2019 (forthcoming). 'Modernity and "Publicness": the career of the Mysore matha, 1880–1940', *The Indian Economic & Social History Review*.

Narayan, Sriman. 1946. *Gandhian Constitution for Free India*. Allahabad: Kitabistan.

Ong, Aihwa. 2000. 'Graduated Sovereignty in South-East Asia', *Theory Culture Society*, 17 (4): 55–75.

Ong, Aihwa. 2012. 'Powers of Sovereignty: State, People, Wealth, Life', *Focaal*, 64: 24–35.

Pinch, William R. 2012. 'The Slave Guru: Masters, Commanders, and Disciples in Early Modern South Asia', in J. Copeman and A. Ikegame (eds.), *The Guru in South Asia*, pp. 64–79. London: Routledge.

Reddy. Gayatri. 2003. '"Men" Who Would Be Kings', *Social Research*, 70 (1): 163–200.

Ripepi, Titiana. 2007. 'The Feet of the Jangama: Identity and Ritual Issues Among the Virasaivas of Karnataka', *Kervan -Rivista Internazionale Di Studii Afroasiatici*, 6: 69–100.

Rousseau, Jean-Jacques. 2007 [1762]. *The Social Contract and Discourses*. Translated by G. Cole. Thousand Oaks, CA: BN Publishing.

Sharma, Aradhana, and Akhil Gupta (eds.). 2006. *The Anthropology of the State*. London: Blackwell.

Sood, Aditya D. 2006. *The Matha State: Kinship, Ascetism and Institutionality in the Public Life of Karnataka*. Unpublished thesis, University of Chicago.

Spencer, Jonathan. 2007. *Anthropology, Politics, and the State*. Cambridge: Cambridge University Press.
Strathern, Marilyn. 1996. 'Cutting the Network', *The Journal of the Royal Anthropological Institute of Great Britain and Ireland*, 2 (3): 517–535.
Thimmaiah, G., and Abdul Aziz. 1983. 'The Political Economy of Land Reforms in Karnataka, A South Indian State', *Asian Survey*, 23 (7): 810–829.
van der Veer, Peter. 1988. *Gods on Earth*. London: The Athlone Press.
Weber, Max. 1978 [1956]. *Economy and Society*. Berkeley: University of California Press.

3

TIME AND THE SOVEREIGNTY OF THE PEOPLE

David Gilmartin

Democracy has a paradoxical reputation. In the modern world, it is an object of deep and persistent yearning, an embodiment of human freedom and progress. Where it is missing it is often the focus of almost millennial expectations. And yet, where it is well established, its workings are frequently an object of disdain, and sometimes even disgust. Its political practices embody some of the worst competitive and self-interested human impulses. While democracy as an idea is sometimes venerated in India, democratic politics are often viewed as a 'dirty' business.[1]

These paradoxes have often been noted. Theorists of democracy have in fact often stressed the multiple contradictions democracy entails, an embodiment of both the best and the worst of human impulses. Beyond this, the huge gap between democracy as an ideal in which the 'people' exercise power, and the reality of the various corrupt, inefficient and inegalitarian systems that 'democracy' has at times been associated with, is striking. Some have tried to traverse this dissonance by drawing a distinction between substantive democracy and procedural democracy, that is, between a system open to 'real' popular influence and one simply defined by the formal holding of periodic elections. But this too is a distinction difficult to sustain in practice, for it is hard to imagine how these could be truly separated.

Perhaps more fruitful is the suggestion from the political philosopher, John Dunn, that the term 'democracy' needs to be dissociated from *any* particular form of governance and political order (since in popular thinking it encompasses a wide range of often conflicting values and visions of government order) and be viewed instead as, in effect, a modern term of political enchantment, 'a sort of spell through which the world's political imagination has come to be bewitched' (Dunn 2014: 6). For Dunn, this is a spell that needs to be broken if we are to think seriously about how 'democratic' systems of governance actually operate in the modern world.[2] But I would suggest that his acute insight in fact points to something of more basic significance in understanding democracy, not only in India but in most other areas of the world as well. Democracy casts a spell because it is at root a term for a principle of *sovereignty*, the sovereignty of the 'people', and not for a specific form of government. And if 'political imaginations' are 'bewitched' by the 'people's sovereignty' (even as critics have long debated the multiple possibilities for giving this political form), this is because forms of sovereignty (both democratic and otherwise) are in their very nature forms of enchantment, even as they also operate to shape the operation of power in the world's most mundane realms. Without 'political imaginations' coming to be in some sense 'bewitched', in other words sovereignty (in its most powerful historical and comparatively compelling meanings) has little meaning.

Such a view is central to the purposes of this chapter, for it highlights a key question for democratic theory, that is, how has democracy as an enchanter of the political imagination based on the sovereignty of the 'people' actually come to be tied in specific places and in specific historical circumstances to distinctive structures of governance and rule?[3] And one key answer, which I'd like to explore for India in this chapter, is through the juxtaposition of varied conceptions of time, linking cosmic worlds to the mundane structure of human politics and social affairs. For at its root, sovereignty's power rests both on the establishment of a pragmatic system of worldly order and on the linking of that order to forces operating outside the realm of objectifiable social and political relations.

Colonialism, sovereignty, and the 'people'

Some have argued that the concept of popular sovereignty gained currency in India as a frame for legitimising the widespread, and often violent, political mobilisation in opposition to colonial rule in the last decades of the British Raj. There is no doubt considerable substance in this argument (Sen 2007). But there can be little doubt that the ultimate constitutional projection of the 'people's sovereignty' in India after 1947 also drew powerfully on the evolving construction of sovereignty that had been long developing under British imperial rule – and, most importantly, on the forms of 'enchantment', rooted in both Indian and European traditions, that the British mobilised to legitimise their sovereign authority. The structure of colonial sovereignty – as much as resistance to it – was thus critical to the forms that the people's sovereignty ultimately took in post-colonial India.

Though the nature of sovereign authority under the British has been the subject of some debate, the key to the sovereign enchantment of British imperial rule after 1857 lay in the projection of a vision of order – and a relation between state and society – linked to what was termed the 'rule of law'. As a concept, the 'rule of law' should not be confused with the nuts and bolts of the law's everyday operation in India, which was varied and subject under the British to a variety of changing political and self-interested influences. But as a principle of sovereign authority, the 'rule of law' was powerfully tied for the British to what has been called the 'enchantment of reason', the idea that the British were the carriers of a culture of objectifying order, visible not only in law but in science, technology, and rational administration, of which the law was the supreme moral expression.[4] As Mithi Mukherjee has argued, it was the power of detached, disinterested reasoning and oversight, perhaps most clearly embodied in the figure of the judge, that defined the 'rule of law' as a concept, delineating for the British (at least in their self-perceptions) a ruling position of power standing conceptually apart from – and outside – the politics and social conflicts defining the structure of Indian society (Mukherjee 2010). The sovereign claims of the law thus lay in the *combination* of its worldly ordering power with its evocation of a particular form of detached sovereign selfhood. In this sense, as Fitzjames Stephen wrote, the rule of law represented a 'moral conquest more striking, more durable, more solid than the physical conquest that renders it possible'. Indeed, its position was comparable to that of a 'new religion' (quoted in Smith 1988: 134).

The comparison of the 'rule of law' with religion is not, of course, to be taken too literally. But, with respect to sovereignty, it points critically to the ways that the rule of law was, for Stephen, *like* a religion, in that it involved not only a vision for the structuring of legitimate power, but also the linking of that power to the imagining of a particular type of moral, sovereign self, capable of the detachment from the pressures of society and politics necessary to project sovereign claims. This was an idea that had deep roots in the history of the European 'enlightenment',[5] but its particular power in India was linked also to its strong resonances with older Indian understandings of sovereignty, within which austerity and asceticism – as avenues of access to cosmic powers transcending human society – had a long and complicated relationship to the enchantment of kingship. This is not to argue that such a vision appealed to all groups equally; what legitimacy British rule carried was probably rooted most widely in the perceived success of the British in establishing a stable order, an order linked to violence as much as to law. But it is nevertheless true that the 'rule of law' as a conception of sovereign power appealed powerfully to India's educated, upper caste leaders, and as Mukherjee demonstrates, to the leaders of the early Congress Party, who saw the law as the surest avenue to participation in the new sovereign dispensation underlying the Raj. As some have argued, it was a power associated particularly with Brahmans and with a Brahmanic vision of legitimation linked not only to law, but to personal self-control and austerity as the ultimate counterbalance to worldly force in delivering sovereign legitimacy.[6] But it was hardly a model tied exclusively to Brahmans. Visions of self-discipline as the key to the accessing of ultimate authority ran through many movements in India, among Hindus and Muslims alike.

Critical to our purposes here, this vision of authority was also associated in late nineteenth- and early twentieth-century India with the framing of a sovereign order that could encapsulate multiple temporalities. On one level, the 'rule of law' was embedded for the British in a strong conception of modern 'linear' time, linked to an enlightenment vision of human 'development'. The triumph of law and reason over the social forces of influence and dependence was, for many Victorians, a long, unfolding process. Indeed, the linear and progressive development of society was itself modelled for many mid-nineteenth-century liberals on the developmental processes of individual maturation, as the individual moved through education and self-awareness to freedom from the constraints of unreason, superstition, and social dependence.[7] It linked 'moral and material progress',[8] and even provided for the British what some referred to as a 'providential mission' (Sen 2007: 52). The linking of the 'rule of law' to the full potential of human consciousness was indeed the major source of its powerful enchantment.

But in practice its application to India was strongly constrained by British perceptions of Indian society as so deeply in the thrall of received traditions that the short-term requirements of order involved a very different approach to rule. This led to the deep contradictions in British rule that have often been noted. The Raj's sovereign projection had two interconnected sides, one aligning their rule with an enchanted future linked to reason and law, which powerfully captured the imaginations of educated elites; the other tied to the perceived requirements of everyday order in 'society' at large. Particularly in the wake of the 1857 revolt, the requirements of stability and order in India assumed such overwhelming importance that India's 'progress' toward the ideals of reasoned maturation came to be grounded on so distant a time horizon that its fruits were, as Uday Mehta has written, now viewed as endlessly deferred (Mehta 1999). Indeed, to make these two seemingly conflicting principles of sovereign authority simultaneously tenable, the British tended increasingly after 1857 to consign Indian state and society to two entirely contrasting realms of time.

This dual vision of time was in fact assimilated into the structure of the 'rule of law' itself. Queen Victoria's proclamation of 1858 maintained the state's rhetorical commitment to progressive ideals (and modern linear time), but at the same time the 'restraint' defining the 'rule of law' dictated that it now abstain from any direct interference with India's 'religions' or any disturbance of its 'ancient rights, usages and customs'. The integrity and authenticity of Indian culture (as encapsulated by the terms 'religion' and 'custom') was thus recognised (and, in effect, validated) by the British, a position viewed by many British officials as critical to stabilising British rule. This was reflected in the significant development by the British of rituals of monarchical incorporation, formally drawing 'traditional' elites into the structure of empire (through imperial *darbars* and titles, for example). But this was accomplished only at the cost of consigning the culture of these elites to an unchanging past, which stood fundamentally apart from the vision of human progress that underlay the sovereign authority of the state itself. The implications inherent in this separation of 'custom' from the modern state's 'providential mission' (as an agency of human 'development') were in fact captured by J. S. Mill. 'To conform to custom, merely as custom', as Mill put it in *On Liberty* (published in 1859), 'does not educate or develope [sic] . . . any of the qualities which are the distinctive endowment of a human being' (Mill 1999: 104). While some certainly saw the formal recognition of Indian 'customs' as an avenue for opening them to currents of 'progress' (and, indeed, for giving the population certain 'rights' within this customary framework), the more common view was expressed by the jurist Sir William Rattigan (in speaking of the spread of 'individualism' in rural society): 'unless I am egregiously mistaken, it is not the policy of our administration to further or hasten this change'.[9] The 'rule of law' was thus structured to maintain the distinction between a state and society operating in two different temporal realms, even as it also served to encompass both in a common system. The law's distinction between *substance* and *procedure* provided the mechanism for structuring this temporal bifurcation. Custom and religion comprised the primary substance of personal law and were signs of the people's deep grounding in the logic of the past. But it was the state's self-disciplined adherence to legal procedure, itself a sign of the detached and objectifying power of reason and self-control, that defined the state's authority in the present.[10]

All of this shaped the distinctive meanings that the 'people' took on within the structure of British colonial sovereignty. On one level, this structure encouraged the persistence and patronage at local levels of older, alternative popular notions of sovereignty, linked to rituals of kingship and religion that had long held potential sovereign implications, such as the performance of Ram's sovereign kingship during the Ram Lila.[11] Yet these were distanced from the sovereign claims of the colonial state itself, largely through their assimilation to the categories of 'custom' and 'religion', protected by the state as part of the people's 'culture' even as they were subordinated to the law's higher, procedural oversight (which included at times the state's adjudication of conflicts over control and precedence in such performances).

The state's relationship to the 'people' as a category was thus highly ambiguous. When forms of popular culture shaded into what the British saw as the 'fanaticism' of unreason, the British engaged in ferocious (and self-righteous) suppression.[12] Yet, state recognition of the *authenticity* of the culture of the people (even as it was labelled as an artefact of the past) also generated at times a powerful language of reciprocity that linked the 'people's' consent to the state's protection of 'custom' and 'religion', a reciprocity that was also embodied in a language of state-recognised 'rights' (including rights to property, commonly defined in essentially historical/customary terms). Such rights were sufficiently delineated that they could even be mobilised at times as the foundation for popular claims *against* the state, shaping movements of political resistance. Threats to suspend customary performances as a form of protest, for example, could be mobilised at times to challenge to the colonial order, suggesting the centrality of state recognition of the people's 'customs' to the entire edifice of sovereign order. But the 'people' in such a framing could never claim sovereign authority as their own, for their voice was fundamentally conflated with a culture that stood outside the realm of progress and reason – whatever the possibilities that they might on some very distant day evolve to a 'modern' condition. Far more than the framing of India as a culture fragmented and divided, it was this temporal structure that attempted to foreclose the 'people's' association with any overarching sovereign claims.

Critically, however, this by no means walled off the state from the educated Indian elites who in many cases identified strongly with this statist vision of sovereignty and were themselves increasingly critical of custom's hold on Indian society. This was reflected in their significant participation in (and in many cases strong identification with) the detached procedural authority of the Indian legal system. It was reflected also in the deep currents of religious and social reform that flowed from the model of colonial sovereignty, which legitimated strong visions among the educated focused on reforming the 'customary' vision of religion (and religious leadership) in order to align it with a vision of individual maturation and self-regulation. Such currents influenced Hindu and Muslim reform movements alike, and found powerful expression in new organisations such as the Arya Samaj, and in reformist pressures among the Muslim ulama as well. Underlying such movements were efforts, in effect, to pull 'religion' away from the constraints of what the British viewed as 'traditional society' and toward the new more dynamic vision of personal 'development' (and the 'rule of law') underlying state sovereignty. 'Religion' itself was thus subjected in this framing to a bifurcation in meaning between the 'religion' of the developed, sovereign human being, shaped by the internalisation of 'scripture' as a foundation for conscience, reason and autonomy, and the 'religion' of 'customary' life, bound into all the social and political pressures of the past and everyday life. Conceptions of sovereign authority thus had a profound impact on the dynamics of 'religious' reform.

Not surprisingly, as Karuna Mantena has argued, early Congress critics of British rule thus attacked the colonial state precisely for the gap between its own, enchanted sovereign pretensions and its worldly subservience to the social and economic pressures of British imperial and racial interests (Mantena 2016: 304–308). Underlying these challenges to British rule was the argument that Indian elites, with their own aspirational assimilation of the sovereign claims of the 'rule of law' (deeply linked to the broader imagining of 'modernity') could do better.[13] It would hardly be an exaggeration to say that an important strand in elite Indian thinking was thus 'bewitched' by these sovereign claims, linked powerfully to science and material progress, but most of all to the self-controlled, moral 'development' of the individual – even as they launched increasingly powerful critiques of the British state's policies and of the state of Indian society alike.

The 'people' and the challenge to colonialism

What, then, were the implications of these developments for the ultimate emergence of an ideology of popular sovereignty, and of democracy, in India? The consignment of Indian 'culture' to a different realm of time from that framing the sovereignty of the state was fundamental to British colonial rule. And one of the key dynamics in the strategies of 'nationalist' actors, from the time of the Swadeshi movement up until India's independence in 1947, was thus the attempt to break this temporal structure, to make Indian culture (and thus the Indian 'people') temporally immanent.

One of the most powerful of the efforts to do this came from Mahatma Gandhi. As a man with training in law, there is little doubt that Gandhi imbibed early on many common elite attitudes about the 'rule of law' as an enchanted frame for imperial sovereignty. And like many elite Indians, he also saw this sovereign principle as a frame for holding British worldly power to account. But by the time of his return from South Africa, Gandhi had grown deeply disillusioned about how the law actually operated in the British empire – and perhaps equally skeptical of Indian elite aspirations to control British injustices without fundamentally challenging their sovereign claims. Gandhi's comments on the actual operation of the colonial legal system in fact grew increasingly damning, so much so that in *Hind Swaraj* he identified the law as an institution that had made Indians complicit in their own 'slavery'.[14] He mocked elite dreams of maintaining 'English rule without the Englishman' (Gandhi 1997: 28).

But if Gandhi was scathing in his critique of the ways the law actually operated in British India, he nevertheless drew on a vision of sovereign authority that, in its strong emphasis on the enchanted power of detached, reasoned, self-controlled asceticism, held deep resonances with the British 'rule of law' and with the commitments of earlier elites. What differed most markedly in Gandhi's approach was his insistence on the embedding of ultimate sovereignty within the Indian 'people' themselves. As a product of ascetic self-control and individual moral development, sovereign authority in his view could only come from within – from within the individual, but also from within the society of which the individual was, in Gandhi's eyes, a microcosm. And he thus sought to demonstrate this through his technique of *satyagraha*, a vision of *self-rule* (or *swaraj*) that marked individual self-discipline and self-control as the most critical arena in which sovereignty was publicly performed.

Here Gandhi drew powerfully on older Indian sovereign traditions, particularly in his association of the image of the *satyagrahi* with the image of the world-renouncing *sannyasin*. But in doing this, he explicitly brought Indian 'tradition' into contemporary time, placing the image of the satyagrahi as a renouncer-in-the-world into direct dialogue with what he saw as the compromised British image of the enlightened modern individual that underlay the state's claims to rule according to the 'rule of law'. 'If the sannyasins of old did not seem to bother their heads about the political life of society', he wrote, 'it was because society was differently constructed'. But today 'politics properly so-called rule every detail of our lives. . . . The State affects our moral being. . . . A *sannyasin*, therefore, being well-wisher and servant *par excellence* of society, must concern himself with the relations of the people with the State' (Gandhi 1967: I, 66). Gandhi's satyagraha was thus directly calculated to break the structure of colonial sovereignty that had temporally separated the state from Indian culture, and in the process to transfer sovereignty from the colonial state to the 'people' themselves.

But Gandhi's vision nevertheless contained its own deep contradictions, which mirrored those embodied by the 'rule of law'. Like the British vision of human 'development', Gandhi's vision of satyagraha too operated against the backdrop of a temporality in which the mass of the people were never quite 'ready' for their sovereign role. It thus shared to some degree in a colonial temporal structure built on a vision of sharp separation between an elite who embodied the disciplined maturity and ascetic self-control necessary to share in sovereignty and those who remained to be transformed. Though the process of satyagraha undoubtedly gave immediacy to the performed *image* of a mobilised (and enchanted) sovereign 'people' (as in his famous salt march), Gandhi himself drew powerful distinctions between the possibilities of a democratic order based on this image, and the reality of the contemporary state of most Indians as a result of lack of education and the demoralising effects of British rule. This was perhaps most dramatically illustrated by his distinction between 'democracy' and 'mobocracy' as he began to organise the first non-cooperation movement (Gandhi 1999: XXI, 245–249). 'It is given to every one of us to cultivate detachment', he said, seemingly conflating the message of the Bhagavad Gita with the emergence of the democratic citizen (Gandhi 1967: I, 66). But the reality was different. 'Democracy disciplined and enlightened is the finest thing in the world. A democracy prejudiced, ignorant, superstitious will land itself in chaos and may be self-destroyed' (Gandhi 1967: I, 60). The people's sovereignty, in such a framework, could only be an act of becoming.

It was thus left to socialists and leftists in India to project a more *immediate*, fully present vision of the 'people' as a sovereign force that could challenge colonialism's temporal structure in the here and now. And this was associated, not surprisingly, with a more fundamental conceptual break with the 'rule of law' as a procedural (and indeed, ascetic) foundation for sovereignty. Here, the 'people' were instead commonly cast as a collective agency of historical progress, the carriers of the revolutionary ideas that would push society from the material inequalities of capitalism and imperialism, toward an era of higher productive development and equality under an independent and socialist state. Linked to the world-wide narrative of capital, this was a historical vision that particularised the temporal structure of British colonialism as merely an artefact of India's place within a larger history, with the agency of the 'people' a reflection, in essence, of their autonomous sovereign role in capitalism's linear historical unfolding.[15] Indeed, from this perspective, Gandhi's calling off of the first non-cooperation after the Chauri Chaura violence due to the people not being 'ready' was an unconscionable denial of the 'people's' immanent sovereign mission. As Subhas Chandra Bose wrote from prison, Gandhi's actions at that time were like a 'bolt from the blue', which amounted, in his view, to 'strangling the movement' (Bose 1948: 107–108). The very oppression of the 'people' by British imperialism and capitalism (as part of a worldwide historical process) devolved on the people what amounted to a sovereign imperative.

But this vision too had to grapple with the realities of popular culture under British rule, and with the problem of developing 'consciousness' (and of 'false consciousness') among the oppressed peasantry, whom many Indian Communists saw as the necessary bedrock of the 'people' as a revolutionary class. Among theoretically inclined Marxists, some saw the 'people' as necessarily evolving through historical stages as India's capitalist economy developed, a vision reflected in many of the policies of the Comintern. But if the 'people' were to speak in the immediate present, they required an intellectual 'vanguard' to give them voice in fulfilling their historical mission (as ultimately reflected, for example, in the concept of the party-based 'mass line' in China).[16] In India, the Congress hardly embraced such a fully vanguardist vision of party development and party sovereignty. Yet for many Indian socialists, such as Jawaharlal Nehru in his famous autobiographical 'discovery' of the Indian peasantry in the 1920s, it was enough to find in the 'people' an inherent revolutionary spirit, however inarticulate, that could empower an educated elite to translate this spirit into rational policy. Nehru and other Congress socialists thus made significant efforts to associate the Congress Party with policies of statist developmentalism, linked to the rational sciences of economic transformation and of elite technical knowledge, and justified by such a vision of the sovereign 'people'.[17] In spite of some significant peasant movements in the late colonial era, to which Congress leaders were to varying degrees involved and resistant, popular sovereignty was defined in this formulation less as an act of the people's mobilisation, than as a framework for authorising the state in the people's sovereign name – a vision in significant tension with the fundamentally anti-statist vision of Gandhi.

The Congress itself thus embodied different, temporal visions of the meaning of the sovereignty of the people within itself. But whatever these contradictions, the mobilisation of Gandhians and socialists alike fed into a larger, emerging image of the Indian 'people' during the late colonial period that was based less on particular ideologies than on the performative aspects of *public* mobilisation itself. Though it took many and variant forms, this was an era marked by the significant spread of performative self-assertion through protests, processions, and collective actions, projecting a powerful image of the Indian 'people' that deeply challenged a vision of culture as the preserve of 'custom' or traditional 'religious' authority. As Sarbani Sen argues, an image of selfhood linked not to asceticism or self-control (or to the 'rule of law'), but to the power of self-directed *action* can be tracked back to the position of some of the early 'extremists' in India, like Tilak, who in challenging the British projected a vision of Indian popular sovereignty tied powerfully to individual 'will' (Sen 2007: 52–63). Although this fed partly into later Gandhian thinking (and, indeed, later socialist thinking as well), it was an idea that overflowed the boundaries of these movements and shaped emerging forms of mobilisation among numerous groups, from Ambedkarite Dalits (ex-'untouchables') to Muslims to urban workers to the Hindu volunteers of the Rashtriya Swayamsevak Sangh (RSS), challenging not only the old temporal structure of colonial rule, but the non-violent constraints of Gandhian satyagraha as well. As Durba Ghosh shows in her work on colonial 'terrorism', violent acts (including individual violent acts) helped to delegitimise a sovereignty of law by goading the British into a wide variety of emergency measures that belied the very sovereign power of self-restraint on which the 'rule of law' was theoretically based (Ghosh 2017).

A critical element in giving coherence to all these movements as an expression of the 'people' was the powerful emergence – across multiple movements – of individual devotionalism as a political act. This of course drew on religious models, rooted in Indian 'traditions'. But it was by no means constrained by religious language or goals, and, most importantly, it pulled those models out of the temporal frame of a 'traditionalism' firmly located in the past, and into the temporal immediacy of India's anti-colonial and political struggles. Drawing on the vision of enchanted individual fulfillment and autonomy (linked to reason) that defined the 'rule of law', this was an image of individual sovereignty now rooted less in the power of ascetic self-control (and law) than in the public projection of individual will, defined by devotion and sacrifice in the name of collective symbols.[18] The power of such models in the last decades of British rule is captured in Christopher Pinney's discussion of the striking prominence in twentieth-century visual culture of images of the executed 'martyrs' of anti-colonial resistance in India, such as Bhagat Singh, whose images came to be almost as popular as those of Gandhi. Bhagat Singh's images were rendered all the more powerful by his common portrayal in English dress, devoid of any 'signs of a colonially instituted alterity' (or links to religion), even as he offered his life in sacrifice (in some images) to the goddess as Mother India (Pinney 2004: 127). Here it was the autonomous power of Indian devotion, sacrifice and 'will', in other words, that defined the presence of a free individual, who could transcend not only the temporal structure of the colonial state, but also, even in death, its legal apparatus (which was here portrayed wholly as an instrument of state oppression).

Time and the Constitution

This was an image of a sovereign 'people' that arguably 'bewitched' many political imaginations as the colonial era came to a close, across a range of ideological orientations. But the meaning of this image of the 'people' for the construction of new 'democratic' institutions remained an open question, and one given added immediacy in the wake of the violence and disorder that accompanied partition. 'We the People' was the phrase that opened the Indian Constitution, but the meaning of the 'people' as a source of sovereign enchantment was in fact deeply influenced by the ideas that had shaped *both* the sovereign claims of the colonial state *and* the varying ideas that had challenged it during the 'nationalist movement'. And it is the argument here that it was the intersection and structuring of multiple temporalities that provides a critical key to understanding how the institutions of Indian democracy came to be constructed.

The strongest ideological blueprint for the state that emerged from the nationalist movement came from socialists like Nehru, and its temporalities exercised an important influence on the constitutional debates that followed India's independence and on how the constitution came to be conceptualised as an expression of the 'people's' will. As Granville Austin argued in his study of the Constitution, India's independence represented for most Congress leaders a critical 'revolutionary' moment that was both a fulfillment of India's past and an *escape* from colonialism's temporal structure.[19] To underscore the 'people's sovereignty' was precisely to underscore a new imperative for India to join in a *worldwide* march of modernity, socialism and linear progress, geared toward the present and the future. But, in an ironic echo of colonialism, central also to this imperative was the idea that, given the stunting legacies of colonialism on the bulk of India's population, such a 'social revolution' could only be led by the state. Ironically, the 'people's' displacement into the past was here a product of colonialism itself, rather than 'tradition'. But the effect was the same. The heart of the constitutional imperative for 'social revolution' was most clearly embodied in the Constitution's 'Directive Principles of State Policy', which were not justiciable, and took on the form of guiding exhortations for state policy, to be fulfilled by parliament and the bureaucracy. 'The Directive Principles of State Policy were envisaged as duties of the state, basic principles fundamental to governance' (Ramnath 2012: 58–59). Even as the invocation of the 'people's sovereignty' thus served to *enchant* the new state, the Constitution's 'Directive Principles' invested practical sovereignty *not* in the people in any immediate sense, but in parliament (and the bureaucracy) as the only institutions capable of bringing to fruition the guiding (and legitimising) 'revolutionary' principles that the Constitution laid out.

But this was hardly the only way that the Constitution engaged with the concept of the 'people' – or with the concept's temporalities. The 'rule of law' also exerted a profound and continuing influence on India's constitutional order after 1947, and on the thinking of many of India's new leaders such as Nehru and Ambedkar. But the 'rule of law' also took on new and transformed meanings as a foundation for the people's sovereignty after 1947, and this can be tracked most clearly in the law's evolving relationship to the structure of *elections*, which came to be central to India's new constitutional order. Elections were first introduced as an important element in India's political structure in the late colonial era (with a limited franchise), and were greatly expanded after 1947 (with universal adult suffrage). But if the expansion of elections in some ways transcended the old temporal bifurcation between state and society that characterised the colonial 'rule of law' in India, in certain other ways they simply gave this structure of temporality new form. And they operated in the early decades of India's independence in significant temporal counterpoint to the socialist vision of popular sovereignty embodied in the Constitution's 'Directive Principles'.

Though elections in some forms date back to the nineteenth century in India, they were introduced as an important structuring element in British colonial politics only by the reforms of 1919. The rhetoric of 'self-determination' was at this time a powerful force in international discourse and the expansion of elections into India represented, at least in part, an effort to legitimise British colonial rule internationally by paying some lip service to this principle. Nevertheless, there can also be little doubt that within India the British expansion of elections represented an effort to strengthen the structure of their control by providing a new frame to bring 'traditional' elites, who they rightly suspected would dominate local elections, into closer association with their authority.[20] The original British establishment of elections can thus be seen as deeply entrenched in the same sovereign structure that shaped the colonial 'rule of law' more broadly. The underlying assumption was that the state, as the bearer of reason and self-control, would institute the rationalising *procedures* (electoral rules) that would frame the choosing of electoral representatives, even as the politics (or *substance*) of elections would revolve around patronage, passions, and culturally particular loyalties rooted in a not-so-rational past. In this sense, the people, still displaced temporally from the present, could hardly be identified through voting as emerging sovereign agents who could challenge the sovereign claims of the British.[21]

Given this framing, it is not a surprise that the Congress Party boycotted the first elections under these reforms. But the Congress soon decided to contest them (with access to considerable patronage on the line) and ultimately came, in many critical ways, to buy into the structural assumptions that shaped them, precisely as an avenue for coming to terms with the temporal contradictions that marked their own position. In some ways, of course, elections changed significantly over the quarter century before the British departure, particularly as party organising came to play a much more significant role in electioneering than when elections were first introduced. Indeed, by the 1937 elections, the Congress had developed a sufficiently strong organisation to win control of nine of the legislative assemblies elected under provincial autonomy. So it would hardly be correct to suggest that the substance of electioneering remained entirely displaced from new Congress claims to sovereign authority. Nevertheless, the process of Congress electioneering, most often involving faction, caste, and local deal-making, shaped an image of voters far different from that projected by the men and women involved in Gandhi's satyagraha, who provided the defining model of the self-ruled sovereign citizen. As we have seen, Gandhi was thus highly suspicious of such electoral exercises, as real 'democracy', for him, lay elsewhere.[22] Indeed, one can in some ways see the entire nationalist movement in the decades before independence as a cycling between Gandhian satyagraha and Congress electoral engagement, each pointing toward alternative images of what 'democracy' and the 'people' meant.

Yet, if colonial elections crystallised the longstanding tension between an image of the free, sovereign individual and the reality of everyday politics, their institution nevertheless defined a framework within which these realms were brought into direct temporal juxtaposition in new ways, a fact illustrative of the deep contradictions in British rule itself. Regardless of the politics surrounding the introduction of elections in India, a central element in the colonial *law* of elections was the protection of the free right of voters to choose, and of candidates to freely stand for election, whatever the pressures of local politics. Such law derived from practice in the UK and was embodied in electoral rules that gave losing candidates the right to petition (before specially constituted election tribunals) to overturn election results on the grounds of a variety of procedural irregularities, prominent among which was the exercise of 'undue influence', that is, the exercise of political (or religious) pressures that might compromise the 'free choice' of the voter. There was thus an important sense in which, whatever the actual nature of the politics that produced election results, elections also put the image of the sovereign voter, defined in law by an almost mystical freedom to transcend the politics in which they were enmeshed, into intimate dialogue with the operations of local politics – however much the colonial 'rule of law' in colonial India continued generally to consign these to separate temporal realms.

This provides a critical backdrop to track the ways that the Constituent Assembly sought to link the people's sovereignty to the conduct of elections. An image of the free, sovereign individual was, of course, also underscored by the Constitution's delineation of Rights (a vison of rights – associated with enchanted individual personhood – that was quite different from the old colonial-era 'rights' associated with 'custom'). But the importance of this image as a backdrop to the institutional structure of the new state was underscored by the creation of a new National Election Commission, a constitutionally delineated body (with no precedent in earlier colonial tradition) that was to administer all national and provincial elections. The mission of the Election Commission was thus to procedurally enable the full capture of Indian politics in the new electoral structure, even as it stood apart from these politics and operated to procedurally protect an underlying image of the free individual voter as the underlying foundation for the people's sovereign authority.

On one level, the Election Commission's mission was all-encompassing: to prepare the electoral rolls in order to make sure that *all* eligible Indians were able to vote under adult suffrage, and that elections would thus encompass the politics of all.[23] Not surprisingly, many educated elites were uneasy with this process, continuing to see the 'masses' as parochial and 'backward' (as yet 'undeveloped'), and politics, in its everyday sense, as reflective of the uncontrolled impulses that low levels of education and development produced. There was thus much skeptical elite commentary and uncertainty as the first general election of 1952 approached.[24] But the leap to adult suffrage, as a sign of the new nation's claim to independent sovereignty in the name of the 'people', meant that few would openly challenge this undertaking, for its very comprehensiveness facilitated the critical equation of the 'people' with the new 'nation' as a central legitimation for the new state.

But skepticism about the electorate was balanced also by the EC's commitment to electoral *process*, which underscored the importance of elections as a moment when the ideal of the autonomous, free, voting citizen was on prominent display, at least in the EC's procedural requirements of free voting (such as the requirement for a secret ballot or in restrictions on appeals to religion and caste that might compromise free individual selection). In this sense, the election was also a massive *performance* of a vision of popular sovereignty rooted not in the current 'state' of the people or politics, but in the ideal vision of a free, individual, a vision of enchanted personhood standing apart from the worldly realities of society, even as Indians participated in what was an inescapably deeply political and worldly process. This structure came to infuse into elections a vision of temporal cyclicality, constitutionally defined by the EC's power to claim personnel from other government departments and to wield special authority during the delimited time of an election campaign.

But if the 'special' time of elections seemed to bring two distinct – and conceptually oppositional – temporal images of the 'people' together, they hardly reconciled them. Images of the free individual and of Congress 'vote banks' jostled uneasily. The continuing tension between these worlds was in fact remarked on by many, including Nehru, who tended to see the process of elections as itself a *pedagogical* process that might ultimately bring these two visions together. It was not a surprise, therefore, that these tensions – and more particularly between the state's independent sovereign mandate through the 'Directive Principles' and the projection of a people's voice through elections – came to a boil – and erupted with long-term implications for India's democracy – during the turbulent era of Indira Gandhi's Prime Ministership and India's 'Emergency' in the 1970s.

The Emergency and the crisis of sovereign authority

Tensions between the sovereignty of parliament, as derived from the 'Directive Principles' and the role of the courts in constraining parliamentary authority in the name of the 'Fundamental Rights' in the constitution (such as the right to property) were long evident during the time of Nehru. But these tensions came to a head in the late 1960s after Indira Gandhi split the Congress in the name of pursuing a more active, socialist, and statist program, even in the face of opposition from provincial party bosses (the so-called 'syndicate') whose political skills lay most fully in the successful Congress Party management of elections and patronage. Using heated populist rhetoric ('*Gharibi Hatao!*' ['Eradicate Poverty!']), Gandhi swept to victory in the elections of 1971 and gained a supermajority in parliament, which she subsequently used to suspend elections and declare a constitutional Emergency in 1975 (largely to foreclose the effects of an election petition case that threatened her removal from office). At the root of this was a clear assertion of the sovereignty of parliament to act in the name of the 'people' to fulfill the revolutionary objectives contained in the 'Directive Principles' of the Constitution.[25] This was in fact directly signalled in 1976 by Gandhi's insertion through the 42nd amendment of the words 'socialist' and 'secular' into the Constitution's preamble as defining principles of the republic.

Given these circumstances, it was perhaps not surprising that a significant element in the ideological resistance to the Emergency lay in the assertion that Gandhi's actions violated the different vision of the sovereignty of the people that was embedded in the Constitution's voting procedures. If the Constitution embodied in its fundamental structural assumptions the people's sovereign 'will', these critics argued, this created an imperative that stood beyond and above the immediate role of parliament as a reflection of the people's voice. Elections were not just about outcomes, but about the principles their procedures embodied. Here the temporality of the 'rule of law' was the key. As some on the Supreme Court now argued, the Constitution embodied a 'basic structure', reflecting the people's ultimate will, which transcended even parliament's power of constitutional amendment.[26] It embodied, in this sense, a timeless dispensation that was now beyond the reach of *any* contemporary political interference (even through the power of amendment by parliament), for it was a product of that extraordinary moment when the sovereign 'people' had spoken (through the Constituent Assembly) to give to the more mundane people who inhabited everyday politics the overarching Law represented by the Constitution. The conflicts of these years thus gave new meaning to elections not only as a moment when the people's voice was registered in *immediate* linear time as they chose a new parliament, but also as a moment when the voice of the 'people' as a timeless emanation of sovereignty came to earth through the mechanism of electoral procedure and law. And it was the Supreme Court rather than parliament that now asserted the sovereign right to protect and interpret this.

This was the vision that seemingly shaped Justice H. R. Khanna's celebrated opinion in the Supreme Court's 1975 judgement that threw out (parts of) the 39th amendment to the Constitution, which had been passed by parliament during the Emergency precisely to bar the courts (and the law) from challenging the elections of key leaders of parliament, including the prime minister herself. What originally prompted the amendment was Gandhi's political effort to render null the judgement of the Allahabad High Court against her election to parliament (for 'corruption') – the event that provoked the Emergency. But as Justice Khanna argued explicitly (in a judgement that in fact let stand the specific overturning of the Allahabad decision even as it asserted a higher principle), the more general subjection of elections to law (that is, legal procedure) was beyond political dismantling, for it was 'basic' to the democratic structure of the Constitution itself. Law (or, the 'rule of law', as others put it) lay at the heart of the Constitution's democratic dispensation, a principle that, in effect, was now asserted to stand apart from any political meddling – that is, to stand outside the temporal frame in which everyday politics was embedded.[27]

This grounding of democracy in a 'basic constitutional structure' that transcended the Constitution's specific amending provisions proved to be of critical turning point in India's electoral system, particularly when this framing of sovereign authority was seemingly confirmed by the people themselves with the repudiation of the Emergency in the 1977 elections.[28] Appeals to the state (and directly to parliament) as the enchanted instrument of historic socialist development by no means disappeared. But with the linking of the people's sovereignty to the sovereignty of law – which was implicit in the 'basic structure' doctrine – a new stress on the importance of cyclical time in the structuring of electoral democracy emerged as a key to the ongoing expression of the people's sovereign will. Even if everyday politics remained a driving force in the people's voice (bound up with the all the 'low politics' of caste, patronage, and local influence), the voice of the people as a higher sovereign force could nevertheless speak, even amidst these politics, when it was contained within a cyclical electoral structure defined by the overarching procedural power of the 'rule of law'. The decades after the Emergency were thus an era when elections as a performance of sovereignty came into their own.

Popular sovereignty, elections, and cyclical time

The dynamic instrument that came to be the key to dramatising this was what was called the 'Model Code of Conduct' for elections. The Model Code emerged in the years after 1977 – and even more dramatically after 1990 – as the key to shifting popular perceptions of the importance of cyclical temporality in India's democratic structure. The Code itself was simply a set of rules issued by the EC for the 'guidance' of candidates and political parties during the time of elections. It was not new in the post-Emergency period; its origins go back to agreements on conduct initially forged among political parties themselves, particularly in some of India's southern states beginning in the late 1950s. But the Code soon came to be associated with the overarching authority of the EC, which began to publish it during the 1960s as a framework for electoral behaviour applicable during the 'special time' of each election cycle. It took on new meaning when, in 1979, a more comprehensive Model Code was published that gave special attention to strictures on the use of state machinery (and even levers of government 'influence') in elections – a clear reaction to the Emergency.[29]

The significance of the Code, however, lay not just in the new prominence given to it by the EC, but in the fact that it cast the rules for electoral behaviour – and thus the authority of the EC in projecting them – less in technical legal terms than as a moral imperative, associated with the sovereign image of the free voter.[30] It took the leadership of the EC by T. N. Seshan in the early 1990s to give this structure a significant purchase in the popular Indian consciousness. Two critical political developments provided the backdrop for this. First was the continuing decline of the dominant Congress Party patronage structure at the local level, a trend reflected in the late 1980s in the rise both of the Bharatiya Janata Party (BJP), and of lower caste and regional political parties, all of which produced a far more fluid electoral structure and a growing sense of crisis among some urban middle-class elites with respect to the control and discipline of the electoral *process*. In some parts of India, this was the era of electoral corruption (including 'booth-capturing') par excellence. But second was the concurrent growth of the public media sphere in India during this period, and along with it the emergence of a discourse of public, middle-class identity cast in sharp opposition to the 'dirty' character of politics and corruption. This went hand in hand, as Lloyd and Susanne Rudolph have pointed out, with the rise of judicial activism by the Supreme Court.[31] It was in this context that Seshan was able to carve out for the EC a new place in public consciousness during the 1990s by stressing the EC's identification with the Model Code, casting itself as the patron and protector of a code transcending *both* the substance of local electoral politics, where patronage, payoffs, and caste mobilisation predominated, *and* the technical structure of the legal system.[32] It increasingly cast its own public authority, through widespread publicity (which could at times be characterised almost as the public shaming of politicians), as deriving from a vision of the sovereign people that (like the basic structure doctrine) stood outside politics itself and was embodied in the Model Code.

It is impossible here to detail the many conflicts during the period of Seshan's leadership of the Election Commission (from 1990–1996) during which this vision crystallised.[33] But critical to the underlying character of all these conflicts was a vision of cyclical time, centred on the EC's management of electoral cycles, but grounded in the essentially timeless sovereign dispensation represented by the Constitution. Some of the key constitutional questions brought to the surface by Seshan's activist use of the Model Code related precisely to the Constitution's framework for delineating special 'electoral time'. Key conflicts thus arose over the EC's full powers to set the dates and temporal parameters for electoral campaigns, independent of government political pressures, and its full disciplinary control over government servants deputed to the EC during election campaigns. In each case, in spite of considerable public controversy, and government opposition, the EC ultimately triumphed in the Supreme Court.[34] In contrast, in Seshan's most contentious clash with the government during these years – over the Congress government's appointment of two additional Election Commissioners to try to dilute his personal authority – it was the government that emerged victorious in the Court. Yet this hardly changed the underlying dynamics. What all these controversies suggested was that the EC projected a power during 'electoral time' that neither politics nor the law could fully contain. Indeed, the EC's most forceful power of sanction for Model Code violations was its power to stop or postpone election campaigns altogether when the Code's provisions were too publicly flouted, a threat it in fact followed up on, with much publicity, in stopping several by-elections.[35] Such powers had relatively little to do with the substance of party politics (though competing parties repeatedly insinuated, by turns, that the EC was favouring their rivals), but they had everything to do with the sovereign meanings infused into election campaigns, a fact that Seshan sought to underscore with his own frequent references to *dharma* as he addressed youthful audiences about the Model Code. To suggest that these powers operated without considerable public controversy would of course be very wide of the mark, for they were the subject of concerted debate and public commentary. But they have nevertheless since the time of Seshan gained a deep hold on popular understandings of elections in India, and in ways that have put cyclical temporality at the centre of any understanding of India's democratic order.

Sovereignty, cyclical temporality, and political theology

Here, reference to the old colonial structure of sovereignty may help us to understand how the cyclical temporalities associated with Seshan's reforms, and with the Model Code, increasingly 'bewitched' a significant element of the Indian public.[36] As Sandria Freitag has argued in discussing the colonial history of performances such as Ram Lila, the annual cyclicality and 'special time' of such performances had long allowed for the projection of images of enchanted sovereign kingship that could be used as templates for measuring 'good rule' in 'normal' times. It is for this reason that she labels these arenas as 'public', not just because of their performance in open spaces, but also because of their analogical connection to the developing 'public sphere' of print and publication (Freitag 1989). They thus linked the people to a sovereign imagining, which, if not deriving ultimately *from* the people (but rather from a higher cosmic ordering), at least defined the 'people' as the carrier of a legitimate sovereign vision to which the state might be (at least theoretically) held accountable. And if the British deflected this during the colonial era – largely by labelling the insertion of contemporary political meanings into these 'customary' performances as inauthentic 'innovation' – the structure of these 'public arenas' nevertheless suggested how such cyclical performances had long played key roles in making popular sovereign imaginings visible.

A key question thus lies in how such temporalities may have shaped popular investment in the temporal structure of elections in the wake of Seshan's reforms. Freitag uses the work of Victor Turner to lay out the specific temporalities of these public arena performances, delineating a movement from everyday political structure, through a state of liminality (moving outside structure), to a realisation of *communitas*, a sense of collective unity transcending everyday structure. This created what was, in effect, an enchanted image of ultimate sovereignty, defining what Turner called 'root paradigms in people's heads', which remained as a powerful force in popular consciousness even as the cycle returned to the conflicted political and social realities everyday life.[37] It is easy to see a similar structure of temporality operating during elections. It was during the 'special time' of elections that the image of enchanted sovereign individuality – performed though the individual act of voting (and through the secret ballot) – was in fact directly juxtaposed against the worldly politics of social pressure, hierarchy, influence, and group competition, which were equally central to electoral structure. To participate in elections meant to participate in open political competition of the sharpest kind, through which all of society's divisions were displayed.

Yet one participated at the very same time, through the legally protected act of individual voting (and through the projection of the Model Code), in a performance of enchanted individual personhood – and through this an imagining of the sovereign 'people'.[38] It was the *simultaneity* of these two sides of sovereignty, worldly and enchanted, that was, in effect, the 'root paradigm' carried in people's heads once elections were over.

To suggest that older temporalities, rooted in religion, shaped newer visions of 'popular sovereignty', rooted in an overtly secular Constitution (and the 'rule of law'), is to enter the realm of what has sometimes been called 'political theology', the idea, first framed by Carl Schmitt, that modern forms of state power and legitimacy, however overtly secular, are often framed by older, theological conceptions of how power operates in the universe (Schmitt 1985: 36). Here the templates linking the secular and the religious were to be found in the common structural requirements of sovereign projections. These required both the effective establishment of worldly order, and, simultaneously, the ability to link authority to the enchanted realms of power lying outside society, whether to forms of divinity or to the extra-social image of an enchanted individual defined by autonomous will. And this is where the structuring of cyclical temporality came to be critical, for it provided a frame through which the fundamental opposition between worldly and extra-worldly realms was made manifest, even as these conflicting realms were juxtaposed and *both* made necessary for legitimate order.

But the concept of 'political theology' also raises other, more complex, issues. If it provides a frame for understanding how older templates gave new vitality to India's electoral structure after the Emergency – and thus gave elections greater enchanted resonance in the popular imagination – we can also ask whether such framings also opened the door to the more overt insinuation of religious ideas not only into the substance but also into the secular procedures of elections themselves. We have already seen hints of this in Seshan's invocation of *dharma* as he publicised the Model Code. And it is noteworthy that the very years of the EC's expanding power and prestige in the years after the Emergency were associated also with the rise of Hindu nationalist politics in India (and with the rise in some areas of lower caste parties as well). The growth of the BJP in these years was in fact intimately associated with the projection of Ram as India's ultimate sovereign icon, a devotional focus that precipitated the dramatic events at Ayodhya in 1992. This was a sovereign image pulled from its earlier place in the encapsulated realm of 'religion' into a central place in a new assertion of the sovereign people's meaning. And it was also associated with a newly invigorated ideology of 'Hindutva' ('Hinduness') as a purported foundation for India's national identity. What relationship, then, did such ideas have to the older model of the 'rule of law' – and to the principles that underlay the EC's management of elections? How did they relate to the temporalities of popular sovereignty?

In some ways the rise of the BJP in the 1980s and 1990s must be seen also as a product of the same disenchantment with the Nehruvian socialist model after

Indira Gandhi's death that shaped the electoral transformations we have already discussed. But to assess the relationship of BJP ideology to Seshan's reforms – and to the invigorated Model Code – is also to confront the inadequacy of the terms 'secular' and 'religious' in shaping this discussion. For if sovereignty fundamentally involves enchantment – that is, the imagining of powers that operate outside everyday social and political worlds – then sovereignty even in ostensibly 'secular' formulations cannot escape a connection to 'religion' (at least in the sense of 'religion' as a field specifically relating to human engagement with the realm of the 'enchanted'). In this sense, Hindutva and the Model Code operated in a common field. Indeed, Hindutva referred less in this context to a cultural definition of the nation than to a vision of enchanted selfhood – a vision of the sovereign individual that, like that animating the Model Code, stood above the 'low politics' of everyday deal-making, casteism, and patronage politics that preoccupied most political parties (including, it should be added, the BJP itself when it came to everyday electioneering).[39] Intellectual advocates of Hindutva thus commonly projected it as a universal Indian vision, linked to asceticism and self-restraint – and indeed, tolerance – that could, in theory, be aspired to by all. This image of enchanted sovereign selfhood was reflected as well in BJP political rhetoric and style – with their own leadership often cast into ascetic, self-controlled idioms (both at the top and through its connections to the RSS). It should not come as a surprise, therefore, that the BJP was just as supportive of the outwardly secular procedural authority of the EC, and the rule of law, as was the Congress – and that this vision of Hindutva was recognised by the Supreme Court as entirely compatible with the structure of electoral law embodied by the Model Code.[40]

Yet in practice the BJP *also* mobilised the idea of 'Hinduness' in highly exclusionary and discriminatory ways. The party's 'higher' vision of an enchanted self as a universalising model for Indian sovereignty was in fact widely displaced in popular politics by a deeply particularised vision of worldly 'Hindu' identity, defined by its contrast to a variety of 'religious' others (most notably Muslims) who were now projected as enemies within, threats to the purity of the 'nation'. Here the forms of religious identity mobilised in elections were sometimes linked to the forms mobilised through religious riots. On this level, the BJP tended to stress the importance of devotionalism in *action* as a public expression of identity, which in some ways harked back to the era of late colonial nationalism. 'Secularism' in such a frame was easily projected as a threat to an already physically embodied identity, a vision of selfhood defined by a temporality that was, in fact, far more 'organic' (and immediate) than 'developmental'.[41] The 'Hindu' self was tied not to a vision of becoming, in either the Gandhian or the liberal sense, but to the mobilisation through performative action of an already formed – and immanent – identity, a vision of identity that seemingly belied the construction of a sovereign 'people' through the cyclical simultaneity of an electoral moment based *both* on particularistic identities *and* on a 'higher' (and universalising) vision of an enchanted national selfhood.

Nor has such a vision of an authentic, ethnically or religiously defined self been confined to the new BJP politics of Hindu nationalism in the last three decades. Indeed, one can see parallels in new forms of political mobilisation among lower castes as well. As some recent ethnographic accounts have suggested, parties such as the Samajwadi party in UP have deployed forms of mobilisation focused largely on the political projection of a competitive ethnic self, with little reference to the model of uplift and becoming associated with many earlier lower caste movements (Michelutti 2008). Rights claims, such as those of Dalits and OBCs ('Other Backward Castes') for reservations, which had roots in the colonial legal structure, gained increasing importance in Indian politics in the years after 1990, less through appeals to law (though these have certainly remained important) than through new forms of competitive self-assertion in electoral politics, based on what some have called the 'ethnicization' of caste identities (Jaffrelot 2000: 756–766). If such movements can be read in some ways as avenues for lower castes to claim full recognition as an equal part of the sovereign 'people', and not just in some distant 'developmental' future, they can be read in other ways as running parallel to the 'ethnicization' of religious identities shaping the BJP as well.

Indeed, both caste and religious-based claims have been associated in political practice with strong local and regional networks of patronage and protection, often under the authority of 'big men', that have frequently seemed to defy the emphasis on the legal protection of individual choice that shaped the Model Code and the new vision of electoral politics that has evolved since the 1990s. The tensions engendered by such forms of politics have been reflected in a range of recent ethnographic accounts focusing on what Hansen and Stepputat have called the distinctive practices of 'de facto sovereignty', that is, a sovereignty relating less to the claims of the state and the law (and of the sovereign 'people'), and more to the forms of local control derived from legal impunity, criminality, and violence (Hansen and Stepputat 2006: 296). Some have related this as well to changes in imaginings of sovereignty associated with the India's ongoing economic 'liberalisation' in the years since 1990. In some ways, a more 'organic' view of the person (such as that shaping new caste and religious mobilisations in India), may have roots, in this view, in its 'elective affinity' to the imperatives of neoliberal capitalism, which have increasingly shaped India since the end of the Cold War. Indeed, we can perhaps see in such imperatives a view of the 'people' linked to what some in India have called the 'animal spirits' of money-making and wealth, a vision, of course, with its own powerful 'magical and redemptive' – and internationally sanctioned – enchantments.[42]

But to project such new images of the 'people' remains highly speculative and hardly suggests that cyclical temporalities of elections have ceased to have meaning in shaping how the 'people's sovereignty' is understood. To underscore the local operation of something called 'de facto sovereignty' is in fact to ignore the critical importance of enchantment to sovereignty's underlying meaning. The relationship of an 'organic' vision of the self to new conceptions of sovereignty – and to the 'people' – thus remains an open question, and one clearly linked not only to the structure of law and politics in India, but also to the evolution of India's place in the organisation of the world economy at large. How the temporalities of such conflicted visions of the 'people's sovereignty' will play out in structures of law and politics – and the market – thus remains to be seen.

Conclusion

Whatever the future may hold, the history of sovereignty and its temporalities is one with deep links to the past. The fundamental link between the 'people's sovereignty' and issues of temporality lies in what we might call 'the politics of enchantment', a politics tied to the underlying nature of sovereignty itself. Sovereignty, as a vision of rule, has always involved both power and enchantment, both equally necessary to the mobilisation of an effective sovereign vision, and yet always in tension with each other. It defines the way legitimate rule has been grounded not only in the effective maintenance of worldly order, but also in the association of rule with an extra-social cosmic order, that is, with the larger ordering of the universe and the place of individuals within it. It thus involves visions of power that transcend everyday social life, and 'bewitch' imaginations, even as they also shape the workings of mundane power structures. It is in juxtaposing (if never fully reconciling) the fundamental oppositions between the worldly and the extra-worldly, the social and the extra-social, that the cyclical temporalities of elections have gained their greatest significance, giving meaning to the people's sovereignty.

But the specific forms that the 'sovereignty of the people' has taken in India have been varied, and, indeed, as we have seen, often competitive. Democracy, as John Dunn has argued, is not just about the 'spell' that the idea of the people's sovereignty casts, but about how it is embodied in distinctive institutions and forms of political culture. The differing images of the 'people's sovereignty' that came to be embedded in the Indian Constitution grew in part from the significant movements of resistance that developed in India during the late colonial period (in both Gandhian and socialist forms), and from the ways that colonial rule itself had structured its own sovereign claims, particularly through a regime ideologically predicated on what the British called the 'rule of law'. The authors of the Constitution thus built on both the structure of colonial rule – with its own powerful links to worldwide intellectual currents – and on the ways an image of the 'people' had been mobilised more concretely in resistance to the British. It was this that produced the distinctive – yet somewhat contradictory – mix of sovereign ideas that shaped the Constitution.

As the Constitution and its meanings have evolved, the very contradictions within it – and the major crises that these produced – have driven the structure of the Constitution into deeper resonances with Indian culture and ideas. This has been particularly evident in the years since the Emergency and its repudiation in the 1977 elections. India is today not only the largest – but among the most vibrant – democracies in the world. But the forms that its institutions and political culture have developed as 'the people's sovereignty' have taken on varied meanings, and remain deeply contested. In this sense, the story of India's particular engagement with democracy – and its competing temporalities – is of potentially wide comparative historical interest. But it cannot be divorced from the larger – and long – history of sovereignty and its enchantments in the subcontinent – and indeed in the world at large.

Notes

* Thanks to Pamela Price, Arild Ruud, and Douglas Howland, and the participants at a seminar organised by Mrinalini Sinha and Manu Goswami in September 2014 at the University of Michigan, on 'Recalling Democracy', for helpful comments on earlier drafts of this chapter.

1 See, for example, Ruud (2000: 115–136). Mukulika Banerjee links this 'dirty' aspect of politics to the term '*rajniti*', referring to the 'corrupt, violent, and immoral world of the powerful'. She contrasts this with popular perceptions of the word 'politics' (an originally English word assimilated into Indian languages), which is less negative and refers to the complex balancing of competing interests (Banerjee 2011: 81–82). In more recent elections, the term 'neech rajniti' (or 'low politics') gained some notoriety as a term of description for this 'dirty' character of much politics.

2 As Dunn remarks, 'Anyone who hopes to see the politics of any democratic polity clearly must learn to look beyond the category itself' (Dunn 2014: 114–115).

3 Such questions are implicit in recent studies of popular sovereignty, for example in Richard Bourke's recent observation that 'the twentieth century was not characterised by the steady ascent of liberal democracy, but by competing visions of popular sovereignty embracing Caesarism, state socialism, libertarianism and welfare liberalism' (Bourke 2016: 13–14).

4 The deep grounding of modern (in this case, American) law in the 'enchantment of reason' is laid out in Pierre Schlag (1998). His book is a critique of this, but his case for the power of this idea is compelling.

5 There is a huge literature on this. This vision of the personal qualities associated with sovereignty was nicely captured by Max Weber's emphasis on 'the strict *objectivity*, the steady sense of *proportion*, the restrained *self-control*, and the capacity for *unobtrusive* action which it calls for' (quoted in Stanton 2016: 331–332).

6 For some thoughts on the special position of Brahman authority within the framework of the Raj, see Srinivas (1956). The universalistic leanings of Brahman authority, as a form of independent power transcending the local bonds of the social, had a particular affinity, as J. C. Heesterman puts it, with the universalistic claims of the 'modern' British regime. 'In this way modernity – in a sense already "transcendent" by the fact of its alienness – falls in line with the transcendent legitimation that Brahminic theory possesses' (Heesterman 1985: 16).

7 For a discussion of the central importance of the concept of maturation and its relationship to the fulfillment of reason in enlightenment thinking (and after), see Owen (1994).

8 The centrality of this phrase to the new visions of sovereignty in India after 1858 was reflected in the annual publication by the government of a *Statement Exhibiting the Moral and Material Progress and Condition of India.*

9 Note by Sir William Rattigan, December 26, 1897, in Punjab (1915: 72).

10 This is not to suggest, of course, that this distinction between procedure and substance was in fact fully maintained. For a discussion of the degree to which British judicial views affected the 'substance' of India's 'custom' and 'religious' law, see Sturman (2012).

11 This was the popular performance of Ram's story drawn from the *Ramayana,* commonly performed at the time of Dussehra.

12 This could also be seen as a prominent element in the state's projection of 'Emergency' powers and its sometimes extra-legal mobilisation of force. This was required in the face of the mobilisation of any form of what could be labelled as 'anti-reason' challenging the state. See, for example, Kolsky (2015: 1218–1246).

13 As, for example, in Dadabhai Naoroji's *Poverty and Un-British Rule*.

14 Lawyers, he said, had 'enslaved' India (Gandhi 1997: chapter 11).

15 Such a vision was connected to Marx's projection of capitalism as having an autonomous historical agency of its own, transcending individual human agency, and encompassing the material world and the agency of individual humans alike in a historical process defined by its own independent dynamics. In such a frame, as Timothy Mitchell puts it, it was not only human beings, but also, 'through exchange, the powers of objects' that manifested 'consciousness and a will' (Mitchell 2002: 30). Here, the concept of the 'people' assumed meaning as an enchanted source of sovereign authority, not simply as an expression of individual autonomy writ large, but as a class collectivity, enchanted by a temporal vision that encompassed but transcended individual agency.

16 Such a concept developed first in Russia. As the institutional embodiment of the 'correct line' for fulfilling the historical mission of the 'people', it was in the party that Leninist sovereign power came to be deeply embedded. As Alexei Yurchak puts it (in contrasting Leninist rule in the USSR with fascism), 'the center of sovereign power in the Leninist polity . . . was located not in the body of the current party leader, but in the body of the party' (Yurchak 2015: 135).

17 This was made clearest in the Congress' adoption of a socialist, progressive vision for India at its Karachi session in 1931.

18 This can be related to what Markus Daechsel has called the 'politics of self-expression', which, as he notes, had links to larger worldwide developments in the economy and, to some degree, fascism (Daechsel 2006).

19 As Austin puts it: the Constitution (the Directive Principles) aims 'at making the Indian masses free in the positive sense, free from the passivity engendered by centuries of coercion by society and by nature, free from the abject physical conditions that had prevented them from fulfilling their best selves' (Austin 1966: 51).

20 This was reflected also in the limited franchise granted under the 1919 reforms. Based primarily on the payment of minimum levels of land revenue, the reforms gave the vote to approximately 3 per cent of the population (though a larger percentage of the adult male population). The franchise subsequently expanded in various ways, so that by the 1946 elections, somewhere between a quarter and a third of the adult population was eligible to vote, varying between provinces. According to a later, post-independence Home Ministry report, the overall percentage who could vote in the 1946 provincial elections constituted 28.5 per cent of the 'adult population of the provinces' (India 1969: part II, 140).

21 This structure was further underscored by the recognition of special electorates for distinctive religions and (in limited cases) for caste groupings in the delimitation of constituencies.

22 As Sunil Khilnani has written, 'Gandhi's view of representation bore an oblique relation to the idea of democracy understood in terms of elections'. As Gandhi wrote, 'to safeguard democracy the people must have a keen sense of independence, self-respect and their oneness, and should insist on choosing as their representatives only such persons as are good and true'. But this bore little relationship to the existing structure of electioneering (quoted in Khilnani 2005: 72).

23 As Ornit Shani has recently shown, the large bureaucratic task of preparing the rolls was begun well before the official, constitutional establishment of the Election Commission under the direction of the Constituent Assembly (Shani 2017).

24 Ram Guha thus takes for his frame for the discussion of these elections a contemporary editor's labelling of them as 'the biggest gamble in history' (Guha 2002: 95–103). The central problem of discipline facing politics in the transition from colonial rule was certainly a deep concern of Nehru (Chakrabarty 2005).

25 See Rudolph and Rudolph (1987: chapter 3). The ongoing debate over the meaning of parliamentary sovereignty is discussed in Krishnapuram (1985).
26 This doctrine was first judicially enunciated in the early 1970s in Kesavanada Bharati vs. State of Kerala, AIR 1973 SC 1461. But it took on far more meaning in light of the events of the Emergency. See Krishnaswamy (2010).
27 Smt. Indira Nehru Gandhi vs. Raj Narain and another, 1975 SCC (2) 159. Khanna's judgement was a concurrence in a result in which justices wrote independent opinions. While he saw the key 'basic structure' issue in the judgement as the maintenance of democracy through free and fair elections, other justices stressed directly the principle of the 'rule of law'.
28 Critical here – again – is the almost mystical reading of the election after the fact, as a reflection of a 'people's voice' transcending the concrete and varied political circumstances in which voters actually decided to vote against the Congress and Indira Gandhi.
29 In his election memoir, later Chief Election Commissioner, James Lyngdoh, identifies this period as the real beginning of the EC's efforts to establish independence (Lyngdoh 2004). For a discussion, see Singh (2012: 152–153, 157).
30 The ambiguous place of the Code between law and morality is strongly argued by Singh (2012). This is in no way to suggest, however, that it was entirely divorced from the 'rule of law'. Many of the Model Code's guidelines were drawn from the Representation of the People Act of 1951, which, among other things, laid out the parameters of 'undue' electoral influence and 'corruption'. and parts of the Code were drawn from the IPC as well. Though the courts were barred from hearing election cases during 'election time'. criminal court cases could in some cases be brought during election time that related directly not to election law, specifically, but to the IPC. Cases were also brought to the SC relating to the adjudication of the constitutional powers of the EC itself.
31 Rudolph and Rudolph (1987). See also Sen (2009). The SC basically supported the increasing power of the EC, though not in every respect. Seshan's most notorious clash with the government was over the government's efforts to dilute his influence by appointing two additional Election Commissioners. This was a move Seshan fought bitterly, and eventually lost when the SC sided with the government.
32 Interestingly, the Dinesh Goswami Committee on Electoral Reform had proposed in 1990 (among many other recommendations) that the Model Code be made legally binding as a way to strengthen the EC. But though Seshan initially supported this, he soon realised that this would undermine the distinctive temporal authority of the EC arising from the fact that the Model Code was *not* subject to direct judicial intervention, which kept the courts at bay and framed the EC's own, distinctive claims to 'moral' authority. He therefore turned against this proposal when it was taken up by the Government, and it was never enacted.
33 For a fuller discussion, see Gilmartin (2009: 247–284).
34 For the former, see *Union of India v. Harbans Singh Jalal and others* (Election Commission of India 2006: IV, 394–397); for the latter, *Election Commission of India v. Union of India and others*. SC writ petition #606 of 1999 (Election Commission of India 2000: III, 35–59).
35 This is in fact reminiscent of the ways state authority could be challenged (both in the colonial period and earlier) by refusals to stage (or participate in) key cyclical rituals (such as Muharram or Ram Lila, for example) that had implications for legitimising sovereign authority. For an example, see Freitag (1989: 109).
36 Some indication of this is evident in Banerjee (2007). See also, Ahuja and Chibber (2012: 389–410).
37 Turner (1974: 96). See also Turner (1977). A powerful evocation of this in its relationship to British colonial rule in India (well before Turner) can be found in E. M. Forster's *A Passage to India*, which deals with the structure of culture as an enduring frame of human division, the transcendence of which, deeply destabilising to moral values, is arguably portrayed as only possible in a context of cyclical time.

38 Mukulika Banerjee has thus used the concept of *communitas* to describe this dynamic, seeing elections as operating 'betwixt and between periods of social time' (Banerjee 2011: 75–98). See also Banerjee (2014).
39 In practice, the BJP attacked 'casteism' even as it saw high-caste privilege as something quite natural.
40 *Dr. Ramesh Yeshwant Prabhoo* v. *Shri Prabhakar Kashinath Kunte & Others*, AIR 1996 SC 1113.
41 For some discussion of this 'organic' self, which could be wounded by the religious practices of others (such as cow slaughter), is itself a story with roots extending back into colonialism, but taking on increasing significance since the 1980s. Many have written on this, but see, for example, Gilmartin and Metcalf (2011: 54–73).
42 'Narendra Modi-Led BJP Wins Big at the Hustings, India Inc Hails Decisive Mandate', *Indian Express*, May 16, 2014. (indianexpress.com/article/business/economy/narendra-modi-led-bjp-wins-big-at-the-hustings-india-inc-hails-decisive-mandate/). See also, 'Economy in Right Direction; Need More Animal Spirit: Rajan', *India Today*, June 8, 2016. (indiatoday.intoday.in/story/economy-in-right-direction-need-more-animal-spirit-rajan/1/687198.html). The term 'animal spirits' was used by Keynes to signify a kind of unselfconscious investment in money-making as a critical element in capitalist growth. On the 'magical and redemptive' fiction of the 'market' as a sovereign force, see Hansen and Stepputat (2006: 309).

References

Ahuja, Amit, and Pradeep Chibber. 2012. 'Why the Poor Vote in India: "If I Don't Vote, I Am Dead to the State"', *Studies in Comparative International Development*, 47 (4): 389–410.

Austin, Granville. 1966. *The Indian Constitution: Cornerstone of a Nation*. Oxford: Clarendon Press.

Banerjee, Mukulika. 2007. 'Sacred Elections', *Economic and Political Weekly*, 42 (17): 1556–1562.

Banerjee, Mukulika. 2011. 'Elections as Communitas', *Social Research*, 78 (1): 75–98.

Banerjee, Mukulika. 2014. *Why India Votes?* New Delhi: Routledge.

Bose, Subhas Chandra. 1948. *Netaji's Life and Writings (Part 2: The Indian Struggle, 1920–34)*. Calcutta: Thacker, Spink.

Bourke, Richard. 2016. 'Introduction', in Richard Bourke and Quentin Skinner (eds.), *Popular Sovereignty in Historical Perspective*, pp. 1–14. Cambridge: University of Cambridge Press.

Chakrabarty, Dipesh. 2005. '"In the Name of Politics": Sovereignty, Democracy and the Multitude in India', *Economic and Political Weekly*, 40 (30): 3293–3301.

Daechsel, Markus. 2006. *The Politics of Self-Expression: The Urdu Middle-Class Milieu in Mid-Twentieth Century India and Pakistan*. London: Routledge.

Dunn, John. 2014. *Breaking Democracy's Spell*. New Haven: Yale University Press.

Election Commission of India. 2000–2006. *Landmark Judgements on Election Law*, v. 1–4. New Delhi: Election Commission of India.

Freitag, Sandria B. 1989. *Collective Action and Community: Public Arenas and the Emergence of Communalism in North India*. Berkeley: University of California Press.

Gandhi, Mohandas K. 1967. *Political and National Life and Affairs*, compiled by V. K. Kher. Ahmedabad: Jitendra Desai, Navajivan Mudranalaya.

Gandhi, Mohandas K. 1997. *Hind Swaraj and Other Writings*, ed. by Anthony Parel. Cambridge: Cambridge University Press.

Gandhi, Mohandas K. 1999. 'Democracy "Versus" Mobocracy', *Young India*, September 8, 1920, in *The Collected Works of Mahatma Gandhi* (Electronic Book), 21: 1 July–21

November 1920: 245–249. New Delhi: Publications Division Government of India. www.gandhiserve.org/cwmg/VOL021.PDF.

Ghosh, Durba. 2017. *Gentlemanly Terrorists: Political Violence and the Colonial State in India*. Cambridge: Cambridge University Press.

Gilmartin, David. 2009. 'One Day's Sultan: T. N. Seshan and Indian Democracy', *Contributions to Indian Sociology*, 43 (2): 247–284.

Gilmartin, David, and Barbara Metcalf. 2011. 'Art on Trial: Civilization and Religion in the Persona and Painting of M. F. Husain', in Sumathy Ramaswamy (ed.), *Barefoot Across the Nation: Maqbool Fida Husain and the Idea of India*, pp. 54–74. London: Routledge.

Guha, Ramachandra. 2002. 'Democracy's Biggest Gamble: India's First Free Elections in 1952', *World Policy Journal*, 19 (1): 95–103.

Hansen, Thomas Blom, and Finn Stepputat. 2006. 'Sovereignty Revisited', *Annual Review of Anthropology*, 35: 295–315.

Heesterman, Jan C. 1985. 'India and the Inner Conflict of Tradition', in J. C. Heesterman, *The Inner Conflict of Tradition: Essays in Indian Ritual, Kingship and Society*, pp. 10–24. Chicago: University of Chicago Press.

India. Ministry of Home Affairs. 1969. *Report of the Committee on Defections*. New Delhi: Government of India.

Jaffrelot, Christophe. 2000. 'Sanskritization vs. Ethnicization in India: Changing Identities and Caste Politics Before Mandal', *Asian Survey*, 40 (5): 756–766.

Khilnani, Sunil. 2005. 'The Indian Constitution and Democracy', in Zoya Hasan, E. Sridharan, and R. Sudarshan (eds.), *India's Living Constitution*, pp. 64–82. London: Anthem Press.

Kolsky, Elizabeth. 2015. 'The Colonial Rule of Law and the Legal Regime of Exception: Frontier "Fanaticism" and State Violence in British India', *The American Historical Review*, 120 (4): 1218–1246.

Krishnapuram, R. Mohan. 1985. *Sovereignty of Parliament in India*. New Delhi: Deep & Deep.

Krishnaswamy, Sudhir. 2010. *Democracy and Constitutionalism in India: A Study of the Basic Structure Doctrine*. New Delhi: Oxford University Press.

Lyngdoh, James. 2004. *Chronicle of an Impossible Election: The Election Commission and the 2002 Jammu and Kashmir Assembly Elections*. New Delhi: Penguin India.

Mantena, Karuna. 2016. 'Popular Sovereignty and Anti-Colonialism', in Richard Bourke and Quentin Skinner (eds.), *Popular Sovereignty in Historical Perspective*, pp. 297–319. Cambridge: Cambridge University Press.

Mehta, Uday Singh. 1999. *Liberalism and Empire: A Study in Nineteenth-century British Liberal Thought*. Chicago: University of Chicago Press.

Michelutti, Lucia. 2008. *The Vernacularisation of Democracy: Politics, Caste, and Religion in India*. London: Routledge.

Mill, John Stuart. 1999. *On Liberty*. Broadview Literary Texts. Peterborough: Broadview Press.

Mitchell, Timothy. 2002. *Rule of Experts: Egypt, Techno-Politics, Modernity*. Berkeley: University of California Press.

Mukherjee, Mithi. 2010. *India in the Shadow of Empire: A Legal and Political History, 1774–1950*. New Delhi: Oxford University Press.

Owen, David. 1994. *Maturity and Modernity: Nietzsche, Weber, Foucault and the Ambivalence of Reason*. London: Routledge.

Pinney, Christopher. 2004. *'Photos of the Gods': The Printed Image and Political Struggle in India*. New York: Oxford University Press.

Punjab. 1915. *Report on the Punjab Codification of Customary Law Conference*. Lahore: Punjab Government.

Ramnath, Kalyani. 2012. '"We The People": Seamless Webs and Social Revolution in India's Constituent Assembly Debates', *South Asia Research*, 32, (1): 57–70.

Rudolph, Lloyd, and Susanne Rudolph. 1987. *In Pursuit of Lakshmi: The Political Economy of the Indian State*. Chicago: University of Chicago Press.

Ruud, Arild Engelsen. 2000. 'Talking Dirty About Politics: A View from a Bengali Village', in Chris Fuller and Véronique Bénéï (eds.), *The Everyday State and Society in Modern India*, pp. 115–136. New Delhi: Social Science Press.

Schlag, Pierre. 1998. *The Enchantment of Reason*. Durham: Duke University Press.

Schmitt, Carl. 1985. *Political Theology: Four Chapters on the Concept of Sovereignty*, trans. by George Schwab. Chicago: University of Chicago Press.

Sen, Ronojoy. 2009. 'Walking a Tightrope: Judicial Activism and Indian Democracy', *India Review*, 8 (1): 63–80.

Sen, Sarbani. 2007. *The Constitution of India: Popular Sovereignty and Democratic Transformations*. New York: Oxford University Press.

Shani, Ornit. 2017. *How India Became Democratic: Citizenship and the Making of the Universal Franchise*. Cambridge: Cambridge University Press.

Singh, Ujjwal Kumar. 2012. 'Between Moral Force and Supplementary Legality: A Model Code of Conduct and the Election Commission of India', *Election Law Journal*, 11 (2): 149–169.

Smith, Keith J. M. 1988. *James Fitzjames Stephen: Portrait of a Victorian Rationalist*. Cambridge: Cambridge University Press.

Srinivas, Mysore N. 1956. 'A Note on Sanskritization and Westernization', *Far Eastern Quarterly*, 15 (4): 481–496.

Stanton, Timothy. 2016. 'Popular Sovereignty in an Age of Mass Democracy', in Richard Bourke and Quentin Skinner (eds.), *Popular Sovereignty in Historical Perspective*, pp. 320–358. Cambridge: Cambridge University Press.

Sturman, Rachel. 2012. *The Government of Social Life in Colonial India: Liberalism, Religious law, and Women's Rights*. New York: Cambridge University Press.

Turner, Victor. 1974. *Dramas, Fields and Metaphors: Symbolic Action in Human Society*. Ithaca: Cornell University Press.

Turner, Victor. 1977. *The Ritual Process: Structure and Anti-Structure*. Ithaca: Cornell University Press.

Yurchak, Alexei. 2015. 'Bodies of Lenin: The Hidden Science of Communist Sovereignty', *Representations*, 129: 116–157.

PART II

Kingship reconfigured

4

DEITIES, ALLIANCES, AND THE POWER OVER LIFE AND DEATH

Exploring royal sovereignty and its tenacity in a former princely state in Odisha

Uwe Skoda[1]

On the 5th of February, 2018, a new 'monumental flag' was hoisted on a 100-foot-high mast in Bonaigarh, meant 'to inspire young Indians to take pride in displaying the National Flag and instil a sense of patriotism among the citizens'.[2] Unfurled by the District Collector in the presence of other government officials, for example the Superintendent of Police, this mammoth *tiranga* or national flag arguably stands as the most towering and most visible symbol of the Indian state locally. Set up just outside the former king's fort, this proximity strikes as a reminder of the many state transformations this former kingdom has undergone – the latest being a rapid industrialisation from 2003 onwards with expanded mining as well as new sponge iron factories arriving together with industrialists in the valley. One of them, Naveen Jindal, is not only Chairperson of Jindal Steel & Power (JSP), which has substantial business interests in the region, but also founder of the 'Flag Foundation of India' that donated this oversized flag. Thus, a close nexus between the Indian state and corporate houses serves literally as backdrop for palace rituals performing royal sovereignty, potentially overshadowed by it.

Going back around 150 years, Colonel Dalton visited Bonai and saw 'a small hilly district lying very snugly isolated from all civilization' with an unimposing fort with 'the river on three sides . . . surrounded by a mud wall and moat, within which are about 150 houses including those of the chief, his court-house, and jail' (Dalton 1865: 1–2). Located in a still relatively remote part of contemporary Odisha populated predominantly by Adibasi (indigenous) communities such as the (Paudi) Bhuiyans, Bonai, then a small 'jungle kingdom' (Schnepel 2002) under several overlords prior to the British arrival, in early twentieth century morphed into a 'princely state'. Under indirect colonial rule the bureaucracy was substantially enlarged to implement new laws such as land settlements, forest regulations, or a 'rule of law' broadly, and to generate more revenue subsequently also invested into palaces and pomp. Merging with the Indian Union in 1948, the rajas lost whatever limited executive power they used to have under colonial paramountcy, before they also lost their privy purses and other privileges such as armed guards in the early 1970s. Yet, the former king continues to celebrate royal 'state rituals' such as Dasara even after Bonai became a sub-division of the new sovereign nation-state. These ritual performances, side by side with rituals of the Indian nation-state such as Republic Day celebrations, indicate a multitude of co-existing claims to or forms of sovereignty in an area, as this brief history and reference to the symbolically loaded landscape outlines, in which such claims have hardly been unitary or static.

The following chapter explores ideas around royal sovereignty primarily focusing on three intersecting aspects: 1) the rulers' family chronicles as textual basis of kingship, 2) the divine manifestations in the kingdom intimately related to the raja, and 3) contemporary ritual performances – thus combining anthropological and historical perspectives. All three contribute to the formation and simultaneous expression of what Nicholas (2013: 6) calls a *sacrificial polity*, that is, a continuum of human and non-human life (Singh 2012: 393) with layered societal and divine structures involving greater or lower deities, greater or lower rulers and so on – constructed in the form of privileged access to or exalted roles in the cult of gods and goddesses. Expressed in rituals, but also texts and temples, lordship and authority emerge and are renewed through different sets of relations. On the one hand, links are established between ruler and powerful deities like Lord Baneshwar, but also Goddess Durga and the raja's tutelary goddess associated with her, both motherly protective as well as potentially ferocious and destructive – the latter (deities) blessing and legitimising the former (rulers). These intimate bonds relate to the idea of a 'ritual sovereignty' (or suzerainty, legitimacy) (Stein 1977) or 'de jure sovereignty' as legally or rightfully exercised (Hansen and Stepputat 2006: 296). On the other hand, one finds pivotal relationships between kings and communities or subjects.

Sovereignty is commonly linked to a state which conventionally implies a '"territorial state" as a geographically contained structure whose agents claim ultimate political authority within their domain' (Biersteker and Weber 1996: 2).[3] Yet, while territory is also a crucial component of sovereignty, especially for modern nation states, clearly bounded realms seemed to have been of lesser importance in case of 'jungle kingdoms' or earlier 'little kingdoms' (Cohn 2001 [1962]; Schnepel 2002; Berkemer 1993) – a point also applicable to Bonai, whose boundaries vis-à-vis neighbouring kingdoms were unambiguously demarcated only in late nineteenth/early twentieth century. Thus, such 'dominions' might be best understood as 'people-cum-territory' or *janapada* (Wink 1984: 269) with a stronger emphasis on relationships between rulers and communities and particularly internal (and external) allies – here first and foremost the foundational and lasting, that is, on the occasion of Dasara, the publically performed axis between the Bonai raja and Bhuiyans.

These privileged and privileging relations or legitimising alliances around the ruler, constituting royal sovereignty and expressed in all the three aspects just mentioned previously (chronicles, divine manifestations, and ritual performances) are entangled with another crucial point – namely the ruler's power over life frequently tied to a similar power of the deities. If one follows Agamben's (1998 [1995]) work on the linkage between sovereignty and bare life, that is, life constantly exposed to death, the capacity to exercise violence, either actual, latent, or imagined, has been foregrounded (see Hansen and Stepputat 2005, 2006), and for Hansen and Stepputat (2005: 10) sovereign power 'is always a tentative and unstable project whose efficacy and legitimacy depend on repeated performances of violence and a "will to rule".' In Bonai, references to violence, force, and conquest permeate ideas of kingship and sovereignty right from the establishment of the realm, when the Bonai Rajas, as the chronicles state, defeated and killed local chiefs. Arriving as 'stranger kings' (see Sahlins 2008; Prager 2010; Platenkamp 2013), they bring in an exterior element implying and substantiating force and the power over life and death, namely the main sword, which in the local constitution of kingship is combined with other idols also manifesting the presence of goddesses as well as marking royal authority and territory at the same time. Nevertheless, royal sovereignty in Bonai understood as a 'bipolar concept' (Singh 2012: 386) combines both, that is, contractual alliances are entangled with threats of force and violence. However, while such a 'de facto sovereignty' in Hansen and Stepputat's terms is frequently alluded to, it is hardly exercised in current practice beyond animal sacrifices. Yet, supposed memories of and rumours about human sacrifices or legends of deities manifest and realise 'spectral violence' in the contemporary sacrificial polity of Bonai, rather than executive power or actual violence taken over and exercised by the Indian state.

Royal chronicles: stranger king, foundational killings, and an alliance

In order to understand ideas of sovereignty and power in a polity of this type, the royal chronicles of Bonai known as *bansaboli* (*vamshavali*) or *Kadamba Gatha* (story of the Kadamba dynasty) offer a rich source, but I will confine my discussion here to the establishment of the realm as a more mythical or 'proto-historical' narrative.[4] This serves as a point of commencement for subsequent events such as temple constructions, land grants, and so on, and the royal lineage more broadly. However, while looking at this foundational legend one needs to keep in mind that many texts were (re-)written, or even fabricated, during the colonial era, the oldest version dating back to very early twentieth century, and in some cases their production was directly stipulated by the paramount power's quest for knowledge and order within the empire (Skoda 2012).

The myth presents a variation of a common trope surrounding kingship in South Asia. The king's conquest of wilderness is frequently presented as an ordeal and he must pass such a test successfully in order to prove his ability to rule (Falk 1973: 2ff). In the process he (followed by subsequent generations) transforms the wilderness, from which he is, however, not completely separated; he rather continues to oscillate between settlement/'settled life' and wilderness/'life in the wastes' (Heesterman 1985: 66). Moreover, the transformation of a forest area (*bana*) – the name Bonai being presumably derived from bana – into a realm is initiated by and ascribed to a Kshatriya (high-ranking) warrior who arrives as an outsider. Such a process, as Sahlins (2008: 177) argued, is, in fact, an 'elementary form of political life', that is, 'sovereignty, the magical source of power, always comes from elsewhere, from the claimed original place, exterior to society' (ibid.: 178). An initial conquest by a stranger king is commonly marred with violence or even murder – documenting a power over life. In fact, in the Bonai myth which I will quote at length later, neither side, stranger king nor autochthonous chiefs, considers any other option than killing the opponent. However, the foundational conquest is an 'ambiguous mixture or contract and chicane' (Sahlins 2008: 179), that is, Pratap Deo as first king does not only kill, but also acknowledges the Bhuiyans and forms a lasting alliance that subsequently shapes the history of Bonai, and is vividly remembered and renewed in ritual practices.

Four aspects of the narrative are particularly striking: 1) the idea of the king arriving as an outsider, who 2) needs a divine intervention and blessing in order to 3) form an alliance with one prominent chief with whose help he 4) kills all other autochthonous chiefs, showing his warrior credentials and finally setting up the realm after this constitutive violence. Let us turn to the narrative:

> The former name of Bonaigarh was Shronita Nagar. Pratap Deo who had come from the Singhal island was its the first king. The name of the state he belonged to was Udepur and his caste was Kshyatriya [high-ranking warrior]. Raja Pratap Deo came with his seven brothers from Singhal to visit Lord Jagannatha.
>
> *(Pramanik and Skoda 2013: 49)*

In this part of the story, the route of the migration is narrated – presumably from Rajasthan: Udepur probably referring to Udaipur, Mewar being considered by many as the former kingdom in Rajputana highest in status. The brothers then moved on to Sri Lanka, to Puri and finally one of them reached Bonai. No reason for the migration to Sri Lanka is given, but Puri is clearly marked as a religious centre, incidentally having exercised or claimed overlordship over several Odishan states in the pre-colonial era. Here the Kshatriyas prove their bravery and truly heroic character – they are not afraid of death even and prefer death to bowing down their heads. Thus, they impress the Gajapati (ruler) and by doing so, after the death of four brothers, the three remaining brothers are granted free access to have a *darsan* (viewing) of Lord Jagannath, the Lord of the Universe. Here the text hints at very a special relationship between royal families and Lord Jagannath as one of the most important gods in Middle India. In the Brahmanic versions, that is, those written by the family of the royal priests, an important initial focus is Puri and the Gajapati, whose power as his inner-worldly representative, deputy on earth and first servant, is rather ambivalent and contested. As overlord he has the power to kill, yet he also recognises the true warriors, establishes relations with them and even privileges them.[5]

Let us turn back to the critical reading of the chronicles narrating the fate of Pratap Deo, who is believed to have arrived in dense jungle already occupied by Bhuiyans and other Adibasis. The Bhuiyans are described as the supreme (*srestha*) group among them. Pratap Deo realises that this state belonged to Banasura (bana=forest; asur=demon) and starts worshipping Lord Shiva, known as Lord Baneshwar, residing on the Brahmani river. Names are apparently used interchangeably in the text – for example Lord Baneshwar and Banasur – but it becomes clear that Lord Baneshwar (literally 'Lord of the forest') is the residing god (*sthanpati*) of Bonai who replaces Banasur, representing wilderness as 'demon of the forest'. Pratap Deo's visits to the Baneshwar temple in order to be blessed by the Lord also mark a shift or at least broadening from a Vaisnava tradition (Lord Jagannath) to a Shaiva one (Lord Baneshwar), who is not only the most important god in the texts, but also plays a prominent role during the coronation rituals of all kings and devotees until today.

The other chiefs (*jamindar*) come to know about the presence of a stranger (*videshi*), that is, Pratap Deo, and conspire to kill him. He has to take refuge in a hollow tree (*gacha khola*), a Kadamba tree after which the dynasty has been named. While Pratap Deo is praying to Lord Baneshwar, a peacock with its tail wipes out his footprints so that the chiefs cannot locate him. It is tempting to read this part in a Leví-Straussian way, discovering a range of oppositions and inversions which are subsequently overcome, for example the migration versus the footprints erased by the peacock or the hollow tree appearing as a womb-like structure out of the which the new raja is subsequently (re-)born. The bird has a wider significance as polysemous symbol equally referring to the Moghul's 'peacock throne' and potential claims of a wider authority, as well as to Bhuiyan legends according to which they have been born out of an egg of a peacock (Dash 1997: 172; see also Roy 1935) and thus implicitly acknowledging their role again. In any case, the myth explains why the peacock occupies the upper position of the royal crest.

Moreover, while the brave Kshatriyas in the initial part of the chronicles do not mind sacrificing their lives, in the latter part Pratap Deo does fear for his life and needs support, which is surprising given the fact that his name *pratap* signifies specifically male power, potency, and valour. However, hiding in the tree Lord Baneshwar appears in a dream and orders him:

> 'Pratap Deo, I make you the King of Shronita Nagar. You will enjoy the kingship without any obstruction.' The raja asked: 'How can I be the King?' [. . . the raja was told]: 'Tomorrow morning whomever you meet in the temple, keep them with you and kill those people. Being the king of this place you have to worship the tutelary deity [ishta debi]. Debi will order you, in your dream.'

The paragraph clearly expresses a divine intervention, that is, the raja is chosen by Lord Baneshwar, who divides the autochthonous population into allies and enemies. The raja also comes to know about his tutelary goddess from Lord Baneshwar (and one of the tribal chiefs), who is marked as local, standing in contrast to the more universal male gods Lord Jagannath and Lord Shiva. The goddess does not play an important role in capturing the state though (unlike other nearby princely states such as Sareikella). However, the sword the raja uses afterwards to kill some of 'those people', namely the chiefs, is identified as main sword (*patkhanda*) and is thus indirectly linked to her, or rather Goddess Durga, as visibly performed in palace rituals (Dasara, see the next section in this chapter).

Empowered by the Lord, Pratap meets Lechada, a Bhuiyan, on the way to the temple, a visit equally triggered by a dream. They recognise each other through this divine intervention. With Lechada's insider knowledge and his help the new raja is able to liquidate all other 'tribal' jamindars who are not protected by the goddess. Their names such as Mahabira ('great hero') and Bira are frequently related to warrior fights and force and some of them demand worship beyond their death, which is granted. These small shrines dot the landscape of Bonai as visible reminders of the establishment of the realm, but such places of worship commemorating a hero's death or even human sacrifice are in no way limited to Bonai alone (see also Singh 2012).

With all other contenders killed, the chronicles state:

> Pratap Deo's anointment [abhishek] was performed. An umbrella [chhatra] was made and offered to Baneswara. Raja Pratap Deo made Lechada the 'Samanta' [feudatory]. From that day till now there have been many kings.
>
> *(all quotes adapted from Pramanik and Skoda 2013: 49–51)*

In terms of the role of the Samanto a later version of the Kadamba Gatha by Surendranath Mishra (in Pramanik and Skoda 2013: 239) is even more explicit. He argues:

> After the victory, Indra Samanta, the Lord of the Soil [Matiswar[6]] placed Pratap on a stone platform at the Great Assembly [Bada Darbar] and placing the turban and the vermillion on his head acknowledged him as the overlord. Indra Samanta was given a fief of about 50 squares with thirteen villages in it.

It is precisely this characterisation of the Samanto as 'Lord of the Soil' which indicates the high status of the Bhuiyan chief, who supports Pratap to become raja of Bonai. By recognising the Samanto the raja does not contest the Bhuiyan claim to indigeneity. This claim is not only marked by the name *bhuiyan*, literally meaning 'earth people', but is also confirmed during every new raja's investiture, the last being performed in 2011. Here the Samanto, also known as Saont, offers a *tika* of the soil of his own tutelary goddess to the raja's forehead, symbolic for handing over the soil to the raja, while the raja sits on the Saont's lap – possibly as motherly, but also a female position, which is frequently ascribed to autochthonous populations together with ties to the earth/soil while establishing a realm (Sahlins 1992 [1985]: 93).[7]

In the royal chronicles, that is, from the raja's or a Brahmanical perspective, Lord Baneshwar clearly favours Pratap. He makes him raja, but in alliance with the Bhuiyans, who are praised as the supreme group and maintain an influential position, for example as ritual specialists in charge of the daily routine at the Baneshwar Temple until today. This crucial alliance, formed with Lord Baneshwar's divine intervention as elaborated on in the myth, last, helps the first and divinely empowered raja to kill all other chiefs – largely executed with the main sword (*patkhanda*) associated with the goddess in contemporary rituals which continue to highlight this special relationship.

Divine manifestations: deities in and around the fort

Claims to sovereignty involving deities are not only found in the chronicles, but also as material manifestations including temples, such as the one of the tutelary goddess; small shrines, for example opposite the palace commemorating Mahabir as mythical figure; hills or caves as abodes of deities such as Ma Kant Debi; crossings (*tirtha*); or especially swords as divine yet mobile manifestations of Bonai. All are part of a symbolic web and sacred geography in the sense of 'a living, storied and intricately connected landscape' (Eck 2012: 2) intersecting with texts and ritual performances. The raja is intimately linked to most of these idols and properties as markers of sovereignty and reminders of power – either as heir, legal owner, and guardian, as in case of the temple of the tutelary goddess Ma Kumari, or also as President of Trusts that were established after merger, for example, the temples of Lord Baneshwar or Lord Jagannath, whose management is shared with state representatives like the Sub-Collector (thereby indicating another limit of the raja's power in post-colonial India). Significantly, these three previously mentioned temples also express an eclectic combination of Shaiva, Shakta, and Vaishnava traditions linked to the royal family.

The largest, wealthiest, and clearly one of the most important temples within the royal framework is the abode of Lord Baneshwar as manifestation of Lord Shiva, whose crucial role in the establishment of the realm and as Lord of the place (sthanpati) has been mentioned in the previous section. Within a curve of the river Brahmani, his temple and the fort are situated on opposite ends, with Lord Baneshwar's temple considered to be located in the wilderness. Periodical visits of the raja to Lord Baneshwar – during the investiture, but also on occasions such as Shivratri or Kartik Purnima, when his *linga* (icon) is elaborately decorated – could thus be understood as symbolic repetitions of the foundational migration process from settlement to wilderness, even though the spreading of the Bonaigarh town over the last decades is increasingly closing the gap. In line with the elevated position of the Bhuiyan community in the chronicles the Lord is served by Bhuiyan priests (*pujari*) with the head priest visiting the palace on a daily basis.

Within the divine configuration of Bonai, Vaishnava elements also appear prominently, yet of slightly lesser importance. According to royal chronicles, Lord Raghunath as the royal family's *ishta devta* (preferred deity) is present in the form of *salegram* stones, in fact discovered together with Kant Debi and included in various rituals, but not the main focus of the performances. Like Lord Raghunath, Lord Jagannath resides inside the fort and his rituals, especially the Rath Yatra (procession), are part of the ritual calendar with the raja performing the role of the Lord's first servant. Moreover, Lord Jagannath together with his wife, Goddess Lakshmi being manifested next to him, expresses ideas of sovereignty linked to Vaishnava traditions, that is, a king can only be king in a conjugal union in the same way as Jagannath can only be the supreme sovereign lord together with his wife (Marglin 1985: 181–182).[8] Yet, historically, the presence and public worship of Lord Jagannath seem to have been later additions rendered possible through the decline of Gajapati rule in eighteenth-century Odisha, with the emergence of Jagannath temples in 'jungle kingdoms' being understood as a symbolic declaration of relative autonomy or even independence vis-à-vis an overlord (Kulke (2001 [1976]: 82ff).

The most important divine tradition in and around the fort, at least with reference to state rituals like Dasara, is the Shakta (goddess) worship. As elsewhere in eastern India, the raja's tutelary goddess, Ma Kumari, is commonly associated with Durga (great goddess) and vice versa. This link is particularly stressed in a prayer (*janan*) in the royal chronicles (Pramanik and Skoda 2013: 38) dedicated to her, in which she is addressed as 'mother', 'Mahisamardini' (demon-slaying goddess), 'caretaker of the whole world', and 'caretaker of the fort' (a universal as well as very specific context of protection) or as 'tutelary deity of Bonai' and 'Durga of the forest', implicitly also linking the royal family to wilderness. Generally, the goddess appears to combine her role as the 'protectress of a site' located on the boundaries of a marked territory to fend off the enemy with her role as the 'protectress of a family' (Biardieu 1989 [1981]: 132). As a case in point, the tutelary deity's temple in Bonai is located at the outer fort, while Durga in other manifestations is also present inside the palace.

In fact, the chronicles mention legends of several goddesses whose temples or small shrines are visible in and around the fort and palace respectively and one encounters them in all directions: North > Ma Kumari; East > Chandi Debi; South > Ma Andhari; and West > Ma Basuli, who plays a major role during the spring festival (Cheitra Parba). All of these goddesses worshipped by the raja or Paudi Bhuiyans, for example during Dasara, belong to the Shakta traditions and are also found inside the palace as swords or as Naba Durga represented as bracelet(s) (*nabadurga kankana*) as well as in anthropomorphic form, that is, as small metal figures depicting the goddess with eight arms. They are considered as *chandi* type, that is, relatively fierce, potentially destructive, benevolent as well as malevolent mother goddesses, rather than as *shanti* type, that is, as relatively peaceful goddesses like Lakshmi. This local distinction chandi/shanti corresponds to widespread classifications of goddesses along the following indicators (Biardieu 1989 [1981]: 140; Michaels 1998: 247):

1) Sri/Lakshmi > wife > prosperity > pure > pacified > passive > mild > vegetarian
2) Durga > virgin/unmarried/childless > warrior > impure > violent > active > wild > non-vegetarian/blood sacrifices

Arguably the most prominent among them is the raja's tutelary goddess Ma Kumari, who is clearly feared by many, some locals also believe to have seen her frightening appearance at night. Yet, she is also approached as caring mother (*ma*) in times of droughts and outbreaks of contagious diseases like smallpox. Her 'terrible' side is described in her legend well known to the Pujaris and locals. It explains her peculiar idol (*murti*) being disfigured after an act of devouring a young boy – commonly related to the goddess' ambivalent position as 'childless mother' yearning for children. The chronicles state that Kumari Debi (i.e. Ma Kumari), as goddess of the fort (*gada debi*),

> takes care of the state's well-being. Once one sage [brahmachari] came here. At that time Bonai was full of dense forest and he stayed at Kumari Debi's place to worship her. He had a student [shishya] with him. He sent the student to fetch water from the river and he went to the village to beg for alms. After returning he saw that water was there but the student was not. The Brahmachari searched everywhere, but did not find the student. Then he saw a pair of footprints in front of the Goddess. He thought that the Goddess had eaten his student. Then he angrily threw the full plate with food offerings [jou] on the face of Kumari Debi and her face has been hidden ever since.
>
> *(adapted from Pramanik and Skoda 2013: 37)*

Other texts, though, indicate an appropriation of a Bhuiyan tradition. As Surendranath Mishra, a former Rajpurohit (royal priest) stated: 'Kumari is the goddess of Bhuyan pitha. She was the tutelary goddess of Samanta. The Kadamba clan established Kumari as the "Goda Chandi" (Chandi of the fort)' (adapted from Pramanik and Skoda 2013: 260). However, Ma Kumari has a special relation with the raja because, according to the royal family, he received Ma Kumari's blessings (*prasad*) in the form of the sword known as *kumari prasad*,[9] though it is not the only sword of the raja. As the chronicles state, Raja Pratap also

> brought one big sword named 'patkhanda' [pat = main, khanda = sword]. The said sword is worshipped at the time of Dasahara or at the time of the coronation ceremony of a new king. In the olden days many, many animal sacrifices and human sacrifices [nara bali] were given. The said sword is

> worshipped with the mantras of 'Bana Durga'. He also received mohana khanda by killing Mohana Kondh . . . and the Kumari prasad tarabari [tarabati = sword, scimitar] which are also worshipped.
>
> *(adapted from Pramanik and Skoda 2013: 37)*[10]

This multitude of swords documents their centrality in the construction of kingship in Bonai. First and foremost they refer to the goddess, and the worship of the Goddess Durga/tutelary goddess in the form of swords is practiced elsewhere in Odisha too (Schnepel 2002; Mallebrein 2004). They are manifestations of divine power publicly displayed during Dasara. In fact, earlier processions to the Dasara field appear as a re-enactment of a raja's initial empowerment, symbolically re-conquering his realm, while at the same time Durga's victory over the demon could be alluded to. In ancient scriptures on kingship the 'sword of state' is often included in the list of central paraphernalia representing royal sovereign authority (together with umbrella, throne, fly-whisks etc.) (Gonda 1956). Here, however, one encounters a combination of allochthonous and autochthonous swords: one (patkhanda) was brought from Rajputana and used to conquer and unite the kingdom, while another one (*mohana khanda*) is believed to have been taken from a tribal chief. While the motif of 'capturing' a potent idol from an enemy is relatively widespread in Odisha (see e.g. Schnepel 2002: 259), this situation also resembles Dasara in Bastar, where Gell (1997: 442) found a certain contradiction in the rituals depicting the goddess as both foreign and local, as well as the raja as both mediator with the outside world and 'vehicle of the goddess', here in the sense of carrying the sword. The combination of swords, central to the establishment of royal power and sovereignty, can be summarised in terms of origin, location or visibility in Table 4.1:[11]

TABLE 4.1 Swords in the fort

Swords	*Kumari Prasad*	*Patkhanda*	*Mohana Khanda*
Origin	from tutelary goddess (process unclear)	from outside the realm, brought by raja into new realm – 'conquering'	from inside the realm, captured by raja in new realm – 'conquered'
Location	inside the fort, but outside of the palace (armoury/temple)	inside the fort, but outside of the palace (armoury/temple)	inside the fort and inside the palace (innermost sphere)
Visibility	every day (representational needs)	once a year	once in a lifetime
Other	temple of Ma Kumari marking a border of the fort		men of royal lineage entitled to consume sacrificial meat on Dasara

With specific reference to the swords, but not exclusively to them, the Rajpurohit emphasised that Goddess Durga has a permanent seat or *pitha* inside the fort, stressing the localisation of the goddess, the sacredness of the place, and her literal grounding (on territoriality, see also Galey 1990). The idea of a divine seat in the fort distinguished the fort rituals, in the Rajpurohit's view, from those more recently established Durga Puja rituals in the market promoting her Bengali form. Instead, he linked the pitha inside the fort to other religious centres and a greater tradition by referring to the locally well known mythological story of Sati or generally the Goddess, that is, a pitha is believed to have come up wherever her body parts fell upon the earth (e.g. Kinsley 1987: 186).

Goddesses are not only present in and around the fort. In contrast to the aforementioned goddesses located in the fort or its relative vicinity, Goddess Kant Debi – also referred to as Kant Kumari or Kant Mahapru – stands out as the only visiting goddess otherwise not firmly located in Bonaigarh, but rather on the periphery of the kingdom. Appearing in the form of a small metallic snake with a cobra-like hood, she is carried by Paudi Bhuiyans to the fort. She too is considered by many to be a form of Durga and a sister of Ma Kumari. This sisterhood may hint at a possible, yet incomplete appropriation of the goddess, because, unlike other Odishan tutelary deities (Kulke 2001 [1984]), she has not moved from hills to the court, but rather has a sister there. An attempt to appropriate a goddess from the autochthonous population is also mentioned in the Rajpurohit's initial statement in this section saying that Ma Kumari used to be the tutelary goddess of the Samanto or raja's Bhuiyan ally in the foundational myth, but this is contested by the current Samanto.

However, a special link between raja, Bhuiyans and Goddess Kant Debi is explained in her legend in the royal chronicles (Pramanik and Skoda 2013: 39ff). Accordingly, the goddess is believed to have come from outside, that is, the neighbouring kingdom of Keonjhar, paralleling the king's entry. She is linked to hills where she and the Bhuiyan, specifically the Paudi Bhuiyans, reside; to the Pano community, which plays a marginal role in her rituals; to the tutelary *devta* in the form of salegram stones representing Vishnu; and to Durga in the form of a bracelet and other holy items. All of these powerful ritual objects were obtained by the raja through killing a visiting Babaji who did not offer them to the raja voluntarily and thereby earned his wrath. The mythical story states:

> After a few years the place where the Babaji was killed was turned into agricultural land and belonged to a person of Pana caste. One day when that Pana was ploughing the land, he could feel that an iron thing struck against his plough. He put it aside and continued ploughing. . . . Finally he could see that it was something like the iron part [sama] of a husking pedal [dhinki]. He thought of taking it home to use it in his husking pedal.
>
> *(adapted from Pramanik and Skoda 2013: 40)*

The story brings up the peculiar 'quaint shape' (Roy 1935: 105) of the goddess, basically 'a roundish fragment of some old metal object' (ibid.), and continues that a visiting money lender (Mahajan) recognises the value of the piece, but finally:

> The Pana . . . dreamed that he should give the sama to the King, otherwise his clan will be wiped out. That night the King also dreamed that whatever he sees in the morning, he should worship it. That night a Bhuiyan of Jala also dreamed that he should go to the King early in the morning and bring the sama from the Rajbati. . . . The Bhuiyan kept it in Jala. After some days again the King dreamed that it [the sama] will be worshipped as Kanta Debi. From that day onwards Kanta Debi is visible on the day of pratipada [the beginning of Dasara].
>
> *(adapted from Pramanik and Skoda 2013: 40)*

The narrative includes very obvious hints at fertility (ploughing as well as the *dhenki* or grinder indicating sexual intercourse) and at wealth (harvesting as well as the moneylender as an expert). Perhaps most importantly, a divine intervention through dreams pre-empts any potential conflict (moneylender, Pano, Bhuiyan, and raja) and, thus, resembles the foundation myth, but this time the goddess is instrumental.[12] She is presented as an allochthonous goddess and, like other goddesses in Kulke's (2001 [1984]: 117–118) developmental scheme of divinities in the former Garhjat states, her presence seems to have been revealed in mythical time without any specific raja being mentioned. However, unlike other states Kulke analysed, this goddess from the 'mountain tribe' did not become the raja's tutelary goddess, but rather his 'personal deity' as the late Rajasahib K.K.C. Deo argued. Thus, he contrasted her with Ma Kumari as the raja's 'chief goddess' or tutelary goddess. At the same time, both are considered as sisters: the latter marking the fort's boundary, while the former preferred to stay in the hills, that is, on the fringes or borders of the kingdom with the Paudi Bhuiyans. This close link between the two goddesses may well hint at royal attempts to appropriate a 'tribal' goddess and to claim sovereignty over the peripheral hills rather than the valley alone.

Their sisterhood as well as the multitude of deities broadly, for example Goddess Durga in the form of swords, however, also express ambivalent dichotomies of inside versus outside or settlement/centre/Ma Kumari versus wilderness/periphery/Kant Debi in the constructions of kingship mentioned earlier. The narratives in the chronicles and the divine manifestations as idols or temples augment and reinforce each other, that is, the myths elaborate on the sacred geography, while the presence of deities offers a tangibility and aura of facticity to the chronicles. Both in turn contribute to the tenacity of kingship. The deities and their abodes, for example the temple of Lord Baneshwar or the patkhanda sword, are key elements of the sacrificial polity and the central alliance with the Bhuiyans. Moreover, these divine manifestations, including the murtis of Ma Kumari or Kant Debi, that first and foremost empower the raja, as well as the narratives surrounding them, are all imbued with references to the power over life.

A sacrificial polity: dasara rituals remembered and performed

Dasara is arguably the most important ritual of kingship throughout India (Fuller 1992: 108), but in Bonai it is also a primary expression of a 'sacrificial polity'. Goddesses and raja are linked to communities or former subjects through offerings and services, while the mobile Bhuiyan Goddess Kant Debi, carried from the hills to the palace, articulates the royal realm in its entirety, spanning from the periphery to the centre. Starting in Bonaigarh, similar to Durga Pujas performed in Bengal or elsewhere, on the sixth day, *Sashti*, of the light fortnight of the month of Asvina and ending on the following full moon, *Kumar Puni*, Dasara entails a range of sacrifices and shows resemblances to other older orders or sacrificial polities such as in Bengal in which:

> Durga Puja aligns the symbols of legitimacy with its substance. The goddess possesses weapons and uses them to destroy those who upend the proper order of heavens. Durga Puja, with a role for dependents and graded responsibilities for various castes, physically assembles the prajas in ranked roles.
>
> *(Nicholas 2013: 176–177)*

Unlike Durga Puja in Bengal, however, Dasara (blood) sacrifices in Bonai include multiple goddesses, even though all are clearly associated with Goddess Durga. And while Durga's myth and victory are well known and alluded to, Dasara in Bonai is saturated with memories of and ideas around human sacrifices (*nara bali, manisha bali*) that indicate a power over life and death in a very elementary sense. Whether such sacrifices have ever been performed and actual violence has ever been exercised or whether they were rather symbolically performed and represent a 'spectral' violence (Hansen and Stepputat 2005: 11) remains an open question. However, these sacrifices perpetuated in the form of stories, (putative) memories, and especially rumours – perhaps the most potent and powerful element surrounding the alleged act (Bates 2006) – continue to inspire awe even decades after their acknowledged end, which intersects with and is reinforced by the often limited visibility of legitimising objects of worship such as patkhanda or mohana khanda.

Remembered rituals: human sacrifices

The power over life and death is brought to the fore not only in the sacred geography with the remarkable presence and multitude of swords, but also in narratives focusing on the annual Dasara rituals and their performance. Many rituals outlined later in this chapter include a public display of weapons and animal sacrifices as crucial elements of the Dasara performance, yet other rituals are or have been hidden from the general public. This secrecy surrounds particularly various forms of human sacrifices, symbolic or otherwise, which many elderly locals believe to have taken place in the not so distant past.[13] They have not been included in visualisations of Dasara such as in an extensive photo album commissioned in the 1930s. Local accounts about such rituals during Dasara differ in details, but many vividly remember their existence though they have probably never attended them and they seemingly became part of a local folklore. The secrecy, however, around some rituals stands in contradiction to the wide circulation of the stories and apparently adds an element of fear vis-à-vis the raja and his assumed power, an element in the constitution of authority in South Asia (see e.g. Price 2006). Invisibilising rituals was presumably also tied to the overlord's position, that is, the British strongly advocating an eradication of the practice as part of their civilising mission legitimising their rule (Bates 2006).

Moreover, implementing the 'Rules for the management of Gurjat Estates' in the mid-nineteenth century curtailed the raja's power over life and death severely by reserving the right to try murder, homicide, and so on for the British Superintendent as colonial overlord, making raja somewhat accountable.[14] Thus, this secrecy around such rituals also suggests a relatively limited sovereignty of the raja vis-à-vis the colonial power strongly disapproving them, of which local actors involved were clearly aware. At the same time the narratives presented in this chapter indicate that the policies to prevent such sacrifices were probably never fully implemented, the colonial power did not fully penetrate the local level, and the practice may well have continued (de facto) despite a stern ban (de jure). An avoidance of an open conflict over the performance or eradication of the sacrifices, through secrecy, nevertheless hints at the multiple sovereignties under colonial paramountcy.

In the following I will briefly summarise stories around two such rituals and alleged human sacrifices – both pointing to a raja's power over life and death embedded in a ritual Dasara context, before turning to the present-day Dasara celebrations, but also to the close connection between raja and Bhuiyans as well as other communities. The first ritual, supposed to have been performed on the day of Vijaydossomi until roughly 40 years ago, is also mentioned in the royal chronicles (making it less hidden than the second example). It involved the presence of the raja, his Rajpurohits, and other Brahmins as well as the Jagirdars and Zamindar. This ritual revolved around two ritual roles – namely Ankulia, usually belonging to the Kansari community, and Baktria from the Bhuiyan community. The families of both more or less hereditary roles are still identifiable and these titles are often explained as 'to begin' (Ankulia) and 'to protect' (Baktria), indicating an internal structure.[15] As the daughter of the supposedly last Baktria explained, both would sit in front of the king clad in yellow cloths with a yellow turban and a garland of hibiscus flowers, understood as symbols of an intended sacrifice. The royal priests would then bring the sword (patkhanda), which was held on the necks of both or possibly only the Ankulia. As the last Ankulia's self-identified brother-in-law described it:

> On the day of Dasara the Ankulia goes there [fort] by worshipping and uttering 'slokas' (religious verses) and as such he observes all the formalities of worship. He looks with his face in a broken looking mirror. That means, he represents the animal for the sacrifice. Only the sword is touched on his neck. Then the worship is done. After the worship is completed nobody is allowed to see his face. On the day of Dasara, he will proceed to the king's house by holding one battle axe in his hand. At that time nobody stands on his way. It was the king's order. If he finds anybody on his front then he will cut his head and kill him. So nobody stands before him. The people know this and become very, very careful and never go before him. Then the royal priest worships him in the king's house.
>
> *(Excerpt of interview conducted by the author, Bonai 2004)*

The sacrificial status of Ankulia and Baktria is clearly expressed as well as a fiction of death by immediately disappearing after the symbolic sacrifice offered to the goddess. In fact, the bansaboli, the chronicles of the royal family, also has a passage on the rituals mentioning the direction where Ankulia and Baktria shall head depending on the day of the week Dasara is celebrated, for example leaving in an eastern direction if the day is a Friday or Sunday. The chronicles also mention that both shall receive raw food and money from the headmen of the village where they shall stay temporarily and that both received land grants from the raja in lieu for this duty. Both families acknowledge the material benefit, but also stressed the drawback and potential danger of this 'work', that is, a potential childlessness in their families, resonating somewhat with the narrative around the idol of the raja's tutelary goddess taking or rather devouring a young boy. The previously mentioned Baktria's daughter argued in the same interview with her:

> Because of that fear [of childlessness or own death] nobody is doing that work. . . . Two persons have done that work. Out of the two one was a Kansari. His family has been finished and he has also died.

While the Ankulia's relative pointed out:

> Nobody has agreed to perform this duty. Because this is the work of animal sacrifice, so nobody agrees. But when a lot of land is given for this work, people have developed an interest to do this work. However, as he continued: Those who were doing this work their race was not continuing. Because the Goddess is there. The sword, which is kept in his [raja's] house, belongs to Goddess Durga.

This suggests not only a symbolic sacrifice of the Ankulia and possibly Baktria to the goddess, but also a perceived potential danger for the families' children, particularly sons, that is, the goddess is not being misled or 'fooled' by a symbolic sacrifice but rather devours both adults or their offspring at any time. The sacrificial 'victim', supposed to remain invisible before being allowed to return later, subsequently becomes, in the local perspective, a real victim after the invitation to the goddess. Significantly, this sacrifice and departure of Ankulia and Baktria on Vijaydossomi is scheduled immediately before the raja used to proceed to the Dasara field to watch the archery and other competitions, which seems to indicate that after the goddess has been properly worshipped and pleased, the raja is able to go on a procession with his main sword that culminates in a celebration of warrior skills and suggest an annual repetition of the initial conquest of the realm.

While the sacrificial victim is invisibilised in case of Ankulia and Baktria, another Dasara ritual people talk about occasionally takes the secrecy around it a step ahead by avoiding to articulate or verbalise any human sacrifice or even any symbolic substitute for it. Accordingly, hardly anything about it is mentioned in the chronicles. The late Raja K. K. C. Deo argued that the raja used to receive or should receive pumpkins (*kakharu*) as symbolic substitutes from three different functionaries: 1) from a Gond-Jagirdar, supposed to give it for the raja's tutelary deity Ma Kumari (handed over to the raja on Dasara, but sacrificed on Kumar Puni); 2) from Sola Pradhani as collective term for 16 Bhuiyan chiefs obliged to give a pumpkin on a day before Dasara for Goddess Kant Kumari; and 3) from the so-called Bandaria (sometimes pronounced as Bandiria also), a Paudi Bhuiyan offering a pumpkin wrapped in leaves intended probably for patkhanda and handed over to the raja before Dossomi day.

Focusing on the last of the three here, the Bandaria family is known in the area and the current head of family told the following on his family's customary duty:

> You know the Siali creeper, we tie the Siali leaf, then we keep some rice in a bamboo basket [tupa] and keep a small pumpkin [kumda – literally: stuff] to it, again we cover it with rice and it will grow into a big one, when we reach [the fort]. On the day, at night, 12 P.M/1A.M on Dasa [10th day]. Puja will be going on, at that time. There, I mean, Raja, Rani will be there, puja will be done there. Like the human blood, that blood is like that. On the day of Kant Kumari, 10th of Dasara, when the sword will fall, on that day we will reach. . . . We will say, Bandaria has come, then Raja will come out suddenly, we will do the Johar, we will give the stuff [kumda]. . . . That thing [kumda] you take, you sacrifice it at Kant Kumari. Sacrifice, at night . . . do the puja on long sword, very old sword, kill with royal sword, head will fall apart on this side and body on that side. Like this, before we were taking human being, human being. Nowadays we are no more getting this. On those days, when truth era was there, on Raja's

> period. We were giving children. Whatever we got, boy child or girl child. Previously old men were bringing and taking it.

Such a link between Bandaria and human sacrifices does not seem to be limited to Bonai alone, if British sources from the mid-nineteenth century are to be trusted, stating that

> [i]t was commonly believed that 'Budurreas' carried off to Keonjhar Garh [neighbouring kingdom of Bonai] such victims and offered in sacrifice by the Rajah. Head and heart are supposed to appease an offended deity.[16]

Yet, in contrast to it, the Bandaria's descendant remembers that three generations ago a shift occurred when the family was unable to provide a human being and a pumpkin was tested instead. Though the initial human sacrifice, if it had been given indeed, had been substituted, the idea of blood remained to play an important role showing parallels to the *rakta handi* or blood pot offered to Goddess Kant Debi nowadays (see the next quote). In fact, as the descendant recollects, the then raja threatened to kill the Bandaria if no blood came out from the pumpkin. However, in the presence of raja, rani, and Goddess Kant Debi, the pumpkin passed the test and was henceforth accepted.

While in case of Ankulia and Baktria the sacrificial victims and their families might be primarily endangered, the Bandaria also stressed that the raja and his family or even kingdom might face dire consequences if the offer to Kant Debi is not given – explaining the raja's insistence on the blood sacrifice. As he stated, Goddess Kant Debi would demand it or

> [o]therwise Raja will be on loss. His child, daughter will not be there. They will die . . . [if the sacrifice is not given] something wrong will happen, something serious will happen, she will come to Raja in the dream 'why are you not giving, if you will not give something will happen.'

That means empowering the raja and blessing him with a sword goes hand in hand with obligations to provide such offerings.

Versions of these narratives vary in detail though. Some locals believe members of the royal family were involved in the transactions as middle men, the offering was actually made to mohana khanda and not Kant Debi, or they believe that the pumpkin used to be given the shape of a human being by fixing small sticks to it. Others argue that the practice of snatching or kidnapping children – the Bandaria's family also mentioned the stealing from the neighbouring state of Keonjhar close to their village – has been discontinued since the 1920s. However, most accounts agree on the secrecy, that is, the pumpkin and/or child was constantly referred to as 'stuff' or simply 'it', while a more precise and possible description as human sacrifice (*manisha bali*) was clearly avoided. Instead, as the late Raja K. K. C. Deo remembered, the raja would just ask the Bandiria: 'Did you bring it?' and the Bandiria might simply reply 'Take it'. The raja would usually not touch it but rather pass it on, also indicating the secrecy and sensitivity of the matter of human sacrifice or even its substitutes.

Being equally aware of it, during an interview the Bandaria, suspecting that I had other than purely scholarly motives, was worried that it might be misunderstood as a contemporary practice. Getting agitated, he proclaimed: 'If I will take a child and it is known by village people, they will cut my head, they will take my life', clearly aware that he may face severe consequences threatening his life, though he might no longer be punished by the raja. In fact, asked about his relation to the raja nowadays, the Bandaria, whose family no longer provides 'stuff' for (symbolic) human sacrifices on Dasara, complained that nowadays the raja

> gives me only one piece of dhoti, money 20 rupees, rice 5 kg and gives some onion. They [raja] didn't give my wages, so I stopped giving. [He also argued that after his father's death the] raja came in a car: 'You have not gone, you will go, otherwise, our puja, we are getting mad', raja told like this. [Bandaria answered] 'Yes Sir, I will go, this year I am in sorrow, one of my brother is no more, I am alone'.

Thus, he cited economic and financial reasons, the raja's limited funds – a shoestring budget for Dasara - for discontinuing a customary sacrificial connection. Claims to sovereignty, constituted in the royal chronicles, linked to divine manifestations and expressed first and foremost in ritual performance of kingship clearly require a certain spending power and a reduction for whatever reason, for example the abolition of the privy purses, affects the sacrificial polity. Even without Bandaria, a wide range of rituals are performed including blood sacrifices with the accompanying weapons to kill, but also a dialogue between raja and Paudi Bhuiyans on the kingdom's affairs, renewing this crucial axis; yet, this enactment of the sacrificial polity may be questioned as not convincing.

Dasara rituals performed

Thanks to the late Rajasahib, who meticulously listed all budget details for example for 2007, there is a clear picture of Dasara exchanges with members of various communities of the sacrificial polity. The central protagonists include 1) the Brahmin rajpurohit, 2) the Paudi Bhuiyan ritual specialist in charge of Kant Debi known as Dehuri, and 3) the non-Brahmin priest or Amat belonging to the Sud community. All of them receive *dasturi*, considered a remuneration for a customary service rendered, but are also entitled to sacrificial meat.[17] Khati, Barik, and Behera supplement their roles and are given dasturi for their more specific roles. For example, the Khati belonging to the Maharona community washes and sharpens the royal swords, while the Barik from the Keunt community is in charge of blood sacrifices, especially he-goats.[18] The Behera belonging to the Hansi community, also known as weavers, prepares an umbrella (*suti chatra*), as symbol of divine (or royal) status, protection, and sovereignty, presented to Ma Kumari.[19] In the pre-merger order all of the previously mentioned families and communities involved in this way had received land in lieu for their services and many continue this tradition with a sense of duty and a certain pride of their somewhat exalted position under the old order, that is, 'that they were somebodies in the past; that the power structure . . . included them' (Samaddar 1998: 31).[20] It appears to be coupled with a genuine devotion to the goddess and to the royal family, which does not exclude simultaneous complaints and frustrations about a miserly performance of rituals by the raja.

In other cases this ritual link has been broken. For example, pots are no longer purchased from a specific Kumbar (potter) family, but in the market. The breaking of such relationships shows a lack of authority on the part of the raja to enforce a participation of communities. In this context it is also noteworthy that frequently an idea is voiced that only a proper performance of rituals involving all customary offerings as well as actors ensures the kingdom's prosperity. This resonates with occasionally expressed opinions that the decline of kingship is directly linked to reduced rituals, instead of linking it primarily to political changes. A deficient performance is often considered as causally responsible for the current situation of perceived decline. A raja's being unable to maintain customary performances or to spend more on them or any performance of kingship and power not being backed up by a certain wealth is hardly convincing (Inayatullah 1996).

However, after other rituals, like the Dasara procession in Bonaigarh itself, have been discontinued, arguably the most important part of Dasara nowadays is related to Goddess Kant Debi and her annual journey from her abode in the hills to the fort and back, covering a full fortnight.[21] This increasingly popular procession of Goddess Kant Debi, carried by the Paudi Bhuiyans to the palace, might have partially also compensated for the abolition of the Dasara procession in town. Its route is customarily drafted by the raja (and his lawyer) and carried by the Dehuri as raja's order, actually a sheet of paper with his royal crest. Apart from attracting the largest audiences and connecting various parts of the former kingdom, hills and plains, or periphery and centre, this journey expresses the special relation between raja and Bhuiyans in a very direct way. On Astami the raja (or his representative) meets the Paudi Bhuiyans just outside the fort to receive the Goddess Kant Debi. This ritual is known as *kant bhet* or 'meeting Goddess Kant'. In the royal chronicles this meeting is presented in the following way:

> Then the goddess comes along with her seat . . . [to] . . . a place named Kantajodi [where] a ritual on a special platform is done for Kanta Debi. Then the Raja Saheb goes with his watchmen drumming the dhol and playing the muhuri to bring Kanta Debi. The Bhuiyan leaves Kanta Debi thinking that the King is coming to kill him. Then Raja asks his followers to search for the Bhuiyan to call him back, but he does not come. Then

> Raja does not wait for him, but takes Kumari Debi and hands her over to his priest [*pujari*] named as Amat. This is called kanta bhet. After finishing the Debi Puja at 12 midnight she meets Kumari Debi and stays with her like a sister in the armoury [*khanda ghar*] in a bowl filled with blood [*rakta handi*].

The chronicles highlight the sisterhood with the raja's tutelary goddess and generally seem to assert the raja's power vis-à-vis the Bhuiyans who run away worried about the raja's intention, providing yet another hint at the power to kill.[22] However, this picture is contradicted by the fact that the Bhuiyans and their chief commanded a significant number of Paiks (peasant-warriors) and were considered a force to reckon with. In fact, there is evidence for occasional Bhuiyan resistance against rajas in the nineteenth century, whenever they tried, for example, to push through land settlements. Thus, the text might have been a creative rendering of the story by a Brahmanical writer in order to downplay the Bhuiyan influence. Or it might indicate a certain shift in their relation in the twentieth century when, under colonial paramountcy, the power balance appears to have tilted towards the raja.

In contrast to that, nowadays the raja often has to wait for the Paudi Bhuiyans in order to receive the goddess. In 2007 the Raja became furious about it and scolded them later on in my presence, though he also shared drinks with them a little later and half-jokingly pointed out that he was the '*bad Bhuiyan*' or 'great Bhuiyan'. However, such delays, so is the impression conveyed, would not have happened earlier and indicate the growing popularity of the goddess' procession with more rituals along the way, but possibly also changing equations between raja and Paudi Bhuiyans after the abolition of kingship. The raja's relative loss of power, which is also expressed by the fact that occasionally and especially during elections he appeals to the Adibasi for their support, might have also contributed to the continuity of those ritual elements within Dasara like kant bhet that highlight mutual care. However, first, the Paudi Bhuiyan Dehuri enquires about the well-being of the raja and his kingdom. The raja answers positively, and only afterwards is the goddess handed over to him, who in turn offers a new silver umbrella, which is attached to her idol (murti). The ritualised dialogue has been documented by Roy (1935: 109–110) for the 1930s, noting:

> The Dihuri . . . comes up to the Raja with the image, salutes him, and enquires of him about the health and welfare, first of himself, then of his Rani, then of his children, then of his servants, then of his elephants, then of his horses, and last of all about the welfare of the land (Prithvi or Earth). The Raja answers 'yes' to every question; and then in his turn, the Raja asks the Dihuri about the welfare of himself and his children and then of the Pauris generally; and to every question the Dihuri replies in the affirmative.

In this form, very close to the contemporary situation, the dialogue seems even more balanced and expresses reciprocal concern for each other, though the raja takes precedence. It is also underlined in Roy's account by the following sequence:

> While the Dihuri hands over the image to the Raja, he addresses the Raja, saying – 'Here is your deity (Deota); we kept it in the hills. Examine and see if the image is broken or intact',
>
> *(ibid.: 110)*

In any case, on receiving the goddess from the Bhuiyans as an initial climax, the raja passes her on to the Amat, who is in charge of Kant Debi in Bonaigarh, but also of Ma Kumari.[23] He worships her and subsequently takes her to her sister, Ma Kumari. This get-together of the sisters remains invisible to the public and even the Amat leaves the temple for a while in order to let the sisters do their 'talking', as he explained. This ritual performance takes place in Ma Kumari's temple and corresponds to statements in the chronicles, though the performance differs slightly from the text, stating that: 'After finishing the Debi Puja at 12 midnight she meets Kumari Debi and stays with her like a sister in the armoury in a bowl filled with blood (rakta handi).'

In contemporary Bonaigarh the *rakta handi* is only present in the rituals on the ninth day, when the Goddess proceeds towards the palace, while being worshipped on certain platforms (*mandal*) to which the public flock in order to take darsan and to offer sacrifices. The goddess is brought to the durbar hall (formerly to the armoury), where she is placed in a rice pot (*handi*) filled with rice (*chaul*) right between the two swords, patkhanda and kumari prasad, already installed there. It is widely believed that this pot used to be filled with blood (*rakta*) in former times – even from human sacrifices as some locals believe, that is (symbolically) linking raja, goddess and the power over life and death. Once the goddess has arrived, the raja takes darsan first of Kant Debi and patkhanda/kumari prasad, and then of Durga/Nabadurga. Finally, he carries goddess Kant Debi into the inner part of the palace, where she is worshipped by the Amat at an altar (*bedi*). He places the goddess in another pot filled with *mahuli* wine, which is later distributed as *bad bhog* (grand offering) among the public that has gathered on the occasion. The Parida community used to produce the alcohol on this occasion, but no longer perform this duty considered as degrading, contributing to a disintegration of the sacrificial polity.

However, after the palace rituals the goddess continues her procession and is finally handed over to the Paudi Bhuiyans. Before the Paudi Bhuiyans cross the river to return to the hills a special cake (*chakuli*) made of bitter neem leaves expressing the bitterness of farewell. It should be offered by a representative of the low-status, 'untouchable' Patro community, whose title is linked to the Pano community mentioned in the chronicles previously quoted to have yet another link between text, location, and performance. Similarly, after the Bhuiyans have left Bonai, the Rajpurohit assists the raja to perform dasara *puja* on the veranda of the former Rajmahal, that is, the patkhanda is held by the raja and moved (*buliba*) in all directions as a symbolic renewal of the kingdom's conquest.

Towards a conclusion

The sad condition of palace buildings including a durbar hall housing many deities during Dasara visibly hints at a decline of kingship. At the same time, new competing rituals, for example, performed as mammoth flag-hoisting ceremonies by the Indian nation-state or coming up as Bengali-styled Durga Puja in the market of Bonaigarh erode or undermine the raja's ritual sovereignty. Both indicate new entanglements between companies and the Indian nation-state that offer novel or grander spectacles and attract large audiences. Especially, Durga Puja, run by an ostensibly more democratic committee, rather than a raja, is generously funded by owners of mines and sponge iron factories. Aware of the fact that the old royal order has changed substantially with the arrival of new powerholders, fellow villagers discouraged the Bandaria to continue with his family tradition of providing 'stuff' for symbolic human sacrifices to the raja. 'Those days are no more', they said, a quote that suggests the realisation of a break-up of a supposedly age-old relationship and the disintegration of the sacrificial polity around the raja, challenged by the emergence of new ritual centres. The quote also refers to a broader detachment between raja and praja (subjects). Yet, the Bandaria very well remembers the earlier rituals as well as the prominent role of his family in them. The secrecy around these rituals inspired and still inspires great awe. He embodies these memories and even agreed to the raja's wish of joining again – without, however, doing anything afterwards.

At the same time, temples such as the raja's tutelary goddess temple have recently been beautified, texts are copied and re-written and, perhaps most importantly, other communities do continue to provide their services despite a rather nominal remuneration. First and foremost, the alliance between raja and Paudi Bhuiyans continues to flourish with reference to Kant Debi. Even 70 years after the formal abolition of kingship, the goddess is still brought annually from her abode in the hills and handed over to the raja, a public procession that might have helped to compensate the end of the older Dasara pageant. Going by the increasingly longer duration of the goddess' procession, more and more locals flock to the Bhuiyan goddess, eager to have a darsan and to get her blessings. In this way, many people are included in a fort-centric sacrificial polity that revolves around the worship of royal swords considered as divine manifestations within a storied sacred geography. However, many locals may actually attend both, Dasara and Durga Puja in the market, and the efficacy of the respective idols might be contested.

Though, the close relationship to the Bhuiyans, expressed especially through Kant Debi as sister of the raja's tutelary goddess, is keenly guarded by the raja as something concerning only him and them, that is, without any role for the Indian state, though he does share the responsibility to manage other temples with its representatives. The Dasara rituals renewing this bond go back to the mythical events described in the chronicles that highlight the pivotal role of Bhuiyans in the foundational killings establishing the realm for a 'stranger king'. Though the form, that is, the handing over of the goddess from Bhuiyans to raja, has apparently hardly changed at least since the 1930s, the raja–Paudi Bhuiyan axis and the concurrent expression of mutual care appears meaningful in new ways in the wake of mining projects. For example, in addition to existing mines the Odishan Government supported a new mine planned by the South Korean steelmaker POSCO in proximity to the goddess' abode and Bhuiyan settlements. This threat, including a fear of potential violence, as occurred while implementing similar projects elsewhere in Odisha (Kalinganagar, Kashipur), loomed large over the area until the project was finally shelved in 2017. It brought raja and Bhuiyans (and others) together as protesters, for example when the late Bonai Raja K. K. C. Deo appeared publicly during rallies, but it also showed that the power over life was concentrated in the hand of the Indian state.

In the Paudi Bhuiyan view this anti-mining protest was often framed in terms of what will happen to the goddess when her abode is affected. In 2008 it was poignantly summarised in an NGO report based on discussions with villagers in the area arguing that:

> [t]he forest and stream of Khandadhar has an immense religious and cultural significance for people of Bonai and adjoining area. The Khandadhar Hills are the abode of 'Maa Kanteswari Devi' [Kant Debi's Sanskritised name – the author], the chariest goddess of local people and deity of Paudi Bhuyans. She comes out of her cave on invitation of Bonaigarh's King in the month of Dushera to give blessing to its worshipers. . . . There is a strong feeling among the local people that any destruction to her temple or the habitat of wild animals and home land of Paudi Bhuyans would create catastrophe in the region.[24]

The report stressed the hills' sacredness with reference to Dasara rituals and pointed at the close relation between raja and Bhuiyans. Thus, mining actually consolidated their alliance, because it exposed the Bhuiyans' vulnerable position, but potentially also the raja's. His royal sovereignty would be even more questioned and overshadowed by the industrialists' increasing money power. Their companies such as Jindal Steel and Power have already begun to substantially 'develop' the 'wilderness', the land of the Bhuiyans as well as wild animals as described in the previous quote. Thus, new powerholders from outside started to curb the raja's potential to symbolically oscillate between 'settled life' and 'wild wastes' and, in fact, to usurp the raja's initial role of transforming the jungle into a realm as described in the royal chronicles, while, ironically, they produce a new kind of ecological 'wasteland' through mining.

However, the privileged link between raja and Bhuiyans clearly goes beyond Dasara rituals. It is also mobilised during election campaigns, as when the late Raja used to allude to deities or the foundational myth stating sentences like 'your ancestors have chosen my ancestors'. But it is clearly grounded in a sacrificial polity and conceptualised with reference to royal sovereignty, which co-exists and competes, also historically, somewhat uneasily with other claims to authority. It is constituted through and embedded in a complex and intertextual linkage of chronicles, divine manifestations, and especially ritual performances, and its combination contributes to its tenacity of royal sovereignty. Yet, while the alliance and several ties with communities, often mediated through deities, continue to be remembered and performed, the raja's power over life and death, in terms of threats and violence has become rather spectral than actual after the merger of the kingdom.

Notes

1 The chapter is based on long-term, yet discontinuous field research since 2003 with the longest periods in 2003–2004 and 2007–2008. The details and observations on Dasara rituals are also abstracted from visits over several years, but refer particularly to 2007 and 2016.

2 http://orissadiary.com/100-feet-high-monumental-flagpole-bonai/ (Accessed March 3, 2018). Being set up in a park named after Biju Patnaik brings in an additional regional political element.

3 It is noteworthy that there is no Odia term directly equivalent to sovereignty in Bonai, that is, locals faced difficulties to translate sovereignty into Odia.

4 In his comparative analysis of Orissan chronicles Kulke (2001 [1987]b: 162–163) distinguishes between three phases the texts usually contain: 1. a mythical 'prehistory' of former ages; 2. a 'proto-history' of legendary dynasties; and 3. a historical period with reliable fact. The first two seems to have merged here.

5 There are other orally transmitted versions, in which the ancestors were not killed, but put behind bars in Puri. As the late Bonai Raja narrated once, while the ancestors were in jail an elephant, royal symbol par excellence, went mad and nobody was able to control him. Only the brave brothers offered their support and managed to catch the wild elephant, which can be construed as a direct challenge to the authority of a centre and specifically the overlord as Gajapati, that is, as 'Lord of the elephants'. It presents a significant inversion when the overlord is apparently powerless and saved by the supposedly lower subjects, yet heroic warriors.

6 Probably 'Lord of the Soil' derived from *mati* = soil, indicating that the Samanto was the original owner of the place or that he is giving a tika of soil/*mati* during the coronation ceremony.

7 However, as the late Raja K. K. C. Deo stressed, the fact that the Saont is the only person for whom the Raja would get up from his chair when the Saont would arrive shows that this position is not simply lower.

8 Referring to royal temple rituals in Puri, Marglin (1985: 182) argues that in the union with her husband, Lord Jagannath, Lakshmi becomes a 'source of sovereignty'. Lakshmi represents auspiciousness – together with hierarchy 'indispensable ingredients of *sovereignty*' (ibid.: 183). The story of Lakshmi showing her power to her husband is also part of the royal chronicles of Bonai.

9 It remains nebulous how exactly the Raja received it.

10 The text mentions another sword named kalapat khanda which is linked to the Samanto's place, Kaleiposh. This reference might also hint at a takeover similar to mohana khanda, but it does not play any prominent role in any ritual and is therefore neglected here.

11 Significantly, the captured and prized mohana khanda sword is kept inside the palace premises, while the other two (patkhanda and kumari prasad) used to be kept in the armoury (*khanda ghar*; nowadays in the Jagannath temple). There are also degrees of visibility, that is, the only occasion for a public darsan (sight) of mohana khanda is the investiture of every new Raja. Moreover, the he-goat sacrificed for mohana khanda during Dasara is consumed only by the men of the royal lineage, that is, processes of exclusion also overlap with gender separations pointing at the link between sword and masculinity.

12 The order of the actions also seems to be important, that is, the goddess is first brought to the raja and afterwards to the Bhuiyans, contesting a Paudi Bhuiyan view that the goddess is their mother.

13 Some similar rituals are still performed during Cheitra Parba, but I will focus here only on Dasara.

14 Vol. I, Old Records Singhbhum, 1833–1854, p. 51.

15 There are various explanations for the term. Some derive the name from *ankul* as auspicious beginning, while others derive it from *an* = without and *kulia* from *kul* = caste and thus explain that the Ankulia was considered as outside the caste system.

16 Singhbhum, Old Records Vol. VII, 1856–1857, p. 281.

17 Especially Dehuri and Amat have additional economic/financial incentives in the sense of receiving the valuable heads of the sacrificed he-goats which are usually sold later on. Without going into the details of all ritual steps here, it is significant that the largest part of the expenses is spent on sacrificial goats accounting for almost half of the budget, as compared to the rather nominal amounts spent on dasturi. Amat, Kant Dehuri and Rajpurohit claim bodies of he-goats as an entitlement. Significantly, the Kant Dehuri also offers heads of he-goats to the raja. The Dehuri is otherwise entitled to keep all heads of he-goats sacrificed for Kant Debi, while their bodies are returned to persons making such public offering. However, passing some of these heads on to the raja, the Dehuri engages in an exchange with him, that is, the Paudi Bhuiyans and their Dehuri receive the body of a he-goat sacrificed by the raja and offer heads of he-goats to the raja later on. Additionally, the raja distributes sacrificial meat at will, primarily to close and favoured friends or servants, but one he-goat sacrificed for mohana khanda is prepared jointly and exclusively consumed by the *biradri*, the male members of the royal family (clan) entitled to it. Thus, meat – often more valuable than the dasturi payments – plays a crucial role in maintaining connections between raja and Bhuiyans, raja and his clan and other ritual specialists who all engage in exchanges to maintain and renew relations during Dasara, however reduced they are nowadays compared to previous or only imagined good old days of the sacrificial polity.

18 Buffalos, in other parts of Odisha often considered as substitutes for human sacrifices, might have been sacrificed earlier, as some people argue.

19 Though his remuneration was not listed as dasturi, the Raja called it dasturi during conversations and explained that it would be handed over prior to the full moon.

20 Samaddar describes how authors of royal chronicles written after the end of the ancient regime are driven by a certain melancholy as well as by a conscious attempt to tell others about their former glory.

21 On the second day of the fortnight (*dwitya*), a group of Paudi Bhuiyans starts a procession from her abode in the hills moving clockwise to the plains and returning on the final day of this fortnight (full moon). The route itself, including overnight stays in the houses of various headmen (Naik) and a Jagirdar of the Gond community (also Roy 1935: 107), connects various Adibasi and non-Adibasi communities.

22 Interestingly the name of the goddess has also been changed from Kanta Debi to Kumari Debi (the tutelary goddess) in the latter part of the text after handing her over, which possibly hints at an attempted act of appropriation of the goddess discussed earlier.

23 The Amat's family presumably took over this duty from Bhuiyans generations ago which also indicates that the Bhuiyans played a crucial role in the kingdom (see Roy 1935: 117).

24 Final Report on National Workshop on Underlying Causes of Deforestation and Forest Degradation in India, 2008, Global Forest Coalition – http://vh-gfc.dpi.nl/img/

userpics/File/UnderlyingCauses/India-Report-Underlying-Causes-Workshop.pdf (Accessed August 17, 2015).

References

Agamben, Giorgio. 1998 [1995]. *Homo Sacer: Sovereign Power and Bare Life*. Stanford: Stanford University Press.

Bates, Crispin. 2006. 'Human Sacrifice in Colonial Central India: Myth, Agency, and Representation', in Bates (ed.), *Beyond Representation: Colonial and Postcolonial Constructions of Indian Identity*, pp. 19–54. New Delhi: Oxford University Press.

Berkemer, Georg. 1993. *Little kingdoms in Kalinga. Ideologie, Legitimation und Politik regionaler Eliten. Beiträge zur Südasienforschung*, 156. Stuttgart: Steiner.

Biardieu, Madeleine. 1989 [1981]. *Hinduism: The Anthropology of a Civilization*. Delhi: Oxford University Press.

Biersteker, Thomas J., and Cynthia Weber. 1996. 'The Social Construction of State Sovereignty', in Thomas J. Biersteker and Cynthia Weber (eds.), *State Sovereignty as Social Construct*, pp. 1–21. Cambridge: Cambridge University Press.

Cohn, Berhard S. 2001 [1962]. 'Political Systems in Eighteenth-Century India: The Banares Region', in Berhard S. Cohn, *An Anthropologist Among the Historians and Other Essays*, pp. 483–499. New Delhi: Oxford University Press.

Dalton, Edward Tuite. 1865. 'Notes of a Tour Made in 1863–64 in the Tributary Mehals Under the Commissioner of Chota-Nagpore, Bonai, Gangbore, Odeypore and Sirgooja', *Journal of the Asiatic Society of Bengal*, 34 (2): 1–31.

Dash, Kailash C. 1997. *Legend, History and Culture of India*. Calcutta: Punthi-Pustak.

Eck, Diana L. 2012. *India: A Sacred Geography*. New York: Harmony Books.

Falk, Nancy E. 1973. 'Wilderness and Kingship in Ancient South Asia', in *History of Religions*, 3 (1): 1–15.

Fuller, Chris J. 1992. *The Camphor Flame: Popular Hinduism and Society in India*. Princeton: Princeton University Press.

Galey, Jean-Claude. 1990. 'Reconsidering Kingship in India: An Ethnological Perspective', in J.-C. Galey (ed.), *Kingship and the Kings*, pp. 123–188. Chur: Harwood Academic Publishers.

Gell, Alfred. 1997. 'Exalting the King and Obstructing the State: A Political Interpretation of Royal Ritual in Bastar District, Central India', *The Journal of the Royal Anthropological Institute*, 3 (3): 433–450.

Gonda, Jan. 1956. 'Ancient Indian Kingship from the Religious Point of View (Continued)', *Numen*, 3 (2): 122–155.

Hansen, Thomas Blom, and Finn Stepputat. 2005. 'Introduction', in Thomas Blom Hansen and Finn Stepputat (eds.), *Sovereign Bodies Citizens, Migrants, and States in the Postcolonial World*, pp. 1–36. Princeton: Princeton University Press.

Hansen, Thomas Blom and Finn Stepputat. 2006. 'Sovereignty Revisited', *Annual Review of Anthropology*, 35: 295–315.

Heesterman, Jan C. 1985. 'Two Types of Spatial Boundaries', in E. Cohen, M. Lissak, and U. Almagor (eds.), *Comparative Social Dynamics*, pp. 59–72. Boulder: Westview Press.

Inayatullah, Naeem. 1996. 'Beyond the Sovereignty Dilemma: Quasi-states as Social Constructs', in Thomas J. Biersteker and Cynthia Weber (eds.), *State Sovereignty as Social Construct*, pp. 50–80. Cambridge: Cambridge University Press.

Kinsley, David. 1987. *Hindu Goddesses: Vision of the Divine Feminine in the Hindu Religious Tradition*. New Delhi: Motilal Banarsidass.

Kulke, Hermann. 2001 [1976]. 'Ksatriyaization and Social Change: A Study in the Orissan Setting', in Kulke, *Kings and Cults: State Formation and Legitimation in India and South East Asia*, pp. 82–92. New Delhi: Manohar.

Kulke, Hermann. 2001 [1984]. 'Tribal Deities at Princely Courts: The Feudatory Rājās of Central Orissa and Their Tutelary Deities (istadevatās)', in Kulke, *Kings and Cults*, pp. 114–136. New Delhi: Manohar.

Mallebrein, C. 2004. Entering the Realm of Durga: Patkhanda, a Hinduized Tribal Deity. in A. Malinar, H. Frese, and J. Beltz (eds.), *Text and Context in Orissa and Beyond*, pp. 273–305. New Delhi: Manohar.

Marglin, Frederique Apffel. 1985. *Wives of the God-King: The Rituals of the Devadasis of Puri*. New Delhi: Oxford University Press.

Michaels, Axel. 1998. *Der Hinduismus: Geschichte und Gegenwart*. Muenchen: Beck.

Nicholas, Ralph W. 2013. *Night of the Gods: Durga Puja and the Legitimation of Power in Rural Bengal*. New Delhi: Orient Blackswan.

Platenkamp, Jos D. M. 2013. 'Sovereignty in the North Molukkas: Historical Transformations', *History and Anthropology*, 24 (2): 206–232.

Prager, Michael. 2010. 'The Appropriation of the "Stranger King": Polarity and Mediation in the Dynastic Myth of Bima', in P. Berger (ed.), *The Anthropology of Values: Essays in Honour of Georg Pfeffer*, pp. 447–470. New Delhi: Pearson.

Pramanik, Rashmi, and Uwe Skoda. 2013. *Chronicles of the Royal Family of Bonai (Odisha)*. New Delhi: Manohar.

Price, Pamela. 2006. 'Changing Meanings of Authority in Contemporary Rural India', *Qualitative Sociology*, 29: 301–316.

Roy, Sarat C. 1935. *The Hill Bhuiyas of Orissa*. Ranchi: 'Man in India' Office.

Roy Chaudhury, P. C. 1958. *Singhbhum Old Records*. Patna: Superintendent Secretariat Press.

Sahlins, Marshal. 1992 [1985]. *Inseln der Geschichte*. Hamburg: Junius.

Sahlins, Marshall. 2008. 'The Stranger-King or, Elementary Forms of Political Life', *Indonesia and the Malay World*, 36 (105): 177–199.

Samaddar, Ranabir. 1998. *Memory, Identity, Power: Politics in the Jungle Mahals 1890–1950*. Chennai: Orient Longman.

Schnepel, Burkhard. 2002. *The Jungle Kings: Ethnohistorical Aspects of Politics and Ritual in Orissa*. New Delhi: Manohar.

Singh, Bhrigupati. 2012. 'The Headless Horseman of Central India: Sovereignty at Varying Thresholds of Life', *Cultural Anthropology*, 27 (3): 383–407.

Skoda, Uwe. 2012. 'Texts, Centres and Authorities: The History of the Royal Family of Bonai', in M. Carrin and L. Guzy (eds.), *Voices from the Periphery: Subalternity and Empowerment in India*, pp. 103–131. New Delhi: Routledge.

Stein, Burton. 1977. 'The Segmentary State in South Indian History', in R. J. Fox (ed.), *Realm and Region in Traditional India*, pp. 3–51. Durham: Duke University Press.

Wink, André. 1984. 'Sovereignty and Universal Dominion in South Asia', *The Indian Social and Economic History Review*, 21 (3): 265–292.

5

DYNASTIC CONTINUITY AND ELECTION IN CONTEMPORARY KARNATAKA POLITICS

Caleb Simmons

In December 2013, the titular Mahārāja of Mysore Śrīkaṇṭhadatta Narasiṃharāja Woḍeyar (1953–2013) passed away as a result of heart failure just days after a successful electoral campaign to be the president of the Karnataka State Cricket Association, a position that brings immense benefits, including the potential of financial gains and boundless prestige. This election had not been the first for the erstwhile Mahārāja. Woḍeyar had entered into politics in the 1980s continuing into the 2000s, running campaigns for a Lok Sabha seat in Indian Parliament six times and successfully winning the seat four times (1984, 1989, 1996, and 1999). In national political history, however, Woḍeyar's political abilities – unlike many of his Woḍeyar predecessors – are largely overlooked or dismissed as ineffectual, at best, or inept, at worst. Renowned Mysore intellectual and professor of History at Karnataka State Open University, Prithvi Chandra Sobhi, summarises this sentiment in his obituary for the newspaper *Indian Express* titled 'Mysore's "last prince" Wodeyar inherited love, loyalty, and great fortune: The legacy of Srikantadatta Wodeyar, who died Tuesday, is not as immense though':

> Despite his considerable electoral success, he rarely made an impact on politics either in Karnataka or in Delhi. . . . Wodeyar's inheritance was immense. His legacy isn't. His royal counterparts from northern Indian states have had greater success both in politics and especially in business. Such success may have eluded him but in Mysore he remained a simple, decent but significant presence, especially during the annual Dasara celebrations. Even though the state government organized the event, he still had a significant ritual role to perform. Despite occasional tension with the new representatives of democratic Mysore, the old prince took care of his responsibilities. He will be remembered primarily for that.
>
> *(Chandra Shobhi 2013)*

This presentation of the Mahārāja's legacy, of course, seems to directly contradict his electoral history, including the results of the KSCA election, and his place in the minds and memory of his constituents. Perhaps the most representative display of his standing in the popular imagination of the region was the overwhelming outpouring of love and grief that accompanied the Mahārāja's death. As the news broke in Mysore, disbelief turned to mourning as shops throughout the city immediately and voluntarily shut their doors for anywhere between two to 12 days. The next morning the government of the state of Karnataka declared a two-day mourning period in which government offices were to be closed, and people from all over Karnataka descended on the Palace City to pay their respects to the royal family and view the body's procession to Madhuvana, the royal family's cremation ground. Within a week, there were even protests demanding that the Deputy Commissioner's Office commission a statue of the late Woḍeyar to be erected in the centre of the busy roundabout at Hardinge Circle (Anon 2016: 7).[1]

The immediate response to the Mahārāja's death from local media was decidedly different than the national obituaries referred to previously. The local Kannada newspapers announced Woḍeyar's death not in terms of his political acumen or his successes and failures in business, but they placed the king and his demise within a much broader conception of political history and mythic time. The headlines of the Kannada daily newspapers for December 11, 2013 perhaps best summarised the region's outlook on the death of the heirless Mahārāja: 'Lineage of the Yaduvaṃśa has ended' (*naṇdida yaduvaṃśa kuḍi*) (Anon 2013b) or 'The Final Sprout of the Yaduvaṃśa has Died' (*yaduvaṃśada kaḍē kuḍi vidhivaśa*) (Anon 2013a: 1). In the local section of the *Times of India* from the same day, the author interviewed R. Jagadeesh, the ambulance driver who had taken the Mahārāja's body from Bangalore to Mysore after his death. When asked about how it felt to have taken Woḍeyar's body in his ambulance, Jagadeesh replied 'I [was] not taking a body. I [was] carrying God' (Kalkod 2013: 1). In both the local newspapers' and Jagadeesh's responses, we see very different understandings of the king and his place in the political and religious history of southern Karnataka. In the local imagination, Woḍeyar was not simply a politician with a mediocre political and business legacy. He was a god on Earth, descendant and culmination of the Yaduvaṃśa, the mythical lineage that emerged at the time of creation starting with Brahmā's birth from Viṣṇu's navel through the deity Kṛṣṇa and the legendary and historical kings of Mysore, like Yadurāya, Rāja (r. 1610–1617), Cikkadēvarāya (r. 1673–1704), and Kṛṣṇarāja III (r. 1799–1868), who were elected by the Hindu deities to rule over the Mysore region.[2]

In this chapter, I explore the tension present in these two very different understandings of politics and the selection of leaders in contemporary India, namely competing notions of democratic and divine election. While some might draw the distinction between the two forms as struggle of a modern, rational political system versus a traditional religious worldview – or even as the British framed it 'the rule of law' versus 'the rule of man' (see Ocko and Gilmartin 2009), I argue that the overlap between the two ways of viewing election is based on the development of political theologies in the early modern period in which sovereignty itself was reconceptualised in the transition from kingdoms to princely states under British control. It is my contention that the court of Mysore during the reign of Kṛṣṇarāja Woḍeyar III created a political theology of Hindu sovereignty that ran parallel to the emerging theories of national sovereignty that grew with, from, and through British notions of imperial sovereignty and its emphasis on the 'rule of law' (Ocko and Gilmartin 2009). Both divine and law-based election, despite their seeming incongruities, are intertwined in the contemporary democratic political context of India. This chapter, however, is not meant to be an exhaustive history that traces the emergence of the contemporary union of divine and democratic election from the early nineteenth century to today. Instead, I wish to highlight how the first half of the eighteenth century in Mysore gave rise to new ways of thinking about sovereignty and its authorisation in relation to temporal rulers and divinity. I do so with the assumption that interactions between colonial and local sovereigns were complex and multidirectional negotiations of political theories, ideologies, and jurisprudence (see Irschick 1994; Price 1996). The influence of British legal and political theory on Indian understandings of sovereignty is evident especially with the implementation of the British ideology of the 'rule of law' that can be seen in several chapters in this book (see Price and Gilmartin); however, I am intentionally privileging the Mysore perspective over the British in order to show how indigenous courts were agents in the development of modern Indian politics, making a space for traditional sovereigns alongside their imperial counterparts.

Election and conquest in premodernity and in democratic politics

Throughout history the ability to rule often comes hand in hand with conflict. In premodernity, these conflicts were often in the form of armed military engagement with sovereignty and power transferring to the victor after conquest. In modern democratic politics the conflict to secure ruling power was shifted to popular elections and democratic processes (though far too often they are still settled with battles and wars). In this section, I examine the role of conquest and the transfer of ruling power and local sovereignty in the political theologies contained in the genealogical texts of premodern Mysore. I suggest that in early representations of the Woḍeyar history, their rise to power in the region was represented through conquest in which Rāja Woḍeyar defeated Tirumala, the Vijayanagara viceroy (*mahāmaṇḍēśvara*) of Śrīraṅgapaṭṭaṇa in order to stake his and his lineage's claim to regional sovereignty. I highlight how his conquest of Śrīraṅgapaṭṭaṇa is framed within the texts through his special relationship with the gods, who authorise his rule through divine election and, thus, empower him in his battles. Next, I transition to place this in the context of modern democratic elections in India in which military conquest is replaced with a war of words, and the will of the gods is, theoretically, replaced with the will of the people, who elect the ruler by casting votes.

Divine election and conquest in premodernity

Throughout the political history of southern Karnataka, what would eventually become the kingdom of Mysore, local dynasties articulated their claims to sovereignty through foundational narratives found in inscriptions and other genealogical literature, namely *vaṃśāvaḷi* texts. These narratives, which begin from the ninth century and continue in contemporary histories of the Woḍeyar dynasty, are remarkably similar in the details concerning each lineage's rise to power. I have explored these narratives and their tropes in more detail elsewhere; so I will not focus on them here (Simmons 2018). It is, however, important to note that one of the primary tropes within these foundational narratives is that the soon-to-be kings are recognised by a local deity, usually a local goddess, who notices their unique capacity to rule and who subsequently elects them to become the new earthly ruler of land (*kṣētra*) associated with the deities' physico-spiritual domain. The newly elected ruler is authorised to rule through initiation into the local ritual and devotional tradition and enacts his new sovereign authority by attacking and defeating the previous ruler. Thus, the foundational narratives throughout the political history of southern Karnataka grounded sovereignty in the appropriation of land through the conquest of previous rulers.

Of course, this type of narrative is hardly something unique to the region of southern Karnataka. Indeed, Carl Schmitt has suggested that such conquest narratives are intimately tied to all forms of political land appropriation with the 'biblical story of the Israelites' land appropriation of Canaan (Deuteronomy 4:4 and Joshua 1 1:23), serving as the 'classic example' (Schmitt 2016: 328–329). Schmitt suggests that through conquest, rulers could claim what John Locke has called 'radical title' over the 'alien land'. For Schmitt, the origin and foundation of a political order were rooted in the ruler's divine 'lot', that is, in the divine providence that is displayed through war and conquest. He concludes that in these cases divine providence serves as the natural law upon which all claims to sovereignty over the domain were based. Thus, for Schmitt – and for our purposes of grounding sovereignty within a particular domain in premodern India - conquest is not the beginning of the sovereign process, but it is the culmination of the ruler's election in which his victory serves as proof of divine election that can be seen in the political theologies of the biblical story of Joshua all the way to modern nationalist claims to land like American Manifest Destiny and within the genealogical materials of the Mysore Woḍeyars.

Indeed, in the earliest genealogical materials from Mysore, it is clear that the Woḍeyar's rise to regional political power was framed through Rāja Woḍeyar's conquest of Śrīraṅgapaṭṭaṇa in 1610 ce. In epigraphic panegyrics (*praśasti*), Rāja Woḍeyar is commonly praised with the epithet 'the conqueror of Śrīraṅgapaṭṭaṇa'.[3] The narrative of his rise is more fully elaborated in the Mysore *vaṃśāvaḷi* literary tradition in which Rāja Woḍeyar's seize of Śrīraṅgapaṭṭaṇa is clearly associated with armed military engagement and his acquisition of the city and region through the 'right of conquest'.[4] Additionally, all of these sources make a point to connect the rise of the Woḍeyar lineage with their relationship with particular deities, including both Cāmuṇḍi in Mysore and Celuvanārāyaṇasvāmi in Mēlukoṭe, in which Rāja Woḍeyar's acquisition of Śrīraṅgapaṭṭaṇa is framed as inevitable because of his and his lineage's divine chosenness and election. In these sources that predate British interference in Mysore's political structures, it is clear that the seventeenth- and early eighteenth-century Mysore Woḍeyar kings' claims to sovereignty over the Mysore kingdom and their capital of Śrīraṅgapaṭṭaṇa were based on conquest as proof of their election.

Popular election, the new conquest?

Jumping forward in time after the end of British rule in India, we can see the shift in political theory and structures that necessarily coincide with a shift in the nature of conquest, that is, a shift toward popular democratic contestation for political authority and power. While at first glance democratic elections seem wildly different from medieval warfare and conquest, if we read modern politics within the frame of its premodern antecedents in India, there are direct parallels in the process. In premodern India, such as in the case of Rāja Woḍeyar and Śrīraṅgapaṭṭaṇa, election and conquest go hand in hand with election serving to ground a ruler's authority and the conquest the means through which the election is proven. Likewise, in modern democratic elections the politician is given the authority to lead by being elected by the people or their representatives. The election process, however, turns into the battlegrounds with the would-be leaders fighting with speeches and slogans covering the landscape with onslaughts from megaphones, banners, and flags.

Indeed, the theories upon which modern democratic politics are based can be traced to the political theologies of the medieval period, which in turn, at least in the European context, grew out of theological conceptions of the relationship between the Christian church and Jesus. Ernst Kantorowicz (2016) was the first to attempt to examine the extent of the theological foundations of political systems and show that the roots of Western democracy can be traced through medieval jurisprudence in which the king was envisioned as a corporation of two bodies, his physical biological body and an incorruptible mystical body that passed from one sovereign to the next. Eric Santner (2011) has recently shown how these political-theological concepts, particularly the mystical body of the sovereign, were transferred from royalty to the corporation of the people who are now the sovereigns in the modern democratic process. He suggests that sovereign surplus that constituted the mystical body of the king was diffused into and through new political structures and controls that united 'the People' into the new corporal sovereign body. While both of these works are important, especially because they highlight the theological bases for modern politics, they both work from the assumption that modern nation states are sovereigns that function solely as corporations, leaving behind the individual agents that function within those bodies to make the individual decisions. Indeed, this same loss frightened Carl Schmitt, who opined the loss of strong decisionist leadership that came along with the democratic process.[5] However, if we consider these individual actors within the political process, what can we make of the relationship between the battles for votes waged between politicians, the medieval 'rights of conquest', and sovereignty in premodern and modern political theologies? Are contemporary politicians, like Śrīkaṇṭhadatta Narasiṃharāja Woḍeyar, and their promotion to leadership a result of an 'electoral conquest'? In modern national, regional, and civic bodies, is election by the people tantamount to election by the gods?

As we reflect on the political-theological roots of modern politics, we must consider the genealogy of contemporary politics and how concepts, such as conquest, election, and sovereignty, develop through different historical contexts. In the Mysore context, divine election and temporal authority were shaped through the colonial period in which conquest became an act of mundane politics and divine election authorised the chosen king to rule over a religio-political realm. Over the course of time, these two, while related, became distinct.

Resisting conquest: divine and political chosenness

While there were certainly many outside stimuli that influenced the development of Indian democratic electoral processes, the political theologies that undergird how people – the electors and the elected – see their role in the process of choosing someone to rule (that is, how leaders are elected) can also be connected to premodern indigenous conceptualisations of sovereignty. In this section, I show how the divine election through the 'right of conquest' was undermined during the negotiation of sovereignty in the reign of Kṛṣṇarāja Woḍeyar III. I suggest that given the politico-historical context in light of the recent defeat of one of the British's most bitter international rivals, the British and the new king of Mysore sought to distance claims to sovereignty based on conquest and instead focused on religio-political claims to divine election that have persisted alongside modern and contemporary democratic processes.

The Ṭipū Sultān problem

The modern history of Mysore is largely shaped on the results of the series of wars, often referred to as the Anglo-Mysore Wars, between the British East India Company forces and the armies of Mysore led by Haidar Āli and his son Ṭipū Sultān. This series of engagements ended in the brief and decisive Fourth Anglo-Mysore War (1798–1799) that result in the death of Ṭipū Sultān in Śrīraṅgapaṭṭaṇa on May 4, 1799. With the death of the powerful ruler, the British installed four-year old Kṛṣṇarāja Woḍeyar III, the son of the last Woḍeyar king, upon the throne of Mysore an act they heralded as the 'restoration of the Hindu kings of Mysore'. Additionally, the British relocated the king's capital from Śrīraṅgapaṭṭaṇa, the site of Rāja Woḍeyar's conquest, to Mysore city, which at the time even lacked a site suitable for the coronation. After moving the Woḍeyar king to the small city of Mysore, the British established their regional headquarters in Śrīraṅgapaṭṭaṇa in Ṭipū Sultān's summer palace. The installation of the young king, the shift of the Mysore capital, and the British's appropriation of Śrīraṅgapaṭṭaṇa mark an important moment for the understanding of sovereignty in the region, splitting the 'right of conquest' and divine election into two distinct but related concepts.

Ṭipū Sultān (r. 1783–1799) had risen to power in Mysore after the death of his father in 1783. Like Haidar Āli, Ṭipū Sultān had acquired territory through conquest, namely conquering the Keḷadi kings of Bidanūru and rising to the rank of royalty in the region. Unlike his father, however, Ṭipū Sultān also ascended the throne of Śrīraṅgapaṭṭaṇa through his military power; though there was no full-scale war through which he wrested control of Mysore from the Woḍeyars, his control over the military made it possible for him to imprison the Mysore king and his family. Thus, Ṭipū Sultān had established his Mysore Sultanate through the same processes as Rāja Woḍeyar, dethroning the previous ruler and claiming the throne as his 'right of conquest'. This, however, would prove problematic for the British.

To truly understand what was at stake in Mysore, we have to consider the role of the British and their policy of non-intervention and lapse. In 1741, the British East India Company implemented an unofficial policy of 'non-intervention' in matters of Indian sovereignty, claiming that they had difficulty securing decent interpreters and were naïve concerning the overall implication that any of their action might have for indigenous politics (*Records of Fort St. George*: 15, 39). This unofficial policy set a precedent for a position of 'non-intervention'. The East India Company employed this unofficial policy when the conflict at hand did not directly affect their corporate dealings, arguing that they were not political entities but merely merchants who were 'disinterested' in Indian political affairs (Dodwell 1920: 177–179). 'Non-intervention', however, went hand in hand with the so-called 'Doctrine of Lapse'. While 'Doctrine of Lapse' postdates the fall of Śrīraṅgapaṭṭaṇa, the British role in Mysore was certainly critical in the development from the policy of non-intervention to the establishment of British sovereignty in India. The 'Doctrine of Lapse' was first enacted in policy after the death of the king of Kittūru (also in modern-day Karnataka) and his 'mysterious' deathbed adoption in 1824, when the British court decided this adoption was not binding because it occurred after the kings then. As part of this decision, the ruling determined that any kingdoms with whom the East India Company entered into treaties could be seized by the Company if the kingdom lapsed on their obligations. In 1834, during a review of a legal position of the British Crown regarding loans given from Lakhnavi bankers to king of Āvadh, John Forbes, the chairman of the East India Company Board, articulated the position of the Company in relation to 'native kings' ('26 February 1834' in *Proceedings . . .* 1834). He declared that the East India Company had the ability to enter into treaties and, therefore, operated within India as an independent sovereign. As an independent sovereign, the Company had the authority to enforce treaties and take control of a kingdom that had 'lapsed'. The position memorandum specifically spells out that a kingdom 'lapsed' both when there was no legal heir and/or the native king failed to uphold his legal and financial responsibilities. In the case of lapse, the East India Company would thereafter be able to 'interfere' in the affairs of native politics (i.e. seize the kingdom through conquest). The policy would only officially become known as the 'Doctrine of Lapse' in 1848 under the command of Lord Dalhousie.

Though the East India Company's position on their sovereignty in India was not articulated until 1834, it is clear that their actions in Mysore 35 years earlier was part of the development toward that end. The letter in which the East India Company Governor-General Richard Wellesley informed Ṭipū Sultān that the Company had declared war on Mysore begins with a long description of their trade and peace treaty that had been violated by the Mysore ruler (Kausar 1998: 260–265). Thus, like the claims of Rāja Woḍeyar and Ṭipū Sultān, the British seized Śrīraṅgapaṭṭaṇa through conquest establishing themselves as the sovereigns over the region. The appropriation of Śrīraṅgapaṭṭaṇa, however, sat uneasily with their policy of non-intervention, and the East India Company knew that for them to effectively administer their business and the region, there needed to be an indigenous king on the throne of Mysore. To 'restore' the Hindu Woḍeyar kings was not an easy decision for the British after the seizure of Śrīraṅgapaṭṭaṇa. There was considerable debate about whether or not the kingdom should be given back to the sons of Ṭipū Sultān (Wilks 1817: 468). In fact, it seems that many amongst the British thought the 'right of conquest' had rendered sovereign authority to the lineage of Ṭipū Sultān and that his conquest had 'extinguished the hopes of the ancient family' (Wilks 1817: 467–468). Ultimately, it was decided, however, that the sons of Ṭipū Sultān posed too large a political liability and that if they were given the crown, future wars with Mysore would be inevitable. Therefore, the British chose to crown the child king Kṛṣṇarāja Woḍeyar III in the cultural and religious capital of Mysore, Mysore city. From his installation on June 30, 1799, Kṛṣṇarāja Woḍeyar III was lauded as the restoration of ancient Hindu kingship in the region and connected with the Yaduvaṃśa and the city's goddess Cāmuṇḍēśvari. Instead of claiming sovereignty through 'radical title' acquired through warfare, Kṛṣṇarāja Woḍeyar III's sovereignty was rooted in divine election based on his birthright, effectively rendering Ṭipū Sultān's claims moot and allowing Kṛṣṇarāja Woḍeyar III to rule alongside the British without challenging their military supremacy in the region.

Chosen by god and man

From his childhood, Kṛṣṇarāja Woḍeyar III (r. 1799–1868) and his sovereign authority were framed through two lenses. On the one hand, Kṛṣṇarāja Woḍeyar III was a Hindu king, chosen by the gods because of his birth in the Yaduvaṃśa ('lineage of Yadu') and born by the grace of the goddess Cāmuṇḍēśvari. On the other hand, Kṛṣṇarāja Woḍeyar III was chosen by the British to rule over the region, which they made abundantly clear on multiple occasions as they slowly stripped him of all administrative powers over the course of his long reign.

The Yaduvaṃśa has been an important religio-political marker of royal identity in southern Karnataka imperial history since 860 CE when the Rāṣṭrakuṭa king Amōghavarṣa claimed to be born into the mythological lineage that includes Brahmā, Kṛṣṇa, and other divine and legendary rulers (*Epigraphia Indica* VI.4). Since this time most rulers from the region have claimed descent from the Lunar lineage of Yadu. The Yādava heritage of the Woḍeyars of Mysore was perhaps first alluded to in the patronage of Rāja Woḍeyar after his conquest of Śrīraṅgapaṭṭaṇa, when he gave a jewelled crown to the deity Celuvanārāyaṇasvāmi of Mēlukoṭe. Though not a direct reference, Mēlukoṭe is traditionally known as Yādavagiri or the 'hill of the Yadus'. Woḍeyar descent from the Yaduvaṃśa was, however, made explicit in the *Kaṇṭhīrava Narasarāja Vijayam* (c. 1648), again in the *Cikkadēvarāya Vaṃśāvaḷi* (c. 1678), and repeatedly in inscriptions from Doḍḍadēvarāja (r. 1659–1673) and Cikkadēvarāja (r. 1673–1704).[6]

During the reign of Kṛṣṇarāja Woḍeyar III his birth and biological succession was of utmost importance. In most inscriptions the birth of Kṛṣṇarāja Woḍeyar III is framed through divine favour as he is typically given the epithet 'born by the grace of Cāmuṇḍēśvari'. Interestingly, however, no details of a miraculous birth are, to my knowledge, ever given in any text or inscription. Born in captivity, it is possible that grace was not simply in reference to the process of his conception and birth but that he was born destined to the be restorer of the Yaduvaṃśa and his family's claims to local sovereignty. Indeed, references to the royal Yādava background of the Mysore Woḍeyars reached new heights as the king and his court emphasised their claim to sovereignty by producing multiple genealogies in a variety of media, including literature and paintings. Two of the most extensive and important genealogical productions of the Mysore court from Kṛṣṇarāja Woḍeyar III's reign are the *Everlasting Lotus* mural from the hall of colours (*raṅgamahal*) in his Jaganmōhan Palace and the *vaṃśāvaḷi* text *Śrīmanmahārājavara Vaṃśāvaḷi* (*Annals of the Royal House of Mysore*), authorship of which is attributed to Kṛṣṇarāja Woḍeyar III himself. In the murals of the hall of colors, the lineage of the Woḍeyar line is visually displayed within the creepers of lotus plant beginning with Vasudēva and his son Kṛṣṇa and ultimately flowering in the centre of the composition where Kṛṣṇarāja Woḍeyar III is shown seated on the golden Mysore throne. In an adjacent room in the palace, an inscription explains that Kṛṣṇarāja Woḍeyar III is the last in a long line of kings that actually began at creation with Mahāviṣṇu. The *Śrīmanmahārājavara Vaṃśāvaḷi* elaborates on this motif, detailing every generation of the Yaduvaṃśa from the moment of cosmic creation down to Kṛṣṇarāja Woḍeyar III. The text, however, continues by connecting the divine ancestry of the Woḍeyar with the foundation of their lineage in Mysore in which their sovereign authority is directly linked to divine election. According to the text, the legendary progenitors of the line, brothers Yadurāya and Kṛṣṇarāya, were ruling in the traditional Yādava homeland, Dvārakā in Gujarat when Kṛṣṇa appeared to them in a dream directing them southward to claim their own kingdom. Then, as they travelled south they were visited by the goddess Vindhyāvāsini, who told them that she had taken up an abode in Mysore and waited for them there. Once the brothers arrive in Mysore, the deity Śiva in his local form as Nañjuṇḍēśvara and the goddess Cāmuṇḍēśvari authorise their rule over Mysore after which they defeat a local chieftain who has been harassing the wife and daughter of the recently deceased king of Mysore. While there is an element of conquest in this foundational myth, it does not connect the lineage to the regional capital of Śrīraṅgapaṭṭaṇa, but it places them in a world of religio-political struggles for the city of Mysore in which the Woḍeyars are elected and authorised by the local deities to rule.

After briefly describing the next few generations of Woḍeyar rulers, the *Śrīmanmahārājavara Vaṃśāvaḷi* slows its pace to describe the life of Rāja Woḍeyar and his acquisition of Śrīraṅgapaṭṭaṇa. In this version of the story, however, Rāja Woḍeyar is not described as the 'conqueror of Śrīraṅgapaṭṭaṇa', but he is given the kingdom because Tirumala, the Vijayanagara viceroy, has become too ill to properly govern.[7] After a consultation between the viceroy and his Vijayanagara overlord, the emperor elects and authorises Rāja Woḍeyar to be the new king of Śrīraṅgapaṭṭaṇa because of his innate qualities that derive from his stock as a descendant from the Yaduvaṃśa, because of his loyal to the empire, and because he had proven himself able through battle. After the emperor's election of Rāja, Tirumala returns to Mysore and installs the Woḍeyar on the throne before retiring to nearby Mālaṅgi/Talakāḍu. Here, Śrīraṅgapaṭṭaṇa was not acquired by the Woḍeyar line through conquest, but it was their lineage, the Yaduvaṃśa, that accounted for their rise to regional political power that in turn was authorised by the political overlord, in this case the Vijayanagara emperor and his representative in Śrīraṅgapaṭṭaṇa.

Together these two narratives create a dual system of election and sovereign authority for the Mysore kings. The kingdom that was given to them by the gods, the kingdom that they were specifically elected to rule over, is the city of Mysore, where they met with gods and conquered rogue villains. Śrīraṅgapaṭṭaṇa, however, was another story. It was not a site of conquest. It was a site of mundane political matters, where temporal politics required the able Woḍeyar kings to step in and administrate. Indeed, Śrīraṅgapaṭṭaṇa was the site where the Woḍeyar kings were authorised not by divine electors, but by powerful outsiders, who installed the king on the throne to rule in accordance to the imperial will. The Woḍeyar king, however, was not just chosen at random, but the same divine succession that had empowered them in Mysore led to his coronation in Śrīraṅgapaṭṭaṇa. The text clearly has resonance with the political situation of Kṛṣṇarāja Woḍeyar III's reign. Kṛṣṇarāja Woḍeyar III had just been installed in Mysore because of his ancient Hindu lineage. By mirroring his own political history into the narrative of Rāja Woḍeyar's ascension, Kṛṣṇarāja Woḍeyar III retroactively creates a precedent for dual streams of authority: true sovereignty came through both temporal authorisation and by the gods granting divine authority. Kṛṣṇarāja Woḍeyar III was not only chosen by the gods, but he too was chosen by the British, temporal imperial rulers, whom the king was to serve, which according the *Śrīmanmahārājavara Vaṃśāvaḷi*, mimicked Rāja Woḍeyar's service to his Vijayanagara imperial overlords. This dual election establishes a complex system of sovereign authority in which the will of the gods and the will of human electors (ought to) align, and one way of establishing the validity of both is through succession from the mythic Yaduvaṃśa.

As a result, the 'right of conquest' is removed from the election of the Woḍeyars. Instead, it is placed within the realm of temporal politics. Śrīraṅgapaṭṭaṇa was framed as the battleground of the non-divine political players, like Ṭipū Sultān and the British, vying for control through their military endeavours, but never owning the proper bloodline or divine call to truly be authorised as sovereign over the religio-political territory of the Mysore kingdom. In the political reality of the period, the British played this role perfectly, framing themselves as mundane administrators and a military power that stood separate from the divine royal sovereignty that was placed on the Woḍeyar lineage through biological succession from the Yaduvaṃśa and through the election by Nañjuṇḍēśvara and Cāmuṇḍēśvari.

Conclusion

Finally, let me return to the case of Śrīkaṇṭhadatta Narasiṃharāja Woḍeyar and his role in contemporary democratic elections in Karnataka. In the same obituary as I quoted previously, Chandra Shobhi (2013) tries to make sense of Woḍeyar's electoral successes:

> Yet, Wodeyar enjoyed immense love and loyalty especially in the rural areas of Mysore region, which often translated electorally too. This was a testimony to the development strategies as well as social justice measures adopted by Wodeyar ancestors, thereby giving the Mysore princely kingdom the image of a modern progressive state.

While I am sure the Woḍeyars' role in the famed modern advances of Mysore played some part in Śrīkaṇṭhadatta Narasiṃharāja Woḍeyar electoral success, I believe this obituary misses a larger point that reflects the development of the electoral process in the region from the foundation of modern politics that were laid in the early nineteenth century in the Mysore court. Instead, when we look to the local Kannada media, we see how the Woḍeyar and his place in local politics was viewed in the popular imagination: he was the culmination of the Yaduvaṃśa. Elected not just by votes that were cast on election day, his election came millennia ago beginning with Mahāviṣṇu. Thus, like Rāja Woḍeyar with the Vijayanagara emperor and Kṛṣṇarāja Woḍeyar III with the British before him, his lineage and the divine election that came along with it caused him to be called upon by temporal electors, chosen to represent the region in Indian national politics.

The importance of these premodern political theologies of divine election and royal sovereignty were not lost on Śrīkaṇṭhadatta Narasiṃharāja Woḍeyar. He was known for continuing to reference the former territory of the Mysore kingdom when speaking to people from Karnataka while he held his seat in the Lok Sabha, claiming a special paternal relationship and authority for their citizens, whom he called 'his subjects'.[8] Further, the erstwhile Mahārāja continued to frame himself through the divine power that came along with his biological lineage, claiming that his excellent memory came from a mantra passed down from his father and that his habit of keeping his eyes half-closed was because his 'eyes are very powerful. It can even turn people to ashes if they try to misbehave with me. I always keep it half closed to see that they are not harmed unwittingly' (Nikam 2013). While this might seem a bit sensational for some, it also reflects the continuation of many of the premodern concepts of sovereignty and authority that are still very much part of contemporary Indian politics in which democratic election and temporal (electoral) conquest continues to be reconciled alongside traditional claims to divine election and the sovereign authority that comes along with it.

Notes

1 This protest was not successful. Instead, a statue of Śrīkaṇṭhadatta Narasiṃharāja Woḍeyar's father Jayacāmarājēndra Woḍeyar was installed in Hardinge Circle in July 2016.
2 The tradition holds that Yadurāya ruled from 1399–1423. However, there is no extent physical evidence to corroborate his reign, and the details of his life and migration to Mysore seem to follow generic foundation narratives found in the region of southern Karnataka. I, therefore, did not include any dates associated with his rule.
3 For example: *Revised Epigraphia Carnatica* V.My.99 (1674) and VI.Sr.24 (1686).
4 For example: *Kaṇṭhīrava Narasarāja Vijayam* (c. 1648) chapter three; *Cikkadēvarāya Vaṃśāvaḷi* (c. 1678) chapter one; *Yādavagiri Māhātmya* (c. 1680s) chapter one; and *Maisūra Dhoregaḷa Pūrvābhyudayada Vivara* (c. 1713).
5 Carl Schmitt (2005). It should also be noted that there is a strong fascist sentiment in Schmitt's work, and he was also employed by the Third Reich to author pro-Nazi propaganda.
6 For example: *Epigraphia Carnatica* XII.Kg.37; *Revised Epigraphia Carnatica* V.My.99.
7 This is not the first text in which the acquisition of Śrīraṅgapaṭṭaṇa is described through a peaceful transition. Instead the first reference that I am familiar with comes from the *Narapati Vijayam* (c. 1800s) that was part of the survey collection of British officer Colin Mackenzie. In this version, the overlap between the contemporaneous political situation and the literary narrative is even stronger because Tirumala is said to have continued to live in Mysore as a 'resident' to counsel the newly crowned king.
8 CNN-IBN Senior Editor and *Indian Express* author D.P. Satish recalled that while he was interviewing Śrīkaṇṭhadatta Narasiṃharāja Woḍeyar in Delhi while he was a member of

Parliament, realising that the reporter was from Shimoga that Woḍeyar exclaimed 'Oh! I see. You are a subject of our kingdom!' (Satish 2013).

References

Anon. 2013a. 'Yaduvaṃśada Kaḍē Kuḍi Vidhivaśa', *Hōsadiganta*, December 11: 1.

Anon. 2013b. 'Nandida Yaduvaṃśa Kuḍi', *Prajāvāṇi*, December 11. www.prajavani.net/news/article/2013/12/11/212394.html (Accessed September 24, 2017).

Anon. 2016. 'Protest Demanding Wadiyar's Statue', *City Today*, December 18: 7.

Chandra Shobhi, Prithvi Datta. 2013. 'Mysore's "Last Prince" Wodeyar Inherited Love, Loyalty and Great Fortune: The Legacy of Srikantadatta Wodeyar, Who Died Tuesday, Is Not as Immense Though', in *India Express*, December 10. http://indianexpress.com/article/india/india-others/mysores-last-prince-wodeyar-inherited-love-loyalty-and-great-fortune/ (Accessed October 1, 2017).

Dodwell, Henry. 1920. *A Calendar of the Madras Despatches Volume I 1744–1755*. Madras: Government Press.

Epigraphia Indica. 1892–1895. Vols. 1–6. Calcutta: Government Press.

Irschick, Eugene F. 1994. *Dialogue and History: Constructing South India, 1795–1895*. Berkeley, CA: University of California Press.

Kalkod, Rajiv. 2013. 'Srikantadatta Wadiyar, Last Scion of Mysore Royal Family, Dies of Cardiac Arrest', *Times of India*, December 11.

Kantorowicz, Ernst. 2016. *The King's Two Bodies: A Study in Medieval Political Theology*. Princeton: Princeton University Press.

Kausar, Kabir. 1998. *The Secret Correspondence of Tipu Sultan*. Bangalore: Karnataka State Archives.

Nikam, N. Niranjan. 2013. 'A Nippy Bowler, Perfectionist, and the Common Man's Maharaja: Senior Journalist N Niranjan Nikam Recalls His Childhood Friend Srikanta Datta Narasimharaja Wadiyar, the Maharaja of Mysore Who Passed into the Ages on Tuesday', *Star of Mysore*, December 11.

Ocko, Jonathan K., and David Gilmartin. 2009. 'State, Sovereignty, and the People: A Comparison of the "Rule of Law" in China and India', *The Journal of Asian Studies*, 68 (1): 55–100.

Price, Pamela G. 1996. *Kingship and Political Practice in Colonial India*. Cambridge: Cambridge University Press.

Proceedings of the Directors of the East India Company with Reference to the Instructions Transmitted to Them by the Commissioners from the Affairs of India to Dispatch a Letter on the Subject of the Claims of Baboo Ram Doss and Baboo Ram Chown Loll, Heirs and Accredited Representatives of the Late Monhur Doss and Seetul Bahoo to the King of Oudh, According to the Tenor of a Draft Sent by the Commissioners to the Court. 1934. London; s.n.

Records of Fort St. George. 1915–1946. Madras: Government Press.

Revised Epigraphia Carnatica. 1972–2009. Vols. 1–16. Mysore: Institute of Kannada Studies University of Mysore.

Santner, Eric. 2011. *The Royal Remains: The People's Two Bodies and the Endgames of Sovereignty*. Chicago: University of Chicago Press.

Satish, D. P. 2013. '"Maharaja" Wadiyar Was a Reluctant MP', *Indian Express: Bangalore Edition*, December 11: 1.

Schmitt, Carl. 2005. *Political Theology: Four Chapters on the Concept of Sovereignty*. Chicago: University of Chicago Press.

Schmitt, Carl. 2016. *The Nomos of the Earth in the International Law of the Jus Publicum Europaeum*. New York: Telos Press.

Simmons, Caleb. 2018. 'Family, God, and Kingdom', in Manu Devadevan (ed.), *Clio and Her Descendants: Essays in Honor of Kesavan Veluthat*, pp. 586–610. New Delhi: Primus Books.

Wilks, Mark. 1817. *Historical Sketches of the South of India, in an Attempt to Trace the History of Mysoor: From the Origin of the Hindoo Government of That State, to the Extinction of the Mohammedan Dynasty in 1799: Volume 3*. London: Longman, Hurst, Rees, Orme, and Brown.

6

CIRCUITS OF PROTECTION AND EXTORTION

Sovereignty in a provincial North Indian town

Lucia Michelutti

Soon after the Uttar Pradesh state elections in March 2012, I attended a debate organised by the *Foundation for Restoration of National Values* at the India International Centre in Delhi.[1] The foundation is dedicated 'to creating a more ethical and value-based leadership, in all walks of life'. Their work is said to be 'driven by the conviction that leadership with integrity creates the most appropriate conditions in our democracy, for all-round national development and the good of all'.[2] The title of the workshop was: 'Urgency of Electoral and Political Party Reforms'. The Justice Minister, Mr. J. S. Verma, delivered the keynote speech and Dr. S. Y. Quraishi, the Chief Election Commissioner, opened the debate. Among the invited speakers was the Oxford-educated former Union Law Minister Mr. Salman Khurshid. For two hours, the speakers and the public discussed the overlap between the political and the criminal spheres in contemporary India and, more specifically, the rising presence of corrupted politicians in the country's national and state legislative assemblies. Concerns about the 'criminalisation of politics', it was pointed out, surpassed worries about endemic nepotism or the mismanagement of public funds. It was emphasised how many 'criminal politicians' were accused not simply of embezzlement, but more so of burglary, kidnapping, and murder, and that the political landscape was seen not only as a corrupt, but also as a highly violent sphere and synonymous with 'mafia/goonda raj' (rule by mafia/gangsters).

During the question and answer session, the former Minister of Law made a very interesting comment. He said that a political leader in Uttar Pradesh can, with a bit of luck, be elected without the support of his/her caste; however no criminal politician could win and rule without caste, clan, and kinship support. He added that academics should look at these linkages: it was not caste and politics that matter in contemporary Uttar Pradesh but kinship, caste, and *goondagardi* (criminal work). Mainstream accounts of Indian criminalisation of politics do not provide insights into such dynamics. Drawing on fieldwork conducted in a provincial town in Western Uttar Pradesh, this chapter asks: What is the role of force (*danda*), kinship and kingship ideals of protection (*suraksha*)[3] in structuring de facto forms of personal/caste (criminal) sovereignty? And what do such forms of authority and power tell us about Mafia Raj morals and 'the rule of law' in contemporary UP and India?

I answer these questions by focusing on a crime that is at the heart of the careers of many of the gangster-politicians and their mafia-like political enterprises: protection rackets. Given the fine line that separates extortion from (informal) taxation, this particular crime has inherent statecraft qualities and therefore provides an ideal ethnographic entry point for studying the tension between power and legitimacy, between processes of power and ideas about sovereignty and political representation. More precisely, I suggest that racketeering dressed up in the language of protection has often the potential to bind people together in intimate complicities and opportunistic partnerships that contribute to cementing kinship/clan/caste bonds and indirectly help the ascendance of sovereign self-interest and violent elected 'gangster-politicians'.

It should be emphasised that in so far as these outlaws overlap with the state, they often resemble not so much Robin Hood/social bandit figures but rather what scholars of strongmen and mafias have characterised as 'violent entrepreneurs' (Blok 1974; Sidel 1999; Volkov 2002), defined loosely as individuals who use private (and state) force as a means of social control and economic accumulation. These are individuals who are officially part of the state: they are not 'informal sovereigns'; they do not work independently from the law; they do not operate on the fringes of the state (Das and Poole 2004); or in formal 'states of exception' (Agamben 1998). Rather the prosperity and survival of these bosses depend as much on the law and its manipulation as on brutal force. Without law, crime does not pay. Thus, what I describe is a situation in which it is impossible to untangle state from non-state sovereignty and 'the law of men' from 'the rule of law', the acquisition of respect from the brutal accumulation of money. Ultimately, Mafia Raj are regimes of governance in which state power and crime power fuse, overlap, and co-function (Michelutti et al. 2018). This symbiotic relation structures threshold spaces in which 'order and disorder, lawful and unlawful, norm and exception, outside and inside conflate. It is in these liminal spaces that arbitrary violence is practiced as legitimate and necessary and where the reality of the intertwinement [the Mafia Raj] takes shape' (Civico 2015: 22).

In this chapter, I examine how a particular form of sovereignty is produced in a multiplicity of entangled liminal domains. I do so by mapping concatenations of circuits of protection and extortion – as 'offers one can't refuse' – and detail situations and traditions in which the protector is both the source of violence and the provider of protection from the violence he/she produces (or threatens) to produce. More precisely I illustrate how 'protection/extortion' functions as a vector between domains that are usually kept apart: the terrain of money and organised criminal systems of protection; established indigenous statecraft models of virtuous kingly protection (*dandaniti*) and related theologies of caste protection; the protection of women and honour; territorial views of democracy and election practices. Ultimately, this exercise shows how 'the ability to kill, punish, and discipline with impunity' (Hansen and Stepputat 2006: 296) that is central to bosses' authority, is capable of producing sovereignty if and when engaged and/or encompassed by other religious/cosmic, material, and legal powers (Singh 2012).

Protection rackets in Western Uttar Pradesh

This section starts by historically contextualising the role of bosses in the state of Uttar Pradesh and the sovereign potentiality of racketeering. Extortion is defined by the Indian Penal Code as the criminal offence of obtaining money, property, or services from a person, entity, or institution, through coercion. In a protection racket the racketeers agree to defend a business/neighbourhood/village/community from an attack in return for money or support. However, they may threaten to attack or attack the object of protection if the protection being offered is rejected. As Charles Tilly pointed out, protection is an ambiguous commodity.

> Which image the word protection brings to mind depends mainly on our assessment of the reality and externality of the threat. Someone who produces both the danger and, at a price, the shield against it is a racketeer. Someone who provides a needed shield but has little control over the danger's appearance qualifies as a legitimate protector, especially if his price is no higher than of his competitors.
>
> *(1985: 170–171)*

Protection theory has been used by economists, political scientists and historians that suggest analytical links between the behaviour of states and that of criminal groups (Shortland and Varese 2014). More recently it has been adopted by scholars of mafia like Blok (1974), Gambetta (1993), Varese (2011), and Volkov (2002) who theorised protection and its sovereign properties in the context of Italy and Russia. By contrast, in anthropology 'protection' has mainly been studied in the context of patronage, lordly styles of leadership and issues of honour. Idioms of patronage have been analysed as forms of protection in the absence of an effective state (see, for example, Gellner and Waterbury 1977) or as 'protection from the state'. In particular, the latter has been a recurrent theme in the literature on Russia and post-socialist countries (Humphrey 2004). Finally, the protection of 'my community', 'my clan', 'my linage' – including their illicit activities – and emphasis on brotherhood and patriarchy are important themes in the literature on Mediterranean and the Middle East.[4] In India these themes are central to the study of dominant castes and related issues of prestige, status, and divine kingly forms of authority. More specifically in North India beyond the world of gangsters, 'the protection offered to your own victims' (Vidal et al. 2003: 20) is a well-rehearsed mode of gaining control and maintaining obedience across a variety of social spectrums of life, including the family and the management of private affairs. In this world 'violence' is one of the constitutive elements used to define the identity of social groups and to maintain caste dominance and hierarchies, and enduring patriarchal systems.

Such realities are particularly alive in the setting under study: Western Uttar Pradesh. This region is widely known for its endemic violence, for being culturally shaped by the 'macho' ethos of its dominant castes, such as the Jats, Yadavs, Gujars, and Thakurs; for being marred by communalism and caste-based conflicts. The statistics and sociological studies available have defined this area as the cradle of 'a subculture of violence' and the home of 'institutionalised riot systems' (Brass 1997). Today, the battle for protection and security has intensified due to the presence of a predatory economy, hyper-electoral competition, and deep political polarisation. For a start, Western Uttar Pradesh has undergone tremendous economic changes over the last 20 years as it is strategically located on the doorstep of the New Delhi National Capital Region (NCR) and the successful industrial suburban areas, such as Noida and Faridabad. The small towns along highway NH-2 (connecting Noida-Agra) that comprise the legendary and mythical land of Brajbhoomi have become goldmines.[5] Demand from investors from Delhi, Haryana, Gujarat, and West Bengal, and indeed global speculators, has intensified. Skyrocketing land prices facilitated the criminalisation of land development and mafia involvement in local politics. This development changed the type of illicit activities local mafias protect.

Traditional illicit activities, such as alcohol production/distribution, smuggling, drugs, and contract killings, have been substituted by the so-called 'land mafia', property and estate development. Local bosses now direct their activities and their investments abroad and have moved on from being 'mohallas' (neighbourhood) protectors to international investors often involved in global speculations (Michelutti et al. 2018: Chapter 6). By moving into land development and joining forces with developers in the lucrative construction industry, the small-town bosses and their associates have transmogrified into well-financed interstate criminal networks whose criminal capital is used to expand their political turf. In short, traditional specialists in violence have stopped supplying their services to the big leaders: they have stopped acting as mercenaries for their landlords and patrons, and instead have begun to use their muscular skills to stage a better life for themselves and their families, and to create their political Mafia-esque clans. This shift has been moulded by a parallel rise in political participation and polarisation. Democratic competition, as Wilkinson (2004) argued, produces an intensified scramble for monetary and political resources, and turns money and muscle-power into pre-requisites for electoral success. Moreover, the need for muscle-power is at its peak in areas with deep community divides where voters want forceful representatives that they perceive can protect their group-based interests most credibly.[6] It has been established that political parties select criminal candidates in those areas where social divisions are the most contested

(Vaishnav 2017); this has been happening in the district under study over the past two decades.

The boss and the king

> Beti, there is no democracy; only the rule of the stick (the lathi). Power is controlled by the danda. The danda is the real king.
>
> (Man Mohan Singh, leader of the local Kshatriya Mahasabha)[7]

In this part of India leaders have been often portrayed as having the duty 'to care for the material interests of [their] followers' (Brass 1990: 96). Pamela Price has described this idea as heir to the persistent, historically embedded models of lordship, pointing out the long-assumed duty of the king to provide (1989: 47). The raja's 'beauty and dazzle', she wrote, 'symbolised the potentialities of wealth for the community as a whole'.[8] The Raja was a servant of *dharma* (virtuous duty) and 'his major two obligations were to protect his realm from outside aggression and to ensure that his people lived together peacefully and in a way conducive to the *rita* [truth/order]/*dharma* complex' (Menski 2004: 14). In order to maintain order and to protect his people, the king has *danda*, the rod of punishment. Danda also means military power. The execution of power is the 'wielding of danda' (*dandaniti*). In Hindu statecraft cosmology, there is a 'hierarchy of protection' at the levels of gods, kingdom/state, caste and family that blurs the distinction between public and private violence, divine, and profane force (Brekke 2005). At the level of communities, it is the concept of dharma, that is, the rights and duties of individuals according to birth, that establish which castes have/can use arms as their profession. Thus, today's bosses' tough reputation and proven capacity to exercise violence brings together the two long-valued potencies of a 'king' – to protect and provide. But how do such normative classical ideals of statecraft mix with forms of protection that are at the heart of criminal mafia-like enterprises? How are they reconfigured and transformed? Below I will start to discuss the figure of the 'king-boss'. Whereas the 'old' kings relied on Brahmins for legitimacy, while the king-boss sovereignty is still precarious as before (see Heesterman 1985) it now also depends on business and entrepreneurship rather than on gods and goddesses, Brahminical authority, and/or law for legitimation.[9] Importantly, today's 'king-boss' is a raja who has given up his/her promise of (genuine) protection to the pursuit of pure extraction, but who nevertheless has not stopped valuing respect. This is a figure animated by a continuous tension between force and disinterested reason, that is, he/she still often frame its authority in terms of sewa (service) and work for the others. Today, violent economic racketeering (and capital accumulation) is framed in reconfigured symbols and actions of honour and revenge, caste mythologies, religious practices, indigenous texts of theology and democratic statecraft. Such socio-cultural and institutional repertoire shapes ideas about who is entitled to violence (and to protect) and who is not, and in the process, transforms violent forms of extortion into appropriate, just, or desired acts of protection, and creates potent Mafia Raj systems of governance.

Today's bosses (like older 'rajas') gain their authority through force and 'dandaniti'. Brute force is often used explicitly (or passively) to achieve authority, and in order to be recognised as someone capable of killing and commanding. Reputations are built by ensuring that there are witnesses to the violence being meted out. Violent crimes – often murders – are at the heart of bosses' biographies and folklores (Michelutti et al. 2018). Being suspected of murder is an accolade for bosses, not a stigma. As Gambetta said of the Italian Mafiosi: 'it provides hard-to-fake evidence that one is "bad", and it spreads knowledge of this trait' (Gambetta 2009: 4). Thus, being objectified by the law as 'criminals' helps bosses to establish their reputation and authority. When a violent authoritative reputation is established, bosses then switch to more sophisticated activities where authority is the means and no longer the goal. In short, bosses start to command and rule. Intimidation is enough. As Volkov points out: 'it [the capacity to kill] becomes similar to a commercial reputation' (2002: 45) – people come to you of their own accord to enforce services or settle disputes or to offer a ticket to contest elections. Importantly, bosses craft and project a capacity of 'getting things done' (see Michelutti 2008, 2010; Witsoe 2009; Price and Ruud 2010) for themselves, their families, and sometimes for their caste/communities (Michelutti 2014). The ability to produce violence and profit is loosely intertwined with the ability to get support and/or votes. It should be emphasised that this type of power is very fragile and needs constant performance (see Michelutti et al. 2018).

Living in a provincial Uttar Pradesh town for a couple of weeks, these characters become easily recognised from their physique, gestures, positions of power, signs of 'muscular strength', and signs of wealth. Crucially, to be a proper boss (locally referred with the terms *bhai* or *dabang*) one needs to have a political seat. Such a position provides the allure and the prestige necessary to act with impunity and also to provide 'state protection'. Proper bosses do not have bodyguards but rather have 'their own men' and 'crew'. They travel in big white 4x4 cars (Mitsubishi Pajero) with a red siren and party flags on the front. Flashy gold jewellery, a big car, and a display of muscle and weapons make a recognisable, assertive style of behaviour. This style is what distinguishes them from other types of criminals (thieves or dacoits, for example). Whereas thieves tend to keep a low profile as they do not want to be caught, bosses need to be visible as they provide a service which, when they are elected, becomes a 'public' service. Bosses do not need to hide and do not care if their acts of 'goondagadi' are caught on camera. They collaborate with the authorities and/or aspire to become part of the authorities.

A trend emerges from the data I have collected by following the lives of six local strongmen: 1) bosses gain authority and a monopoly on a territory through violence and money (mainly from acting as an enforcer); 2) they enter into politics and get democratically 'elected' authority; 3) they try to form a 'political dynasty' in order to secure authority and wealth for their family. Basically, bosses run protection rackets with the advantage of 'democratic' legitimacy and all the glory and prestige that comes with being a legitimate 'little king' or 'little queen'. In the next sections I will begin to examine how their sovereignty is produced and performed by looking at normative logics of protection/extortion and how these materialise at the level of the household, family, the caste/community, the divine, and the law. I illustrate how 'the protection offered to their own victims' strategy is also deployed to govern caste and family matters, to hide domestic violence, and to monitor caste/gender behaviour. Such normative kinship forms of authority and honour ideals are deeply connected to contemporary boss-kingly sovereign repertoires and the opaque powers of democratically elected Mafia Raj.

Violent kinship: protection and extortion in the family/caste kingdom

> This is the land of Krishna where brothers kill fathers and fathers kill sons.
> (Arun Chaturvedi, criminal lawyer)

> In this region, we re-enact the Mahabharata everyday.
> (Muslim leader and local intellectual)

'Mahabharat bana denge' is a threat that is heard time and again in Western Uttar Pradesh. Literally it means we will re-create the Mahabharata and with it its famous fratricidal war. In 2013 this slogan made the headlines when two Dalit girls were found hanged from a mango tree after being gang raped in Badaun in so-called Yadav caste 'territory'. The alleged rapists were Yadavs. The police officers who alledgedly failed to intervene and investigate were also Yadavs. It is difficult not to avoid sensationalism in describing this type of case, which illustrates how rape is used to establish caste sovereignties and protect families and community honour. But these events are everyday routine in UP. News such as this is not generally covered in the press. The culprits are mostly 'protected' by the population that live in their territories. Only when there is retaliation and brave rebellion do the cases emerge, reach the national news, and capture the attention of the police and politicians. The father of the two girls told the reporters that his family have been threatened. 'They say, once the media leaves, Mahabharat bana denge'.[10]

In a world where 'the rule of law' is visibly absent and where the authorities and the legal system are deeply mistrusted, people are increasingly taking refuge in their families, friends, and 'their' blood-related 'king-bosses'. Elected bosses become guarantors of provision of protection and often share kin or fictive kin relations with the people they 'protect' (Michelutti 2014). This is visibly happening in matters of justice. Caste courts and extra-legal forms of adjudication are becoming more and more relevant. Informally, 'blood money' is often sanctioned by caste/community *panchayats* or by bosses who act as adjudicators, which shows the increased role of informal adjudication processes in enforcing caste and gender-specific behaviour such as honour killings.[11] It should be noted that in terms of gender, the bosses' stance is often hyper-masculine and 'traditionally' patriarchal. Western UP Mafia Raj offers a reassuring vision of a conservative, male-dominated world.

It is in this context that bosses are also called 'brothers' (*bhai* or *dada*) and their racketeering is normalised in the language of kinship, family, and *izzat* (honour). It should be noted that the language of kinship and parenthood is widely used both in politics and in the criminal world in North India. Across South Asia the idea of a protector as parent (relative) is also a strong cultural construct. Traditionally, patron-gods and kings have been referred to as parents: *maa-i-baap* (mother-and-father) in Hindi. Kinship terms such as *bapuji* (honourable father), *bhai* and *dada* (brother), *behenji* (sister) are used by Hindi speakers to refer to politicians or local leaders who are seen as treating their supporters with love, self-sacrifice, and devotion. As discussed previously, terms such as *bhai* and *dada* are also used to refer to bosses (a term apparently derived from Middle Dutch that originally meant 'uncle'). This is not specifically a South Asian phenomenon as the usage of terms such as 'godfather'/*padrino* clearly indicates. Such language metaphorically suggests nurturing and caring for the others. It is deeply embedded in strong paternalistic/lordly styles of authority that are used to justify the legitimacy of power by showing interest in others and in the public good. It follows that these relations have been mostly understood and described in a positive light – even if protection goes hand in hand with intimidation and much structural and symbolic violence. Nancy Scheper-Hughes has pointed out that the family is often one of the most violent social institutions (2003: 3). The violence and the symbolic violence that permeates the Indian family in a provincial town in North India 'in the name of protection' is overwhelming and mostly invisible and under-researched. It is certainly not boasted of as the violent bravado of bosses but is rather kept secret and concealed. However, I suggest it is this familial violence that contributes to producing and maintaining the Mafia Raj type of sovereignty.

*

In February 2013, I conducted a survey in a *mohalla* (neighbourhood) of the town under study; I wanted to ask about 'suraksha' (protection/security) and fears in the neighbourhood. My aim was to try to quantify levels of trust and feelings of security or insecurity across communities. I also asked several questions about local leaders and their role as bosses. What I did not realise at the time was that I was about to enter the dark interiors of family lives. In the survey I asked the following questions: What is the main source of insecurity in your neighbourhood? Who are you most afraid of? Which kind of person are you most afraid of? Importantly the perception of security in the neighbourhood varied according to the caste/community the respondents belonged to, and their gender. Generally, Yadav men (who at the time were in power at the state level) felt secure because their caste mates/kin were running the show. On the opposite spectrum Dalits felt very insecure. Dalits were in the government from 2007–2012. At that time, they were running the state and allegedly persecuting the Yadavs during their rule. Now, the Yadavs were back and they were taking revenge. Muslims said they feared Yadavs (or Hindus). Yadavs said they did not fear anybody but that they were concerned about Muslims. Some said they just feared God. However, women seem to live in a different world. Many women across caste/communities say that they fear their husbands, their brothers-in-law, and their brothers.

In the family domain, these figures are the one who possess 'dandaniti', that is, the right to kill, punish, and discipline with impunity. I did the pilot survey study soon after the Delhi gang rape incident in December 2012, an incident which generated public protests in India. In this context the survey became an excuse, a sort of ice breaker, to talk about rape and sexual harassment. A veritable Pandora's box opened up to me as I started to collect narratives about sexual abuse, emotional blackmail, female infanticide; women despising their mothers more than anybody else for not having protected them or for pushing them to marry the wrong guy; for loving their brothers more than them; for blackmailing them and not allowing them to be with their sweethearts. Several women said that they did not feel safe at home. For the men – in particular among the Yadav, Jat, and Rajput castes – the protection of 'their' women is a question of 'izzat'. If you can't protect your own women, how can you be a credible 'protector' in other spheres of life? Hence, there is a widespread 'informal ideology of personalised administration' (Price 1996: 200) and 'the existence of political values which focus on the development and protection of domains of personal influence is of the utmost importance' (ibid.: 201). The family and household are the husband's jurisdiction in microcosm, and their state of order or disorder is indicative of his ability to rule. In this respect, controlling women's sexuality and display of respect, deference, and modesty is often a crucial element of the strongman's political reputation. This requires having women voluntarily or involuntarily participating in the production of macho power; what looks like unthinking obedience may in fact be a consciously and continuously manufactured contribution to the family's reputation. By the same token what happens to women who challenge it? Can they disobey?

*

There has been a lot of discussion lately about women's security in public places. But there is still a veil of silence about violence within the home. Many conversations I had with girls and more mature women tell the story of women feeling alone and powerless even if they live in large extended families. Silence, forgetting, and pretending that all is fine are usually the coping strategies used by women. Emotional blackmail (psychological coercion – referred to in Hindi as *pratadhit* or *yatna*) is part of the everyday lives of many families. This includes the threat of being rejected by her family or disapproved of by members of the community, and being guilt-tripped by someone she loves or respects. Family and clan/caste coercion is still overwhelming. When I asked a well-educated, English-speaking woman recently married in the mohalla: Why don't you go to the police and put an FIR against the guy who has been stalking you for months? She looked at me terrified: 'We live in the Mafia Raj – women who rebel end up like the girl in Delhi, gutted.' Many women believe that if she had not put up a fight against her rapists they would not have killed her. Women in the mohalla rarely go out. They are in purdah (un-displayed), guarded and protected by their own men who are sometimes also their greatest threat. Thus, family lives are deeply shaped by 'offers that cannot be refused'. Such forms of 'gender-extortion' are deeply entrenched in the local caste sovereignties of Rajput and semi-Rajput castes as I will explore in the next section, but are also spreading across lower castes that adopt honour as a tool for social mobility (Still 2014).

Caste theologies of protection: defending communities and society

> I am the protector of my caste.
>
> (Rajput boss, Western UP)

'Yadavs used to be the muscle power of Brahmins and Thakurs [Rajputs]'. A powerful Yadav government administrator reminded me: 'We (Yadavs) were always active in the industry of violence – but now rather than doing it for the Brahmins and Rajputs – we do it for ourselves . . . we became self-employed – it is for this reason we did much better than the Kurmis.'[12]

As mentioned in the previous section, danda (force) is still one of the constitutive elements used to define the identity of social groups in North India. As a 'martial' caste (as they were classified during the colonial time, see Michelutti 2008: Chapter 3), and a caste of wrestlers, Yadavs are considered to have the skills and the reputation to be 'protectors'. During British Rule, middle or higher status castes whose fighting skills were highly valued were classified as martial; however, if they were of lower status they were classed as 'criminal castes'. Yadavs in Western Uttar Pradesh fell under the former category. Interestingly, if one looks at the caste background of the current 'criminal politicians' elected in the UP Vidhan Sabha Assembly, a large number comes from Rajput/semi-Rajput castes: they come from the dominant local castes and not from lower castes or 'criminal castes'. Rajputs and semi-Rajput castes (such as Jats, Yadavs, Gujars) still describe themselves as natural protectors and as the 'ones' who can legitimately administer justice ('We have justice in the blood', they often say). In the district under study, young male Rajputs are still reluctant to engage in any productive activity, 'they do not want to work, even if their land does not sustain the family anymore . . . they still think that their occupation is to go to war, to fight, to govern or to do sports. Basically, they think that they can get money without working – just by mastering force and intimidation' (Sunita Sisodia, 37 years old, police constable). Today, capturing wealth through force and intimidation is turning out to be a profitable and honourable activity. These castes dominate the local sand and oil mafias (Michelutti forthcoming).

In a study of the village of Palanpur (Western Uttar Pradesh, just 30 km from my fieldwork site), Dreze and Khera 2000 noted that most murders over a 20-year period were committed by Thakurs. The authors analyse the persistent influence of military values among the Thakurs, who still had the monopoly on guns in the village, spent time body-building, strove to get jobs in the army and the police, and so on. The 'Kshatriya' (high-ranking warrior) template is still very persistent. People refer to the idiom of blood and to Kshatriya metaphors and by doing so they render violence 'natural'.[13] It should also be noted that despite 15 years of government by lower castes, Thakurs still hold a disproportionate share of political representation across the state. Crucially, they also remain the second most affluent caste. The 'kingly'/'martial' role of particular castes conceived as 'natural' protectors is so entrenched in the locality that since Independence political parties have never risked putting a Brahmin candidate forward to contest a national parliamentary election. A local seasoned Jat Congress party leader explained: 'When it comes to the Lok Sabha elections there are three main vote blocs in the constituency: Jats, Brahmins and Rajput. Since Independence political parties have never risked putting forward a Brahmin candidate.' He continued, 'Brahmins vote for Jats and Rajputs – but no Rajput or Jat will ever vote for a Brahmin . . . this is a scientific fact.' Intrigued by this remark I pressed him to explain the reasons behind such folk theory of voting behaviour and representation. He answered, 'Everybody knows that Brahmins need to be protected by Rajputs or Jats – they cannot protect us, they do not have the skills . . . take for example the Banias [merchant caste] . . . they are useless . . . they get easily scared.' This quasi-Dumontian view of power and sovereignty highlights how ideals of protection are still informed by the classical Brahmin-king relationship.

As a matter of fact, Yadav muscled their way into politics by portraying themselves as natural protectors of the Other Backward Classes, explored at length in *The Vernacularisation of Democracy* (Michelutti 2008). Yadavs draw on their 'pastoral and rural roots', presenting themselves as rustic cow-herding-politicians, all the while claiming aristocratic (Kshatriya) pedigree via descent from princely Krishna. The Krishna invoked in political speeches is the 'martial' Krishna from epics who 'defends the poor and the marginalised'. As his heirs, the Yadav caste is said to be traditionally committed to fighting for 'freedom' and to protecting weaker people against injustices.

In the Hindu cosmology of violence, sacrificial violence is legitimate. Murders committed while protecting do not lead to any serious guilt or impurity for the perpetrators; on the contrary, they provide saintly and heroic status. 'Violent protectors' are transformed into hero-gods. And members of particular communities, such as the Ahir/Yadavs, are considered to be more prone to becoming hero-gods than members of other castes. The Yadavs are said to have 'heroic substance' (Coccari 1989: 260), and their hero-gods (*kuldevtas*) are often glorified strongmen cow herders who defended the community's herd and the community itself from being exploited by higher castes or Muslims. In the Yadav hierarchy of suraksha the god Krishna is the primary warrior and community/caste defender. The need for protection is a strong motivation for worship in Hinduism. Vishnu's many incarnations (*avata-ra*) are involved in protective campaigns on behalf of chosen humans, and the most prominent of the incarnations – Krishna and Ram – are gods who sometimes actively intervene to protect people.

Caste protection and honour may transform senseless violence into meaningful violence and, in the process, produce sovereignty. Yadav politicians and local leaders often maintain and cultivate this 'heroic' and martial heritage and use it to legitimise their engagement with violence, in the army, in the police, or in politics (Michelutti 2008, 2014). Over the years, I have had many conversations with leaders who refer to classical Hindu texts of statecraft such as the Manu Smirti, the Arthashastra, or the famous Mahabharata, and emphasise how 'danda' is necessary and 'good' violence because it is used to protect your own people and provide them with safety, security, and order. Thus, Yadavs have built up a credible reputation for violence that has been legitimised by the language of warrior sacrifice and kingship, and was sanctioned by their inclusion in the martial castes by the British Government. Today this reputation is used in the mafia industry of protection. 'After all, as the Arthashastra emphasized long ago, the good of the kingdom is identical to the king's struggle to retain power, and this kind of argument . . . can be adopted by mafia-like organisations as showed by Heuze' (Vidal et al. 2003: 21).

Mafia Raj as a cycle of caste/party revenge

The Samajwadi Party has a reputation for protecting not only the interests of the Yadavs and Muslims (and more recently also of the Rajputs) but of protecting 'criminals' in Uttar Pradesh. Over the past 20 years the party has been in power twice; 2002–2007 and 2012–2017. It was during its 2002–2007 term that the media started to describe it as a 'party of gangsters'. Mulayam Singh Yadav allegedly surrounded himself with local mafia dons who gave him support in exchange for protection. Managing state economic activities was said to be in the hands of mafia syndicates. Bureaucrats, politicians, and the police were said to be part of criminal enterprises in the state.

The Samajwadi Party lost the 2007 election to its rival Bahujan Samaj Party, partly because of issues related to law and order. During the election campaign for the 2012 election, Mulayam Singh Yadav put his son Akhilesh Yadav forward as the new, clean face of the Samajwadi Party. One of the party members, who was in charge of the election campaign in 2012, mentioned to me: 'We needed to soften our goonda image, so we gave the following recommendations to the prospective candidates: no gold chains, no leather jackets, no showing off, button up your shirts . . . yes to white kurta pyjama and Blackberry but please not dark glasses.' 'Dark glasses' are supposedly perceived as a sign of being a goonda or of embracing a 'dark political culture'.

In spite of Akhilesh Yadav's campaign promises and his vocal commitment to purging UP and the Samajwadi Party of all its 'anti-social elements', as soon as the SP came into power a string of offences committed by criminals associated informally and formally with the SP started to be published in the media. In Western Uttar Pradesh Dalit leaders were beaten up and villages were burnt to the ground while the new SP rulers re-established their sovereignty after five years of Mayawati's government. The Election Commission was pleased to inform the world that no murder was committed during the 2012 UP Election and only 100 incidents were reported compared to the 300 incidents during previous elections. However, post-election violence was not reported. As SP Y. (SP and caste association leader, 65 years old) said in an interview: 'We are still in post-election violence. The current Mafia Raj is very much about revenge. Mayawati made us sit on carpets and touch her feet. When you humiliate people, you can only expect retaliation.' So, systems of Mafia Raj are often legitimised by its perpetuators as a reaction to a crime rather than as a crime in itself and a reaction to an offence against personal, family, and caste pride/honour.[14] During the first 18 months of government the SP's 'criminal face' and capacity to inflict violence by its representatives was not only visible on the streets, but also increasingly on videos recorded on CCTV cameras and/or mobile phones.[15] Such crimes were often justified locally as part of the 'war' of retaliation. This phenomenon reiterates the importance of cultures of honour and their reconfigurations in contemporary politics and criminal worlds. It also reflects another aspect of classical Hindu statecraft, namely the fact that 'one cannot find real and significant distinction between the violence directed against outward enemy societies and the violence directed against criminal and seditious elements within the king's own territory' (Brekke 2005: 82). In a world where the paradigmatic king receives the highest honours, SP retaliation takes on the characteristics of a small-scale civil war. In the process, democracy and the state are infused with kingly, warlike violence. This emphasis on war rather than crime shaped the ways criminal groups and gangs have been conceptualised and studied in South Asia. Sen's study of vigilante groups and Hindu muscular political organisations shows that these are indeed armed and dangerous groups with gang-like and 'mafioso' behaviour; nevertheless, they are not usually treated as such. Their violence is often transformed into non-criminal violence by the usage of a particular vocabulary. For example, among vigilante-gangs in Hyderabad members

> use words such as 'soldiers' (*sepahi*) instead of 'gangs' and 'war' (*ladai/yudh*) instead of 'vigilantism,' and they employ these categories to position

themselves in (their impression of) an urban 'warscape' – for them, the city is 'war' (*yeh sheher ek jung hain*).

(Sen 2007: 70)

It follows that authorities (and academics) do not treat them as delinquents but as 'social workers' or 'party workers'.

The extraction of 'goonda tax' and illegal economic accumulation

The new, 'clean' face of the Samajwadi Party began to crumble when the well-known gangster politician Kunwar Raghuraj Pratap Singh (alias 'Raja Bhai') was made (ironically) Minister of Prisons in the newly appointed government in March 2012. Raja Bhai has 48 murder cases, 32 extortion cases, and 12 kidnapping cases, amongst other multiple civil and criminal charges pending against him. He is considered a hero by many of my Rajput and Yadav informants. He epitomises the 'gangster politician', the kingly (*raja*) gangster who kills with impunity. The story goes that in 1995 he torched two dozen houses, killed four women, and threw their bodies into a river in a small village in Pratapgarh district. This was done in retaliation as a Muslim man refused to pay the goonda tax to the local musclemen.

Crucially, the extraction of the goonda tax – known locally as '*chauth vasuli*' – which refers to the early modern Maratha practice of collecting 25 per cent of profit/production for protection – is the backbone of many of the careers of locally elected bosses. If a member of the public is asked to describe what the Mafia Raj is, they will offer a simple and telling explanation: 'When the SP is in charge criminals are on the streets, they are able to operate and flourish – the Samajwadi Party protects them and they get revenues from them – it is all about 'goonda tax."' Thus, groups which are engaged in conventional criminal (or legal) activities develop under the political protection of the party (see Martin and Michelutti 2017). This protective blanket it is popularly known to ensure a secure environment for criminals to conduct their business. It follows that in the constituency under study, the local ruling party representative allegedly protected the bosses involved in shielding the local 'sand mafia', 'land mafia', 'oil mafia', as well as traditional thieves. This service is provided in exchange for money, favours, and votes. In the area, the SP name/logo itself began to function as a token of protection and a deterrent because it communicates a certain reputation. As scholars of mafia have elaborated, reputations are key in the business of protection. Between 2012 and 2016, I witnessed a variety of people from businessmen, unemployed people, and aspiring 'big men' who associated themselves with the SP and started their career as 'violent protectors'. 'You need *jugar* in this world to get rich' Rakhesh (35 years old) told me. In Western UP, jugar means to improvise, to be resourceful and entrepreneurial. Jeffrey et al. (2008) have shown how young employed men live in a highly competitive world in which source, force, and the need to improvise become paramount concerns (2008: 5). Protection, extortion, and enforcement are particularly attractive avenues because, as Paoli (2003) argues, they do not require high initial investments, they carry low managing costs, and they are relatively low risk investments, particularly where state protection is unreliable or inadequate. Moreover, in today's world one does not even need 'real' fighting abilities, nor particular preparation: 'You just need a pistol, courage and to get involved in the Bhumi (land) mafia' (see Michelutti forthcoming). The result has been a multiplication of competing predatory centres of power which enhance mistrust and fuel the demand for protection.

'Guddu bhai': conversations about sovereignty with a local boss

The boss I am about to introduce is a man in his fifties who is popularly known by the nickname 'Guddu Bhai'. Bosses often have nicknames which symbolise and brand their uniqueness. Conversations with him became a window to exploring how Mafia Raj sovereignty relates to popular ideas on kinship and its relationship to state authority, and examining which aspects of classical kingship are reconfigured. Crucially, Gudduji's story shows that there is a fine line between being perceived as a protector (and provider) and a racketeer. And juggling this fine line in competitive democratic contexts is an art in itself (Michelutti et al. 2018).

Guddu is a very creative and entrepreneurial character. He comes from a relatively politically influential Rajput family. His brother has been elected multiple times as MLA in a nearby district. When I started to do fieldwork on crime and politics I was advised by long-term informants and acquaintances to meet Gudduji: 'You need to meet Guddu Bhai – he will tell you all about goondagardi and politics', I was told and so I did. I did not pre-arrange the meeting. On a cold winter morning, I paid him a visit. In the courtyard, a few members of his crew were playing cards. They were heavily armed. One of them, Rakeshji, knew me. Rakhesh used to live in a neighbourhood in the nearby town where I conducted fieldwork 15 years ago. He started to brief his mates. The first thing he said was: 'She worked with Yadavs'. The rest of the crew looked at me more attentively. The Yadav 'connection' locally signalled protection and power. One of the men went inside and I overheard him explaining to the boss who I was. He came back after few minutes and asked me to follow him. I entered a very extravagantly decorated sitting room, expensive leather sofas, gold leather chairs and upholstery, with an enormous chandelier crowning the room. There he was – sitting in a red armchair – he looked like 'a king' surrounded by his court. Four men were attending this private and intimate *darbar.* I soon learnt that they were all local powerful businessmen and very prominent in the local hotel industry.

Before that January morning I had collected several portrayals of Gudduji. In the local folklore (and local press) he is well known for having run a very successful extortion racket in the late 1990s. Later in life he became involved in the local 'land mafia'. By the early 2000s he was a key player in the regional 'cooperative mafia'. He contested MLA elections with an SP ticket in 2007 and at the time of writing he was the Director of the District Cooperative Bank. This is a very powerful and profitable position. Cooperative society is locally synonymous with graft and criminal activities.

Between 2012 and 2016, I had many conversations with Gudduji and observed him in a variety of situations in the field. Gudduji turned out to be a very gentle, soft-spoken, and cultured man. He loved to talk about statecraft and how detached he was from vested and personal interests. However, in his mid-fifties he still actively participated with his crew in 'muscular' raids. I witnessed him in action when he intimidated polling officers in the 2014 parliamentary election. During our meetings, he obsessively talked about a local leader (and also a distant relative) who is locally nicknamed Chanakya because of his political acumen. Chanakya (a.k.a. Kautilya) is the writer of the ancient text, the Arthashatra, and is globally known as the Indian Machiavelli. In *Politics as a Vocation* Weber famously wrote that the true radical realpolitik 'is classically expressed in Indian literature in the Arthashastra of Kautilya (written long before the birth of Christ, ostensibly in the time of Chandragupta [Maurya]).' Weber added, 'compared to it, Machiavelli's The Prince is harmless.'

Gudduji's interest in Chanakya was so deep that he decided to write a PhD thesis on the philosophy of Indian statecraft. While discussing his dissertation topic he said: 'It is about the art of ruling as lined up in the Mahabharata. . . . I am not sure if you know it but Chanakya was about no nonsense. He was purely concerned with matter-of-fact politics.' In his writing, Chanakya put a lot of effort into describing what force is; how (and when) it should be used to expand influence and maintain control over territories and populations. Guddu Bhai concords with Chanakya and said that before 'killing' (his words), 'peaceful negotiations and forms of collaboration should be preferred'. Such tactics include 'weakening the enemy' through bribery, blackmail, and by causing internal fights among the rival factions. In such an endeavour, being able to acquire information is crucial. 'Rulers', he said, 'depend heavily on local knowledge' and an extensive network of friends and accomplices, many in the political and criminal justice systems, who must be cultivated face to face daily. Mafia Raj are thus closely connected with the concept of war and to ideas of the state as a segmented unit.

At the heart of commanding lies not only force (or threat of force), but money too. Gain and profit are the main goals of war and they are the most visible and pragmatic gains of Mafia Raj extractive forms of governance, too. Money is used to measure one's success and thus it needs to be shown off. Largess and acts of generosity are important tropes of good leadership in South Asia (Price and Ruud 2010). Gudduji also believes that he is serving 'his people' through the Cooperative Bank he is currently head of: 'We give loans to farmers, so they can buy fertilisers, wheat, oil, sugar and other items and in the process, we contribute to reducing poverty.' Gudduji's words echo state-led rural finance programmes. In practice, however, in Western Uttar Pradesh the state control of the banking sector implies that political, not economic and social considerations, determine the flow of credit across sectors and to individuals. In Western Uttar Pradesh, formal subsidised funds are today concentrated in the hands of the powerful few, such as Gudduji. District Cooperative Banks are 'colonised' by caste/mafia families today. Very few works on Indian politics analyse the role that cooperative banks play in controlling territories and voters ('borrowers').[16] As an informant put it crudely, 'Gudduji does not have followers but only kin and bonded-borrowers'. The cooperative network is often used to accommodate relatives. The 'loans' are often not given to cultivators, but they become a 'rent' (one of many) that local political bosses and their henchmen collect.

Mafia raj sovereignties: concatenations of 'offers one can't refuse'

Protection is a 'shadowy contract' (Strathern 2012: 401) in which force, money, personal interests, kinship, divine kingship, and state discourses of 'law and order' intersect (Strathern 2012: 401). Its moral ambivalence manifests itself in different spheres of life: protection/extortion codes are diffused from the intimate realms of the household to the political economy of the area and to public authoritative spaces. The understanding of how physical force works normatively in different domains of life and how such ideas connect with one another in the production of sovereignty is still largely inadequate.[17] Exploring different protection/extortion systems and how they intertwine allowed me to identify who is entitled to protect (and who is not) in a region that is witnessing unprecedented economic transformation, a marked democratisation of violence and high levels of political participation. I argue that it is precisely the concatenation of 'criminal', 'divine', 'kingly', and 'family' ideas of protection that allow brutal violence and coercion to be accepted at given times, or to quote Bourdieu to be 'misrecognised' for something else. Crucially, this something else is often good and with high moral values (not bad – *galat kam*). Ultimately, I hope to have shown that understanding how racketeering becomes seen as sovereign power is crucial to understanding the persistent role of caste and hierarchies in contemporary Indian politics, and why cultures of violence and criminality may be so inexorably central to it.

*

In 2017 the Samajwadi Party Mafia Raj was defeated by the BJP, the Hindu nationalist party. The party won the election on an 'anti-Mafia Raj' ticket. The newly appointed Chief Minister, Yogi Adityanath, a controversial spiritual figure with a respectable criminal record himself, made his reputation by transforming a gangster-dominated constituency, Gorakhpur, into a 'safe' Hindu territory.[18] The charismatic Kshatriya Yogi fuses in his persona divine kingship and democratic popular sovereignty (Chaturvedi 2017). Ultimately, he is also a 'king-boss'. In Gorakhpur, he combined democratic majoritarianism with the vigilante-protective practices of his youth gang/organisation: the Hindu Yuva

Vahini. This is an armed and dangerous group with gang-like behaviour that took over the extortive role of the gangsters that populated the district in the late 1990s. In March 2017, the chief minister, upon taking office, told officials that law and order was among his top priorities. While it is certainly too early to assess if and how the Gorakhpur 'law and order model' is going to be replicated across UP,[19] daily news programmes report that 'the Mafia Raj' is still very much alive and hiding behind 'saffron scarfs' and Hindutva values of protection.[20] This masquerade allows key players to keep breaking the law with impunity, much in the same manner as the SP supporters did for the previous five years. In the locality under study, the key Thakur/Rajput and Jat bosses have conveniently moved in with the BJP, resulting in the local criminal/political leadership remaining intact. However, under the new Thakur Chief Minister, Rajput bosses feel stronger and emboldened.[21] Since Adityanth's appointment caste riots rather than communal riots have been rampant in Western Uttar Pradesh.[22] The Thakurs are taking revenge against the Dalits and backward castes that have been in power for the previous 15 years. Multiple revenge wars are unfolding. These 'battles' spread further insecurity and with it a need for protection that provides a fertile ground for Mafia Raj/Hindu sovereignty to grow and prosper, and reinvent itself this time in the name of Hindu Rashtra (polity) and its dharma.

Notes

1 Research for this paper was conducted within the framework of a large collaborative anthropological project of which I was the Principal Investigator. The project was charting the terrain of power, muscle and money in 15 sites across India, Pakistan and Bangladesh, and was funded by an ERC Starting Independent Grant (2012–2016). I conducted 12 months of fieldwork over three years during the period 2012–2016. Fieldwork was conducted in a provincial town and constituency at the edge of Western Uttar Pradesh in North India. Throughout the chapter localities and informants' names are anonymised.

2 http://home.valuefoundation.in/index.php?option=com_content&view=article&id=44&Itemid=53 (Accessed July 13, 2017).

3 In standard Hindi, the common translation of 'protection'/security is *suraksha*. 'Guarding', 'defence', and 'safety' are also actions conveyed by this term.

4 See Still (2014) for a review of this literature, regarding issues of honour and patriarchy in particular.

5 On Noida development see the official site www.noidaauthorityonline.com/connectivity.html (Accessed June 9, 2009). On Yamuna Express development see Yamuna Expressway Industrial Development Authority.

6 See Michelutti and Heath (2013, 2014) for a study of these dynamics in this area of Uttar Pradesh.

7 The quote was originally in mixed English and Hindi.

8 See also, among others, Shulman (1986) and Dirks (1987) on 'bandit-kings' and lordship styles of rule.

9 I explore the nature of criminal economies in Mafia Raj systems in a Forthcoming co-edited volume with Barbara Harriss-White entitled: *Wild East: Criminal Political Economies in South Asia.*

10 See www.youtube.com/watch?v=bX-t5WGaSr4 (Accessed July 19, 2017).

11 On *khap panchayats* in India see Kaur (2010).

12 The Kurmi is another Other Backward Class that despite being a numerous community and well organised, did not manage to get a central political leadership role in the state of Uttar Pradesh.
13 On the role of Thakur caste idioms in shaping local criminal political economies and in particular 'the sand mafia' and 'the oil mafia' see Michelutti (Forthcoming).
14 For an analysis on the role of revenge and honour in the production of 'criminal' bosses in Punjab (Pakistan) see Rollier (2016).
15 'Goondagardi' caught on camera:

1) Mathura thana; humiliating SP workers see video www.youtube.com/watch?v=JaP9dXxAPdg
2) Ram Gopal Yadav's muscleman beating up a chemist in Delhi http://ibnlive.in.com/news/case-against-guards-of-sp-leaders-relative-for-assaulting-chemist/424596-3-244.html
3) Yamuna Express highway: toll mafia. www.youtube.com/watch?v=GwkVvp0kmrQ
4) SP minister caught slapping www.ndtv.com/article/india/akhilesh-minister-caught-slapping-a-person-on-camera-464879. www.youtube.com/watch?v=uCLGcGCQh3w

16 An exception is the study by Witsoe (2009: 90–102) on the Yadav Raj in Bihar.
17 One exception is the work by Ayuvero (2007).
18 For a detailed exploration of this process see Chaturvedi et al. (2019).
19 What distinguishes these squads from gangs is an ambiguity among local authorities in relation to these groups – which are not treated as delinquents but as 'social workers' or 'party workers'.
20 See Firstpost: www.firstpost.com/politics/akhilesh-yadav-attacks-yogi-adityanath-govt-on-law-and-order-what-lies-beneath-sp-leaders-sudden-anger-3409700.html (Accessed April 28, 2017); Times of India: City: http://timesofindia.indiatimes.com/city/agra/team-under-ssp-mathura-to-probe-assault-on-cops-in-agra-by-right-wing-men-dig-agra-range/articleshow/58382278.cms (Accessed April 28, 2017); Firstpost: www.firstpost.com/politics/hindutva-mixed-with-lawlessness-why-restoring-law-and-order-is-up-cm-yogi-adityanaths-biggest-challenge-3401374.html (Accessed April 28, 2017).
21 Scroll.in: https://scroll.in/article/830346/why-the-thakurs-of-uttar-pradesh-stoop-to-conquer-at-the-time-of-elections (Accessed June 15, 2017); Aljazeera: Features: India: www.aljazeera.com/indepth/features/2017/05/dalit-thakur-simmering-conflict-170526124705563.html (Accessed July 15, 2017); Economic and Political Weekly: www.epw.in/journal/2016/53/uttar-pradesh%E2%80%94vortex-change/identity-equations-and-electoral-politics.html
22 livemint: www.livemint.com/Home-Page/YfaZFWuenE9U4ScnusVAWK/Why-the-rhetoric-of-caste-vs-development-in-UP-polls-rings.html (Accessed June 15, 2017).

References

Agamben, Giorgio. 1998. *Homo Sacer: Sovereignty and Bare Life*. Stanford: Stanford University Press.

Auyero, Javier. 2007. *Routine Politics and Violence in Argentina: The Grey Zone of State Power*. New York: Cambridge University Press.

Blok, Anton. 1974. *The Mafia of a Sicilian Village, 1860–1960: A Study of Violent Peasant Entrepreneurs*. New York: Harper & Row.

Brass, Paul. 1990. *The Politics of India since Independence*. Cambridge: Cambridge University Press.

Brass, Paul. 1997. *Theft of an Idol: Text and Context in the Representation of Collective Violence*. Princeton: Princeton University Press.

Brekke, Torkel. 2005. 'The Concept of War and the Ethics of War in India and Europe', *Numen*, 52 (1): 59–86.
Chaturvedi, Shashank. 2017. 'Khichdi Mela in Gorakhnath Math Symbols, Ideas and Motivations', *Society and Culture in South Asia*, 3 (2): 1–22.
Chaturvedi, Shashank, David Gellner, and Sanjay Kumar Pandey. 2019. 'Politics in Gorakhpur since the 1920s: The Making of a Safe "Hindu" Constituency', *Contemporary South Asia*. doi:10.1080/09584935.2018.1521785.
Civico, Aldo. 2015. *The Para-State: An Ethnography of Colombia's Death Squads*. Los Angeles: University of California Press.
Coccari, Diane M. 1989. 'The Bir Babas of Benares and the Deified Dead', in A. Hiltebeitel (ed.), *Criminal Gods and Demon Devotees: Essays on the Guardians of Popular Hinduism*, pp. 251–269. Albany: State University of New York Press.
Das, Veena, and Deborah Poole (eds.). 2004. *Anthropology in the Margins of the State*. Santa Fe, NM: School of American Research Press.
Dirks, Nicholas. 1987. *The Hollow Crown: Ethnohistory of an Indian Kingdom*. Chicago: Chicago University Press.
Dreze, Jean, and Reetika Khera. 2000. 'Crime, Gender, and Society in India: Insights from Homicide', *Population and Development Review*, 26 (2): 335–352.
Gambetta, Diego. 1993. *The Sicilian Mafia: The Business of Private Protection*. Cambridge, MA: Harvard University Press.
Gambetta, Diego. 2009. *Codes of the Underworld: How Criminals Communicate*. Princeton, NJ: Princeton University Press.
Gellner, Ernest, and John Waterbury. 1977. *Patrons and Clients: In Mediterranean Societies*. London: Duckworth.
Hansen, Thomas Blom, and Finn Stepputat. 2006. 'Sovereignty Revisited', *Annual Review of Anthropology*, 35: 295–315.
Heesterman, Jan. 1985. 'The Conundrum of the King's Authority', in Jan Heesterman (ed.), *The Inner Conflict of Tradition: Essays in Indian Ritual, Kingship and Society*, pp. 108–127. Chicago: University of Chicago Press.
Humphrey, Caroline. 2004. 'Sovereignty', in D. Nugent and J. Vincent (eds.), *A Companion to the Anthropology of Politics*, pp. 418–436. Oxford: Blackwell.
Jeffrey, Craig, Patricia Jeffrey, and Roger Jeffrey. 2008. *Degrees without Freedom? Education, Masculinities and Unemployment in North India*. Stanford, CA: Stanford University Press.
Kaur, Ravinder. 2010. 'Khap Panchayat, Sex Ratio and Female Agency'. *Economic and Political Weekly*, 45 (23): 14–16.
Martin, Nicholas, and Lucia Michelutti. 2017. 'Protection Rackets and Party Machines: Comparative Ethnographies of "Mafia Raj" in North India', *Asian Journal of Social Science*, 45 (6): 693–723.
Menski, Werner. 2004. 'From Dharma to Law and Back? Postmodern Hindu law in a Global World', *Heidelberg Papers in South Asian and Comparative Politics*, 20: 1–21.
Michelutti, Lucia. 2008. *The Vernacularisation of Democracy*. New Delhi and London: Routledge.
Michelutti, Lucia. 2010. 'Wrestling With (Body) Politics: Understanding "Goonda" Political Styles in North India', in P. Price and A. E. Ruud (eds.), *Power and Influence in South Asia: Bosses, Lords, and Captains*, pp. 44–69. New Delhi and London: Routledge.
Michelutti, Lucia. 2014. 'Kingship Without Kings', in A. Piliavsky (ed.), *Patronage as Politics in South Asia*, pp. 283–302. Cambridge: Cambridge University Press.

Michelutti, Lucia. 2017. 'Mafia Raj', in A. Ledeneva (ed.), *The Global Encyclopaedia of Informality*. London: UCL Press.

Michelutti, Lucia. Forthcoming. 'The Inter-State Criminal Life of Sand and Petrol in North India', in B. Harriss-White and L. Michelutti (eds.), *The Wild East: Criminal Political Economies in South Asia*. London: UCL Press.

Michelutti, Lucia, and Oliver Heath. 2013. 'The Politics of Entitlement: Affirmative Action and Strategic Voting in Uttar Pradesh, India', *Focaal: Journal of Historical and Global Anthropology*, 65: 56–67.

Michelutti, Lucia, and Oliver Heath. 2014. 'Cooperation and Distrust: Identity Politics and Yadav-Muslim Relations in Uttar Pradesh, 1999–2009', in R. Jeffery, J. Lerche, and C. Jeffrey (eds.), *Development Failure and Identity Politics in Uttar Pradesh*, pp. 128–164. New Delhi: Sage.

Michelutti, Lucia, Ashraf Hoque, Nicholas Martin, David Picherit, Paul Rollier, Arild Ruud, and Clarinda Still. 2018. *Mafia Raj: The Rule of Bosses in South Asia*. Stanford: Stanford University Press.

Paoli, Letizia. 2003. *Mafia Brotherhoods: Organised Crime Italian Style*. Oxford: Oxford University Press.

Price, Pamela. 1989. 'Kingly Models in Indian Political Behaviour', *Asian Survey*, 29 (6): 559–572.

Price, Pamela. 1996. *Kingship and Political Practice in Colonial India*. Cambridge: Cambridge University Press.

Price, Pamela, and Arild Engelsen Ruud. 2010. 'Introduction', in P. Price and A. E. Ruud (eds.), *Power and Influence: Bosses, Lords and Captains*, pp. xix–xxxiv. New Delhi: Routledge.

Rollier, Paul. 2016. 'Vies de caïds et justice informelle à Lahore (Pakistan)', *L'Homme*, 219–220: 63–92.

Scheper-Hughes, Nancy, and Philippe Bourgois (eds.). 2003. *Violence in War and Peace*. London: Wiley-Blackwell.

Sen, Atreyee. 2007. 'Everyday and Extraordinary Violence: Women Vigilantes and Raw Justice in the Bombay Slums', in P. David and A. Sen (eds.), *Global Vigilantes: Anthropological Perspectives on Violence and Vigilantism*, pp. 69–92. London: Hurst.

Shortland, Anja, and Federico Varese. 2014. 'The Protector's Choice: An Application of Protection Theory to Somali Piracy', *The British Journal of Criminology*. doi:10.1093/bjc/azu046.

Shulman, David. 1986. 'The King and the Clown in South Indian Myth and Poetry', review by Norman Cutler in *The Journal of Asian Studies*, 45 (5): 1108–1110.

Sidel, John. 1999. *Capital, Coercion, and Crime: Bossism in the Philippines*. Stanford: University of California Press.

Singh, Bhrigupati. 2012. 'The Headless Horseman of Central India: Sovereignty at Varying Thresholds of Life', *Cultural Anthropology*, 27 (2): 383–407.

Still, Clarinda. 2014. *Dalit Women: Honour and Patriarchy in South India*. Delhi: Social Science Press.

Strathern, Marilyn. 2012. 'Gifts Money Cannot Buy', *Social Anthropology*, 20 (4): 397–410.

Tilly, Charles. 1985. 'War Making and State Making as Organised Crime', in P. Evans, D. Rueschemeyer, and T. Skocpol (eds.), *Bringing the State Back*, pp. 169–191. Cambridge: University of Cambridge Press.

Vaishnav, Milan. 2017. *When Crime Pays: Money and Muscle in Indian Politics*. New Haven, CT: Yale University Press.

Varese, Federico. 2011. *Mafias on the Move: How Organised Crime Conquers New Territories*. Princeton: Princeton University Press.

Vidal, Denis, Gilles Tarabout, and Eric Meyer (eds.). 2003. *Violence/Non-Violence: Some Hindu Perspectives*. New Delhi: Manohar Publications.

Volkov, Vadim. 2002. *Violent Entrepreneurs: The Use of Force in the Making of Russian Capitalism*. Cornell: Cornell University Press.

Wilkinson, Steven I. 2004. *Votes and Violence: Electoral Competition and Ethnic Riots in India*. Cambridge: Cambridge University Press.

Witsoe, Jeffrey. 2009. 'Territorial Democracy: Caste, Dominance and Electoral Practice in Postcolonial India', *Political and Legal Anthropology Review*, 32 (1): 64–83.

PART III

The nation and the sovereign imagination

7

MESSIANISM AND THE CONSTITUTION OF PAKISTAN

A. Azfar Moin

Dr. Abdus Salam, the only Pakistani scientist to win the Nobel Prize, had lived and worked in Europe but wanted to be buried in his own country. Upon his death in 1996, he was laid to rest in the town of Rabwa in the province of Punjab with an epitaph that read: 'The First Muslim Nobel Laureate'. This statement roused the Pakistani state to take action. A magistrate accompanied by police visited Dr. Abdus Salam's grave and had the word 'Muslim' erased from the gravestone (Cowasjee 2006; Khan 2016).[1] The law was on the government's side. The distinguished physicist had belonged to the Ahmadi community, which had been declared in a 1974 constitutional amendment to be outside the fold of Islam. The exclusion and criminalisation this small group has faced at the hands of the state was not simply a case of majoritarian discrimination against a national minority (Saeed 2007: 132–152). A more fundamental dynamic seems to have been at work, one that was at once constitutional and constitutive of sovereignty.

In this chapter, I explore why it was that the Ahmadis – as opposed to other religious minorities such as Christians, Hindus, Sikhs, or even Ismailis – played such a pivotal role in the conception and practice of sovereignty in Pakistan. My hypothesis is that it had something to do with messianism. I use the word messianism in two distinct senses, doctrinal and sociological. In the doctrinal sense, the explicit 'myth' of messianism in the Abrahamic monotheistic traditions, which is often but not always connected with apocalyptic or end-time notions, foresees the arrival of a saviour figure who would overturn the existing order and replace it with a truer or purer dispensation (Madelung 2011). Such doctrines often formed the basis of revivalist movement in Judaism, Christianity, and Islam. In the sociological sense, messianism refers to the intense collective expectations of impending change in the affairs of the world that gain ground in times of great peril or upheaval. The psychological pressure of extreme disruption can give rise to 'millennial dreams' (Thrupp 1970) of a plentiful and secure utopia along with the expectation that a great leader – the messiah in an implicit sense – would guide the affected group to deliverance.

What might be the link between the two types of messianism, one doctrinal and explicit and the other sociological and implicit? A clue to an answer lies in the 'decisionist' type of sovereign claim that messianism implies. It was the German and Catholic jurist Carl Schmitt who defined sovereignty in terms of the ability to decide on the exception, that is, the sovereign is the one with the power not just to make or execute law but also to decide when to suspend it altogether by declaring a state of exception or emergency. Schmitt, as is well known, criticised enlightenment and liberal notions of sovereignty founded on a system of law derived from human reason and consensus (Schmitt 2005).[2] The point here is that the messianic desire to dissolve the existing juridical order amounts to the same totalising impulse that Schmitt upheld as sovereignty's truest form.[3] However, since messianism could engender cycles of violence and counter-violence, the majoritarian traditions of Judaism, Christianity, and Islam typically projected the coming of the messiah onto a far distant future, that is, to the eventual as opposed to the imminent end of the world. Doing so can be understood as an attempt to curtail the radical power of the messianic sovereign to take the ultimate decision and suspend all law, and to promote instead the relatively conservative ideal that sovereignty is an aspect of the established system of law and belongs to those with the authority to interpret or incrementally amend the rules. Nevertheless, such preventive mechanisms that use the 'rule' to contain the 'exception' in politics – what Schmitt equated with 'miracle' in theology (Schmitt 2005: 36–42) – can be overwhelmed by massive disruptions such as large-scale war, famine, or natural disasters that render the established system of rules meaningless. Such 'messianic' moments enable a decisionist sovereignty that is unconstrained by the operation of law just as a miracle breaks free from the operation of nature. The leader who can absorb this exceptional or miraculous power can wear the saviour's mantle and use it to establish a new state of affairs.

In a country like Pakistan, which was founded for a monotheistic religious community, the two types of messianism – doctrinal and sociological – tended to blend into and feed off one another. Consider, for instance, the fact that the Ahmadi movement was a messianic one. This meant that a public focus on the Ahmadis kept explicit discourses of biblical messianism in Pakistani cultural memory. Consider also that the Ahmadis were declared outside the bounds of Islam after Pakistan experienced its most perilous moment in 1971, when its eastern wing broke away after an exceptionally violent civil war to form the independent state of Bangladesh. Not only was the country shorn in half but its foundational idea – that all Muslims of South Asia constitute a single nation – lay in tatters. At this moment of crisis, Zulfiqar Bhutto emerged as the populist leader – a saviour – of what remained of Pakistan. Instead of finding an alternative to Islam as the foundational idea of Pakistan, Bhutto reinforced it and passed the constitutional decree that declared Ahmadis to be non-Muslims. The issue I am raising here is whether the Ahmadis, an explicitly messianic movement, became unwitting victims of a particularly violent conjuncture of myth and history in post-1971 Pakistan, when messianism became an implicit idiom for sovereignty. However, to glimpse and make sense of this dynamic – the interlocking of doctrinal and sociological messianism that led to the official excommunication and criminalisation of Ahmadis in a Muslim state – one has to look beyond the conventional history of sovereignty in Pakistan that takes as its object the establishment and operation of the law. This is not to deny the significance of law in the conception and functioning of sovereignty. Rather, it is an attempt to merge the history of what Walter Benjamin called law-making and law-preserving violence – the basis of executive and administrative authority of the state – with the history of law-destroying violence, which he enigmatically termed divine or sovereign violence but might also be called messianic violence (Benjamin 1986: 277–300). However, first, it is helpful to begin with a brief synopsis of the conditions in late colonial India in which the Ahmadi movement took shape.

The Ahmadi movement

The Ahmadi movement began in 1889 in the town of Qadiyan in what is today Indian Punjab (Friedmann 1989: 1–46; Qasmi 2014; Kamran 2015). The place of the movement's birth became a way to refer to the community pejoratively as Qadiyani and the movement as Qadiyaniat. The founder, Mirza Ghulam Ahmad (d. 1908), belonged to a respected family known for its service to Sikh and British rulers of the Punjab. He was learned in Islamic religious and mystical traditions but had led a reclusive life until, upon making a claim of receiving divine guidance, he began to gain a following. Over time, he declared himself the promised messiah (*masih-i maw'ud*) and a prophet (*nabi*) of Islam. While this appears to be a jarring assertion from a doctrinal perspective, Yohanan Friedmann argues that Mirza Ghulam Ahmad did not see himself as abrogating Islam, but rather as someone continuing the spiritual guidance of the community in the tradition of the prophet Muhammad. He claimed to be a 'shadow' (*zilli*) or 'manifestational' (*buruzi*) prophet – a term fully explored below – who had been verified by Prophet Muhammad, the seal of the prophets (*khatim al-nabiyyin*). Yet in the eyes of his critics, Mirza Ghulam Ahmad stood for the rejection of the central tenet of majoritarian Islam that all forms of prophethood had ended with Muhammad.

As it developed momentum, the Ahmadi movement drew sharp criticism from many sections of Muslim society and religious leadership in India. The Ahmadi leader had made his mark by engaging in heated public debates on the truth of Islam with Christian missionaries and the Arya Samaj, a Hindu revivalist movement.[4] This alarmed the traditional Sunni 'ulama (religious scholars), many of whom were associated with the major north Indian madrasa (school) at Deoband. They wrote polemics against the Ahmadis, declaring them infidels for denying that Prophet Muhammad was the final prophet. The traditionally educated Muslim scholars were joined by Muslim modernists such as Muhammad Iqbal (d. 1938), the poet, philosopher, and politician who famously outlined the demand of an autonomous homeland for India's Muslims (Saeed 2016: 57–64). He wrote that the because of the Ahmadis the 'solidarity of the Muslim community in India under the British is far less safe than the solidarity of the Jewish community was in the days of Jesus under the Romans' (quoted in Sevea 2012: 169). In another historical reference, he compared Mirza Ghulam Ahmad to the 'heretic' seventeenth-century Jewish philosopher Spinoza (Devji 2013: 160), who had been excommunicated. Iqbal thus publicly lobbied British colonial government to declare the Ahmadis as non-Muslims. In a 1935 letter to the *Statesman*, he argued that they represented a religious community independent of Muslims and should be recognised as such for legal and political purposes by the British.[5] To make his case, Iqbal cited the precedent of the Sikhs whom the colonial government had recognised as distinct from the Hindu majority even without the latter's 'formal representation' for this recognition.

The Ahmadis were also seen as a threat because of the expressed loyalty of their leader to the British. The colonial government did not interfere with Ahmadi efforts to spread the movement, which was in keeping with the *laissez faire* policy that the British had come to practice toward the religions of India, enabling in some cases vibrant new religious forms (Green 2011). Yet, at the same time, the British courts took on the responsibility of defining 'religion', which prompted a series of cases to settle matters among Indian communities and led to the widespread adoption of the colonial state's categories of knowledge.[6] Mirza Ghulam Ahmad had not only acknowledged in his writings that it was under British imperial rule that the Ahmadis could flourish but also developed the conviction that Queen Victoria had a 'secret predilection' for Islam (Friedmann 1989: 35). Partly driven by such motives, the Ahmadis as a group remained aloof from the nationalist movements of the Muslim and secular variety as these gathered steam in early twentieth century. The community was not able to avoid confrontation or controversy, however. The Punjab Muslim League declared Ahmadis non-Muslims and banned them from membership. The Ahrar, a religiously motivated political movement in the Punjab, which itself was ambivalent towards the demand for a separate nation for Muslims, launched a violent agitation against the Ahmadis (Kamran 2015: 1853–1858). In 1934, the Ahrar demanded, unsuccessfully, for the removal from office of a prominent Ahmadi politician, Zafarullah Khan, who was a Muslim League leader and a Muslim member appointed to the Viceroy's advisory council.

In the decades approaching independence, comparing one's opponents to the Ahmadis had become an effective insult in Indian Muslim politics, one that even Iqbal used against a rival, the Deobandi religious scholar Hussein Ahmed Madani, who was a Congress party supporter and against the creation of Pakistan (Zaman 2002: 35). Thus, by the time British India was partitioned in 1947, the Ahmadis had become the target of Muslim religious parties as well as Muslim modernist thinkers. Some of this was to be expected because of the Ahmadi movement's missionising impulse that targeted not only non-Muslims but all other Muslims. Unlike other Muslim minority sects with heterodox beliefs and practices, such as the Ismaili followers of the Agha Khan, the Ahmadis had not kept their religious principles out of public view and avoided the political arena.[7] Thus, their critics could claim that the Ahmadi founder had crossed a political line with his loyalty to the British and a religious one with his claim of being the promised messiah.

Sovereignty and messianism: history and theory

Based on the previously mentioned historical sketch, it may seem obvious why the Ahmadis drew the ire of the Muslim establishment, both of the traditional scripturalist variety and modern nationalist one. Yet, upon closer inspection it explains neither the Ahmadi resort to messianism, which mired them in religious controversy and all but ensured their marginality among the majority of Muslims, nor the enduring reaction against this small group that came to shape the identity of an entire Muslim nation, even if it was primarily via official exclusion and persecution of the Ahmadis. Taking up controversial positions on Islamic doctrine or inventing new religious institutions were common enough among prominent Muslim leaders and intellectuals in British India. The founding father of Muslim modernism, Sir Sayyid Ahmad Khan's 'naturalist' explanations of religion in the manner of enlightenment philosophers (Troll 1978) and, later, Muhammad Iqbal's writings on Islam and prophecy, inspired by Nietzsche and informed by Orientalist scholarship (Devji 2013: 157–160, 2005: 124), were hardly the stuff of orthodoxy. Even the supposedly orthodox Deobandi 'ulama had reinvented the institution of madrasa in the aftermath of the disastrous Mutiny of 1857 and reoriented traditional Islamic education toward new ends (Metcalf 2005: 87–137). In many ways, early twentieth-century South Asia was no different than Europe in experiencing religion as a 'heretical imperative' (Berger 1979), an expression which highlights the choice ('heresy' derives from the Greek verb *hairein*, 'to choose') made available by the separation of religious from political spheres (a process of secularisation) and the subsequent retreat of the former from public life (the rise of secularism). These developments occurred at a time when with the introduction of the election as an instrument of politics, what had become sacred was the individual – an enchanted 'self' in a disenchanted world – who now possessed an 'almost mystical autonomy' in giving the gift of sovereignty (Gilmartin 2012: 411).

If religion had lost its orthodox bearing under colonialism then neither had any traditional concept of politics survived. Loyalty to the British was, at least until the end of World War I, the default stance among a majority of Indian politicians and remained so for Muslim nationalist leaders until the 1940s. Even after Gandhi managed to make anti-imperialism a popular political stance after World War I, most elite politicians, especially of the Muslim League, remained more faithful to the empire than not. For instance, Iqbal, who became the president of the Muslim League in 1930, had received a knighthood in 1922. In the following years, leading up to independence, when going to jail for the sake of independence became a rite of passage for Congress politicians, no major leader of the Muslim League spent a day in prison. So what was it that made the Ahmadis appear so vastly different in their religio-political position than other Indian Muslims?

To appreciate the particularity of the Ahmadi case, it is helpful to examine, as Gilmartin suggests in the introduction, the processes of sovereignty and the ideas of sovereignty at play in the history of South Asia and the place of the Ahmadi movement within these. Over the nineteenth century, the processes of sovereignty were progressively taken over by the British as they gained a near monopoly on the legitimate use of violence across South Asia. The British formalised their dominance after their victory in 1857 against the rebels and mutineers of their own 'native' army, the responsibility for which they laid at the feet of the powerless octogenarian Mughal emperor Bahadur Shah Zafar because the rebels had rallied around him as a figurehead. However, what the rebels had done in 1857, the British themselves were guilty of a century earlier. When the East India Company had gained control over Bengal's treasury, it had asked for recognition from the reigning Mughal emperor, whom the company had militarily defeated.

The rebellion of 1857, which ended with the exile of the Mughal emperor, marked a watershed in the history of sovereignty in South Asia (Moin 2017). Although the Mughals had lost central authority over much of the subcontinent after the death of Aurangzeb (d. 1707), almost all the regional powers had continued, in the eighteenth and nineteenth centuries, to draw formal authority from the powerless emperor. Even those who did not, such as the Sikhs or the Jats, had continued to emulate the symbols and rituals of the Mughal court. It was as if sovereignty was unimaginable without the presence or imitation of the Mughal emperor, a reality enshrined in the eighteenth-century canonisation of the Mughal style in the architecture of post-Mughal regional powers (Dadlani 2018). When analysed over the *longue durée* in South Asia, the phenomenon of the emperor surviving the empire appears limited to the Mughals. One reason why this happened was that the Mughals had struck upon a durable mechanism of universal sovereignty – what I have elsewhere called 'millennial sovereignty' – by which they could incorporate the diverse ethnic and religious identities in their imperial system while still holding the body of the emperor above all religious and cultural distinctions (Moin 2012, 2019 [forthcoming]). What is of particular relevance is that Mughal millennial sovereignty was based on messianism of a kind that shares many parallels with the claims of the founder of the Ahmadis.

It was the third Mughal ruler, Akbar (r. 1556–1605), who transformed the unstable conquest state he had inherited from his father and grandfather into a highly functional empire. He launched his imperial scheme at the highly charged moment of the end of the first Islamic millennium when a grand change in world affairs was expected at the hands of a sacred figure, an emperor or prophet, who would inaugurate a new universal dispensation. This expectation was in line with the messianic myths of Islam as well as widespread conceptions of political astrology. In effect, Akbar had taken advantage of the 'miraculous' occasion of the millennium to proclaim his status to be above any previous laws, including that of his ancestral religion, Islam, and to issue a new set of imperial codes in a manual called *Ain-i Akbari* (*Institutes of Akbar*). In terms of religion, the 'millennial' ethic inculcated among courtiers and soldiers, especially those in the emperor's inner circle, was that of *sulh-i kull* or 'peace with all'. This ethic entailed that all religions and sects be allowed to practice their traditions without interference or persecution, and no one should attack another on the basis of religious difference. In the generations following Akbar, the Mughal imperial scheme with its principle of holding all religious identities equidistant to the state had become ingrained among those who worked for and benefited from the empire (Kinra 2013). Although this situation may appear in hindsight as a form of secularism, it was in fact the product of a sacred enactment in which the monarch was held to be a saviour figure or even divinity made flesh.

The millennial sovereignty practiced in the Mughal empire can throw new light on the case of the Ahmadis. In historical terms, Akbar's millennial project highlights the vast storehouse of Sufi cosmologies and rituals available to Muslim saints and rulers alike for fashioning their sovereign selves. As has often been noted, Akbar's chief ideologue Abul Fazl, drew upon these forms of knowledge to portray the emperor as a saint and sovereign. However, what is even more telling is the way in which the emperor's critics also used the idiom of messianism to attack him. One of Abul Fazl's rivals at court, a Muslim scholar named Abdul Qadir Bada'uni, known for this 'orthodox' stance, had criticised Akbar's assertions of holiness as religious deviance while openly supporting the messianic claims of past Sufi masters like Sayyid Muhammad, the Mahdi of Jawnpur (d. 1505), and Sayyid Nurbakhsh (d. 1464). According to Bada'uni there could be more than one messiah of the age. To explain the phenomenon of multiple messiahs, he turned to the metaphysical mechanism of *buruz*, that is, 'manifestation' or 'projection' of the soul that had been originally elaborated by Nurbakhsh (Moin 2009: 390–402; 2012: 47–49, 158–159). The proponents of projection of the soul held that the most accomplished of saintly bodies could receive the projection of the divine soul and so unveil themselves as the promised messiahs. When the Ahmadi leader called himself a buruzi prophet, he was laying claim to such a spark of divinity.

As Bada'uni's writings show, in the sixteenth century, the concept of being a 'buruzi' messiah could be defended as being within the pale of Islam.[8] Indeed, such metaphysical concepts were needed as a way to justify the messianic claims made by monarchs and saints. Messianism as a route to sovereign status had become rationalised and institutionalised in both Sufi and imperial cultures in the fourteenth and fifteenth centuries, when Mongol imperial universalism had combined with the culture of saints and shrines in the eastern Islamic world to shape a new style of sovereignty (Moin 2019 [forthcoming]). However, as this paradigm ended with the rise of European imperialism, messianism lost its place as a viable form of knowledge. Even though it surfaced in times of stress and war, such as the rebellion of 1857, it had become part of what C. A. Bayly calls the 'mutiny of subordinated knowledges' (Bayly 1996: 330, quoted in Moin 2017: 331). No longer associated with empire and mainstream religion, messianism had become a mark of collective marginality and individual madness by the time the Ahmadi leader came on the scene. Thus, even a lay intellectual like Iqbal could dismiss the Ahmadi founder's claim of being infused by a projection of the divine soul as the assertion of a 'Magian in disguise' (Iqbal 1974a: 109–139, 1974b).

If by the turn of the twentieth century, messianism no longer provided an avenue to sovereignty, then why was the Ahmadi movement taken seriously as a religious and political threat? To find an answer, we must closely examine the monotheistic doctrine of messianism. The notion of a saviour figure expected to appear at the end of history and institute a final judgement makes its appearance in the Hebrew Bible in the Book of Daniel as the 'son of man', which informed later Christian and Muslim notions of the 'son of god' and the *mahdi* (the guided one), respectively. It is thought that the relevant section of the Book of Daniel was composed ca. 165 BCE around the time of a Jewish rebellion against Seleucid rule known as the Maccabean revolt (Assmann 2014: 113–129, 122). The biblical apocalypse or 'unveiling' was thus premised not only on a religious hope but also on a political one, which was to overthrow the tyranny of sacred kingship and replace it with the justice of God's rule.

The idea that the monotheistic God of the Bible was the only true sovereign had been established centuries before the Maccabean revolt and the composition of the Book of Daniel. Nevertheless, it had remained an idea. God's sovereignty had been impossible under non-monotheistic rule, such as that of the Seleucids who demanded that sacrifices be offered in the Jewish temple to deities other than Yahweh. The spark that lit the Maccabean rebellion was a violent refusal to comply with the royal decree of cultic mixing. Of note is Jan Assmann's observation that this resistance led to the encoding of a new semantic in which the principle of association and dissociation – of friend and foe (Schmitt 2007) – was derived from loyalty not to an earthly sovereign but to a divine one. This dynamic led to 'total religion', that is, the intensifying tendency of a religion to institute a codified will of God over all spheres of culture, including, most significantly, politics.[9] Pagan religion – or more precisely, cosmotheism, that is, the worship of a cosmos suffused with divine immanence – had maintained a symbiotic relationship with sacred kingship without requiring the rule of the gods to replace human rule on earth (Assmann 2010: 39–56). However, biblical monotheism brought with it a political theology in which the sovereignty of an earthly ruler was rendered secondary or, depending on the intensity with which the demand for God's rule on earth was enacted, null.

Particularly important for our argument is the observation that total religion was not only a matter of upending the tyranny of kingship, but also a way of marking the boundary of the community. The struggle for cultic purity in monotheism is linked, in a crucial sense, to the struggle for developing a community of political loyalists. In this scenario, what is more threatening than the pagan outsider is the compromised insider, the collaborator who becomes the 'outsider within'. That is to say, the worst foe in this model of community is not an outsider, the follower of another king and the worshipper of another god, but the insider who is willing to serve an outside power and thus put the very principle on which community is defined in deep jeopardy. Thus, as Assmann points out, the rules of extraordinary warfare in the Hebrew Bible – rules that are meant to apply to 'nearby' enemies who populate the promised land – demand total annihilation so as to prevent any possibility of mixing that would lead to disloyalty (Assmann 2014: 121).[10] While total religion was and remains a historical impossibility – it originated as an imaginative scheme, that is, not as 'history' but as 'literature' – it possessed the potential of shaping history. It exerted a moral force that could structure politics, especially in times of distress and acute collective vulnerability – what Carl Schmitt called *Ernstfall* or state of exception – that could give rise to a type of sociological messianism.

It is important to note, however, that total religion contained within it the seeds of its own subversion. This was because its structural logic hinged on a paradox: the messiah, the agent of total religion, was a 'king' whose mission was to end sacred kingship. Upon gaining power, the saviour could just as well usurp divine sovereignty and become the ultimate king. Perhaps in recognition of this danger, the traditional writings on the coming of the messiah are rife with warnings of the antichrist, the false messiah. Indeed, these dire prophecies came true more often than not as they did in the Mughal empire. When at the end of the first Islamic millennium, the emperor Akbar declared himself the holiest of beings and instituted 'peace with all' religions in his realm, his critical courtier Bada'uni lamented (Bada'uni 1973, 2: 313, 1976, 2: 323):

> I see in 990 two conjunctions,
> I see the sign of Mahdi and that of Antichrist;
> Either politics or religion must change,
> I clearly see the hidden secret.

In sum, messianism offered a totalising vision of sovereignty that could be attained in two conflicting ways, as God's rule or as sacred kingship. In the form of sacred kingship, it exposed the aspirant to the risk of condemnation by monotheists who would reject him as the antichrist. This was the accusation that Akbar had to live with when he declared his millennial sovereignty. In the form of God's rule, however, messianism in its intensified form required the total exclusion of the compromised insider, the 'outsider within'. This was the price paid by the Ahmadi community as the Pakistani state moved closer toward total religion.

The Ahmadis, the Islamists, and the constitution of Pakistan

After 1947, when work began in earnest on the constitution of Pakistan, the religious leadership comprising of the 'ulama and the Islamists, most notably Abul 'Ala Mawdudi, the leader of the Jama'at-i Islami, campaigned for the framing of the new constitution according to Islamic principles. They achieved a measure of success when the pre-constitutional 'Objectives Resolution' of March 12, 1949 vested sovereignty, not just over Pakistan, but also over the 'entire universe' to God (Saeed 2007: 136). This resolution allowed a permanent legal foothold for Islamist parties and others who wanted the establishment of an Islamic State. It subordinated to God, in theory if not in practice, the power of the state to make or suspend the law. In a sense, the Objectives Resolution was a first but crucial step towards total religion by a process of 'desecularisation', that is, a collapsing together of the spheres of politics and religion (Saeed 2016: 24–40). However, the desire to create a theocratic state was difficult to operationalise because the major institutions of the state were under the control of a secular-minded and Westernised elite that held British colonial ideals. This status quo had to be upended if man-made law was to be replaced with God's law. As if to create such a disruption, the Ahrar, which had lost momentum after the creation of Pakistan, launched itself in the new country by leading an anti-Ahmadi campaign. This resulted in the widespread and violent agitations against the Ahmadis in the Punjab in 1953–1954.

The Ahrar reignited the Ahmadi controversy in order to reestablish itself politically (Nasr 1994: 132–141; Qasmi 2014: 35–63; Saeed 2016: 94–97). Specifically, they combined socialist politics with a call for Islamisation in an attempt to destabilise the central government. The Ahrar used wheat shortages and anti-Ahmadi feeling in the province to link the demand for socio-economic justice with the suppression of Ahmadis. They compared the wealth of the Ahmadis with the downtrodden peasant masses of Punjab, and asked that if Pakistan had been founded for the betterment of Muslims, then how it was that the Ahmadis – non-Muslims according to the Ahrar – were reaping all the benefits. The Ahrar was successful enough that Nawab Daultana, the Chief Minister of Punjab allied himself with the movement to bolster his support in an apparent attempt to bring down the central government and then make a bid for the office of prime minister.

One of the demands of the Ahrar was that Zafarullah Khan, now the foreign minister of Pakistan, be dismissed from his post. The government ignored this demand. Zafarullah Khan had good relations with the American and British governments and his dismissal on religious grounds would have caused embarrassment to the new nation-state. When, in 1952, Zafarullah Khan admitted publicly that he was an Ahmadi, it lent support to the Ahrar's conspiratorial claim that the government was controlled by Ahmadis, a community allegedly supported by imperialist powers (Nasr 1994: 133). Zafarullah Khan was made into the symbol of the 'outsider within'. Indeed, the Ahrar threatened mass riots if Zafarullah Khan did not resign.

All this time, as the leader of the Jama'at-i Islami, which like the Ahrar had also found itself organisationally and ideologically disoriented by the partition of British India, Mawdudi had tried to keep his energy focused on the Islamisation of the emerging constitution of Pakistan. He maintained the somewhat opaque position that Ahmadis would be reconverted to Islam once a proper Islamic government came into power. He had eschewed violent confrontation or public polemics against the group until it became clear that the Ahrar were going to carry the field with their rioting. Inspired by the Ahrar, Mawdudi too turned away from the 'rule' toward the 'exception'. Setting aside his work on constitutional Islamisation, he produced a sharp polemic entitled *The Qadiyani Problem* (*Qadiyani Mas'ala*) (Nadvi et al. 1993: 31–63; Maudoodi 1979). It became an instant success, propelling Mawdudi to the forefront of the anti-Ahmadi struggle.

Written in flowing Urdu prose, Mawdudi's work offered what appeared to be a systematic exposé of the Ahmadi movement's allegedly nefarious designs on the new nation of Pakistan. First, he made clear that this anti-Ahmadi agitation was not simply sectarian strife that had always existed in Muslim societies because the Ahmadis, by accepting Ghulam Ahmad as a prophet, were no longer a sect but a separate religious community. Furthermore, he argued, other minority Muslim sects present in the country were static, self-enclosed communities in contrast to the Ahmadis who were aggressively spreading their faith. Citing Ghulam Ahmad's professions of loyalty to the British crown, Mawdudi maintained that the Ahmadis did not want an Islamic state, but preferred an infidel one. He quoted from one of Ghulam Ahmad's letters to a British government officer in which the Ahmadi leader had explained his antagonistic position against the Christian missionaries as follows: Ghulam Ahmad was afraid that the missionaries, by insulting the prophet of Islam, would incite the hot-blooded Muslims to revolt against British rule; so, he vehemently attacked the missionaries in public to assuage Muslim anger and to prevent *jihad* against the British (Nadvi et al. 1993: 53–55). That the Ahmadi leader had tried to diffuse Muslim religious zeal that could have led to an armed struggle (*jihad*) against the British was an accusation that continued to echo in the Pakistani press and was repeated by conservative writers like Z. A. Suleri in 1974, when a second major wave of anti-Ahmadi politics swept the country (Saeed 2007: 142).[11] It would appear that Mawdudi was successful in casting the Ahmadis as collaborators, the outsiders within, who, in *Ernstfall*, become the worst of foes.

Mawdudi argued that the Ahmadis had wanted to be counted as Muslims in British India so they could gain influence out of proportion to their numbers. According to this scheme, he alleged, the Ahmadis first had obtained jobs reserved for Muslims. Then by enrolling other Ahmadis, they sought to increase their influence at the expense of Muslims. Mawdudi offered proof that after the creation of Pakistan the Ahmadis had attempted to use similar tactics to gain power beyond their numbers. He quoted from a speech given by an Ahmadi leader in the province of Baluchistan, in which the latter emphasised that Ahmadi missionaries should first target the sparsely populated province of Baluchistan. Since Baluchistan formed a whole 'unit' in the Pakistani federation, it carried a political importance greater than that implied by its small population. The implication was that if successful there, the Ahmadis would have a province of their own to use as a 'base' from which to operate (Nadvi et al. 1993: 50–51).

Ultimately, Mawdudi saw the Ahmadis as an existential threat that, like a cancerous sore (*sartani phorha*), must be cut out and removed from the body politic of Pakistan. The only way to accomplish this, he argued, would be for the government to formally declare the Ahmadis non-Muslims, and curtail their political rights. To not act, according to him, would be against democratic principles because this rational (*ma'qul*) demand was supported by the force of public opinion (*rai-i 'am*) (Nadvi et al. 1993: 60–64).

Despite Mawdudi's whole-hearted entry into the fray, the anti-Ahmadi struggle of 1953–1954 ended in disappointment for the religious political parties. The secular bureaucratic-military elite that held power at the centre was too strong. The state dismissed the Punjab government and imposed martial law in the province. Mawdudi was among those arrested and tried. A military tribunal even sentenced him to death on the charge of inciting hatred and public unrest. Although Mawdudi's sentence was eventually dismissed after two years, and he emerged from prison with his prestige enhanced, the first and second constitution of Pakistan in 1956 and 1962 contained nothing of the Islamic principles that Mawdudi and the 'ulama had demanded (Kennedy 1992; Nasr 1994: 137–138).

In 1954, a judicial committee, led by Justice Munir Muhammad published a report on the anti-Ahmadi agitations – later known as the Munir Report – that underlined the irrationality, incoherency, and fractiousness of the religious leadership. Justice Munir observed that the most well-known 'ulama and Islamists of the country could not even agree on how to define a Muslim (Nasr 1994: 138–139, 142; Qasmi 2014: 119–164). If such a basic principle of Islam escaped consensus, the thinking went, the demand for a modern Islamic state had little hope of being institutionalised. This cynicism is perhaps why the secularists in power had little difficulty with the insertion in the Objectives Resolution of the principle that sovereignty belonged only to God. In any case, the point that escaped Justice Munir's incisive analysis was that the one thing that all religious parties had agreed upon was that the Ahmadis were non-Muslims. There was a consensus, even if it was a negative one. Moreover, the rioting had demonstrated to all the usefulness of anti-Ahmadi feeling in summoning people's anger against the establishment. It had also exposed the fact that the state still derived its sovereign authority from the unpopular British-era model of the 'transcendence of the law'.

Largely because of colonial-era inertia, the first two decades of Pakistan's history are typically viewed in retrospect as the heyday of secularist politics. In the 1950s and 1960s, Westernised elites held power in the army and bureaucracy. Professors trained in British universities controlled higher education and set the curriculum for public schools. The population at large had little say in the matter because no general elections were held in Pakistan until 1970. For good reason, Saeed calls the defence of the minority rights of the Ahmadis by the undemocratic state in Pakistan's first two decades as an era of 'authoritarian inclusion' (Saeed 2016: 97–102). However, the apparent secularism among those in power in Pakistan's early decades did not mean that the majority was moving toward an acceptance of the principle of separation of religion and state. In fact, quite the opposite transpired. In the 1960s, Pakistan – like many other post-colonial states – experienced a massive demographic shift from rural areas to cities. This population movement occurred largely because of the efforts to industrialise the economy. However, as Gilles Kepel argues in his comparative study of the rise of political Islam across the Muslim world, the *en masse* movement to the cities weakened traditional religious practices rooted in village shrines and kinship networks (Kepel 2002: 65–69). It also created large concentrations of people who had access to modern education and aspired toward a better economic future but found themselves politically disenfranchised. Islamism became the rallying call of these recently urbanised and atomised individuals who were literate, but not in Western languages; and who were politically ambitious, but not invested in the Western colonial-era model of sovereignty. By the end of the 1960s, the effort by this emergent demographic to gain a political voice became the impetus behind the process of desecularisation and the turn toward 'total religion'. What was needed to make a play for sovereignty was a moment of large-scale disruption.

The crisis arrived in 1971. Pakistan had held its first unrestricted general election in 1970 but then refused to hand over power to the winner, the Awami League Party, which represented the Bengali-speaking majority of East Pakistan. The result was one of the region's worst civil wars, by some accounts more violent than the partition of British India in 1947. At the war's end, Pakistan stood less than half its size and thoroughly humiliated. It had not only lost the civil war with the Bengali separatists but also a military confrontation with its archenemy India. The country had yet to recover from this catastrophe and the state of emergency was still at play, when, in 1974, there began another round of anti-Ahmadi demonstrations in the Punjab (Saeed 2007: 141–145, 2016: 116–122). As previously described, the political and sociological context had changed radically from what it had been in 1954. The first-generation elite's hold on the state had weakened. The armed forces were no longer a bastion of secularism with a growing number of its officers now belonging to the more pious and religiously observant lower middle classes. Finally, the student wing of the Jama'at-i Islami, the Jami'at-i Talaba-i Islam (JTI), had emerged as an effective cadre organisation, modelled along the lines of the Egyptian Muslim Brotherhood's militant arm. Its ranks filled with upwardly mobile young men from rural areas and small towns, JTI had entrenched itself in major public university campuses and was capable of launching violent demonstrations. In 1974, it was the JTI that led the anti-Ahmadi agitation, and the campaign against the government of Zulfiqar Ali Bhutto (Nasr 1994: 171–181).

Bhutto had campaigned on a populist socialist agenda but upon gaining power allied himself with the landed feudal elite to maintain power. He also resorted increasingly to autocratic methods to suppress dissent. When faced with opposition from the religious parties, and having alienated his support base in Pakistani labour groups and middle-class leftist intellectuals, he began to make compromises with the Islamists and the ‘ulama. Under such pressure, it is conventionally believed, Bhutto passed a constitutional amendment in 1974 declaring the Ahmadis to be non-Muslims. However, Sadia Saeed has argued against the conventional view and shown, instead, that Bhutto actively sought the charisma that would inhere to the leader who declared the Ahmadis outside the fold of Islam. There are indications that he had privately made it clear to all elected parliamentarians that he wanted them to vote for the constitutional amendment. One opposition Member of the National Assembly (MNA), interviewed by Saeed, attributed the unanimous vote for the constitutional amendment against the Ahmadis to Bhutto's authoritarianism, comparing it to that of Hitler and Mussolini: ‘Nobody dare vote against Bhutto's wishes’ (Saeed 2016: 135–139).

The journalist and politician Hussain Haqqani observes that in 1974 Bhutto did three disparate things to construct a powerful image as a leader of Islam. He hosted the Islamic Conference, a major international event involving the heads of state of much of the Muslim world, where he declared Pakistan to be the fortress of Islam. He also launched the development of the nuclear bomb, which became fondly known as the Islamic bomb. And, third, he modified Pakistan's constitution to declare Ahmadis as non-Muslim (Haqqani 2005: 106–107). When seen through the prism of messianism, Bhutto's three actions do not appear to be so disjointed in their symbolism. The unification of Islam under one flag, the deployment of military capability of apocalyptic proportions against the external enemies of Islam, and the extirpation of an internal threat posed by a heretical and global conspiracy against Muslims mesh well with the basic tropes of doctrinal messianism. The messiah, according to doctrinal tradition, will unite Muslims under a single banner and then lead them in a final set of battles against united forces of antichrist (Madelung 2011). In Bhutto's three-part enactment of this ritual scheme, the Ahmadis were cast into the last category as supporters of antichrist. If Bhutto's fateful embrace of Islamism can be interpreted as a move toward total religion (an intensified desecularisation) in a time of *Ernstfall* (the civil war and the loss of East Pakistan), his treatment of the Ahmadis appears to follow a particular sovereign logic. The national community that such a move envisioned had no place for the Ahmadis because it was predicated on their total exclusion as the outsiders within.

Bhutto's turn toward Islamic rhetoric and messianic symbolism did not ensure his political longevity. He, like the emperor Akbar, had tried to absorb the charisma of a messianic moment to raise his stature, but was unable to translate it into an enduring form of sovereignty. His conservative and Islam-inclined Army chief, General Zia-ul-Haq, overthrew Bhutto's government in a military coup in 1979 and later tried and sentenced Pakistan's first democratically elected prime minister to death for the murder of a political opponent.

General Zia was an admirer of Mawdudi's writings on Islam, and echoed the latter by publicly calling for the eradication of the ‘cancer’ of Qadiyanism (Friedmann 1989: 46). He employed Mawdudi's ideas as well as his organisation, the Jama‘at-i Islami, to enact a gradual Islamisation of Pakistani state and society (Kennedy 1992). Most significant is his Ordinance XX, issued in 1984 and entitled, 'Anti-Islamic Activities of the Quadiani Group, Lahori Group and Ahmadis (Prohibition and Punishment) Ordinance'. This law, which followed the third concerted anti-Ahmadi movement led by the Islamist parties, made it a punishable offence for Ahmadis to use any Islamic phrase or symbol publicly in their religious practice (Saeed 2016: 156–165). Ahmadis could, and indeed were, sent to prison for writing 'bismillah' (in the name of Allah) on marriage invitations or, as discussed later, wearing badges which had the Muslim profession of faith, called 'kalima' in Urdu. In short, these laws encouraged criminal charges to be brought against Ahmadis, who could now be persecuted at ease with the help of the police and the courts (Friedmann 1989: 45–46, 192–194).

Zia's anti-Ahmadi policies had captured the religious mood of the country. Literature targeting Ahmadis became widespread. Even children's books written in Urdu included anti-Ahmadi messages. There began to appear in the 1980s several pages of anti-Ahmadi polemics at the end of Urdu novels written by Ishtiaq Ahmad, Pakistan's most popular author of detective stories and youth fiction, who wrote prolifically at the rate of four books a month and reached a mass audience of both young and adult readers across Pakistan. This atmosphere of anti-Ahmadi exuberance did not abate after Zia's death. Indeed, not everyone was satisfied with General Zia receiving all the accolades for Islamising Pakistan and dealing firmly with the Ahmadis. Sayyid Muhammad Sultan Shah, a Bhutto supporter, published a book in 1993 – when Benazir Bhutto, Zulfiqar Bhutto's daughter, was in power – to remind Pakistan that it was Bhutto and not Zia who should get credit for acting against the Ahmadis. Notably, Shah's book was in Urdu with a title that echoed the famous polemic written earlier by Mawdudi, *Bhutto and the Qadiyani Problem* (*Bhutto aur qadiyani mas'ala*).

The fact that Shah wrote in Urdu is significant. The Urdu-language public sphere in Pakistan had by this time become Islamised. Urdu newspapers in the 1990s carried Islamist and anti-Western opinions and stories that routinely did not make it into the Westernised English-language press. This bifurcation of Pakistan's public sphere into a Westernised and Islamised one is a reflection of the demographic shift, described earlier, that by the 1970s produced a disenfranchised, urbanised political class. Under Zia, this politicised class began to assert itself in an oppositional non-Western idiom that was Islamist and often conspiratorial. In his book, Shah deployed such an idiom, asserting that Bhutto had been warned not to touch the Ahmadis by the Americans. He specifically mentioned Henry Kissinger's meeting with Bhutto and pointed out that Kissinger was a Jew (Shah 1993: 13–16, 145–150). The suggestion of a link between the Ahmadis and Imperialist-Jewish forces aligned against Pakistan and Islam is a revival of the same conspiracy theory that had surfaced in the first agitations against the movement in the 1950s.[12] Shah argued that Bhutto, despite knowing the danger to his government and his life, went ahead with the 1974 constitutional amendment against the Ahmadis. In revenge, according to Shah, the Ahmadis engineered Bhutto's death. The evidence Shah gave for this claim was that the police officer who had given testimony against Bhutto in the murder trial leading to his execution had been an Ahmadi.

It is hard to take Shah's conspiracy theory seriously as political analysis despite its presentation as a scholarly argument complete with footnotes and appendices. Nonetheless, it demonstrates how by the 1990s the Ahmadis had become the very embodiment of religious pollution and political subversion. To neglect this perceived threat was to risk losing one's Islamic credentials, a major liability in a country where Islam, rather than language, territoriality or ethnicity, had become the primary factor in imagining the nation and its history (Jalal 1995). With the intensification of desecularisation, anti-Ahmadi action, once a subversive tactic used by the struggling Ahrar in the 1950s to establish itself in rural Punjab, had become a widespread convention of politics. Violence against Ahmadis was no longer a transgression of the law but a ritual of sovereignty.[13]

Sovereignty between law and miracle

In 1993, three years before the death of the Nobel Laureate Dr. Abdus Salam, the Supreme Court of Pakistan heard an appeal filed by three men of the Ahmadi community who had been sentenced to one year of rigorous imprisonment for 'posing as Muslims'. Their crime had been wearing badges with the Muslim profession of faith written on it. The panel of five judges, in a majority decision with one dissenting vote, rejected the appeal of the Ahmadis.[14] The text of this court decision is revealing on several accounts. In clear terms, the judges emphasise multiple times that the secular courts have the onus of deciding what proper, authentic religion is.[15] The practice of defining religion via the courts, as Radhika Singha has shown, is a legacy of British colonial rule (Singha 1998). According to her, the British in India had declared it their intention to govern Indians by their own religious law, but in the process ended up changing the meaning and place of both religion and law in India. Law became the mechanism through which colonial despotism was imposed on Indian society, as the British courts took it upon themselves to legalise or criminalise religious practices. In other words, it was British judges, not experts in religious law, who decided matters of religion in colonial India. Pakistan continued this policy. Even under General Zia, who did the most to Islamise Pakistan, the final authority to rule on matters of religion was given to the secular courts not Muslim jurists (Kennedy 1992; Saeed 2016: 198–200).[16]

Even so, the question remained: who could decide upon the definition of Muslim? In 1954, Justice Munir had pointed out that Muslim jurists and Islamists, despite being united in opposition against the Ahmadis, were unable to agree on such a definition. However, by 1993, the Supreme Court judges who heard the Ahmadi's appeal had found an answer. In their written decision against the Ahmadi defendants, whom they declared as non-Muslims and refused to release from prison, the judges did not mention any authority in the traditional Islamic sense, either in the form of a text or institution. They did not seek a *fatwa* or juridical response from a shari'a expert. Instead, the justices simply cited the

1974 Constitutional Amendment against the Ahmadis and quoted the words of Muhammad Iqbal.[17]

This turn toward Iqbal, I would suggest, indicates a break from colonial-era precedence. It abandons the Orientalist notion that religion is to be found in some ancient and unchanging textual tradition. Instead, the mere words of the man who first saw the 'dream' of Pakistan – the nation's patron saint, in a way – sufficed.[18] Moreover, this was a shift away from the bureaucratic and abstract form of authority inherited from colonial rule, and a return to an older notion of concrete and embodied authority reminiscent of the high era of Mughal rule (Moin 2017).[19] The Pakistani state had issued a legal judgement that derived its force not just from the constitution and the law but also from the words of a charismatic founder. It had gone beyond the law to set the words of its holy man against that of the Ahmadi messiah. To paraphrase Schmitt, the state had demonstrated its sovereignty not just by reason but also by miracle.

Conclusion

Power cannot legitimate itself simply by reference to itself but must do so with 'respect to larger, *extrapolitical* processes of power (even if hidden and ineffable) in the cosmos – processes operating outside the realm of the overtly "social" or "political"' (Gilmartin 2017: 80–88, 81). I have attempted to trace how such processes shaped sovereignty in Pakistan with reference to the Ahmadis. In 1954, the newly founded post-colonial state, still confident in its ability to manage religion as a separate sphere of culture, had defended the Ahmadis against the Islamists. Sovereignty appeared to be at the time simply a matter of upholding the supremacy of law. However, with increasing Islamisation of society, and especially after the devastating 1971 civil war, the Ahmadi position in the national community became precarious, leading to their formal exclusion in 1974 and criminalisation in 1984. No longer protected by the law, they were banned and abandoned by it – as Giorgio Agamben puts it, 'exposed at the threshold of the law'.[20] A symptom of this abandonment is how anti-Ahmadi action became ritualised. When the state sent out its agents to erase the word 'Muslim' from the epitaph of Dr. Abdus Salam, it required these men to play the role of priests. In other words, if sovereignty is a limit concept (Schmitt 2005: 5; Agamben 1998: 11, passim), then marking the boundary of the law is surely a rite of purification.

Notes

1 Several Pakistani newspaper columns written on the tenth anniversary of Dr. Abdus Salam's death mentioned this incident. A photograph of the defaced gravestone is published in the BBC report (Khan 2016) which also catalogues the recent cautious steps taken by Prime Minister Nawaz Sharif to celebrate Dr. Abdus Salam's scientific achievements.

2 Schmitt's work still inspires considerable discussion (Vatter 2016), not least for his trenchant criticism of what he believed to be the 'disenchanted' political theology of liberal secularism (Yelle 2010).

3 As Giorgio Agamben notes: 'From the juridico-political perspective, messianism is therefore a theory of the state of exception – except for the fact that in messianism there is no authority in force to proclaim the state of exception; instead, there is the Messiah to subvert its power' (Agamben 1998: 57–58).

4 These public debates were started by British missionaries and tended to be formulaic and predictable (Metcalf 2005: 198–234).

5 Iqbal's June 10, 1935 letter to the 'Statesman' is reprinted in Appendix III of *The Qadiani Problem* (Maudoodi 1979: 65–69).

6 Religion in colonial India was often defined in British courts (Singha 1998), which was part of a larger pattern of colonial forms of knowledge shaping cultural categories and practices (Cohn 1996; Dirks 2001).

7 Indeed, Jawaharlal Nehru had compared the Ahmadi case to that of the Ismailis when he warned that to paint one group as 'heretic' would open the way for a whole series of denunciations (Devji 2013: 155).

8 The projection of the soul, according to Bada'uni, was not the same thing as the transmigration of the soul. The latter was considered a heretical notion because it shared similarities with the idea of reincarnation in Indic and Manichean traditions. In transmigration, a soul was thought to be reborn into a new body. In projection, however, it was believed that the divine soul emanated itself into a person whose soul had achieved a high degree of purity.

9 In total religion, 'All other spheres of culture are subordinated to religion and controlled by the [divine] law that forms the basis of the covenant: art by the prohibition of images, law and economy by corresponding regulations, cult by the ritual laws, and, above all, the political, the institution of kingship that is now clearly and completely subordinated under the Torah [that is, God's law]' (Assmann 2014: 113–129, 125).

10 Note also that this biblical requirement of total annihilation of the enemy inside the holy land with no recourse to the courts of law is akin to treating the foe or the 'outsider within' in manner of the *homo sacer* defined by Giorgio Agamben as someone brought to the threshold of the law – neither inside nor outside – who can be killed by anyone but cannot be sacrificed or legally executed (Agamben 1998).

11 The anxiety and paranoia surrounding the Ahmadis has invited comparisons with the status of the Jews in Nazi Germany (Qasmi 2014: 220).

12 Nasr also hinted at this conspiracy theory when he observed that Bhutto was forced to act against the Ahmadis because of politically damaging rumours that the Ahmadi movement supported his government (Nasr 1994: 172).

13 An unforeseen consequence of these endeavours, however, was an increase in sectarianism and sectarian violence in Pakistan. The techniques of organised violence, propaganda, and legal argumentation that were used against the Shi'a from the 1980s onwards in Pakistan had been first honed in campaigns against the Ahmadis (Zaman 2002: 113–114, 119).

14 This 1993 Supreme Court decision case is discussed in Saeed (2016: 200–206). The text of the decision is available online via a website dedicated to anti-Ahmadi literature (Rahman et al. 1993).

15 For example, one judge states that 'It is further held that it is for the courts to determine whether a particular practice, constitutes essential and integral part of the religion or not? In that view of the matter, these practices have to be stated and proved so, from the authentic sources, of the religion, to the satisfaction of the court' (Rahman et al. 1993).

16 Kennedy also argues that the Islamic religious parties, disappointed with the legislative route, had begun to resort to judicial activism under Zia to bring about Islamisation of the law.

17 The judges wrote: 'Allama Iqbal says, "I became suspicious of the Quadiani movement when the claim of new prophethood, superior even to the prophethood of the Founder of Islam, was definitely put forward, and Muslim world was declared 'Kafir' (infidel). Later, my suspicion developed into a positive revolt when I heard with my own ears

an adherent of the movement mentioning the Holy Prophet of Islam in a disparaging language" (See Thoughts and Reflection of Iqbal, page 297–1973 Edition)' (Rahman et al. 1993).

18 Iqbal's words on the matter are an integral part of most anti-Ahmadi literature. Even the Islamist party, Jama'at-i Islami published Iqbal's English-language writings on the Ahmadis in an appendix to a translation of Mawdudi's book against the Ahmadis (Maudoodi 1979).

19 There is some parallel between the bureaucratisation of law under the British and the situation described by Brinkley Messick in his discussion of the Yemeni practice of Shari'a, which transformed in the nineteenth century from the personalised and embodied to the impersonal and abstract under the modernising influence of the Ottoman state (Messick 1993).

20 The Ahmadis' position became analogous to those who are exposed at the threshold of law: 'He who has been banned is not, in fact, simply set outside the law and made indifferent to it but rather abandoned by it, that is, exposed and threatened on the threshold in which life and law, outside and inside, become indistinguishable. It is literally not possible to say whether the one who has been banned is outside or inside the juridical order' (Agamben 1998: 28–29).

References

Agamben, Giorgio. 1998. *Homo Sacer: Sovereign Power and Bare Life*. Stanford: Stanford University Press.

Assmann, Jan. 2010. *The Price of Monotheism*. Stanford: Stanford University Press.

Assmann, Jan. 2014. 'Total Religion: Politics, Monotheism, and Violence', in Assmann, *From Akhenaten to Moses: Ancient Egypt and Religious Change*, pp. 113–129. Cairo: American University in Cairo Press.

Bada'uni, Abd al-Qadir ibn Muluk Shah. 1973. *Muntakhab-ut-Tawarikh*. 1st ed. 3 vols. New Delhi: Idarah-i-Adabiyat-i-Delli.

Bada'uni, Abd al-Qadir ibn Muluk Shah. 1976. *Muntakhabu-t-Tawarikh: By 'Abdul Qadir bin-Muluk Shah Known as al-Badaoni*, trans. by George S. A. Ranking and Wolseley H. Lowe. 1st in Pakistan ed. 3 vols. Karachi: Karimsons.

Bayly, Christopher A. 1996. *Empire and Information: Intelligence Gathering and Social Communication in India, 1780–1870*. Cambridge: Cambridge University Press.

Benjamin, Walter. 1986. 'Critique of Violence', in Benjamin, *Reflections*, pp. 277–300. New York: Schocken Books.

Berger, Peter L. 1979. *The Heretical Imperative: Contemporary Possibilities of Religious Affirmation*. Garden City, NY: Anchor Press.

Cohn, Bernard S. 1996. *Colonialism and Its Forms of Knowledge: The British in India*. Princeton: Princeton University Press.

Cowasjee, Ardeshir. 2006. 'Lest We Forget', *Dawn*, November 26, Cowasjee Corner. http://dawn.com/weekly/cowas/20061126.htm (Accessed December 16, 2006).

Dadlani, Chanchal B. 2018. *From Stone to Paper: Architecture as History in the Late Mughal Empire*. New Haven, CT: Yale University Press.

Devji, Faisal. 2005. *Landscapes of the Jihad: Militancy, Morality, Modernity, Crises in World Politics*. Ithaca: Cornell University Press.

Devji, Faisal. 2013. *Muslim Zion: Pakistan as a Political Idea*. Cambridge, MA: Harvard University Press.

Dirks, Nicholas B. 2001. *Castes of Mind: Colonialism and the Making of Modern India*. Princeton: Princeton University Press.

Friedmann, Yohanan. 1989. *Prophecy Continuous: Aspects of Ahmadi Religious Thought and Its Medieval Background*. Berkeley, CA: University of California Press.
Gilmartin, David. 2012. 'Towards a Global History of Voting: Sovereignty, the Diffusion of Ideas, and the Enchanted Individual', *Religions*, 3: 407–423.
Gilmartin, David. 2017. 'Imperial Sovereignty in Mughal and British Forms', *History and Theory*, 56 (1): 80–88.
Green, Nile. 2011. *Bombay Islam: The Religious Economy of the West Indian Ocean, 1840–1915*. Cambridge: Cambridge University Press.
Haqqani, Husain. 2005. *Pakistan: Between Mosque and Military*. Washington, DC: Carnegie Endowment for International Peace: Distributor Brookings Institution Press.
Iqbal, Muhammad. 1974a. 'Islam and Ahmadism', in A. R. Tariq (ed.), *Speeches and Statements of Iqbal*, pp. 109–139. Lucknow: Academy of Islamic Research and Publications.
Iqbal, Muhammad. 1974b. 'Islam and Ahmadism'. www.koranselskab.dk/profiler/iqbal/ahmadism.htm (Accessed October 5, 2016).
Jalal, Ayesha. 1995. 'Conjuring Pakistan: History as Official Imagining', *International Journal of Middle East Studies*, 27 (1): 73–89.
Kamran, Tahir. 2015. 'The Pre-History of Religious Exclusionism in Contemporary Pakistan: Khatam-e-Nubuwwat 1889–1953', *Modern Asian Studies*, 49 (6): 1840–1874.
Kennedy, Charles. 1992. 'Repugnancy to Islam: Who Decides? Islam and Legal Reform in Pakistan', *The International and Comparative Law Quarterly*, 41 (4): 769–787.
Kepel, Gilles. 2002. *Jihad: The Trail of Political Islam*. Cambridge, MA: Belknap Press of Harvard University Press.
Khan, M. Ilyas. 2016. 'Why Has This Nobel Winner Been Ignored for 30 Years?', *BBC News*, December 8, Asia. www.bbc.com/news/worldasia38238131 (Accessed December 16, 2006).
Kinra, Rajeev. 2013. 'Handling Diversity With Absolute Civility: The Global Historical Legacy of Mughal Sulh-i Kull', *The Medieval History Journal*, 16 (2): 251–295.
Madelung, Wilfred. 2011. 'al-Mahdī.', in P. Bearman, Th. Bianquis, C. E. Bosworth, E. van Donzel, and W. P. Heinrichs (eds.), *The Encyclopaedia of Islam*, 2nd ed. Brill. www.brillonline.nl (Accessed January 1, 2007).
Maudoodi, Syed Abul 'Ala. 1979. *The Qadiani Problem*. 1st ed. Lahore: Islamic Publications.
Messick, Brinkley Morris. 1993. *The Calligraphic State: Textual Domination and History in a Muslim Society*. Berkeley, CA: University of California Press.
Metcalf, Barbara D. 2005. *Islamic Revival in British India: Deoband, 1860–1900*. New York: Oxford University Press.
Moin, A. Azfar. 2009. 'Challenging the Mughal Emperor: The Islamic Millennium According to 'Abd al-Qadir Badayuni', in B. Metcalf (ed.), *Islam in South Asia in Practice*, pp. 390–402. Princeton: Princeton University Press.
Moin, A. Azfar. 2012. *The Millennial Sovereign: Sacred Kingship and Sainthood in Islam*. New York: Columbia University Press.
Moin, A. Azfar. 2017. 'The "Millennium" of 1857: The Last Performance of the Great Mughal', in Z. Benite and S. Geroulanos (eds.), *The Scaffolding of Sovereignty: Global and Aesthetic Perspectives on the History of a Concept*, pp. 322–339. New York: Columbia University Press.
Moin, A. Azfar. 2019. 'Millennial Sovereignty and the Mughal Dynasty', in R. Eaton and R. Sreenivasan (eds.), *Oxford Handbook of the Mughal World*. Oxford: Oxford University Press.
Nadvi, Abul hasan Ali, Syed Abul 'Ala Maudoodi, and Shaikh Muhammad Khizar Husain. 1993. *Qadyaniyat*. New Delhi: Markaz-i Maktabah-yi Islami.

Nasr, Seyyed Vali Reza. 1994. *The Vanguard of the Islamic Revolution: The Jama'at-i Islami of Pakistan*. Berkeley, CA: University of California Press.
Qasmi, Ali Usman. 2014. *The Ahmadis and the Politics of Religious Exclusion in Pakistan*. New York: Anthem Press.
Rahman, Shafiur, Abdul Qadeer Chaudhry, Muhammad Afzal Lone, Saleem Akhtar, and Wali Muhammad Khan. 1993. 'Judgment of Supreme Court of Pakistan'. Idara Dawat-o-Irshad, USA, Inc. www.irshad.org/exposed/legal/pkcort93.php (Accessed September 22, 2017).
Saeed, Sadia. 2007. 'Pakistani Nationalism and the State Marginalization of Ahmadiyya Community in Pakistan', *Studies in Ethnicity and Nationalism*, 7 (3): 132–152.
Saeed, Sadia. 2016. *Politics of Desecularization: Law and the Minority Question in Pakistan*. New York: Cambridge University Press.
Schmitt, Carl. 2005. *Political Theology: Four Chapters on the Concept of Sovereignty*. Chicago: University of Chicago Press.
Schmitt, Carl. 2007. *The Concept of the Political*. Chicago: University of Chicago Press.
Sevea, Iqbal Singh. 2012. *The Political Philosophy of Muhammad Iqbal: Islam and Nationalism in Late Colonial India*. Cambridge: Cambridge University Press.
Shah, Sayyid Muhammad Sultan. 1993. *Bhutto aur Qadiyani Mas'ala*. Lahore: Jang Publishers.
Singha, Radhika. 1998. *A Despotism of Law: Crime and Justice in Early Colonial India*. New Delhi: Oxford University Press.
Thrupp, Sylvia L. (ed.). 1970. *Millennial Dreams in Action: Studies in Revolutionary Religious Movements*. New York: Schocken Books.
Troll, Christian W. 1978. *Sayyid Ahmad Khan: A Reinterpretation of Muslim Theology*. New Delhi: Vikas Publishing House.
Vatter, Miguel. 2016. 'The Political Theology of Carl Schmitt', in J. Meierhenrich and O. Simons (eds.), *Oxford Handbook of Carl Schmitt*, pp. 245–268. New York: Oxford University Press.
Yelle, Robert. 2010. 'The Trouble with Transcendence: Carl Schmitt's "Exception" as a Challenge for Religious Studies', *Method & Theory in the Study of Religion*, 22 (2/3): 189–206.
Zaman, Muhammad Qasim. 2002. *The Ulama in Contemporary Islam: Custodians of Change, Princeton Studies in Muslim Politics*. Princeton: Princeton University Press.

8

SOVEREIGN SENSIBILITIES

Gunday and the nation as the self

Arild Engelsen Ruud

At a press conference in 2016 a senior party leader of the governing party in Bangladesh defended a new law. This law prohibits organisations that receive funding from abroad from criticising the constitution of Bangladesh and its parliament. This law was taken by many to be a restriction on civil liberties, and it was widely criticised. In defence of the new law, ruling party leader and government minister Suranjit Sengupta evoked notions of sovereignty. He held that the national parliament is a sovereign parliament (*sarbobhoumo shongshod*), and because it is a sovereign parliament no 'foreign body' (using the English terms) could 'use abusive language' (*gali*) against it. Criticism by organisations financed from abroad could not be permitted, he held, because then the sovereignty (*sharbobhoumotvo*) of the national parliament would be lost. Such criticism is not allowed anywhere in the world, he claimed. However, he pointed out, criticism of the parliament was of course permitted for the Bangladeshi media. Bangladeshi media may criticise parliament because the constitution has given them this freedom (*shongbidhan gonomadhyomke shadhinota diyechhe*). But foreign bodies had no such right (*odhikar*) (*Prothom Alo* 2016).

Sengupta's statement had clearly a very immediate political objective, to deflect criticism of a particular law that was being passed and more generally to deflect criticism of a government perceived as increasingly autocratic and sensitive. However, Sengupta was also a very seasoned politician and astutely aware of how to phrase an argument. The statement is interesting for the ways it portrays widespread notions of Bangladeshi sovereignty. His statement resonated well with popular perceptions that came out, as we shall see, in an online outburst of anger at an Indian 'Bollywood' film three years earlier. There are in particular three aspects raised by Sengupta that are salient.

The first is the suspicion he rallied against 'foreigners' or those funded by foreigners. His government had for years been criticised by organisations in what is commonly referred to as 'civil society', many of which, and probably a majority of the more prominent ones, receive funding from abroad.[1] Sengupta tied the term 'foreign bodies' to the suggestion that such organisations were potentially opposed to the sovereignty of the nation, an allegation that in the context of Bangladesh and its bloody war of independence is a serious one. A second aspect was the demand that the country's sovereignty must be respected, which implies that it often is not. This lack of respect from outside or an incomplete acknowledgement by outsiders of Bangladesh's rightful place in the world is, as we shall see, a powerful trope that also has wide circulation in popular imaginings. A third aspect of his statement is that the right to speak against the parliament was given to Bangladeshi media by its constitution. The way in which the statement was phrased – 'the constitution has given this freedom' – suggests that the right to criticise parliament was given by an entity above those who receive the right, an entity separate from the individual or from the collective of individuals that make up the nation. Sengupta seems to have suggested a notion that the constitution, as an expression of the sovereignty of the nation, was somehow above the collective of individuals and organs of society.

This chapter is an investigation into these popular notions, these ideas to do with the independence of the nation and its people's right and duty to defend it. As such, this is an investigation into the relationship between popular notions, narratives and ideas on the one hand and the way in which 'the nation' thinks about itself at an aggregate level. This is not to suggest that nations have 'souls' or anything similar, but to investigate why nations act on particular stimuli and why the reaction takes the shape it does.

The voter-sovereign

Sengupta's take on the constitution as something above the people is not his alone. The notion that the sovereignty of the nation is embodied in 'the people' yet also above it is found in a number of contexts, including, as we shall see, in the reactions to this film. This double nature of the nation's sovereignty is not specifically Bangladeshi, but it is also Bangladeshi. In the case of Bangladesh, the double nature is encapsulated in its constitution, for instance, where a distinction between the nation as a collective of citizens and the nation as something sublime and independent of the individual is made. In the Preamble to the constitution it is stated that it was 'We, the people of Bangladesh' who proclaimed independence in 1971, who fought 'a historical struggle for national liberation' and who finally established an 'independent, sovereign People's Republic of Bangladesh'. But then the text changes the pronoun and somehow shifts the perspective, lifting the constitution to somewhere above this 'we'. The rest of the text talks about 'our' people, not 'we'. The constitution states for instance that high ideals inspired 'our heroic people' and 'our brave martyrs' to dedication and sacrifice. The remainder of the text of the constitution retains this 'from above' perspective.

Surveys and ethnographic investigations suggest that the people of Bangladesh are like the people of India and other parts of South Asia: their support for electoral democracy is high, but their trust in state institutions, political parties, the rule of law and so on is low (Shastri et al. 2017). There is little evidence to suggest that voters perceive of any state institution as the embodiment of their (the people's) sovereign rights. And yet the notion that 'the people' as the sovereign is strengthened by an omnipresent emphasis on 'the people' as the source of power and legitimacy. The phrase 'the people is the source of all power' is found for instance in school textbooks (National Curriculum and Textbook Board 2012: 6). It is found in the constitution, where article 7(1) says that 'all powers in the Republic belong to the people'. Political scientist Mubashar Hasan (2014) points out that 'Politicians in our country often use the phrase "people are the source of all power"'. The republic is known as the People's Republic of Bangladesh (*Gonoprojatontri Bangladesh*), where the 'proja' of the name indicates that it is the ordinary man and woman who have been lifted to the centre of the republic's legitimacy. Rather than state institutions, it is 'the people' that is at the core of the state.

Historically it was the king who held this position both in India and in Europe, as both active in society (ruling, collecting taxes, dispensing punishment) and a moral agent above society, its ultimate representation. The double nature of historical kingship has long been the subject of investigation and different aspects of the double nature have been sought and captured in phrases such as 'the king's two bodies', 'the kingly conundrum' or 'the stranger-king' (Heesterman 1985; Hansen 2001). It is in this place the voter now stands. That the voter is supreme is underlined in modern electoral democracies by the powers of the vote as a means through which rulers are chosen. In an article from 2012, David Gilmartin points out that embedded in the modern construction of democracy lies a vision of the individual voter 'as both an active player in the world, and yet, at the very same time, as an autonomous moral agent, transcending the bonds of society' (Gilmartin 2012: 411). The voter *qua* voter will supposedly consider his individual wordly interests as he decides on how to vote. At the same time the voter should also and at the same time consider the interests of the community as a whole. This is underlined in the secret ballot and in the curtain that shields the voter in the crucial act from outside interference. 'The image of the free individual voter, separated from society, was asserted, even for illiterate voters, through a technology of secret voting based on electoral symbols' (Gilmartin 2012: 417). Thus the citizen in exercising his or her powers in a modern electoral democracy is both a voter who votes according to his or her particularistic interests and at the same time a sovereign transcending the boundaries of society. This voter-sovereign has taken the place of the king, and in the same way as the king-sovereign, the voter-sovereign is double-natured. The conflict between self-interest on the one hand and obligation towards the community on the other is built into the very idea of voting and democracy. The voter-sovereign is both of society and above it.

In a traditional or religion-inspired vision of society, man is obligated to God in his actions. 'God fearing' means just, righteous, and law abiding. In the secular and disenchanted democratic vision, that obligation is founded on the more fuzzy notions of human equality, dignity, and reciprocal recognition. These are increasingly widespread notions, but they are less absolute and entail a less certain onthology, more open to negotiation. Claude Lefort has pointed out (in Thomas Blom Hansen's reading) that modern democracy inaugurated an experience in which society is constantly searching for its own foundation (Hansen 2004: 24). Political power has become something abstract that could be held by no one – as it belonged to 'the people' and only could be represented temporarily. As a consequence, society has become unrepresented and unrepresentable, because 'all markers of certainty were disappearing'. Hansen uses this to underline how community, society, or the nation is in constant search of general and accepted representations, and because everything is contested and oppositions made visible, there is a need (desire?) for 'ever new forms of representation – in elections, in texts in speech and images' (Hansen 2004: 24). It is in this new ontological reality the voter is to make his or her choices in the voting booth.

This sociology of the marker-deficient society points us in an important direction. The omnipresence of democracy as an ideal should not lead us to believe that the voter-sovereign is alike all over. That the voter-sovereign is not outside time and space but very much part of his or her time and culture is convincingly exemplified by Lucia Michelutti's ethnographic investigation into 'vernacularised' understandings of democracy of north India, and by Anastasia Piliavsky's suggestion that conceptions underlying our understanding of democracy, such as equality, may not be shared everywhere (Michelutti 2008; Piliavsky 2014). An interesting angle for investigating the particularities of the relationship between the voter-sovereign and his/her community can be had from Bonnie Mann's investigation into how nations are gendered. In *Sovereign Masculinities* she draws our attention to the close relationship between the imagined national individual and policy making – including foreign policy and decisions about war (Mann 2014).

In Mann's reading, the particularities of the early twenty-first-century US hero are exemplified in the blockbuster movie *The Hurt Locker*. Here, the main protagonist, the hero who defuses bombs, is courageous and skilled in the use of all sorts of technological devises. But he is also excentric and certainly reckless in his complete and self-effacing dedication to his bomb-defusing tasks. As war veterans pointed out in their reactions to the film, that was not how the Iraq war was fought. But in the popular screen rendering the hero is not calm and rational – he is slightly mad, emotional, and able to grasp a situation in ways he is not able to verbalise. He has all possible technological devises at his disposal, but in the end scene he rejects these and relies instead on guts and instinct. The parallel to the political reaction to a terror attack is strong. A war without planning, without rationale; an emotional gut reaction. Mann uses her reading of the film to illuminate the US reactions and rhetoric after 11 September 2001 (the film came later, but expresses the sentiments), a 'fantasy of masculine sovereignty'.

The maleness of the national ideal is a crucial aspect. To Mann, the notion of national manhood ties to ideas of sovereignty. Building on Simone de Beauvoir she emphasises the contrast between intersubjective vulnerability and dependency on the one hand and invulnerability and independence on the other. In de Beauvoir's view this is the female subordination under men. In Mann's reading it is not necessarily about dominance, it is about freedom from dominance and vulnerability. To be dominated is to be feminine, to be undominated and invulnerable is to be male. This independence is what constitutes to be sovereign and defines intersubjective sovereignty. For nations the ultimate aim is independence, sovereignty, and as unfree nations strive towards independence their masculinity is being formed through a conversion from vulnerable to invulnerable and sovereign.

As Mann acknowledges, there is no straight relationship between bodily gender and the gender of nations. They are at best 'strange cousins', and 'national manhood' and similar ideas are imaginary formations that 'cannot, properly speaking, be said to exist' (Mann 2014: 10–11). Her point and the point we take away is, nonetheless, that certain values associated with sovereignty and independence are also associated with maleness and that this notion of gendered nationhood affects the nation's understanding of itself.

Interestingly, the excentric protagonist of *The Hurt Locker* is quite different from the sensible, law-upholding John Wayne-type hero of American popular culture from the 1950s and onwards. Early twenty-first-century American maleness is a culturally and historically distinct formation of notions and values. While we agree that nations may have a gendered identity, we also need to account for differences in time and place. As the gendered nations and their values are constituted by the voter-sovereigns in modern electoral democracies, the particularities of the constructions depend on the processes through which the individual self-identifies with the larger collective entity. These are the processes Jean Bethke Elshtain calls 'soft self-sovereignty' (Elshtain 2008), wherethrough the self is absorbed in a collective to become one with the larger entity. It is by being in this collective that the self takes part in sovereignty and that the self *is* the sovereign. 'One finds the full triumph of the self and the will-to-power and self-transcendence in and through a group project', writes Elshtain (2008: 205). It is this form of self-fulfillment that was promised by the totalising ideologies of the twentieth century, fascism and communism, but it is evident in most (all?) forms of nationalism or identity formation that lay claim on the individual. In such modern ideologies there is no transcendent truth, no God; there is only the immanent will of the group, of those within the magic circle (Elshtain 2008: 207–208).

Closer to home, Fabian Maxwell's interesting reading on youth rebellion in Kashmir bears out some of these points. He argues that the conflict is not only heavily gendered, it is gendered on both sides. On the one hand, the Hindu nationalist masculinity experiences itself as 'always vulnerable to the exposure of the self as non-masculine', which contributes to the intractability of the conflict

(Hartwell 2017: 126). On the other hand is the observation that for Kashmiri young men, stone throwing serves as a 'rite de passage' in a society in which other forms of passage from young to adult (including premarital sex or economic independence) are largely unavailable (Sanjay Kak 2017, cited in Hartwell 2017: 130). Among equivalents from other parts of the world, Hartwell points to Palestine where it is suggested that the simmering rebellion 'will be sustained as long as the oppressor allows no other way for boys to become men'. Clashes with the Israeli army play an important part in the construction of young Palestinian men's sense of gender roles. This resonates with the Kashmiri experience, and is summed up succinctly in Seema Mustafa's answer to the question 'Why do boys take to militancy?': 'Because it is there', and it is their way out of the system (Mustafa 2016). Assertion of an imagined ideal manhood becomes central to the intractability of the conflict and to the ways in which political sentiments are expressed.

As we shift our focus to a less violent and yet still very assertive incident from Bangladesh, some of the same issues make an appearance: The defence of the nation as something imperative on ordinary citizens, the sensitivity to outside disrespect, the sense of sovereignty challenged, and not the least the national and popular narratives that fired the assertive nature of a reaction to what might have seemed to others a very small affair.

Blasting a movie

The Bollywood movie *Gunday* ('goonda' or thug) tells the story of two small-time criminal friends who grew up together in Kolkata. The opening scenes place them as young boys and orphans coming to Kolkata from the war in what was to become Bangladesh. The year was 1971. Originally the movie received rather favourable reviews. In an online *New York Times* review it was characterised as 'downright enjoyable' even if at times a little preposterous (*New York Times* 2014).

And yet in Bangladesh the film was the target of an almost immediate outpouring of anger. Some 55,000 Bangladeshis reacted by voting *Gunday* the worst film ever on the online international movie database (IMDb). They also wrote 903 almost entirely angry user reviews on *Gunday* on IMDb. This number is quite high. Famous Bollywood movies such as *Lagaan* or *3 Idiots* have a mere 122 and 385 user reviews respectively (October 2016). Even *The Godfather* has only a little more than twice the number of user reviews that *Gunday* has.

The protests were so numerous that for a while *Gunday* figured at the absolute bottom of this database of about four million films and television shows. The online community celebrated this as a major victory. Some two years later the film has achieved a small lift and the rating 2 out of 10. This lift is largely due to a number of votes rating it 10 out of 10 – most probably from India and the Indian diaspora. In total there were close to 55,000 votes, of which 46,000 rated it 1 out of 10. Among those who have given their gender, almost 90 per cent were male. Most reviewers were in the age brackets 18–29 (almost 30,000 men and 4000 women) and 30–44 (another 7700 men and 800 women). These figures are significant and interesting. Collier and Hoeffler claim that 'the most likely people to participate in militancy are men between the ages of 15–24' (Collier and Hoeffler 2004: 563). Taken together these two age brackets accounted for almost all male voters.

The controversy had to do with what was being said in the voiceover at the start of the film. Translated from the original Hindi it said: 'On the 16th of December 1971 the third war between Hindustan and Pakistan came to an end. Ninety thousand Pakistani soldiers were captured by the Hindustan soldiers. A new country had been born, Bangladesh.'

It was the phrase 'the third war between Hindustan and Pakistan' that riled the online community of Bangladeshis. The war was, of course, the third war between India and Pakistan – after the wars in 1947 and 1965. But the two-week formally declared war between India and Pakistan in December 1971 came only as the last leg of a war of independence that had already raged for close to nine months. For Bangladeshis 1971 is the Bangladesh war of liberation. It was a war fought by civilians and slowly forming military units against the Pakistani occupation forces. It was long and bloody, and it was for their own national independence.[2]

Other protests appeared on Facebook pages specially set up, on Twitter with several hashtags, on the Facebook page set up by YashRaj Films (the filmmaker) for its promotional programme, and quite extensively in the online newspaper commentary sections.[3] The protests even made it to a commentary post on the *Wall Street Journal* blogpost, 'Why "Gunday" Angered Bangladeshis' (Arafat 2014). Here the commentator, a Bangladeshi political scientist, suggested that the film's version of events amounted to a 'denial' of the months between the outbreak of the war of liberation in March 1971 and the Indian intervention early in December the same year. This echoes the general sentiment, as we shall see. He acknowledged that the Indian intervention quickened the end of the war, but held that the final victory was not due to the Indian intervention alone but to the fact that the Pakistanis had been weakened by months of resistance from the Bangladeshis themselves.

The comments were mostly harsh and angry, and indicated a deep sense of hurt. Under the heading 'Manipulating Bangladesh's Liberation War history' one reviewer wrote: 'The film begins with narrator saying Bangladesh was born out of Indi-Pak War of 1971. What The Hell??'[4] Of the 1,718 people who rated this review, almost all (1,659) found it 'Useful' – which in this context indicates that they agreed. Other reviewers expressed the same sentiment. India's participation was 'only a sidekick' to some, and the statement that it was primarily an Indo-Pakistani war was 'Traditionally fake, ridiculous . . . & offensive (most importantly)'. Other headlines and statements read 'Misrepresentation of History'; 'Full of Lie, manipulation of the history and insulting our language'; and 'This is one of the most severe films you can sturdy process which are complete of traditionally unsuitable, incorrect and foolish events!!!!' By 'traditionally' the author probably meant 'historically'. Others wrote that the storyline is 'historically inappropriate' and many wrote that it is a distortion of history and a 'misrepresentation'.

This was the main objection in this 'melodrama of nationalism' (Hoek 2017). The film had ignored the effort made by Bangladeshi freedom fighters to the war. There were a few other points raised in the comments that the reviewers found objectional. Among these were the fact that all the characters in the film spoke Hindi, which was construed in the commentaries as a suggestion that Bengalis speak Hindi, and thus 'offending countless Bangladeshis'. This added insult to injury and constituted 'an issue of excellent disgrace' created by 'foolish and insensitive' scriptwriters. Another insult was the portrayal of some freedom fighters, in particular the suggestion that some of them engaged in embezzlement and illegal activities. Such representations of 'the best children of the nation' could not be permitted, one reviewer held. Another reviewer pointed out there were probably no female police officers in the 1970s, and certainly not in tight-fitting skirts and pants. But these were minor points. It was the statement that this had been a war between India and Pakistan that riled most of the commentators.

The comments were mostly angry. The more moderate ones characterised the film as simply 'idiotic' or 'bad'. But most reviewers were explicit: ':/ How could you people make this king of shitt!!'; 'stupidity of ignorant director and writer'; 'Illiterate and uneducated' producers; and 'bloody Hippocates'. One suggested that the film's representation of the 1971 war could be compared to a film that claimed Hitler won World War II. The Facebook page 'Ban Gunday' stated that the film 'disrespected' the history of Bangladesh and its 1971 liberation war, and that the film is 'tottaly insane nd should be BANNED.' Many used the term 'history manipulation' and a few called it 'hate speech'.

Online protesting is relatively simple. In order to write a user review and to rate the film, one needs to register and create an account. This is not a major undertaking for the individual. But the unanimity and the numbers were still surprising and made the production company as well as policymakers sit up. The energy and anger of the commentaries were such that the Government of Bangladesh formally protested and the film producer apologised for the offence.

Over the few days of active protesting, more elaborate comments were made as the 'debate' evolved. These comments fell into four main categories: chest thumping, sense of hurt, anti-India, and introspection.

Chest thumping

Basic to the reviews and comments was an interpretation of the war of 1971 as a war of great sacrifice, a unique and prestigious historical moment, and a proud example to the world. 'The freedom fighters and a leader such as Bangabandhu [the liberation movement's undisputed leader Mujibur Rahman] have never been born in this part of the world, and never will be'. This war was globally and historically unique, many held. The reason for this unique place in world history is that Bangladesh, they held, is the only country that has fought for independence on the basis of its language. Moreover, many claimed it is the only country where ordinary individuals had sacrificed their lives in order to protect and promote their mother tongue. It is, wrote one, 'the only fearless nation who had reduce their bloods for declaring their native language'.

The most prominent cause for anger at the film's misrepresentation, though, was that it ignored the more than eight months of war that preceded the Indian intervention.[5] This was a period of hardship and violent opposition to the Pakistani forces, of sacrifice, suffering, fear, and loss. It is because these months of resistance were ignored in those 11 minutes that so many insisted that the film ignored the suffering and heroic sacrifice. One wrote that the movie makers do not have 'the right' to misrepresent the central historical event of a nation ('the core birth history') for business purposes. More specifically, it was the contribution to the military opposition to the Pakistanis that cannot be ignored, most argued. The storyline of *Gunday* 'makes insignificant the valiance of our army'. This reviewer and others pointed not only to the resistance from the regular military units, but from the forces that at least in an early phase were irregular, such as the Mukti Bahini and the various units made up of students and farmers. Individual reviewers pointed to a number of names and features to underline that the war was fought by Bangladeshis, not the Indians: names of legendary sector commanders such as Colonel Taher and Khaled Mosharraf were listed, along with the almost mythical guerilla groups led by Kader Siddiqui, Siraj Sikder, and others. 'BANGLADESH won the war against fuckistan. BANGLADESHI freedom fighter fought a brave war against fuckistan, India help us nothing more did u understand??????'.

Others again pointed to the heroics and horrors of the war, the fingernails pulled in torture, the rescue of individuals and daring acts of guerilla warfare. These horrors were construed as sacrifices to be proud of. 'Bangladesh earned its independence the hard way and justifiably wants that to be appropriately acknowledged.' Someone else pointed to the number of dead and raped, and emphasised that 'we have paid lots of blood.that was not gifted by india'.

> This were we, the Bangladeshis. Our War of Liberation started not in 1971, it has been started from 1952. . . . We, the Bangladeshis' are very much grateful to Indian civilians and Indian government about what they did for us in 1971!

On the Facebook page 'Gunday the Film' (set up by the filmmaker as part of its PR campaign), the objection to the film's portrayal of the war was summarised in one particularly angry comment. The comment pointed out that to Bangladeshis the war and the narrative of the war are 'sacred'.

> You people told the incident as a fiction. But keep in mind that, it may be merely a fiction to you but it is our sacred history regarding our independence. . . . [We] will never tolerate any propaganda regarding our history and its vandalism.

The 'we' in the commentaries encompassed all Bangladeshis and all of Bangladesh in its modern history. The three million who died and the 300,000 who were raped all belong to this large 'we'.[6] It was the same 'we' who were engaged in the struggle that started in 1952 and who 'sacrificed themselves for the sake of mother language, Bangla'. 'This were we, the Bangladeshis', and this 'we' identified the authors of those commentaries with the memorable ideals of that war of liberation: sacrifice, patriotism, and that particular Bangladeshi quality of love for the mother tongue Bangla.

Humiliation and hurt

A second set of concomitant sentiments that were expressed had to do with humiliation and pain, and underlined how the film and the first 11 minutes had 'hurt' sentiments. Other terms used a lot included 'respect'/'disrespect', 'offense, 'insult' and 'shame'/'shameful'. These were used to characterise both 'the Indian behaviour' or the maker's 'attitude' as well as their own sense of hurt. As one reviewer formulated it, the way in which historical events had been portrayed was both 'perverse and insulting' (*bikriti ar opoman*). Words relating to feelings of hurt, pride, and respect were common in the reviews. Many used words to suggest hurt and humiliation. One wrote, for instance, that this 'dreadful film often humiliates the Bangladeshis' and that this misrepresentation of its history amounts to 'real pain'. Several reviewers used words of honour, shame, and humiliation to express their feelings. 'The proud contribution of our freedom fighters is humiliated!!!!' wrote one, while another wrote that the representation of the war was 'terribly hurting an entire nation' and that the film 'humiliates us on several scenes'. Several reviewers felt that the humiliation was such that it would be impossible for the Indians to 'correct the mistake and apologize to us', as one put it. Another said:

> You have no right to steal our history, our pride. Don't provoke us to refuge [refuse? reject?] you. . . . Don't try to make us fool. . . . I will never forgive you. never, ever. Our liberation war is out pride. We lost many of our men and women on that war. About 30 lakhs people were died, 2 lakhs women sacrificed their awe. You can't erase this history. You have no right to do that. I think you have done a great fault. You have to say sorry.

The word 'humiliated' appears often in the 900+ reviews on IMDb partly because a few texts were copied from an original and reproduced by many. Also, on the filmmakers' outreach Facebook page there are a good many identical entries. Some of the latter ones were polite in tone, and sought to reach out to the filmmaker. The polite language of the comment nonetheless set the anger in the context of humiliation. 'Do you understand that this project of yours has humiliated the Bangladeshi people? Hopefully the mistakes were done unintentially'. It then went on to list the errors made in the film and repeated the belief that the mistakes were unintentional.

Towards the end, this politely formulated comment on the film ended in an ominous threat: 'Therefore apologize to us and correct the mistakes. Or else we will have to take different action. Thank you.' Other comments had less veiled threats, and in less polite language. 'But, beware! Don't try to insult our history! Don't try to show the War of Liberation 1971, in a different format. BEWARE!'

There were more threats in the comments. Several demanded that the government 'should protest this humiliation' and one wrote that it was 'Time for legal action against these low class dogs!!' There were some who made more fuzzy forms of threat. 'Don't make us crazy. Say sorry & edit or remove your film. Either it will be bad for you'.

These threats are interesting, for it is unclear what is being threatened. As we shall return to, these were the threats of a man injured and angry, they were spluttering objections against perceived injustice. They were not specific, and they were not intended to be specific. They were not necessarily a sign of intent of violence, but expressions of anger and sincerity. They were saying 'we are angry and upset'. As we shall see, in the tale Bangladeshis often tell of themselves as spontaneous, emotional, and ready to fight for even the smallest thing of beauty. In his study of Bangladeshi speech acts, Wilce hints that 'a willingness to commit violence – sometimes described as "fearlessness"' – is part of the construction of male Bangladeshi identity (Wilce 2004: 198).

Anti-Indian anger

A large number of comments claimed that the film's portrayal of the war was typical of India's attitude towards Bangladesh. The comments on the Facebook page called 'Ban Gunday', for instance, suggested that the omission in the first 11 minutes somehow characterised India. 'It is not enough to ask them to applogise on Facebook', wrote one, while another wrote: 'what can you expect from these *shalas* [brother-in-law, a common insult]'. And a third held: 'india is worse than pakistan cz pakistan was our face yo face enemy but india is a back stabber'.

Many of the exclamations were targeted at India, and the film company was made out to represent the entire country. There were quite a few perfectly spluttering curses directed at India: 'Indians are stupid'; 'Stupid . . . India'; 'Bloody Indians!'; 'what Bengali thinks today, India thinks a day after . . . All people of Bd hate them due to their obnoxious activities'; 'the size of india in land .is oppsite to size of their mind'; 'bustard'; 'india never like our good'; and 'shiiittttttttttttttttttttttttttt'. And finally someone grunted, 'India Huh My bathroom Is more clean Thn Their freaky country "India"'.

That the perceived insult to Bangladeshi pride and history came from India may have exacerbated the reactions, at least it did not dampen it. India was blamed for most of what ails Bangladesh, including its 'backwardness', not because India is richer or superior but because the Indians are cunning and sly. 'Because of some Indian chamchas and dalals we are behind' (*pichhiye achhi*). The accusation was not unusual. India is often portrayed as untrustworthy, sly and a neighbour that has evil designs on Bangladesh. Someone else wrote that nothing will come out of these protests, because India is 'our big brother' (*amader boro dada je*). The Bengali term dada means elder brother and is used as a euphemism for the neighbourhood bully, as it is in Hindi.

The enemy within

Quite a few of the comments turned the table on Bangladeshis themselves, claiming they as a collective have failed to protect the country's honour. As Ayesha Jalal has pointed out in *Self and Sovereignty*, the inclusionary nationalism of modern states has a problem dealing with difference; it ends up in 'a narrative construction of an exclusionary majoritarian identity' (Jalal 2001: 630). In the commentaries to *Gunday*, many felt that the insult to Bangladesh was such that all true Bangladeshis had to react with fury. This rallying around the national pride and identity did not permit dissenting voices. Anger and fury were the only legitimate forms of reaction, and other points of view were explained away or even condemned. The larger enemy was the internal doubter rather than the external enemy. The internal doubter was a traitor because he attacks what Rousseau referred to as 'the general will' that animates the collective body. In Rousseau's thinking, the collective is larger than the sum of its parts and if a part is destructive it may be discarded (Elshtain 2008: 133). In the outcry against *Gunday* there were a few voices calling for calm, who sought to say that it was 'only' a Bollywood movie and not a documentary sponsored by the Indian government. But such voices were shouted down in a manner not dissimilar to the 'gaali' of the online Hindu nationalist commentaries in Sahana Udupa's study (Udupa 2017).

> No one can bear [*sojyo*] insults to one's own country. . . . They [the doubters] say that this is only a film. But they have not understood the matter. With this film the whole world has learnt that it was a war between Hindustan and Pakistan, not a Bangladesh liberation war. I wish they could learn to love their own country. I wish their ignorance [*oggota*] could be dispelled.

The majority were less generous. One strand complained that certain sections of Bangladeshi society did not protest because they secretly or implicitly were India's allies. The finger was pointed at the so-called Shahbagis and the Gonojagoron Moncho organisation. The Shahbag demonstrations about a year earlier had been a momentous moment that pointed to deep tensions in contemporary Bangladeshi society. Many hundreds of thousands assembled over a few weeks at this central Dhaka intersection in what was both a show of protest against leniency for those convicted of 1971 war crimes and at the same time a vivacious celebration of the country's rich history and culture (for details see De 2017). Gonojagoron Moncho was the organisation set up by 'Shahbagis' to sustain the momentum and spread the message of a secular Bangladesh. This was very much a country-wide mobilisation of the cultured and intellectual 'elite' around values of secularism and religious and cultural tolerance. A year later it was clearer that not all shared these values or the way in which they had been represented. *Gunday* protesters felt that the Shahbagis and the Gonojagoron Moncho were not sufficiently patriotic and when their spokesmen did not protest *Gunday*, the questions were asked with a certain glee: 'Where are the Shahbaghis? Where are the people of the culture business?' ran one typical comment. 'The Gonojagoron Moncho is nowhere to be seen here [*ei bishoye tiktitao dekha jaye na*]'. And in an ironic tone: 'Thanks India and thanks Hasina'. Sheikh Hasina was the Prime Minister and leader of the dominant Awami League, known as generally more friendly to India than its main rival, the Bangladesh Nationalist Party.

Some comments that named Gonojagoron Moncho tended to dismiss them as pro-Indian and lackeys of the Indians. 'And Gonojagoron Moncho?! They do not have the courage [*shahosh*] to say anything against the Indian government.' The Shahbaghis, many held, were too close to India, too friendly with India, to complain. 'No protest on this issue from these so called patriotics', one wrote, even if the film misrepresents Bangladeshi history and 'negatively presents the Bangladesh Army'. Someone else followed this up and suggested that Gonojagoron Moncho would not take up the issue because they would not do anything against India, 'and india is their father'.

It seems clear that for many of the commentators one could or should not be able to be rational or calm about this insult. It is as if there could not be two opinions about this, there could only be one. Any other opinion, any doubt, constituted an enemy within. One is reminded of what Canetti calls a 'discharge' – the shedding of difference in the transition from a heterogeneous group of individuals into a living crowd (Canetti 1973: 18–19).

The weak self

Lastly, there was a significant element of self-flagellation in these commentaries. The Indians may be bad, they seem to say, or the leftists or the cultural elite, but the main culprit is the Bangladeshis themselves and an inherent weakness in their character.

> They [the Indians or the filmmakers] are making crores and crores of rupees of business selling our liberation war history. And we, Bengali heroes [*bir bangali*], with our selfrespect [*attoshomman*], the conscious citizen takes the CD of that movie and downloads for his amusement. The selfindulgent Bengali [*ahare bangali*].

The reason given for setting up the Facebook page to protest against *Gunday* was that Bangladesh had not been able to protest properly against the film. The 'About' section of the page explained that Bangladesh's honour had been challenged, but the response was not consummate to the crime. There had been protests, but the protest had been weak and ineffectual. And this, said the text, was a shameful thing. 'We have not been able to protest, we could not protect the honour of the country' (*amra kono protibad korte parlam na, parlam na e desher shomman rokkha korte*). The text did not blame the Indians; it blamed instead 'us', the large 'we' who were heirs to the sacrifice of 1971. What sort of men are we, the text seemed to say, who cannot defend the honour of our country? It sought to shame its readers into action, alleging that strong action was necessary when the honour of the country had been challenged.

It then suggested that a proper form of protest would be to boycott Indian goods, in particular Indian clothing. It claimed that young Bangladeshi girls for Eid and other festive occasions were often dressed up in Indian-made clothing and made up to look like Indian (Hindu) goddesses. 'Why dress up young girls in Indian made dresses for Eid?' To stop buying Indian merchandise would have been a tangible mark of protest. But even such an easy protest, the text said, was beyond the weak and ineffectual Bangladeshis. 'We can't even do that' (*amra tao korte pari nai*). And if we are that ineffectual, if we cannot achieve even this, 'then whose fault is it [that the country's honour is challenged]?' (*tobe ekhane kar dosh bola chole?*). The answer offers itself: it is all of us, the large 'we' (*amra*) and our weaknesses. 'The fault is in our mind, our way of being, our whims' (*doshta ashole amader moner; amader manosikotar; amader pochonder*).

Here others took up the cue and joined in on the general self-flagellation.

> We Bengalis are very selfish [*swarthopor*]. The film has reduced our honour to dust [*amader man shomman dhoolioshat kore dilo*], and what did we do? how did we respond? We opened an Event on Facebook. Many joined, opened the page, but few even pressed Like or shared it. In reality our patriotism [*deshprem*] is not genuine [*okritrim*]. We are not capable of protest. We are a nation of great selfishness.

In the end Yash Raj Films apologised on their blog. For most of the commentators, however, this apology was insufficient. A blog was not considered official enough, not weighty enough. The Facebook activists demanded instead an official press conference, and that the controversial part be taken out of the film and the apology be positioned in its place. The humiliation was such that it could only be condoned after a sincere apology. The Facebook page organisers in particular kept encouraging their fellow patriots to continue the struggle until this aim had been achieved.

> We have proved it. We can. We can do harder. The first eleven minutes of this film must be taken out, must be removed. Or this film will be banned [*nishiddho*]. There is a movement, and the movement will continue [*andolon cholche; andolon cholbe*].

The last line would remind readers of the rhythm of slogans shouted in processions (Banerjee 2014: 80–83; Spencer 2007: 3–4). It suggested a movement that would go on and on until the demands were met, in a time-honoured form of protest – the street demonstration. It suggested that the 'we' needed to keep rallying around the values of the country and to use these forms of protest to harden the resolve.

The unnamed hero and misunderstood courage

In both popular and official narratives of the war of liberation two strands stand out. There is an emphasis on the popularity of the cause of the war and on the enthusiasm, courage, and sacrifice of ordinary members of society. This emphasis on the ordinary man or woman is stronger than in comparable nationalist narratives and helps explain the second strand: the special features of Bengaliness as explanation for why Bengalis rose against the oppressors. The Bengali may look soft on the outside, the narrative tells us, but it is misunderstood. The soft love of poetry and language hides determination and a will to sacrifice – as proven in 1971. The war of independence thus becomes both proof of this quality and the rallying cry for its upkeep.

The war of independence is, for Bangladesh, what Hannah Arendt thought of as a founding moment or 'foundation', the event from which authority springs (Arendt 1961: 32–33). The independent republic was founded after a bloody war, and it was given an ideological direction in its new constitution – a constitution that established, first and foremost, independence and democracy as core values, but also secularism and socialism.[7] This founding is a central political action, the one great deed that establishes the public-political realm and makes politics possible.

In school textbooks the war is given much space.[8] It is the only political topic mentioned until Class 5 and it is the only topic in history until Class 5. Even after Class 5 the war of liberation continues to occupy a prominent place. To convey a correct understanding of the war was part of the mandate of the committee that revised the textbooks, and the need to give the children a proper understanding of 'the spirit of the Language Movement and our Liberation War' (according to the Introduction) had been a major objective for the revisions (National Curriculum and Textbook Board 2012).[9]

'Every nation has its heroes', write Reicher and Hopkins (2001: 2/20), and point to how national narratives often come with 'exemplary figures' whose exploits are well known and summarised in tales that are told and retold. School textbooks often highlight how the nation imagines itself and how it wishes to portray itself. In this respect the heroes it chooses for itself are interesting. Such heroes are represented also in portraits in official buildings or statues in many nations. In Bangladesh that hero is just one man, Bangabandhu Sheikh Mujibur Rahman.

Bangabandhu's portrait is on bank notes, stamps, in every public office, in every school class room, in advertisements and in large posters that adorn major thoroughfares in the capital and elsewhere. His name is used for public buildings and institutions. Important dates in his career are public commemorations (such as his homecoming)[10] and public holidays (his independence speech, his birth, and his assassination). Even the political opposition has come to accept the narrative that places Bangabandhu at the pinnacle of national historiography as 'the father of the nation'.[11] Beyond this extraordinary figure only a small handful of people are named in school textbooks or national narratives: his predecessors, the four shot by the police in 1952 that set off the language movement, and a handful of war heroes or liberation leaders. But these are names introduced to the pupils only once in the course of an entire school life, whereas Bangabandhu is omnipresent. Where India had a whole set of extraordinary figures in Gandhi, Nehru, Netaji, Patel, Rajaji, Ambedkar, Bhagat Singh, Lala Lajpat Rai, Tilak, and countless others whose stories are told and retold and whose standardised features are reproduced in popular art all over India (Pinney 2004), Bangladesh has only one – Bangabandhu.

However, he was imprisoned during the entirety of the war, which was instead fought by the ordinary man and woman. This is the crux of the narrative. Inspired by Bangabandhu, the ordinary man and woman took to arms and fought the enemy and crushed him. In school textbooks there are stories of unnamed peasants, workers, students, women who rise in anger to resist the oppressor (Ruud 2013). This ordinary Bangladeshi hero is characterised in the school textbook stories by qualities such as perseverance, courage, and sacrifice. Their qualities are brought out in stories that emphasise how the beauty of the landscape and the eternal pastoral tranquillity of village life was ruined by the onslaught of the demon Pakistani forces. In the school textbooks these stories are presented side by side with poems or song lyrics. The opposition to beauty and the courage necessary to protect beauty in face of Pakistani violence is a recurrent contrast in national narratives. In this strand of the narrative, emphasis is on the apparently contradictory elements of the Bengali character – the love of poetry and language on the one hand, and the determination and readiness for war on the other. The narrative is also found in songs sung on special commemorative occasions to mark important events in the independence struggle. A popular song that recalls the war is called '*Mora ekti fulke banchabo bole juddho kori*', 'We will fight to save even one flower'. The 'fight' is not the poet's struggle, but war, the warrior's war, *juddho*. The text goes on to say: 'we take up arms for the sake of a smile . . . we fight to write a new poem . . . we fight for a song'. The pledge contains the contrast, to war for the sake of flowers, songs and smiles. The pledge underlines that within the sensitive poet lives a courageous and determined soul.

Another popular song that makes the idea of the sensitive Bengali man its central point ('*Maa go bhabna keno*') starts with the line 'Mother, dear, do not worry // we are your peace-loving quiet boys [*shantipriyo shanto chhele*] // but we can take up arms if the enemy appears // do not be afraid, mother, we know how to resist [*protibad korte*]'.

The notion that the foreign occupiers – Pakistanis or British – held Bengalis to be effeminate and emotional is well known among the educated and beyond. While most object to such stereotyping, others will acknowledge that the idea of the emotional Bengali has some merit. It is used, for instance, to explain why political protests erupt regularly and why there is such widespread radicalism. 'We want revolution. Any revolution!', a student leader once put it to me (interview Dhaka April 2013). The notion of the emotional Bengali carries 'ontological weight', to use Mann's expression, it is sufficient to precipitate action. The poems and the songs and school textbooks all underscore the stereotype of the soft Bengali by simultaneously emphasising the contrast. The fear of being misinterpreted means the need is strong for the contrast to be reemphasised.

Conclusion

Democracy as an institutional set-up underlines through 'the vote' the right and obligation of the individual to be part of and defend the community. The obligation on the part of the voter to be both self-interested and altruistic on behalf of the community is emphasised in the secret ballot, as pointed out by David Gilmartin, putting the voter in the same position as the sovereign of old – as both part of and *in* society and its moral conscience and *above* society. The present contribution argues that the voter-sovereign also has to be placed in time and space in order to understand the particular expressions of this position. Expectations of the nation may be gendered, but, as Bonnie Mann points out, even if the gendered nature of the nation demands independence and sovereignty, the freedom from dependency, the nuances of that particular gendered expectation are still formed through layers of popular culture, history narratives, and contemporary politics. The individual's self-identification with the larger community demands that one yields to the expression that has been formed.

In the Bangladeshi reactions to the Bollywood film *Gunday* one finds the voter-sovereign expressing anger at a perceived slight in the opening scenes of the film. The Bangladeshi historical narrative – both popular and official – is formed around ideas of the ordinary Bengali rising against the oppression, rising because of his or her love for language, poetry and the land – a narrative that allowed the online community to identify with that ordinary Bengali. This figure may appear soft to the untrained eye but – the Bangladeshi voter-sovereign will insist – it is still someone courageous and determined. The suffering and heroism of 1971 are central to the national myth-making, and the self-identification with these ideas is expressed in the outburst of anger that followed the launch of *Gunday*. The ordinariness of the heroes in the narratives of 1971 embraces widely enough to include the ordinary young and young adult men (mostly) and women of the twenty-first century. The self-identification is bolstered by another central strand in the national myth, that the Bangladeshi is fundamentally misunderstood, that his emotional attachment to poetry and language is mistaken for a soft and effeminate character by outsiders. On the contrary, the comments to the film sought to convey that Bangladesh is a nation of determination and courage, and the nation's immense sacrifice and suffering in 1971 due to its love of language and poetry is testimony to that.

In this light, the slight in the film becomes acutely important. The slight was more than a slight to the state or even the nation, it was a personal insult, a slight to the individual who wanted to identify with the sacrifices and suffering of 1971. It became imperative on the individual voter-sovereign to protect the reputation and image of his community, and to press the government into action. The government, then, is no more than a tool in the hands of the voter-sovereign, an entity that must do the voter-sovereign's bidding, and not a sovereign in its own right. When the minister in the opening paragraph of the present contribution held that outsiders could not criticise the constitution and the nation's parliament because it would undermine the country's sovereignty, he was not talking on behalf of the government or making a legal argument. He appealed to popular ideas of a nation whose determination is misunderstood and its courage and sacrifice unappreciated, ideas that obligate every citizen as a voter-sovereign to take part in the resistance to any infringement on its reputation.

Notes

1 Organisations that have been prominent critics of the Government include Amnesty International and Transparency International, and local organisations such as Ain o Shalish Kendra, Sujon and other rights organisations.

2 There is no doubt that the Indian intervention tipped the scale, even if the Pakistani resolve had been considerably weakened by the independence fighters by then. In the blog 'Alal o Dulal', one writer points out that the version of events portrayed in *Gunday* in fact are similar to the Pakistan Government's version of events in 1971, that the secession of Bangladesh was an Indian ploy.

3 The matter was discussed in other media as well. On Twitter there was the hashtag #'Gunday'HumiliatedHistoryOfBangladesh, and there were several Facebook pages – including 'Ban "Gunday"' and 'Khoma Chaibar Dabite Yash Raj Films-er Kache Protibadlipi Preron'. The latter had 15,000 members. Commentaries to a news item on the controversy in the *Daily Star* newspaper, the largest English language daily in Bangladesh ('Bangladesh condemns "Gunday"', *Daily Star*, February 20, 2014). The comments used here have mainly been taken from the film's official Facebook page, the Facebook pages set up to protest the film, the IMDb page, comments to a *Daily Star* news item on *Gunday*, and a Twitter hashtag.

4 To the extent possible I have kept the original text, including spelling, punctuation, and choice of words. This has been done to convey the sense of anger and yet of the flurry of the posts. It also means some of the posts are open to interpretation.

5 The war of independence started with the declaration of independence on March 25, 1971 by Sheikh Mujibur Rahman, the movement's undisputed leader. Although India supported the budding armed warfare, its formal entry into the war came on December 3. The war ended two weeks later, on December 16.

6 These figures are subject to debate. The number of casualties has been placed between 300,000 and three million. The figure of three million (*tirish lokkho*) is firmly established in Bangladeshi political vocabulary, however. The number of rape victims is commonly put between 200,000 and 300,000, and the number of refugees close to ten million.

7 The preamble of the Constitution listed these four as core values of the state.

8 I refer here to the textbooks introduced in 2012. These textbooks were revised versions of the previous textbooks.

9 Personal communication, Liberation War Museum director, who was member of the committee.
10 Sheikh Mujibur Rahman was in prison in West Pakistan for the duration of the war. His return to Bangladesh in January 1972 is officially commemorated every year.
11 See for instance the admission in Tarique Rahman's speech March 27, 2017 where he seeks to argue that his father be given similar recognition (www.youtube.com/watch?v=SiPlxgvNMGM); or Ahmed (1984).

References

Ahmed, Moudud. 1984. *Bangladesh: Era of Sheikh Mujibur Rahman*. Wiesbaden: Franz Steiner Verlag gmbh.

Arafat, Kabir. 2014. 'Why "Gunday" Angered Bangladeshis', *The Wall Street Journal blogs* commentary.blogs.wsj.com/indiarealtime/2014/02/24/why-bollywoods-gunday-angered-bangladeshis/ (Accessed February 10, 2014).

Arendt, Hannah. 1961 [1954]. 'What Is Authority?', in *Between Past and Future*, pp. 91–141. London: Faber and Faber.

Banerjee, Mukulika. 2014. *Why India Votes?* London: Routledge.

Canetti, Elias. 1973. *Crowds and Power*. Harmondsworth: Penguin. Translated from the German by Carol Stewart.

Collier, Paul, and Anke Hoeffler. 2004. 'Greed and Grievance in Civil War', *Oxford Economic Papers*, 56 (4): 563–595. https://doi.org/10.1093/oep/gpf064.

De, Sanchari. 2017. 'Memory, Imagination and Political Mobilization: The Case of Pro-Shahbag Bloggers'. PhD thesis, Jadavpur University, Kolkata.

Elshtain, Jean Bethke. 2008. *Sovereignty: God, State, and Self.* New York: Basic Books.

Gilmartin, David. 2012. 'Towards a Global History of Voting: Sovereignty, the Diffusion of Ideas, and the Enchanted Individual', *Religions*, 3: 407–423. doi:10.3390/rel3020407.

Hansen, Thomas Blom. 2001. *Violence in Urban India: Identity Politics, 'Mumbai', and the Postcolonial City*. Delhi: Permanent Black.

Hansen, Thomas Blom. 2004. 'Politics as Permanent Performance: The Production of Political Authority in the Locality', in John Zavos, Andrew Wyatt, and Vernon Hewitt (eds.), *The Politics of Cultural Mobilization in India*, pp. 19–36. New Delhi: Oxford University Press.

Hartwell, Fabian. 2017. 'Burhan Wani and the Masculinities of the Indian State', *Journal of Extreme Anthropology*, http://dx.doi.org/10.5617/jea.4688.

Hasan, Mubashar. 2014. 'Life Isn't Getting Better', *Dhaka Tribune*, May 22. dhakatribune.com/uncategorized/2014/05/22/life-isnt-getting-better-2 (Accessed January 17, 2019).

Heesterman, Jan C. 1985. *The Inner Conflict of Tradition: Essays in Indian Ritual, Kingship, and Society*. Chicago: University of Chicago Press.

Hoek, Lotte. 2017. 'Cinema and the Melodrama of Nationalism', *Himal*, March 15. himalmag.com/hindi-urdu-cinema-nationalism-bangladesh/ (Accessed June 27, 2017).

Jalal, Ayesha. 2001. *Self and Sovereignty: Individual and Community in South Asian Islam Since 1850*. New Delhi: Oxford University Press.

Kak, Sanjay (ed.). 2017. *Witness / Kashmir 1986–2016 / Nine Photographers*. India: Yaarbal Press.

Mann, Bonnie. 2014. *Sovereign Masculinity: Gender Lessons from the War on Terror*. Oxford Scholarship Online. New York: Oxford University Press. doi:10.1093/acprof:oso/9780199981649.001.0001.

Michelutti, Lucia. 2008. *The Vernacularisation of Democracy: Politics, Caste and Religion in India*. New Delhi: Routledge.

Mustafa, Seema. 2016. 'Kashmir, Before and After Burhan Wani'. focusweb.org/content/kashmir-and-after-burhan-wani (Accessed March 31, 2017).

National Curriculum and Textbook Board. 2012. *Bangladesh and Global Studies* (various classes). Available at nctb.gov.bd (Accessed January 15, 2019).

The New York Times. 2014. 'Bandit Buddies Separated by a Woman: "Gunday", a Bollywood Action-Thriller'. nytimes.com 16 February (Accessed November 20, 2014).

Piliavsky, Anastasia. 2014. 'Introduction', in A. Piliavsky (ed.), *Patronage as the Politics of South Asia*, pp. 1–37. Cambridge: Cambridge University Press.

Pinney, Christopher. 2004. *'Photos of the Gods': The Printed Image and Political Struggle in India*. London: Reaktion Books.

Prothom Alo. 2016. 'মতপ্রকাশের স্বাধীনতা এনজিওর জন্য নয়: সুরঞ্জিত' (Freedom of Expression is not for NGOs: Suranjit). Online version. https://www.prothomalo.com/bangladesh/article/1002593. 19 October (Accessed October 20, 2016).

Reicher, Steve, and Nick Hopkins. 2001. 'Lessons in National History', in *Self and Nation: Categorization, Contestation and Mobilization*. London: Sage, Online Publication May 31, 2012. doi:10.4135/9781446220429.

Ruud, Arild Engelsen. 2013. 'Narratives of 1971', in *Bangladesh Genocide and the Issue of Justice*, pp. 61–66. Dhaka: Liberation War Museum Publications.

Shastri, Sandeep, Suhas Palshikar, and Sanjay Kumar. 2017. *State of Democracy in South Asia (SDSA). Report II*. Bangalore: Jain University Press.

Spencer, Jonathan. 2007. *Anthropology, Politics, and the State: Democracy and Violence in South Asia*. Cambridge: Cambridge University Press.

Udupa, Sahana. 2017. 'Gaali Cultures: The Politics of Abusive Exchange on Social Media', in *New Media and Society*, 1–17.

Wilce, James M., Jr. 2004. 'To "Speak" Beautifully in Bangladesh: Subjectivity as Pāgalāmi', in Janis Hunter Jenkins and Robert John Barrett (eds.), *Schizophrenia, Culture, and Subjectivity: The Edge of Experience*, pp. 196–218. Cambridge: Cambridge University Press.

AFTERWORD

We have other ideas

Jonathan Spencer

The sovereign turn

In the first two decades of the new century, there has been an enormous expansion in reflections on the idea of sovereignty, both in public discourse, and in the more muted tones of political theory. But, as Clifford Geertz once reminded us, political theory, for all its appeal to the lofty and universal, is always and everywhere 'a specific response to immediate circumstances' (2000: 218). If we are to take Geertz's warning seriously, then the question this excellent collection provokes is this: what is the question to which the sovereign turn is the answer? What has happened, or is happening, in our world that we think can be clarified, or understood better, by thinking about the question of sovereignty? Or, more precisely, what is happening in South Asia that makes sovereignty now such an appealing object of reflection?

In his incisive and exhaustive Introduction, David Gilmartin covers the dominant version of sovereignty at play in the world of International Relations, the hybrid experiments of colonial sovereignty, competition between religious and other sources of sovereignty, the sovereignty of the people at work in post-colonial democracy, the echoes of kingly sovereignty in the present, and the lure of national sovereignty. All of these find fruitful illustration in the chapters that follow: Price, Ikegame, and Gilmartin on competing sources of sovereignty; Skoda, Simmonds, and Michelutti on kingship and kingly idioms; Moin and Ruud on sovereignty in the imagination of the nation. Given the range of topics illuminated by the sovereign lens, how useful is a concept which is, as Gilmartin acknowledges from the start, 'ambiguous and contested', and yet also omnivorously broad in its application? Why indeed did we need a sovereign turn at all?

Let me start by identifying some different strands at work in the analyses here. One is clearly historical. Attention to sovereignty allows us to track the persistence of different idioms of power and rule through the colonial period and on into the world of post-Independence South Asia. This is a theme which has animated Pamela Price's scholarship throughout her productive career (Price 1989, 1996). A second concerns performance, symbolism, and, often, spectacle. These are neither epiphenomena of some realer, more fundamental zone of rational politics, nor irrelevancies that distract our attention from the capillary workings of modern power; they are instead constitutive features of our political worlds. A third concerns violence, the distributed violence of actually existing colonial and post-colonial sovereignty which defies the received platitudes about the state's supposed monopoly of legitimate force. That in turn raises questions about our understanding of 'the state' and its relation to that other powerful abstraction, 'the nation'. What links these strands is the capacity of questions about sovereignty to destabilise familiar approaches to important topics, and if the sovereign turn is most useful for the questions it raises, rather than the answers it provides, that is, as I shall argue at the end of this Afterword, entirely in keeping with the long history of South Asian reflection on the topic.

One government or none?

To test the usefulness of the language of sovereignty, and to supplement the answers already implicit in the Introduction, rather than reiterate the points made by Gilmartin, let me instead think through two rather different examples from my own work in Sri Lanka, during and after the civil war, before returning to the bigger question.

Colombo, October 26 2018: Surrounded by enthusiastic supporters and in the presence of senior figures from the army and the police, Mahinda Rajapaksa is sworn in as Prime Minister of Sri Lanka to the astonishment of almost everyone not actually in the room with him. Rajapaksa had served as Prime Minister from 2004 until his election to the Presidency in November 2005. He was unexpectedly defeated in the Presidential election of January 2015 by his former ally and cabinet minister, Maithripala Sirisena, who had defected to head a coalition of opposition parties united against Rajapaksa's increasingly authoritarian rule. It was the same Sirisena who invited him back into government and announced the summary dismissal of the incumbent Prime Minister in 2018.

So far so grubby, another move in the long history of dirty politics in Sri Lanka, of which Rajapaksa was an acknowledged master. On the face of it, what happened next would be simple. Although Rajapaksa could not as yet muster a majority in Parliament, it was widely expected he would win the elections scheduled for 2020. Till then it was simply a matter of inducing enough cross-overs from the incumbent government benches, possibly boosted by an offer of cabinet places and patronage to the smaller parties representing minority communities, to build the necessary majority. Except the plan failed to work. Ruling party MPs refused to budge. Minorities were unswayed by the new 'government'. (The leader of the Sri Lanka Muslim Congress took his MPs for an unexpected pilgrimage to Mecca to keep them away from temptation.) The necessary majority did not materialise. The incumbent Prime Minister stayed put in his official residence. The President suspended Parliament. He then attempted to dissolve Parliament and call elections. But his own government had passed a constitutional amendment explicitly limiting the President's power to dismiss Prime Ministers and dissolve Parliaments. The Supreme Court issued an interim judgement, suspending the dissolution of Parliament. When Parliament was eventually recalled, it formally voted down Rajapaksa's new government. Or rather it tried to: on three separate occasions an attempted vote of no confidence was disrupted by Rajapaksa loyalists physically attacking their opponents, hurling objects at the Speaker, and generally performing extreme ungovernability.

As I first drafted this Afterword, the country awaited the full Supreme Court hearing on the dissolution. At that point, it had either two parallel governments, or no government at all, depending on who you asked. Like all journeys into politically uncharted water, there was a strong sense of transgression, of some kind of fundamental and unresolved challenge to the moral order about all this. The times were out of joint and the politicians on all sides were widely believed to have failed the people.

Not everything in this drama was completely new, but where there were precedents, they were deeply unpropitious. After winning re-election to the Presidency in 1982, J. R. Jayewardene invoked a new constitutional power and held a referendum to extend the life of the sitting Parliament (where his party had a comfortable two-thirds majority which allowed them to amend the constitution they had themselves only just written on a more or less weekly basis) rather than take the risk of a general election, in which a newly introduced system of proportional representation was bound to reduce his huge majority. The referendum that followed was widely believed to be rigged. The party thugs who had played the central role in delivering the necessary majority were the same thugs who organised most of the anti-Tamil pogrom in July 1983. Disenfranchised youth took to extra-parliamentary opposition in their thousands. In the north and east, Tamil youth joined the LTTE and the other militant organisations pursuing the goal of a separate state. In the south, Sinhala youth joined with the JVP in a violent, doomed assault on state power.

Jayewardene's 1982 attempt to unwrite the rules of popular sovereignty led directly to the twin insurgencies, Indian intervention, and a catastrophic slide into civil war.[1] The 2018 repeat ended rather less in tragedy and a great deal more in farce. In mid-December, the Supreme Court ruled the President's actions unconstitutional. With no parliamentary majority and no legal case, Rajapaksa announced his resignation as Prime Minister, a position he had never really held in the first place. On social media, satirists offered to follow suit in their hundreds as part of what one memorably named National Prime Minister Resignation Day.

Satire was one response to the extraordinary events of late 2018. Protest was another. A dogged group of civil society activists kept up a daily vigil at one of central Colombo's busiest road junctions. Their protests were imaginative, and often very funny, but the proliferation of witty signs in English reminded passers-by that this was something less than a mass movement. For bigger numbers one had to look to rallies organised by the political parties on each side in the impasse. As far as one could tell, the general mood was less one of fearful anxiety, and more of cynical resignation: the politicians were at it again, all were as bad as each other, and the government elected on a promise of good government in 2015 had signally failed to deliver on that score.

There is something about the events of late 2018 in Colombo, like the earlier events in the 1980s of which they seem to be a distorted echo, which challenges the prosaic explanatory frames of conventional political science. The 2018 crisis was a curious blend of transgression and enchantment. MPs arrived in Parliament with chili-infused water to throw at their opponents. The Speaker, who emerged as the central player in the emerging drama, required an escort to make it in and out of the chamber unscathed. The increasingly child-like behaviour of Rajapaksa's parliamentary supporters served to set off the transcendent properties of certain positions and procedures: the Speaker, the Constitution, the Supreme Court, the rules of procedure and the proper mode of conduct in Parliament. Viewed in the dominant idiom of South Asian dirty politics, what happened in late 2018 simply makes no sense at all. If the contributions to this volume are to be believed, what happened might be better captured if we attend to the notion of sovereignty, understood in that broad sense of a principle of rule that cannot justify itself, but always needs to supplement its own practice with an appeal to something elsewhere, transcendent, or as Gilmartin has it in his own chapter, enchanted. Briefly, and to the astonishment of those watching, appeals to procedure, to following the rules and rituals of parliament, of attending to the wording of the constitution, eclipsed the brawls, threats, and attempted bribes of politics as usual.

Sovereignty is above all a puzzle, a conundrum, a paradox capable of producing a hall of mirrors of further paradoxes. It is, as Shulman puts it in the context of Tamil kingship, 'less a fact than a concern' (1985: 15). As a source of law, it cannot be justified by law. As a principle of power with the capacity to act on mundane matters, it must derive its power from something or some place beyond the mundane. Many of the contributors to this volume use sovereignty as a lens through which to analyse, in Bernard Bate's memorable phrase, 'the newness of old things' (Bate 2009: xv): renouncers as modern political actors, kings, and rituals of kingship in contemporary settings.

But this is not simply an exercise in political exoticism: new things, as well as old ones, are also part of the puzzle of sovereignty, as Gilmartin has shown in his masterly unpicking of the idea of 'popular sovereignty' in Indian democracy. The procedures of electoral democracy have become ritualised, and thus sacralised (as Mukulika Banerjee [2007] has eloquently pointed out). The rhythms of democracy, the repetitive but ever new cycle of elections, are ritual rhythms, guarantors of the proper order of things and the proper order of people. These are the rhythms that were disrupted by Jayawardene so disastrously in 1982, and were being disrupted again by Rajapaksa as I started to write. Thus the unexpected and apparently disproportionate unease that followed Rajapaksa's attempted power grab. The grubby business of politics as usual is, just about, liveable with so long as it knows its place and follows its lines.

Violence and its limits

A second example, this time from the years of civil war in Sri Lanka. In the Tamil-speaking areas of the North and East, the Liberation Tigers of Tamil Eelam carried out an extended experiment in more or less spontaneous sovereignty. Their repeated claim to be the sole legitimate voice of the Tamil nation was accompanied by demonstrations of sovereignty in multiple registers. During the years of cease fire and fruitless negotiation in the early 2000s the LTTE administrative centre in Killinochchi was home to LTTE courts, speeding motorists were flagged down by the LTTE traffic police, and visiting journalists and academics were shown endless examples of the LTTE's capacity to perform sovereignty by 'acting like a state' (Wedeen 2003; cf. Stokke 2006). At the same time, an elaborate cult of leadership and death was worked up, centred on the figure of Prabhakaran, the LTTE leader, and on the bodies of the fallen cadres, the martyrs. A 1990s BBC documentary showed footage of the funeral of one such martyr, the body bedecked by LTTE flags, and buried to the words of an LTTE liturgy as the martyr's family members sobbed: the film then cut to a Colombo talking head, counter-intuitively assuring the viewers that the LTTE was an 'entirely secular' organisation.

But there were curious limits to the LTTE's assertions of sovereignty. In the bureaucratic register, Sri Lankan government offices continued to function in LTTE-controlled areas, children sat national exams at schools, teachers were paid by the Colombo government, civil servants worked both with the LTTE and with the government (Klem 2012). In the ritual arena the LTTE didn't entirely know how to deal with the opposition. Although political challenges to the LTTE were brutally suppressed, other kinds of politics carried on more or less as usual: I refer to the politics of precedence and honour at the big Hindu temples in LTTE-controlled territory. Mark Whitaker (1997) describes this well for the temple village of Mandur in the 1990s, where what he describes as the 'nonmodern' politics of temple honour carried on as ever, alongside the 'modern' politics of national assertion and the LTTE's relentless efforts at what Benjamin called 'law-making' violence (Benjamin 1978).

The LTTE's relation to the temples was not simply a matter of parallel projects operating in isolation of each other. There are signs that the LTTE would have preferred to extract some kind of sign from the temples to acknowledge their own claims for comprehensive sovereignty over everything. In the diaspora this was forthcoming: the LTTE controlled many temples and used them as bases for fundraising and mobilisation (Maunaguru 2015; Maunaguru and Spencer 2018). In Sri Lanka itself, though, the LTTE often steered clear of overt challenges to the authority of the deities, and their attempts to engage with temple politics often ended badly. In a forthcoming article Maunaguru (in press) describes a series of incidents in which the LTTE attempted to sort out the internal affairs of various temples in Sri Lanka. In each case their attempt was unsuccessful, and they retreated to a position of relatively passive coexistence with the sovereign deity of the temple, a deity who, in each instance, operated in quite different registers of sovereignty from the 'totalizing violence' of the LTTE. In an earlier analysis with Bart Klem, Maunaguru wrote of the LTTE's 'citational' approach to sovereignty, mimicking different models in constructing its own idiom of power (Klem and Maunaguru 2017). In the case of the temples, Maunaguru suggests, the LTTE eventually ended up mimicking the deities. But in the diaspora, the temples, and with them the deities, increasingly took on attributes from the LTTE in what could be read as a process of counter-mimicry.[2]

This example from war-time Sri Lanka is important because it at once builds upon one of the most powerful recent applications of ideas about sovereignty in South Asia, and reminds us of its limitations. I am referring to Hansen and Stepputat's creative reworking of aspects of Agamben's ideas to create a template for a new, historically informed, political sociology of violence. Agamben himself starts his argument in *Homo Sacer* with an affirmation of a position from Schmitt which should be entirely familiar to students of Indian kingship: 'the sovereign is, at the same time, both outside and inside the juridical order' (Agamben 1998: 15; cf. Schmitt 1985). The point is, to put it no stronger, compatible with Heesterman's chapter on 'The Conundrum of the King's Authority', which Gilmartin acknowledges in his Introduction to this collection (Heesterman 1985). Agamben, though, links this point about sovereignty's necessary appeal to something outside its own field of operation, to Foucault's concern with 'life' as the object of new forms of modern power, the biopolitical. His concern is to address and rectify two related problems in Foucault's writing on power. One is the implausibly complete break posited between early modern ideas of power which focus on the figure of the sovereign, and those new techniques of government which focus instead on abstractions like 'population' or 'economy'. The other is between the capillary and usually unrecognised working of power on and through the individual body and the persistence of spectacle and symbol in modern political fields (Agamben 1998: 1–12).

With Agamben as their point of departure, Hansen and Stepputat (2005, 2006) have created a powerful template for understanding colonial and post-colonial manifestations of sovereignty, and Hansen (2005) has put this to use in an illuminating essay on political authority and violence in colonial and post-colonial India. Hansen and Stepputat valorise violence as the central component of what they call de facto sovereignty: 'the ability to kill, punish, and discipline with impunity' (2006: 295). De facto sovereignty is inherently pluralistic and fragile: multiple claims to sovereignty may jostle against each other, and violence is as necessary as a performative reminder of the sovereign's capacities – or claims – as it may be for more narrowly instrumental purposes. In their fullest account of this vision, the 2006 chapter in *Annual Review of Anthropology*, their opening illustration and analytic point of departure is the confused, contested, and hyper-violent landscape of post-invasion Iraq (Hansen and Stepputat 2006: 296). In Hansen's own chapter on India, the equivalent point of departure is Paul Brass's Hobbesian depiction of the Uttar Pradesh countryside in *Theft of an Idol*, a countryside with 'no law and order', in which the identities of law-breaker and law-enforcer are hopelessly overlapped and blurred, and in which violence, and the possibility of violence, is ubiquitous (Brass 1997: 75).

Michelutti's chapter in this book provides a fine example of the insights that have now been built upon the foundations laid down by Hansen and Stepputat (cf. Michelutti et al. 2018). The warscape of northern and eastern Sri Lanka in the 1990s and 2000s would seem if anything even better suited to understanding in terms of competing de facto sovereignties. What they say of Iraq seems if anything even more suited to the hinterland of Jaffna and Trincomalee after more than two decades of war:

> Here, multiple, fragile, and contested centres of military might, welfare, and ethno- religious and local loyalties claim sovereignty over people and land – both legal sovereignty as in the legitimate right to govern and de facto sovereignty as the right over life (to protect or to kill with impunity).
> *(Hansen and Stepputat 2006: 296)*

And yet. And yet, here is a scene from a journey across this landscape just after the end of the war in 2012.[3] With my friend and fellow anthropologist, Sidharthan Maunaguru, I am trundling on a bumpy dirt road across paddy fields a few miles outside the town of Jaffna in northern Sri Lanka. As the van carrying us lurched its ponderous way round potholes and ruts, a curious sight appeared in front of us. Nestled among a grove of trees in the otherwise flat, featureless landscape was a pair of Hindu temples, their walls brightly painted. In front of the first temple was a low compound wall, which had been decorated with a series of portraits. The portraits were of Sri Lanka's leading post-Independence politicians. Here, on one section of the wall, we see Ranasinghe Premadasa, whose Presidency was abruptly terminated by an LTTE suicide bomber in 1993; Chandrika Kumaratunga, President from 1995 to 2005; her successor Mahinda Rajapaksa; the then current President, Ranil Wickremesinghe, who as Prime Minister in 2002 signed the ill-fated Norwegian-brokered ceasefire agreement; and J.R. Jayewardene, who was President in the late 1970s and early 1980s when the war started.

All of these were Sinhala politicians, elected by voters far from Jaffna, but other sections of the wall included prominent Tamil and Muslim politicians. We were, to put it mildly, intrigued. Although portraits of politicians are everywhere to be seen in Sri Lanka's public culture, they are invariably presented on quite strict partisan lines. Members of opposing parties are not routinely depicted alongside each other, and even members of rival factions within the same party would avoid casual juxtaposition: Chandrika, for example, is never seen in the ubiquitous portraits of Mahinda Rajapaksa that adorn Sri Lanka's towns and highways. In any case, partisan alignments aside, what were these people doing on the walls of a temple? We went inside to enquire and were told that they were entirely the idea of the chief priest of this temple. He was next door, hanging out with the priest of the neighbouring temple, which is where we found him, with a couple of lay worshippers preparing tea. We sat down with him and asked him to tell us about the story of his temple, hoping it would lead on to the murals and his explanation of their origins.

It did. This is what he told us on that first encounter. 'Why these people?' we asked. 'What do they have in common?' 'These are all the people who tried to solve this problem', came the reply. 'Tried – but failed'. The portraits were the idea of the deity of the temple, Lord Pillayar, the elephant-headed god Ganesh. They came to the priest in a dream which revealed that 'this problem' – an obvious euphemism for the Sinhala-Tamil divide that shaped the war – would never be resolved until Lord Pillayar himself appeared and sorted it out once and for all. What of the one key player missing from the mural – the LTTE leader Prabhakaran? 'Of course he is there also' (but just happened not to be depicted on the walls). The priest then proceeded to tell us the details of his dream, which must have come to him at some point in the second half of the 1990s, when Chandrika was President, newly elected on a peace ticket but bogged down in an increasingly fruitless war with the LTTE. He dreamed that Chandrika would be supplanted by another leader and Prabhakaran and the LTTE would suffer their military defeat. But he also dreamed – and here we pricked up our ears – that Chandrika would eventually return to power, and before that happened, Prabhakaran himself would also return and temporarily prevail. But nothing would lead to a long-term resolution, until Lord Pillayar himself appeared to take charge of the situation.

'I wrote a letter to Chandrika herself, to tell her what was to happen. But she didn't reply', he went on. Then she lost an eye in an attempted LTTE assassination at an election rally. He wrote again: 'See, I told you this was going to happen.' This time she did reply and conceded he was correct in his appraisal of the history, and in his prognosis for the future. Or so he told us.

This is a very short account of a much longer story, a story we listened to raptly as we sat with the priest and his neighbour in the neighbour's temple. Then, abruptly, our narrator stood up and announced he had business to attend to at his own temple. Once he had gone, his neighbour, the other priest, looked at us with an air of resignation, and said, 'All that, of course, is his opinion. We have other ideas.'

We have other ideas. That would serve quite nicely as the epigraph to this book, and therefore as the beginnings of an answer to the question with which I started: what is the question to which the sovereign turn is the answer? In South Asia, as Hansen's work and the recent work of Michelutti and her team (2018) demonstrate, the question could be the place of violence in political life and the emergence of hybrid 'criminal politicians'. But it could also be many other potential sources of that appeal to transcendence which seems to be a necessary accompaniment to the exercise of worldly power. It may simply be the transcendence inherent in the position of the renouncer, whose place outside the social order makes him a perfect arbiter of disputes within that order (Ikegame). It may be the transcendent figure of 'the people' implicit in the workings of popular sovereignty, and sedimented in the sacred procedures of electoral democracy (Gilmartin). We might find it unexpectedly in the borrowed rituals and conventions of a post-Independence parliament. To explicate those other ideas, we need obviously to attend to what is being done and said in the present, to capture the nuances of sovereignty in the vernacular, as so many of the chapters here do. But we also need to attend to the past, not simply the colonial past (which is where Hansen and Stepputat draw the analytic line), but older pasts, and especially, what we might call the vernacular past (Singh 2012). If sovereignty is best understood as a conundrum, a problem, a question, the sovereign turn may be seen as an attempt, however limited and modest, to expand the known set of potential answers to that question, and in doing so, expand our sense of what might be politically possible. I have already cited Shulman's summation of Tamil ideas about kingship as always problematic, as 'less a fact than a concern, a congealed longing always in danger of dissolving back into despair' (1985: 15). Looking around our troubled present, I'd say that ambivalent longing will be with us for some time yet.

Notes

1 For more on these earlier events, see the on-the-spot reports collected in Manor (1984), Moore's (1993) powerful analysis of the 1980s JVP, and my own overview of the links between democracy and conflict in Sri Lanka (Spencer 2008).

2 Maunaguru, in this analysis of the limits of LTTE's claims to sovereignty, is taking a cue from other writers who have queried the narrow horizons of currently fashionable ideas about sovereignty, the state of exception and bare life. Agamben's (1998) exploration of a Schmittian political theology is deeply Eurocentric, and therefore not surprisingly rooted in Judeo-Christian monotheism. Das (2013a; 2013b), in a pair of recent papers, has explored the vulnerability attendant upon acts of violence in texts like the Mahavamsa, and their consequences for understanding differing conceptions of sovereignty in the Hindu world. Other places – like India – might be expected to develop political theologies that build on more fluid, polytheistic ideas of divinity; these in turn might then turn attention back to lower forms of divine life of a sort that also appear in popular Christianity and Islam (Singh 2012). Das' project, like Singh's and Maunaguru's, is expansive and, in her case at least, explicitly ethical.

3 This closing section draws on Spencer (2018); Maunaguru has also published his own analysis of this thought-provoking encounter (in press).

References

Agamben, Giorgio. 1998. *Homo Sacer: Sovereign Power and Bare Life*. Stanford: Stanford University Press.

Banerjee, Mukulika. 2007. 'Sacred Elections', *Economic and Political Weekly*, 42 (17): 1556–1562.

Bate, Bernard. 2009. *Tamil Oratory and the Dravidian Aesthetic: Democratic Practice in South India*. New York: Columbia University Press.
Benjamin, Walter. 1978. *Reflections: Essays, Aphorisms, Autobiographical Writings*. New York: Schocken.
Brass, Paul. 1997. *Theft of an Idol: Text and Context in the Representation of Collective Violence*. Princeton: Princeton University Press.
Das, Veena. 2013a. 'Violence and Nonviolence at the Heart of Hindu Ethics', in M. Jerryson, M. Juergensmeyer, and M. Kitts (eds.), *The Oxford Handbook of Religion and Violence*, pp. 15–40. Oxford: Oxford University Press.
Das, Veena. 2013b. 'War and the Mythological Imagination', *Anthropologia*, XIII (16): 25–36.
Geertz, Clifford. 2000. 'The World in Pieces: Culture and Politics at the End of the Century', in C. Geertz (ed.), *Available Light: Anthropological Reflections on Philosophical Topics*, pp. 218–264. Princeton: Princeton University Press.
Hansen, Thomas Blom. 2005. 'Sovereigns Beyond the State: On Legality and Authority in Urban India', in T. B. Hansen and F. Stepputat (eds.), *Sovereign Bodies: Citizens, Migrants and States in the Postcolonial World*, pp. 169–191. Princeton: Princeton University Press.
Hansen, Thomas Blom, and Finn Stepputat (eds.). 2005. *Sovereign Bodies: Citizens, Migrants and States in the Postcolonial World*. Princeton: Princeton University Press.
Hansen, Thomas Blom, and Finn Stepputat. 2006. 'Sovereignty Revisited', *Annual Review of Anthropology*, 35: 295–315.
Heesterman, Jan. 1985. *The Inner Conflict of Tradition: Essays in Indian Ritual, Kingship and Society*. Chicago: University of Chicago Press.
Klem, Bart. 2012. 'In the Eye of the Storm: Sri Lanka's Front-Line Civil Servants in Transition', *Development and Change*, 43 (3): 695–717.
Klem, Bart, and Sidharthan Maunaguru. 2017. 'Insurgent Rule as Sovereign Mimicry and Mutation: Governance, Kingship and Violence in Civil Wars', *Comparative Studies in Society and History*, 59 (3): 629–656.
Manor, James (ed.). 1984. *Sri Lanka: In Change and Crisis*. London: Croom Helm.
Maunaguru, Sidharthan. 2015. 'Amman as Social Auditor: Financial Misconduct vs Charitable Giving by the Tamil Sri Lankans in UK', *Contribution to Indian Sociology*, 49 (3): 369–388.
Maunaguru, Sidharthan, and Jonathan Spencer. 2018. '"You Can Do Anything with a Temple": Philanthropy and Politics in South London and Sri Lanka', *Modern Asian Studies*, 52 (1): 186–213.
Maunaguru, Sidharthan. Forthcoming. 'Vulnerable Sovereignty: Sovereign Deities and Tigers' Politics in Sri Lanka', *Current Anthropology*.
Michelutti, Lucia, Ashraf Hoque, Nicholas Martin, David Picherit, Paul Rollier, Arild E. Ruud, and Clarinda Still. 2018. *Mafia Raj: The Rule of Bosses in South Asia*. Stanford: Stanford University Press.
Moore, Mick. 1993. 'Thoroughly Modern Revolutionaries: The JVP in Sri Lanka', *Modern Asian Studies*, 27 (3): 593–642.
Price, Pamela. 1989. 'Kingly Models in Indian Political Behavior: Culture as a Medium of History', *Asian Survey*, 29 (6): 559–572.
Price, Pamela. 1996. *Kingship and Political Practice in Colonial India*. Cambridge: Cambridge University Press.
Schmitt, Carl. 1985. *Political Theology: Four Chapters on the Concept of Sovereignty*. Cambridge, MA: MIT Press.
Shulman, David. 1985. *The King and the Clown in South Indian Myth and Poetry*. Princeton: Princeton University Press.

Singh, Bhrigupati. 2012. 'The Headless Horseman of Central India: Sovereignty at Varying Thresholds of Life', *Cultural Anthropology*, 27 (2): 383–407.
Spencer, Jonathan. 2008. 'A Nationalism Without Politics? The Illiberal Consequences of Liberal Institutions in Sri Lanka', *Third World Quarterly*, 29 (3): 611–629.
Spencer, Jonathan. 2018. 'Pillayar and the Politicians: Secularization and Toleration at the End of Sri Lanka's Civil War', in H. Iqtidar and T. Sarkar (eds.), *Tolerance, Secularization and Democratic Politics in South Asia*, pp. 191–214. Cambridge: Cambridge University Press.
Stokke, Kristian. 2006. 'Building the Tamil Eelam State: Emerging State Institutions and Forms of Governance in LTTE-controlled Areas in Sri Lanka', *Third World Quarterly*, 27 (6): 1021–1040.
Wedeen, Lisa. 2003. 'Seeing Like a Citizen, Acting Like a State: Exemplary Events in Unified Yemen', *Comparative Studies in Society and History*, 45 (4): 680–713.
Whitaker, Mark. 1997. 'Tigers and Temples: The Politics of Non-modern Violence in Sri Lanka', *South Asia*, 20: 201–214.

INDEX

Adibasi (indigenous) communities 109, 113, 128
Agamben, Giorgio 20–21, 59–60, 111, 191, 192n3, 192n10, 221, 224n2
Ahmad, Ghulam 177, 178, 185
Ahmad, Ishtiaq 189
Ahmadis 25, 26, 176–177; Ahrar's violent agitation against 178, 184; Constitution of Pakistan and 183–190; exclusion and persecution of 179; Imperialist-Jewish forces and 189; Iqbal on 177–178, 179, 180, 182, 191, 193n18; JTI and 187; loyalty to the British 178; Mawdudi's anti-Ahmadi struggle 184–186; messianic movement of 177–179; Munir Report 186; Muslim establishment and 178–179; as non-Muslims 176, 178, 186, 188; Shah's conspiracy theory 189–190; as target of Muslim religious parties and modernist thinkers 178–179; as a threat 178, 186
Ahrar's violent agitation against Ahmadis 178, 184
Ain-i Akbari (*Institutes of Akbar*) 181
Aiyangar, V. Bhashyam 50
Aiyar, S. Subramania 50
Akbar (Mughal emperor) 180–181, 183, 188
Alam, Muzaffar 8–9
Ali, Haidar 141, 142
Allahabad High Court 92
Andhra Pradesh 44
Anglo-Mysore Wars 141
Anjaneya, H. 70–71
anthropology of sovereignty 58–61
Arbitration Act 68
Arendt, Hannah 210
Arya Samaj 83, 177
Asad, Talal 68
Assmann, Jan 182
Aurangzeb 180
Austin, Granville 88
autonomy 60
Awami League Party 187
Ayodhya 96

Bada'uni, Abdul Qadir 181
Baluchistan 185
Baneshwar (Lord) 110, 113–114, 115, 120
Bangabandhu (Sheikh Mujibur Rahman): as liberation/national hero or leader 203, 210, 211
Bangladesh 27; civil society 197; constitution 196, 197, 198; double nature of sovereignty 197; electoral democracy 198; foreign bodies 196–197; independence from Pakistan 27, 176; media 196, 197; notion of emotional Bengali 211–212; as republic 198; right to criticise parliament 196, 197; war of independence/liberation 202–205, 210–211; *see also Gunday* (Bollywood movie), Bangladeshis anger/reaction to
Bates, Crispin 66
Bayly, C. A. 182
Benjamin, Walter 177
Bhagavad Gita 85
Bharatiya Janata Party (BJP) 63, 70; devotionalism in action 97; growth/

rise of 96–97; idea of Hinduness and Hindu nationalism 97–98
Bhuiyans 112, 113
Bhutto, Benazir 189
Bhutto, Zulfiqar 26, 176, 187–188, 189–190, 192n12
Bhutto aur Qadiyani Mas'ala (Shah) 189
Bidanuru 142
Bildung 5
Blackburn, Stuart 40
blood money 157
Board of Revenue 43
Bombay High Court 38
Bonai (former princely state), Odisha 22, 109–132; Dasara rituals 110, 121–130; deities and divine manifestations 115–121; human sacrifices 121–126; king's conquest of wilderness 111–112; overview 109–111; route of the migration 112; royal chronicles 111–115; stranger kings 111–115
Book of Daniel 182
Bose, Subhas Chandra 85
bosses, in Western Uttar Pradesh 154–156; authority 155; as brothers *(bhai/dada)* 157; reputations through violence and force 155
British colonial rule: challenge to 83–87; mathas under 37–51; peasant movements 86; popular culture 86; public mobilisation against 86–87; religious law and 190; state and society under 79–83; *see also* rule of law
Burghart, Richard 42

caste: Mafia raj 161–163; theologies of protection 159–161; violent kinship 156–159; *see also* protection/extortion
Chanakya (Kautilya) 165
Chauri Chaura violence 85
chinna jiyangar 44
civil society 197
Collier, Paul 202
colonialism, modern 2
communitas 95
Congress 52, 70; British rule and 80, 83, 86, 89; colonial elections and 89; India's independence and 88; leaders of 80; rural development policy 66; socialists 86; split 91
Connolly, William 60, 61
Constitution of Bangladesh 27
Constitution of India 19, 87–91; concept of the 'people' 88; Directive Principles 19, 88, 91, 101n19; elections 88–91; Emergency in 1975 91–93; Fundamental Rights 91; independence and 88; 39th amendment to 92
Constitution of Pakistan 183–190
criminalisation of politics 150–151
criminal politicians 150, 223

Dalhousie, Lord 143
Dalton, Colonel 109
Dasara rituals, in Bonai 110, 121–130; human sacrifices 121–126; *kant bhet* 127–128; procession 127–130; *rakta handi* 129
dasturi 126; *see also* Dasara rituals, in Bonai
Daultana, Nawab 184
de Beauvoir, Simone 200
deities, Bonai and 115–121
democracy: as an enchanter of political imagination 79; Dunn on 78–79; modern 198, 199; paradoxical reputation of 78; theorists of 78; vernacularised understandings 199
Deo, K. K. C. 120, 124, 126, 131, 132n7
Deo, Pratap 112, 113–115
Deoband 177
dharma: king and 62, 154; morality 67, 68; renouncer heads of mathas 39; Seshan's invocation of 94–95, 96
Dharmakarta 41
Dharmapuram Adhinam 42
Dharmarakshana Sabha 49, 50
divine manifestations, Bonai and 115–121
Doctrine of Lapse 142, 143
Doss, Dharma 46–48
Doss, Ramakisore 49–50
Doss, Seva 44, 45, 46
Dumont, Louis 61
Dunn, John 78–79
Durga (great goddess) 110, 114, 116; swords 117–119; *see also* Dasara rituals, in Bonai

East India Company (EIC) 43; Doctrine of Lapse 142, 143; Mysore and 141, 142–143; *see also* British colonial rule
East Pakistan 187; *see also* Bangladesh
education, transformative power of 5
Election Commission (EC) of India 90–91, 162; general election of 1952 90; mission 90; Model Code of Conduct 93–95, 96, 97, 98, 102n30, 102n32
elections, India 88–91, 139–141; cyclical temporalities 95–99; Emergency in 1975 91–93; expansion of 88; Model

Code of Conduct 93–95, 96, 97, 98, 102n30, 102n32; 'special time' of 91, 93, 95; structure of 88
Eliott, E. F. 47–48
Elshtain, Jean Bethke 200
Emergency in 1975 91–93
emotional blackmail 158–159
equality 199
Ernstfall 188
Everlasting Lotus mural 144
extortion: defined 152; goonda tax 163–164; *see also* protection/extortion

Facebook page, protest against *Gunday* (Bollywood movie) 203, 205–206, 208–210
Fazl, Abul 181
Flag Foundation of India 109
Forbes, John 142–143
Foucault, Michel 59, 60, 221
Foundation for Restoration of National Values 150
Freitag, Sandria 95
Friedmann, Yohanan 177

Gajapati 112
Gandhi, Indira 91–92, 97
Gandhi, M. K. 63, 66, 84–86, 87, 179; non-cooperation 85; non-violent constraints of 87; satyagraha 84–85
Gandhian Constitution for Free India (Narayan) 66
Geenens, Raf 4
Geertz, Clifford 59, 216
gendered nations 199–201; bodily gender and 200
Ghosh, Durba 87
Gilmartin, David 18, 52, 62, 198, 216, 217, 219, 221
Godfather, The 201
God fearing 199
God of the Bible 182
Gonojagoron Moncho 207–208
goonda tax, extraction of 163–164
Gorakhpur, UP 166–167
Gunday (Bollywood movie), Bangladeshis anger/reaction to 27, 201–210; anti-Indian anger 206–207; Facebook page 203, 205–206, 208–210; humiliation and hurt 205–206; misrepresentation of war of independence 202–205; social sections/organisation not protesting against 207–208; user reviews and rating 201–202
Gupta, Akhil 60
guru (religious leadership): as an embodiment of community 63; authority of 61; capturing people's political imagination 63; celibacy and incorruptibility 63–64; decision-making power 71–73; kinship 62–63; moral authority 68; political power and networking 70–71; power of 64; as sovereign renouncer 61–64; *see also* mathas, under British imperial rule

Hansen, Thomas Blom 21, 24, 59, 111, 199, 221–222, 223
Haqqani, Hussain 188
Hartwell, Fabian 200–201
Hasan, Mubashar 198
Hathiramji Mutt case 38
heads of mathas 39; as embezzlers of funds 39; poor reputation of 40; power of 42
Hebrew Bible 182
Heesterman, J. C. 1–2, 61–62
Hijras 63
Hind Swaraj 84
Hindu nationalist masculinity 200–201
Hindu Religious Endowments Board (Madras Act II of 1927) 51
Hindu self 97
Hindutva 96–98; asceticism and self-restraint 97; intellectual advocates of 97; Model Code and 97
Hindu Yuva Vahini 166–167
Hobbes, Thomas 13–14, 30n20, 59, 60, 222
Hoeffler, Anke 202
Homo Sacer (Agamben) 221
Hopkins, Nick 210
human autonomy 4
Hurt Locker, The 200

IMDb 201
imperial rule of law 38
inclusionary nationalism 207
independence: invulnerability and 200; sovereignty and 200
India International Centre in Delhi 150
Indian Law Reports 41
Indian Punjab 177
inequality 4
institutionalised riot systems 153
intersubjective sovereignty 200
Iqbal, Muhammad 177–178, 179, 180, 182, 191, 193n18
Iraq 199, 222
Islam 176; 'buruzi' messiah 181; messianic myths of 181; *see also* Ahmadis; messianism

Islamic bomb 188
Islamic Conference 188

Jackson, Robert 3
Jaffna, Sri Lanka 222
Jaganmohan Palace 144
Jagannath (Lord) 114, 116
Jalal, Ayesha 207
Jama'at-i Islami 183, 184, 187, 188–189, 193n18
Jami'at-i Talaba-i Islam (JTI) 187
Jayewardene, J. R. 218, 222
Jewish community 178
Jindal, Naveen 109
Jindal Steel & Power (JSP) 109
JTI *see* Jami'at-i Talaba-i Islam (JTI)
judicial activism 94
judicial officers 37
JVP 218

Kant Debi (goddess) 115, 116, 119–121, 125, 126, 127; *see also* Dasara rituals, in Bonai
Kantorowicz, Ernst 140
Karnataka Janata Paksha (KJP) 70
Karnataka State Cricket Association (KSCA) 136, 137
Kartik Purnima 115
Kashmir: stone throwing in 201; youth rebellion in 200–201
Kepel, Gilles 187
Khan, Agha 179
Khan, Sayyid Ahmad 179
Khan, Zafarullah 178, 184
Khanna, H. R. 92
Khurshid, Salman 150
king and kingship: ancient India 1–2, 62; conquest of wilderness 111–112; double nature of 198; paradox in 62
Klem, Bart 221
Kshatriya (high-ranking) 112
Kumaratunga, Chandrika 222–223
kumari prasad 117

Lagaan 201
land mafia 153, 163, 164, 165
Latour, Bruno 64
law-making violence 220
Lechada 114
Lefort, Claude 199
Leviathan (Hobbes) 60
Liberation Tigers of Tamil Eelam (LTTE) 218, 224n2; administrative centre 220; BBC documentary 220; citational approach to sovereignty 221; claims for sovereignty 220–221; cult of leadership 220; political challenges to 220; temples and 220–221; *see also* Sri Lanka
LTTE *see* Liberation Tigers of Tamil Eelam (LTTE)

Maccabean revolt 182
Madani, Hussein Ahmed 178
madrasa 179
Madras High Court 67
Madras Law Journal 41
Madras Legislative Council in 1871 49
Madras Village Courts Act of 1889 67
Mafia Raj: as a cycle of caste/party revenge 162–163; defined 151; sovereignties 166–167; *see also* protection/extortion; Uttar Pradesh (West)
Maine, Henry 6
maleness of national ideal *see* masculine sovereignty
Mandur, Sri Lanka 220
Mann, Bonnie 199–200, 212
Mantena, Karuna 6, 83
marker-deficient society 199
masculine sovereignty 199–201
mathas, under British imperial rule 37–51; administration 43–46; head/leadership 41–43; litigation 49–51; management 48–51; renouncers and 46–48; spiritual lineages 41
Maunaguru, Sidharthan 222, 224n2
Mawdudi, Abul 'Ala 183–186, 188–189
Maxwell, Fabian 200
Mayawati 162
Mehta, Uday 81
Member of the National Assembly (MNA) 188
messiah 188
messianism: as collective marginality and individual madness 182; defined 175; history and theory 179–183; twentieth century 182; types 176; *see also* Ahmadis
Michelutti, Lucia 23, 24, 53, 199, 216, 222, 223
Mill, J. S. 81
millennial dreams 175–176
Mishra, Surendranath 117
Mitchell, Timothy 9
Model Code of Conduct 93–95, 96, 97, 98, 102n30, 102n32
modern colonialism 2
Modi, Narendra 63–64
Moin, Azfar 8
monotheism 182
Montagu-Chelmsford reforms 51
Mosse, David 67

Mughals 8, 9; millennial sovereignty 180–181
Muhammad (Prophet) 177
Muhammad, Munir (Justice) 186, 190
Muhammad, Sayyid 181
Mukherjee, Mithi 80
Muslim Brotherhood, Egypt 187
Muslim League 179–180
Mustafa, Seema 201
Mutiny of 1857 179, 180
Mysore: Anglo-Mysore Wars 141; East India Company and 141, 142–143; election and conquest 138–141; Sultan, Tipu 141–143

Narayan, Shriman 66
nationalism 200; inclusionary 207
nationalist movement 87–88
national maleness 200
national manhood 200–201; *see also* gendered nations; masculine sovereignty
National Prime Minister Resignation Day 218
Navalar, Arumukam 40
Nehru, Jawaharlal 86
Nelson, J. H. 41
New Delhi National Capital Region (NCR) 153
New York Times 201
Nicholas, Ralph W. 110, 121
Nietzsche 179
Nurbakhsh, Sayyid 181
Nyaya Peetha (seat of justice) 18, 64–66; being conservative 73; equal voice at 73; as a guardian of social structure 73; legal boundaries and compliance 68–69; mediators at 68; mining companies case 69–70, 72; morality 67–68; as place for counter-politics 72

Objectives Resolution of 1949 26, 184, 186
O'Hanlon, Rosalind 5
On Liberty (Mill) 81
Orientalist scholarship 179

Pakistan: civil wars 187; demographic shift from rural areas to cities 187; emergency 187; first general election 187; Islam as the foundational idea of 176; Islamisation of 184–189; secularist politics 186–187; Urdu-language public sphere 189; *see also* Ahmadis
Palestine, Israeli army and 201
Paoli, Letizia 164
paper revolution 5
Pax Britannica 37
Pedda Jiyangar Matha 44, 45, 46
pedda jiyangars 44, 45–46
Persian cosmopolis 8–9
Piliavsky, Anastasia 199
Pillai, Mayuram Vetanayakam 40
Pillayar (Lord) 223
Pinney, Christopher 87
political Islam 187
political power: in modern democracy 199
political theology 20–21, 25, 26, 96–98, 224n2; biblical monotheism 182; Hindu sovereignty 97–98, 138
Politics as a Vocation (Weber) 165
Pollock, Sheldon 8
Prabhakaran 220, 223; *see also* Liberation Tigers of Tamil Eelam (LTTE)
pracharak 63
Premadasa, Ranasinghe 222
Price, Pamela 16, 20, 154, 217
proclamation of 1858 81
protection: as ambiguous commodity 152; in anthropology 152; in Hindu cosmology 154
protection/extortion 151–152; caste theologies of 159–161; goonda tax 163–164; racket/racketeering 152–154; as shadowy contract 166; *see also* Uttar Pradesh (West)
protection of property 38
protection of worship 41
Protestant Christianity 40
Punjab Muslim League 178
Puri 112

Qadiyan 177
Qadiyani Problem, The (Mawdudi) 185
Quraishi, S. Y. 150

Raghunath (Lord) 116
Rahman, Sheikh Mujibur *see* Bangabandhu (Sheikh Mujibur Rahman)
Rajapaksa, Mahinda 217–220, 222, 223
Ramanuja 46
Ram Lila 82
Ramnad Zamindari in Madras Presidency 46
Rashtriya Swayamsevak Sangh (RSS) 63
Rattigan, William 82
reason 3–5; autonomy of 4; sovereignty and 4–5
Regulation VII of 1817 43
Reicher, Steve 210
religion: British courts and laws 178, 190; colonialism and 179; as a heretical imperative 179; total religion 182–183

Religious Endowments Act XX of 1863 47, 49
right of conquest, Wodeyar and 140, 141, 142, 143, 146
Rousseau, Jean-Jacques 17, 60–61, 64, 72, 73, 207
Roy, Sarat C. 128
RSS *see* Rashtriya Swayamsevak Sangh (RSS)
Rudolph, Lloyd 94
Rudolph, Susanne 94
rule of law: concept 79–80; customs and 81–82; human consciousness and 81; India's constitutional order and 88; linear and progressive social development 80–81; maintaining distinction between a state and society 82–83; Mukherjee on 80; religion compared with 80
Ruud, Arild 27

sacrificial polity 110
Saeed, Sadia 186, 188
Sahlins, Marshall 112
Salam, Abdus 175, 190, 191n1
Samajwadi Party (SP) 161–162, 163, 165, 166, 167
Samanto 114–115, 119
Santner, Eric 140
satyagraha 84–85
Scheper-Hughes, Nancy 157
Schmitt, Carl 20–21, 31n30, 59, 96, 139, 141, 176, 181, 191n2, 221
science 4
secret voting 198
Section 539 of the Civil Procedure Code 49–50
secularism 97
Self and Sovereignty (Jalal) 207
self-determination 89
self-fulfilment 200
self-rule 60
Sen, Sarbani 86
Sengupta, Suranjit 196–197
September 11, 2001 199
Seshan, T. N. 93, 94–95, 96, 97, 102n31–32
Shah, Sayyid Muhammad Sultan 189–190
Shahbagis 207–208
Shanmukappa 70
Sharif, Nawaz 191n1
Shiva (Lord) 113, 114; *see also* Baneshwar (Lord)
Shivamurthy Shivacharya Maha Swamiji *see* Sirigere guru
Shivratri 115
Shobhi, Chandra 146
Shulman, David 219, 224
Sikhs 178
Simmons, Caleb 22
Singh, Bhagat 87
Singh, Raghuraj Pratap 'Raja Bhai' 163
Singha, Radhika 190
Sirigere guru 64, 65, 69–71
Sobhi, Prithvi Chandra 136
Social Contract, The (Rousseau) 60–61
social death 62
social revolution 88
society: marker-deficient 199; traditional/religion-inspired vision of 199
soft self-sovereignty 200
Sovereign Masculinities (Mann) 199
sovereign paradox, anthropology of 58–61
sovereign people 62
sovereign renouncer 61–64; celibacy and incorruptibility 63–64; kinship 62–63; social death 62
sovereignty: academic literature on 2–3; Agambenian theory of 59–60; anthropology of 58–61; attention to 216–217; colonial and post-colonial manifestations of 221–222; as a concept 3; de facto 221–222; Foucault's view on 60; kingship and 1–2; principle of 3; Rousseau on 60–61; state and 3, 110; views on 60
Spinoza 178
Sri Lanka: anti-Tamil pogrom 218; authoritarian rule 217; civil war in 218, 220; dissolution of Parliament 218; militant organisations 218; politics and government in 217–220; portraits of politicians 222–223; referendum 218; *see also* Liberation Tigers of Tamil Eelam (LTTE)
Sri Lanka Muslim Congress 217
Srimanmaharajavara Vamsavali (Wodeyar III) 144–145
Srirangapattana: British and 141–142; Raja Wodeyar's conquest of 138, 139–140, 143; Tipu Sultan and 141, 142, 143, 146; Wodeyar kings and 145
Statesman 178
Stephen, Fitzjames 80
Stepputat, Finn 21, 24, 59, 111, 221–222, 224
Sufi cosmologies and rituals 181
Suleri, Z. A. 185
Sultan, Tipu 141–143
Sunni 'ulama 177
Supreme Court of India 92, 94, 97; judicial activism 94
Supreme Court of Pakistan 190–191, 192n14

'The examples raised across the essays in this volume . . . present legitimacy as a function of sovereignty, unstable and contradictory as [it tends] to be . . . The essays demystify the enchantments of sovereign kings or voters and the kinds of violence they legislate. This is deconstruction at its best.'

– **Uday Chandra**, *Georgetown University, Qatar*

'This fascinating collection of essays interrogates sovereignty through its tensions with the legitimacy of political power and authority in South Asia. As they move from kingship and nationalism to legal and religious institutions, these interdisciplinary contributions provide a rich historical context that greatly illuminates how international imperialism transformed indigenous structures in the South Asian subcontinent. The solid empirical work here will resonate with studies of modern colonialism in other parts of the globe.'

– **Douglas Howland**, *Buck Professor of Chinese History, University of Wisconsin-Milwaukee, USA*

'We live in an age of clamouring sovereignties. Every current social and political movement, from Kurdish nationalism to the LGBT, grounds its claims in calls for self-determination and rule. This carefully crafted volume reaches deep into the clamour of South Asian politics to reveal how it draws on and clashes against the transcendent. This is as much a book for scholars of South Asia as it is for anyone interested in the chaos of politics around the world.'

– **Anastasia Piliavsky**, *India Institute at King's College London, UK*

Supreme Court of Sri Lanka 218, 219
Swami, Govindaraja 44
Swami, Venkateswara 44
Swamigal, Ramalinga 40

Taralabalu Jagadguru Brihanmath 64
temples: LTTE and 220–221
Theft of an Idol (Brass) 222
3 Idiots 201
Tilak, B. G. D. 86
Tilly, Charles 152
time: rule of law and 81
Tirumala (Vijayanagara viceroy) 138, 145
Tirumala Tirupati Devastanams (TTD) 38; administration at 43–46; competition among renouncers 46–48
total religion 182–183
transformative power, of education 5
Turner, Victor 95

Udupa, Sahana 207
'Urgency of Electoral and Political Party Reforms' 150
Uttar Pradesh (West) 23; bosses 154–156; Brass's Hobbesian depiction of 222; caste-based conflicts 153; conversations with 'Guddu Bhai' (local boss) 164–166; Election of 2012 162; goonda tax *(chauth vasuli)* 163–164; jugar 163–164; protection rackets/racketeering 151, 152–154; violence 153; violent kinship 155–159

Vaishnava, in Bonai 116
Verma, J. S. 150
Victoria, Queen 81, 178; proclamation of 1858 81
village courts 66–67
village panchayats 66
violence 220–224; de facto sovereignty and 221–222; law-making 220; political sociology of 221; *see also* Uttar Pradesh (West)
voter-sovereigns: autonomous moral agent 198; gendered nations and 199–201; modern electoral democracies and 198–199, 200; powers/right to vote 198

Wall Street Journal 202
war of independence, Bangladesh 202–205, 210–211
Wellesley, Richard 143
Western Uttar Pradesh *see* Uttar Pradesh (West)
Westphalian system 3
Whitaker, Mark 220
'Why "Gunday" Angered Bangladeshis' 202
Wickremesinghe, Ranil 222
Wilkinson, Steven I. 153
Wodeyar, Krsnaraja, III 137; chosen by gods and British 143–146; crowning/enthroning 141, 143; Hindu sovereignty 138; *Srimanmaharajavara Vamsavali* 144–145, 146
Wodeyar, Raja: conquest of Srirangapattana 138, 139–140, 143; election and conquest 140; *Srimanmaharajavara Vamsavali* (Wodeyar III) 145; Yadava heritage 144
Wodeyar, Srikantadatta 23, 136–137, 146–147
worldwide system 3

Yadav, Akhilesh 161–162
Yadav caste 156
Yaduvamsa 137, 143–145, 146
Yash Raj Films 209; *see also Gunday* (Bollywood movie), Bangladeshis anger/reaction to
Yeddyurappa, B. S. 70
Yogi Adityanth 166–167
youth rebellion in Kashmir 200–201

Zafar, Bahadur Shah 180
Zia-ul-Haq, M. 188–189, 190

For Product Safety Concerns and Information please contact our EU representative GPSR@taylorandfrancis.com
Taylor & Francis Verlag GmbH, Kaufingerstraße 24, 80331 München, Germany

www.ingramcontent.com/pod-product-compliance
Lightning Source LLC
Chambersburg PA
CBHW070828300426
44111CB00014B/2489
9780367312701